STRATEGIC
NONVIOLENT
CONFLICT

STRATEGIC NONVIOLENT CONFLICT

The Dynamics of People Power in the Twentieth Century

PETER ACKERMAN *and*
CHRISTOPHER KRUEGLER

With Forewords by
Gene Sharp *and* Thomas C. Schelling

PRAEGER

Westport, Connecticut
London

Library of Congress Cataloging-in-Publication Data

Ackerman, Peter.
    Strategic nonviolent conflict: The dynamics of people power in the twentieth century /
Peter Ackerman and Christopher Kruegler; with forewords by Gene Sharp and Thomas
C. Schelling
      p. cm.
    Includes index.
    ISBN 0-275-93915-4 (hc : alk. paper).—ISBN 0-275-93916-2 (pb : alk. paper)
    1. Nonviolence.   2. Protest movements.   3. Power (Social sciences)
I. Kruegler, Chistopher. II. Title.
JC328.3.A28   1994
303.6'1—dc20   93-2870

British Library Cataloguing in Publication Data is available.

Library of Congress Catalog Card Number: 93–2870
ISBN: 0-275-93915-4
     0-275-93916-2 (pbk.)

First published in 1994

Praeger Publishers, 88 Post Road West, Westport, CT 06881
An imprint of Greenwood Publishing Group, Inc.

Printed in the United States of America

The paper used in this book complies with the
Permanent Paper Standard issued by the National
Information Standards Organization (Z39.48-1984).

10 9 8 7

Copyright Acknowledgment

The narrative portion of Chapter 7 ("El Salvador: The Civic Strike of 1944") is digested
from *Nonviolent Insurrection in El Salvador: The Fall of Maximiliano Hernández Martínez*, by
Patricia Parkman and is used by permission of the University of Arizona Press, copyright
1988.

To Joanne and Gillian

Contents

Foreword

Gene Sharp

In his classic study of military strategy, Sir Basil Liddell Hart concluded what to many may seem obvious, "the conduct of war must be controlled by reason if its object is to be fulfilled. . . . The better your strategy, the easier you will gain the upper hand, and the less it will cost you."[1] It is unfortunate, indeed, that this fundamental insight has more often than not been neglected by leaders and organizers of a different, yet tremendously powerful form of struggle, that of nonviolent conflict.

The technique of nonviolent action, often referred to as "people power," has been employed by groups in diverse cultures as the central means of fighting for political freedom, democracy, human rights, social and economic justice, and a variety of other objectives. In recent years, nonviolent action has been at the core of the most powerful struggles of the day: the Solidarity movement in Poland, the South African anti-apartheid struggle, the East German, Czech, and Slovak struggles of 1989, and the independence movements of the Baltic states come quickly to mind.

With certain exceptions, most nonviolent struggle organizers have not taken Liddell Hart's insight into account. Nonviolent movements have often been merely reactive, often relying on spontaneous mobilizations and tactical countermoves rather than focusing on maintaining the initiative and the wise "calculation and co-ordination of the end and the means."[2] With such neglect to the role of strategy in nonviolent struggle, especially in comparison to military conflicts, it is surprising that so many nonviolent campaigns have indeed succeeded. Many have of course failed.

Peter Ackerman and Christopher Kruegler seek to correct this neglect with their masterful study *Strategic Nonviolent Conflict*. Through careful and historically rich comparative analyses of six important nonviolent struggles, the authors have developed a set of strategic principles that should form the core of any analysis about launching and conducting mass nonviolent action. Through this work, Ackerman and Kruegler have thrown the door wide open for the expanded strategic development of nonviolent conflict.

The central hypothesis of the book is that the "comprehensive adherence to a set of strategic principles enhances performance, which bears importantly on the outcome" (p. 318). In other words, develop and apply wise strategies and you are more likely to win. Ackerman and Kruegler convincingly make the case that leaders of people power movements cannot afford to neglect twelve key strategic principles of nonviolent conflict. These address such problems as: formulating functional objectives, expanding the repertoire of sanctions, attacking the opponents' strategy for consolidating control, maintaining nonviolent discipline, and adjusting offensive and defensive operations according to the relative vulnerabilities of the protagonists.

In recent decades, three developments in nonviolent struggle have occurred. First, its practice has grown world-wide in frequency and political significance. People power has been applied on a scale and with an impact which was not previously imagined, although the circumstances have frequently been unfavorable. Second, some individuals and groups have deliberately sought to develop and plan for the practical application of nonviolent struggle in advance of and during various acute conflicts. Third, scholars have attempted to more clearly formulate several fundamental aspects of nonviolent action, such as the theory of power upon which this technique of action rests (that is, the dependence of governments on the populace for their sources of power), the dynamics of this technique in action, and even strategic considerations in nonviolent struggle. *Strategic Nonviolent Conflict* advances the study and practice of strategy in nonviolent struggle far beyond these previous efforts, providing the most sophisticated analysis of the subject to date. A new standard for studies of strategy in nonviolent struggle has been established.

Strategic Nonviolent Conflict deserves careful reading to grasp in depth its insights and finely tuned nuances. With due recognition of the dangers of "a little knowledge," the careful reader will benefit in two important ways; he or she will gain a thorough understanding of the key principles of strategy in nonviolent struggle and will be more able to develop his or her own strategic analytic skills.

The present volume is of profound relevance to a number of different audiences. General readers, students, and professors interested in modern politics and the study of conflict will do well to study this analysis. Its contents has deep implications for several academic disciplines, namely political science, sociology, and strategic studies, and it provides a greatly needed context for understanding contemporary social, political, and international developments. For practitioners and leaders of nonviolent struggle, *Strategic Nonviolent Conflict* is required reading. Given the power wielded by this technique of action and its concomitant risks to its participants, the insights in this volume cannot and should not be ignored.

In reflecting on the 1989 Chinese movement for democracy, Shen Tong (who was active in the student movement and who managed to escape secretly to the United States after the brutal June 4 crackdown) has stated the following:

> I would also like to talk about the reasons why our movement failed. There are many reasons. The primary one is that sight of our goals was lost. Our original plan was to return to the campuses, regroup, and continue our movement through broadcasting stations, the newspapers, and the tremendous support we had gained from the people. But the movement got out of control. . . . Rather than moving to achieve something positive, the students started merely to react. If the government did nothing, the students remained in the Square doing nothing. If the government made some statement, or did something, then the students proposed another hunger strike. Some students even proposed to set themselves on fire in protest. For no constructive reason. We prevented this.[3]

Shen Tong's words point to several key issues involved in the conduct of nonviolent action: the clarity of objectives, the required discipline and leadership, the importance of seizing and maintaining the initiative, the need for tactical actions to support strategic objectives, and the danger of relying on a narrow range of methods. There are of course many others. Ackerman and Kruegler carefully and soberly call attention to these vital aspects of nonviolent conflict. As the events in China revealed, the costs of neglecting careful strategic calculation are very high.

Two important characteristics of nonviolent struggle are demonstrated by the strategic analyses and case studies in this book. First, this technique makes possible the mobilization of the power potential of the oppressed, the subordinates, the presumably powerless. Second, the technique can weaken, and even disintegrate, the effective power of oppressors, the superordinates, the once supposedly omnipotent rulers. The use of this technique, when applied with wise strategies, may allow the practitioners of nonviolent struggle to exert significant control even over their *opponents'* capacity to repress the defiant population.

Strategic Nonviolent Conflict clearly reflects the many years of academic and professional involvement both authors have devoted to the field of nonviolent action. While rigorously laying out the evidence that nonviolent conflict is a potent and often successful means of struggle, Ackerman and Kruegler avoid the hyperbolic claims of many advocates of nonviolent action. While noting the successes, the authors are earnestly clear on the dangers and failures of past nonviolent struggles. The book also benefits from the skilled use of the work of four highly qualified research consultants: Patricia Parkman, Lennart Bergfeldt, Ronald McCarthy, and Jan Zielonka, who worked with the authors to develop the Salvadorean, Danish, German, and Polish cases respectively. All six cases have been subjected to critical analysis. The descriptive case studies are superb.

In past years I have often suggested—without any hard data—that with the benefit of advance strategic analysis, preparations, and planning, future cases of nonviolent struggle could be made ten times more effective than the most successful past cases. Whether that projection turns out to be accurate remains to be seen. It is clear, however, that Peter Ackerman and Christopher Kruegler have made a most important contribution to increasing the effectiveness of nonviolent struggle in that direction. This can, and I believe will, have profound consequences.

In a world in which dictatorships, oppression, injustice, wars, and mass violence often appear endemic, the increase in the effectiveness of nonviolent struggle and its progressive application in place of violent options offers a great sign of realistic hope. This possibility merits the serious attention of everyone.

NOTES

1. Liddell Hart, Sir Basil, *Strategy: The Indirect Approach* (New York: Frederick A. Praeger, 1954), p. 369.
2. Liddell Hart, Sir Basil, *Strategy: The Indirect Approach, 2nd ed.* (London: Faber and Faber, 1967), p. 322.
3. Shen Tong, speech at Martin Luther King Center, Atlanta, Georgia, January 13, 1990. In Han Minzhu, ed., *Cries for Democracy: Writings and Speeches from the 1989 Chinese Democracy Movement* (Princeton, NJ: Princeton University Press, 1990), p. 380.

Foreword

Thomas C. Schelling

Twenty years ago, when I had been a student of strategic violence for at least fifteen years, Gene Sharp asked me for a foreword to his *Politics of Nonviolent Action*. I was not surprised, and he did not expect me to be. With rare exceptions, like Sir Basil Liddell Hart whom Gene likes to quote, most writers on military strategy had been primarily interested in how to defeat an enemy in combat. My interest was in how military capabilities might be and had been used, successfully or unsuccessfully, to influence an adversary. I had written a book on the subject, with the word "influence" in the title.

A focus on "influence" is what brings the two subjects, the strategic use of potential violence to influence an adversary and the strategic use of nonviolent capabilities toward a similar purpose, into alignment with each other. Twenty years ago I said of Gene Sharp's book that we lacked an equally comprehensive and careful study of the politics of *violent* action!

In the intervening two decades the study of "strategy as influence" has come a long way. A new and expanded version of Alexander George and William Simon's *The Limits of Coercive Diplomacy* (in press) is a subtle, perceptive presentation of the theory of what I once called "the diplomacy of violence," with a rich selection of case studies to display both the strengths and weaknesses and the successes and the failures of international military violence as influence. Peter Ackerman and Christopher Kruegler have brought up-to-date the best thinking on strategic nonviolence, together with their impressive menu of case studies. Even "people power" has its violent as well as its nonviolent interpretations; Napoleon was a master of people power as much as he was a master of artillery. All of these parallels I find fruitful.

I stress these parallels because the required quality of the reasoning, and the required honesty of the historical studies, are nearly identical for the study of both strategic violence and strategic nonviolence. The style of the reasoning too, is necessarily similar. Many of the topical headings are the same: command, control, communication, intelligence, recruitment, training, discipline, logistics, surprise, terrain, and timing.

Ackerman and Kruegler, no less than Gene Sharp before them, have been willing students of violent conflict the better to understand their own subject. Students of military policy can immensely enrich their insight into their own subject by examining the reasoning, and pursuing the case studies, that Ackerman and Kruegler present.

When Gene Sharp's first book was published in the early 1970s it was not yet easy to identify eager audiences outside academia, and not many inside. Sharp had to be as concerned to explain what his subject was not as to expound what it was. I was interested that among those who took his work seriously were a number of fairly senior people in the military professions; they recognized good strategic thinking when they saw it.

The Ackerman-Kruegler work is being issued into a world full of potential audiences, including undoubtedly some who can wish the authors had finished their book a few years earlier. But a few years ago they still had a lot of hard thinking and a lot of hard arguing to do. At last the book is ready, and I hope to see it translated into many languages.

Acknowledgments

This study culminates a lengthy intellectual journey for both of us, characterized by a common interest in the relationship between strategic theory and nonviolent action in acute conflicts. Early in this collaboration we shared the belief that comparative historical data might yield a carefully delineated set of principles that could enhance our understanding of nonviolent conflict. Throughout this work we have discovered many areas of disagreement, but our mutual commitment to that basic assumption has never varied.

Often after a long journey, travelers feel indebted to those who provided sustenance along the way. We are grateful to the many people whose encouragement and help have been vital to this project's completion.

Anyone undertaking to write about nonviolent action necessarily stands on the shoulders of Gene Sharp. His work provides many of the conceptual tools that make this effort possible. Beyond that, he has helped each of us, over many years, as a teacher and friend. His indefatigable efforts to develop nonviolent action as a topical field and a policy alternative have inspired many, not the least ourselves.

A perennial problem in the literature on nonviolent action has been that authors interested in theoretical and policy issues have often not been equipped with the requisite language skills to conduct deep primary research in diverse cases. This shortcoming has led to weakly supported conclusions or to an overemphasis on single case studies with little or no comparative or theory-testing element. We sought to overcome this deficiency in our own work by engaging as research consultants four outstanding scholars to help us develop some of the case studies that follow.

Dr. Lennart Bergfeldt (Denmark), Professor Ronald McCarthy (the Ruhr), Dr. Patricia Parkman (El Salvador), and Professor Jan Zielonka (Poland) each made a major contribution to our understanding of their respective cases. As consultants, they conducted all primary research in the languages in which the conflicts were fought and drafted narrative descriptions of the cases for us. In analyzing the cases, we have altered their narrative treatments as little as possible so that our assessment will be well grounded in context and history. Portions of Chapter 7 that overlap with Dr. Parkman's own published work appear with the kind permission of The University of Arizona Press. Text and quotations that also appear in Dr. Bergfeldt's doctoral dissertation, as cited in Chapter 6, appear here with the permission of the author. We assume full responsibility for the use made of their work and for all interpretations and judgments arising from it.

Many friends and colleagues gave us the benefit of their critical comments on both the substance and style of this study. Their candor and thoughtfulness were invaluable to us, and we hope we have made good use of their insights. We are especially grateful to Hans Binnendijk, Douglas Bond, John Chipman, Joanne Leedom-Ackerman, Mary Locke, Roger Powers, Gillian Price, and William Vogele. Additional editorial work by Joanne Leedom-Ackerman, Mary Locke, and Roger Powers will allow readers to enjoy a crisper text. Julia Wheatly and Susan Wilson policed repeated drafts of chapters to ensure that they would meet technical standards. Kendra McCleskey provided indispensable word processing support.

We would like to thank everyone at Praeger Publishers, and especially our first editorial contact there, John Harney, for invaluable help and support throughout this project. Finally, we would like to acknowledge the hospitality of three institutions: the Albert Einstein Institution, Harvard University's Center for International Affairs, and the International Institute for Strategic Studies. Each welcomed us warmly and provided a stimulating intellectual environment while our work was in progress.

Introduction

The term "people power" became a household word during the period in which this book was written. It was widely used to describe the processes leading to Ferdinand Marcos' fall from power in the Philippines in 1986. The mass use of nonviolent direct action by civilian populations seemed to proliferate throughout the late 1980s and early 1990s. The revolutions throughout East Central Europe, the Chinese student uprising of 1989, resistance to the failed Soviet coup in 1991, the nonviolent aspects of the Palestinian Intifada and the South African struggle against apartheid, the "Civilian Crusade" against the Noriega dictatorship in Panama, and efforts to advance democracy in many other places have depended largely, and with varying degrees of success, on people applying methods of nonviolent action.

Clearly, the phenomenon of "people power" helps explain the recent past, and, partly for that reason, may be an important guide to the near future. Without jumping to conclusions about the efficacy of this technique of conflict, most analysts would agree that it has become a regular part of our national and international life and should be explored and understood.

The term "people power" is more evocative than precise. We see its contemporary manifestation as part of a surprisingly long and robust tradition of waging conflict by nonviolent means. We prefer the phrase "strategic nonviolent conflict" to describe the process under discussion since it conveys intent as well as content. People use nonviolent methods, more or less strategically, to achieve vital objectives in conflict. The process varies with time and place and ends in failure as well as success, with a vast array of factors bearing on the likely outcome. We invite the reader to join with us in an effort to understand more precisely what strategic nonviolent conflict is all about and what promise it holds.

Many past cases involving nonviolent action have been more improvised than planned, more reactive than strategic. We see the degree of careful premeditation that goes into an episode of "people power" as a variable, rather than a defining condition for the phenomenon. However chaotic or unplanned, past cases yield important clues about the process. Strategic thinking about nonviolent conflict can be improved, and we believe that prospects for attaining such important objectives as democracy, human rights, and security can be increased. Strategic nonviolent conflict, in short, is among those human enterprises that can be enhanced and extended through careful thought and skillful action.

Nonviolent conflict has been idealized, scorned, made into a panacea, or mystified, or it has been completely overlooked. It has sometimes been improvised at the expense of its participants, leading to cynicism and premature rejection of the technique, or even the uncritical adoption of violent alternatives. Other times it has created successes so dramatic and unexpected that the ingredients of success were never properly analyzed or were facilely attributed to unique circumstances. Our goal is to develop a more precise understanding of how nonviolent conflict actually works. We use a series of case studies to create an explanatory framework that can account for the relationship between strategic performance and outcome. Simply put, this book is about who wins based on who makes best use of the resources and options at hand.

Readers who place overwhelming importance on structural explanations may quarrel with the thrust of this book. They will expect it to indicate what conditions are necessary for successful nonviolent conflict, and what objective realities constrain or even prohibit its use. For example, isn't nonviolent conflict always easier to wage in a liberal democracy than in a repressive autocracy? Or they will be disappointed when we do not spell out the range of alternatives and specify a cut-off point beyond which nonviolent alternatives are of no avail. Many thoughtful colleagues have advised us to take such an approach. We must say that we have quite deliberately resisted their advice.

Structural constraints are real, and they precede the waging of conflict, both violent and nonviolent. But time and time again we see historical examples of people using nonviolent action to alter those very constraints and to change the environment of conflict in their favor. Is this so surprising? We are all familiar with cases of military conflict in which David beats Goliath despite starting from an objectively inferior position. In any case, real constraints are case specific, and do not seem to set general limits on the technique.

The will to repress nonviolent struggle violently, for example, is widely regarded as a given that naturally limits the exercise of "people power." But we have observed that violent repression often fails, has unintended consequences for its sponsors, or simply is not chosen by parties for whom it might have proved successful. We have to ask why. Repression begins to look to us like yet another variable, one that interacts in complex ways with many others to form part of an explanation.

We are therefore able to make what seems to us a modest but compelling argument: that the quality of strategic choice by practitioners of nonviolent conflict is a critical variable that must be taken into account. The scope for choice varies from case to case, but within that margin, performance counts and can improve results.

If this perspective is sound, what is its import? Strategic nonviolent action is not necessarily the most important feature of every social and political conflict, but it is an important feature of many. Perhaps it is more relevant to the emerging agenda in contemporary international and security affairs than is widely supposed.

Many contemporary observers, for example, are concerned with the apparent erosion of national sovereignty and a corresponding increase in the number and kinds of opportunities for nonstate actors to wield power. Nongovernmental organizations, corporations, transnational social movements, and the like are asserting themselves on issues from the environment and human rights to international trade and monetary policy. They represent an important challenge to a state-centered view of the international system. In acute conflicts of the near future, how will they act and what role will they play? Nonstate actors may find that their particular attributes and capabilities make them especially well suited to waging nonviolent conflict.

Another dominant concern now and into the foreseeable future is ethnic conflict. Bitter clashes along ethnic lines have been a defining feature of this century in most parts of the world. Many observers feel that the breakup of the Soviet empire has opened a Pandora's box of new, inevitably violent horrors among groups struggling for recognition and resources in an ambiguous and fluid arena. But must every ethnic conflict descend into the lowest possible hell of atrocity and genocide? We think it likely that some important ethnic claims will be advanced in the coming period by means of nonviolent action. The sheer cost of losing an ethnic conflict is so high that many leaders will be loath to escalate fights beyond their capacity to control costs for their own people. They may want to garner for their struggle the advantages of legitimacy and international support that sometimes come with adopting a nonviolent approach. Groups that have been militarily defeated, and perhaps nearly obliterated, may find it necessary to reconstitute themselves and reassert their most basic interests using the only means objectively left to them: nonviolent ones.

Terrorism has often been the preferred methodology of marginal or disenfranchised groups. There is appropriate concern that the technical capabilities of terrorists are increasing. The miniaturization and availability of certain new weapons, along with the growing vulnerability of complex societies, conspire to make political terrorism more of a threat. Yet groups employing terror have often failed to achieve their stated goals in any reasonable time frame. This fact may lead populations that have formerly sheltered terrorists to the rediscovery of other approaches, including the strategic use of nonviolent action.

The growing emphasis on multinational intervention in response to human rights abuses may create a further incentive for groups to adopt a nonviolent stance to expose those abuses and gain a hearing for their own claims. Using nonviolent action is no guarantee of an adequate response from the international community. However, it at least obviates the possibility that potential interveners would be caught between two equally violent hostile fronts, a prospect frequently advanced as an argument against intervention.

The intrasocietal use of nonviolent conflict can be coordinated with the application of international economic and diplomatic sanctions, even in cases in which third party intervention is not possible, likely, or desirable. This range of sanctions has been a crucial part of the strategic mix in numerous contemporary struggles. Those commentators who find economic and diplomatic sanctions irrelevant need to pay greater attention to the role they have actually played in the recent past. Our perspective would lead us to think they will continue to play a role and that their potential should be understood and exploited.

Just as some are inclined to dismiss economic sanctions, others think that the national security applications of nonviolent conflict are bound to be negligible. Perhaps they have not looked at the problem of regional security from the perspective of many small states who, if attacked, have no realistic military options at their disposal for the successful defense of their territories and societies. For example, in some of the successor states to the Soviet Union, notably Estonia, Latvia, and Lithuania, serious policy consideration is now being given to an option known as civilian-based defense, or the prepared use of nonviolent resistance by civilians as a means of national defense. It is highly probable that a civilian-based defense component will figure to some degree in Baltic security policies of the near future, in large part due to the positive role played by nonviolent action during these countries' independence struggles. Anyone wishing to support Baltic security will need to understand this development and its implications.

The past decade has seen a worldwide wave of democratization, and great attention will be paid to defending and sustaining it. There is an unmistakable correlation between democratization and the strategic use of nonviolent action, but what is the relationship? It is typically thought that a relatively democratic environment is necessary to perform nonviolent action, but the reverse may very well be true. Effective nonviolent conflict may be shown to precede, abet, and defend the democratizing process. Nonviolent action may be the prevailing means by which civil society first asserts, and then defends itself from counterattack.

A final factor that is transforming the environment of conflict is technology, and especially communications technology. Since organized social conflict requires communication, improved access to cheap, efficient, and discreet communications should make strategic nonviolent conflict both easier to perform and more relevant. Indeed, new technologies from personal computing to fax machines, beepers, and cellular telephones have already created a whole new range of opportunities for practitioners of nonviolent struggle. Despite many impressive examples of strategists exploiting these new opportunities, we must note that technological advances confer no permanent advantage on those who are democratic and nonviolent. The same tools can be used for domination and repression. They do not relieve nonviolent strategists of their fundamental strategic obligation: to outperform their adversaries.

Strategic nonviolent conflict, then, should not be seen as an isolated or special subject. It is not only intimately bound up with many of the major events of our recent past. It is also part and parcel of some of our gravest concerns in the present and immediate future. Whether we are concerned with collective or common security, ethnic strife, conflicts of the post–Cold War era, the future of democracy, alternative means of defense, international sanctions, or the role of technology in conflicts, the strategic performance of nonviolent action will be an essential part of the process.

The question is no longer whether nonviolent action "works" in the abstract. It is no longer appropriate, if indeed it ever was, to dismiss nonviolent conflict as an alternative by hypothesizing some extreme degree of violent opposition against which it cannot contend. We know that real conflicts rarely involve such absolutes, and that strategic performance by all parties, violent and nonviolent, has a bearing on the outcome of fights. "People power" simply is, and will continue to be, part of our political experience. The important questions now are about when and how nonviolent action is operating, and whether it can be improved upon, made more effective, and rendered comprehensively strategic. We will argue that it can.

Chapter 1

The Emergence
of Strategic
Nonviolent Conflict

As the twentieth century draws to a close, and the twenty-first begins, a startling feature emerges in most of the significant conflicts of our time. From Santiago to Moscow, Johannesburg to Beijing, Rangoon to Manila, the great social and political struggles of this era have been shaped by the methods of nonviolent action. The struggles in East Central Europe leading to the end of the Cold War and the downfall of Soviet communism were no exception.

Some have argued that the appearance of nonviolent action as the weapon of choice in acute conflicts is increasing, either in absolute terms[1] or relative to episodes of predominantly violent conflict.[2] Others contend that it is the magnitude and importance of the contests in which it appears that makes "people power," as it is sometimes called, a factor to be reckoned with in international affairs. Unarguably, the mobilization of civilian populations for nonviolent direct action and governmental use of nonviolent sanctions have contributed to the withering away of the Soviet empire, the dismantling of apartheid in South Africa, and the strongest challenges to date of communist autocracy in China.

The drama, power, and human triumph of these events are not without their dark contrasts in other parts of the world. Many brave and astute practitioners of nonviolent conflict have met with bitter and costly defeat. A few examples from the 1980s might include the Tibetans, Burmese, and Panamanians (prior to the U.S. military invasion of Panama in 1989). In each of these countries, well-conceived nonviolent campaigns against dictatorial rule were waged and lost (in the sense that the stated objectives of the nonviolent opposition were not met in the near term).

Neither policy makers, students of conflict, nor journalists have yet satisfactorily explained the role and dynamics of nonviolent action in comparable events. While it is well established that nonviolent action is *possible* in intense conflicts, it is becoming increasingly urgent to understand what circumstances are *conducive* to its success.

This book describes a process we call *strategic nonviolent conflict*. Our hypothesis is this: *the quality of the strategic choices made by nonviolent protagonists matters to the outcome of nonviolent struggle.* At first glance, this statement appears to be self-evident. After all, in any human enterprise, to think well about something should enable one to do it more effectively. So, to think clearly about the exigencies of nonviolent struggle and the good and bad effects of certain kinds of choices should result in more successful campaigns, more gains and fewer losses. One should need only to *do* the strategic thinking to improve performance.

This has not been obvious, however, to many observers of nonviolent conflict. Strategy does not matter, it is sometimes argued, because there will always be some decisive variables that lie outside the control of the would-be strategist. These might include the character and competence of the opponents, economic constraints, the inherent uncertainty of events, the opponents' relative will to repress with violence, and so on. Our claim is that these and other factors, while important in certain cases, perhaps even decisive, do not determine all cases. We view strategic performance as likely to be a significant, possibly the dominant, factor in the outcome of nonviolent struggle.

An additional question that arises is whether and how nonviolent strategy develops. Are people learning, or can they learn, to wield nonviolent action more efficiently and effectively, or are they at the mercy of factors that are not tractable to deliberate human action? Is mastery of the technique of nonviolent action getting any easier? Is strategic competence becoming a more or less important factor in contemporary conflicts? Can the margin of victory for strategic nonviolent conflict be widened? To begin to approach these questions, we need to be more precise about what we mean by *strategic nonviolent conflict*.

Conflict is an inherently adversarial process involving the direct exchange of sanctions, either violent or nonviolent, with a view to inflicting costs on one's opponents, inducing them to change their behavior. The protagonists in conflict act unilaterally to overwhelm opposition and to secure outcomes they deem to be in their interest. Whether the objectives being fought over are realistic or not, negotiable or not, tangible or not, the process of conflict exceeds the bounds of normal politics and consensus-building processes.

We take the view that while no *particular* conflict can be judged a priori to be inevitable, necessary, good, or bad, some conflicts are always likely to occur over issues that the belligerents will consider worth fighting for, despite high risks. Thus, while the simple avoidance of conflict or its creative resolution is often appropriate, it is also worthwhile to consider the means by which conflict may, in some cases, be waged. By creating a better risk-reward relationship, nonviolent methods may make waging conflict a more efficient option than either violent conflict or compromise.

In considering conflicts to include in this work, we focused on four attributes. First, the conflict has to be a major one for the society or societies fighting it. We are interested in contests in which large numbers of people are mobilized for action or have a significant stake in the outcome. The second criterion is duration: the contest needs to last long enough for certain dynamic processes to be manifested, observed, and analyzed. Third, all of the cases in this book have a quality of intensity. The participants are so committed that they are willing to inflict or sustain very serious damage to pursue their goals. In particular, at least one protagonist in these conflicts is willing and likely to employ massive repressive violence. Finally, we chose conflicts in which at least one party exhibited significant use of nonviolent methods as sanctions.

NONVIOLENT SANCTIONS

Nonviolent sanctions are methods which, in conflict, serve as instruments of power. Whether we look at the "people power" revolution in the Philippines in 1986, or Solidarity's struggle in Poland during the 1980s, or the student uprising in China in 1989, one of the principal things these episodes have in common is the recurrence of methods of nonviolent action being brought to bear as sanctions. Strikes, boycotts, defiance campaigns, the creation of parallel institutions, civil disobedience, and the like are all actions which create costs for some parties to a conflict, and in doing so, contribute to a shift in the relative power of the contestants.[3] Nonviolent sanctions are seen here as methods capable of bringing pressure to bear against even the most ruthless opponents, by mobilizing social, economic, and political power, without recourse to killing or otherwise causing direct physical injury to the opponents or their agents.

It is important to note at this point what our definition leaves out. As behavioral phenomena, nonviolent sanctions are not equivalent to or synonymous with any of the philosophies of principled nonviolence, such as pacifism or satyagraha.[4] In fact, in the overwhelming majority of known cases of nonviolent conflict, there is no evidence that concepts of principled nonviolence were either present or contributed in a significant way to the outcome.

Nonviolent sanctions as behaviors are different from the value systems of the people who may occasionally engage in them. Once this distinction is made, it becomes possible to observe that most of the known cases of nonviolent struggle have been motivated by the need to defeat a particular opponent with the most effective and least costly means at hand, rather than by a principled commitment to the avoidance of bloodshed as an end in itself.[5] Often nonviolent action is chosen because a viable military option is simply not available.

When citizens of Germany's Ruhr region were faced with a Franco-Belgian military occupation in 1923, for the ostensible purpose of securing reparations payments that were in arrears, they were encouraged by their government to adopt a policy of what was then called "passive resistance." This included the refusal of German civil servants to obey any orders of the occupation authorities, the noncooperation of coal miners and transport workers who were expected to ship coal to France in lieu of the debt payments, and various forms of strikes, demonstrations, and boycotts by the general public. After a year of struggle that was bitter and costly for both sides, France (by then fairly isolated in world opinion) agreed to the reexamination of Germany's ability to pay her war debts by an international commission. The decision ultimately went in Germany's favor, and the reparations in question were never paid.

The Weimar Republic's decision to encourage passive resistance (which was, on the contrary, quite active) cannot have been based on a moral commitment to nonviolent behavior in all conflicts. Instead, it must have derived, in large part, from the fact that Germany had been effectively disarmed by the terms of the Treaty of Versailles. In other words, a society with no particular predilection for pacifism found it expedient to employ nonviolent sanctions in a specific situation and did so with some success, without its entire population experiencing a mass conversion to a new philosophy of conflict.

Historically, nonviolent sanctions have most often been used by people who needed to make practical choices under very difficult circumstances, rather than by people committed to the avoidance of bloodshed for ethical reasons. This fact, in itself, argues for the investigation of nonviolent sanctions in purely pragmatic terms. To be sure, this approach must bear in mind that the presence or absence of principled actors may be a variable in nonviolent conflict, not to be confused with the conduct of nonviolent action itself.

If the use of nonviolent sanctions is not equivalent to a commitment to principled nonviolence, neither should it be confused with the somewhat misleading phrase "nonviolent conflict resolution." That phrase usually denotes a dispute settlement process, such as negotiation or mediation, that is characterized by a relative absence of violence. All conflicts, violent and nonviolent, ultimately get resolved. What typifies conflict by means of nonviolent sanctions is not that the resolution as such is less violent, but that the conflict itself is waged by sanctions which eschew violence en route to resolution. Strategic nonviolent conflict does not start from the premise that resolution of differences is the highest good, but rather that valid societal objectives must sometimes be defended or advanced by some active means. In other words, we are talking primarily about a technique for the prosecution and not the resolution of conflict.[6]

Finally, our definition does not, as is sometimes supposed, reduce the concept of "sanction" to include merely third party economic and diplomatic sanctions, such as those collectively imposed from time to time against an errant state. While such measures obviously fall within our definition, we want to use the term in its more radical sense, including all direct methods of punishment and persuasion at the nonviolent protagonists' disposal. Table 1.1 gives an indication of the range and types of such methods or sanctions that are available to strategists for consideration.[7]

Choices from among this range of methods in conflict have often been haphazard, involving a very high degree of improvisation. Systematic selection of the optimum sanctions to achieve clear strategic objectives is much rarer. Some observers have even found a virtue in this fact, attributing the successes of nonviolent action to its alleged

Table 1.1
Methods of Nonviolent Action

Protest and Persuasion	Noncooperation	Intervention
mass demonstrations	civil disobedience	overloading facilities
petitions	strikes (all types)	sit-ins
protest funerals	economic boycotts	creating parallel institutions
walk-outs	tax withholding	nonviolent blockades
renouncing honors	credit withholding	teach-ins
picketing	legal obstruction	seizure of assets
mock awards	providing sanctuary	alternative markets
fraternization	rent withholding	guerrilla theater
vigils	diplomatic non-cooperation	counterfeiting
speeches/advocacy	resignation of posts	forcible exposure of identity
mock elections	draft refusal	nonviolent invasion
symbolic public acts	social boycotts	nonviolent sabotage
parades and marches	nonrecognition of appointed officials	seeking imprisonment
"haunting" officials	judicial noncooperation	dumping commodities

"spontaneity" and its elemental force.[8] We disagree. It is our view that the conduct of nonviolent conflict can and should be *strategic*. Improving strategic performance by leaders of nonviolent action improves the efficiency and effectiveness of the technique. What, then, makes nonviolent conflict strategic?

DIMENSIONS OF STRATEGIC CHOICE

Strategy, in the broadest sense, is the process by which one analyzes a given conflict and determines how to gain objectives at minimum expense and risk. As with conflict, strategic calculation must necessarily foresee an adversarial process, since the objectives in question must be achieved at the expense of opponents who are engaged in a similar process.[9] The strategist wants to know which resources, including human resources, material resources, and specific sanctions, deployed in which manner, given the likely response of opponents, will offer the most cost-effective route to success.

Up to this point we have referred to the whole process of decision making as "strategy." Now we need to acknowledge what students of military affairs have known for hundreds of years, namely, that the process of conducting conflict proceeds on several distinct levels, one of which is properly called strategy. For now we will concern ourselves with just three: policy, strategy, and tactics.[10] Decisions taken on the level of policy are ones which define a group's objectives, determine what price may be paid for them, what an acceptable outcome may consist of, when to commence the conflict, and when to stop fighting. It is at the level of strategy that plans for securing the objectives are adjusted to real-life, real-time circumstances. Strategic decisions coordinate all of a group's resources and actions to pursue desired outcomes in a fluid process of interaction with opponents. On the next level down, tactical decisions govern behavior toward the opponents and their agents in specific encounters.

These distinctions and their significance will be developed in much greater detail in the next chapter. Suffice it here to say that a comprehensively strategic nonviolent effort does not confuse tactics with strategy, nor does it pursue ill-defined objectives on the basis of inadequate planning. A nonviolent strategist understands what level each decision is pertinent to, and will therefore automatically see if important issues are being overlooked on any level. Any given choice in conflict, then, may have an impact on one or more of the levels described above.

The next dimension we need to consider is that of offense and defense. Each discrete choice may also affect the mode of conflict each protagonist pursues along a spectrum of possible offensive and defensive postures. Is an action designed to undermine the opponents' objectives, or to protect one's own capabilities and allow the nonviolent strategists to continue the conflict? Both types of options will be necessary in most conflicts, and it will be important to recognize and prepare for them.

The logic of strategic choice, approached conceptually in more or less similar terms to those above, has informed the conduct of military affairs throughout the course of most of recorded history. Our purpose is to ask what happens when strategic concepts are introduced systematically into the arena of nonviolent conflict. There is a long tradition of strategic discourse that speaks to the conduct of war, and there is no reason why the same logic and methods may not be applied fruitfully here. Indeed, there have been several attempts to do just that already. In 1973, Gene Sharp wrote in his major work, *The Politics of Nonviolent Action*, that individual sanctions

> will be most effective if they fit together as parts of a comprehensive whole, so that each specific action contributes in a maximum way to the development and successful conclusion of the struggle. The optimal combination of specific actions is therefore best achieved where leaders with an adequate grasp of the situation and the technique are able to chart the course of the campaigns.[11]

Sharp's *Politics* was predicated on the notion that power relationships can be altered if nonviolent sanctions are used systematically to erode an opponent's source of tangible support. The intellectual pedigree of this approach goes back at least as far as the sixteenth-century essayist, Etienne de la Boétie, whose "Discourse of Voluntary Servitude" reasoned that tyrants thrive because the oppressed afford them the cooperation they need to retain power. Gandhi's experiments with the methods of nonviolent action were informed by this conception as well, and implicitly so are all cases of struggle in which the withdrawal of consent is a feature.

The genius of Sharp's *Politics*, however, is that it combines not only a relational theory of power with an expanded array of nonviolent weapons, but it also incorporates more sophisticated strategic assumptions from sources such as Machiavelli, Clausewitz, and Liddell Hart.[12] So, in the quotation above, we see the beginnings of a transition from a broad political construct to something more operationally precise. The general knowledge that power can be taken and wielded by collective action begins to encounter the more challenging reality that the truth of that statement never ensures victory in a particular case. What must be done to best a specific opponent is not revealed in the theory. Schelling presents well the inherent unpredictability of the outcome of a battle between violent and nonviolent protagonists:

the tyrant and his subjects are in somewhat symmetrical positions. *They* can deny *him* most of what *he* wants—they can, that is, if they have the disciplined organization to refuse collaboration. And *he* can deny *them* just about everything *they* want—he can deny it by using the force at his command. They can deny him the economic fruits of conquest, he can deny them the economic fruits of their own activity. They can deny him the satisfaction of ruling a disciplined country, he can deny them the satisfaction of ruling themselves. They can confront him with chaos, starvation, idleness and social breakdown, but he confronts them with the same thing and, indeed, most of what they deny him they deny themselves. It is a bargaining situation in which either side, if adequately disciplined and organized, can deny most of what the other wants; and it remains to see who wins.[13]

The statement that "it remains to see who wins" is about as far as strategic discourse in this field has managed to get. A number of factors have militated against further refinement. We have noted that in the past the phenomenon of nonviolent conflict has been misidentified with, or reduced to, particular principled ideologies. That tendency, in turn, has kept much of the history of nonviolent action (and therefore much grist for analysis) hidden. Instead of understanding it as purposeful and potentially strategic behavior, nonviolent action has often been seen as an expression of goodness or heroism—something not easily subject to explanation or development.

In the next chapter we elaborate a set of "principles" for strategic nonviolent conflict. Organized into three broad categories—principles of development, principles of engagement, and principles of conception—they are intended not as mechanistic formulas for winning fights but as a comprehensive guide to the types of problems and challenges involved in using this technique of struggle. The principles are derived from the history of nonviolent struggle, including the cases which follow, as well as from the theoretical literature about it and the literature of strategic discourse in general. These principles, constituted as a set, are offered as an explanatory framework to assess the relationship between strategic performance and "who wins."

CAMPAIGNS

There is virtually no such thing as a case of exclusively nonviolent conflict. Empirically, violent and nonviolent methods nearly always coexist to some degree in major social and political conflicts. Even when some violent methods are not acted out by one party, the possibility that they might be is usually part of the other parties' calculations. For example, we will see shortly that while the Indian independence movement was predominantly nonviolent, the British colonial government needed to concern itself with occasional violent outbreaks and with the continuing possibility that the movement as a whole might change course.

In the absence of a more refined strategic problematic, the kind of improvisation that has typically characterized nonviolent conflict is bound to continue. Our purpose is to move further from the general political construct that nonviolent action can wield power to a more fully realized operational framework. We want to move from politics to strategy.

Chapters 3 through 8 of this book will present historical treatments of a selection of cases of predominantly nonviolent conflict spanning the twentieth century. These include: the Russian revolution of 1904 to 1906, resistance to the Franco-Belgian occupation of the Ruhr region in 1923, the Indian independence movement from 1929 to 1931, Danish resistance to Nazi occupation from 1940 to 1945, the nonviolent insurrection in El Salvador in 1944, and the Polish Solidarity movement in 1980 and 1981. These cases were selected both for the ways in which they are similar and for the ways in which they differ.

While the six conflicts vary in duration from one month to three years, each of them lasted long enough to bring into play most of the variables explored in Chapter 2. All were intense conflicts, in that the opponents were prepared to use violent repression ruthlessly (and in varying degrees did so), while the populations wielding nonviolent sanctions were equally committed to success. Another similarity is that of magnitude. Each struggle enjoyed the active support and participation of a very large segment of the society in which it occurred.

Finally, each case represents a clearly discernible "campaign." A campaign, in this context, is a sequence of strategic interactions in which the participants try to pursue more or less known objectives. A campaign (as distinct from a social movement that might go on for decades or generations) tends to have a recognizable beginning, middle, and end. We contend that it is in the context of a campaign that the logic of strategic choice and consequence expresses itself and is meaningfully analyzed and compared. Even in a losing effort it is possible that certain choices might be seen to have long-term beneficial effects. While not denying that possibility, it is our purpose to look at these cases strictly at the campaign level, in order to determine which types of choices produce the best results within the framework of the immediate conflict.

The cases differ radically in three respects. The first is the degree to which nonviolent sanctions were part of a deliberate, internally consistent strategy. The Russian revolution, though it followed an active tradition of many years of urban strikes and demonstrations, peasant uprisings and agitation even among the professional classes, was essentially spontaneous.

The Indian independence movement presents a completely different picture. Here nonviolent sanctions had been utilized and refined for several years prior to the campaign in question, with varying results. The events of the 1929–1931 period were a deliberate attempt by the Indian National Congress, the leading nationalist party, to revitalize a long-standing conflict. In the Indian case, nonviolent action was a carefully conceived strategy to attain independence. Those who promulgated the policy were personally committed to it; they were well-entrenched leaders, respected by their peers and the overwhelming majority of their nation's people.

In other cases, violent sanctions were rejected because they did not provide a viable alternative due to particular conditions (the Ruhr region, for example, had been demilitarized) or because of a fear that they would provoke intolerable reprisals. This will be seen in the case of El Salvador, where an abortive violent insurrection preceded the successful nonviolent one. In both of these cases, nonviolent sanctions were chosen more or less by default, and their use did not follow a coherent strategy.

Another major way in which the cases differ is according to the character of their objectives. In Russia and El Salvador, the goal was to dislodge a long-entrenched indigenous regime. In the Ruhr and Denmark, nonviolent activists worked to defend their societies from recent encroachments by an external power. In India and Poland, one could argue that either was the case, depending on how "long-entrenched" and "external" are defined. It seems quite possible that the strategic principles pertinent to one type of threat may not be the best guides to strategy against another.

A final way in which the cases differ is in the degree to which violent sanctions were either present in the predominantly nonviolent movement or were believed to be an implicit threat if the nonviolent sanctions should fail. In Russia and the Ruhr, terrorist bombings and assassinations accompanied the mass nonviolent struggles, while in Denmark nonviolent resistance to occupation was one part of a wide spectrum of action taking place in the context of the Second World War, in which military sanctions were, of course, paramount. Gandhi, on the other hand, insisted on consistency and discipline among his nonviolent followers. However, he was not above implying that if the British could not resolve matters with his party, they might well find themselves faced with an array of groups that were prepared to use violence.[14] The degree to which violent and nonviolent sanctions can be effectively combined in pursuit of a common goal has been a long-standing question in this field, and the range of difference exhibited by this group of cases should enable us to make some preliminary judgments on the issue of mixed strategies.

We do not purport to offer exhaustive histories of these contests, any one of which could (and in most cases does) constitute a field of study in its own right. We will attempt, however, to look carefully at the following aspects of each struggle. What is the background to the conflict? Who are the parties and what are their objectives? What resources can they muster? What main lines of strategic interaction unfold? What is the outcome, as represented by the status of stated objectives at the end of a campaign? Is there evidence of critical junctures at which the quality of the protagonists' choices can be seen to affect the outcome materially?

As we work through the cases, we will be asking three questions about the strategic principles set out in Chapter 2. Are they operative? Do the actors conform to them? Does the answer to the previous question make any perceptible difference to the outcome, that is, are they important? Chapter 9, "Strategy and the Margin of Victory," summarizes our answers to these questions and explores how adherence to the principles improves the performance of strategic nonviolent conflict. Here we will be asking whether the principles are comprehensive, in the sense that they anticipate all major problems inherent to this type of conflict.

The cases examined illustrate the principles. They do not test them. Indeed, in this work, the study of cases and the articulation of principles have been simultaneous and reinforcing. Examination of additional cases might well lead to further refinements to this set of strategic principles, and we welcome and encourage further research toward that end.

Chapter 9 concludes by addressing questions of contemporary and future relevance, and returns to the issue of whether strategy develops. Using some of the most significant cases from the 1980s and 1990s, we look for evidence that the conduct of nonviolent conflict becomes more efficient and consistent over time—that the technique, in effect, becomes easier to master and use effectively.

RED HERRINGS

There are four arguments that will inevitably be leveled against a book on nonviolent conflict. These arguments have functioned historically as red herrings,[15] serving to delay the emergence of strategic nonviolent conflict by throwing up spurious ideas about its nature and potential. These criticisms are persistent, widespread, and subtle in their capacity to confuse thinking. We want to confront them at the outset.

First, someone will surely argue that any attempt to identify "strategic principles" is reductionist and mechanistic. No conflict is ever so simple that a cookbook of how-to concepts can be meaningfully used to assess it at any point. Look at the damage that has been done throughout the course of military history by formulaic notions when they have been simplistically applied! Nothing ever happens as expected, and there is no reason why it should be any different for nonviolent conflict.

We agree with this basic sentiment. The principles we outline are heuristic devices rather than formulas for easy victory. The best response to this line of criticism is not to give up thinking about the subject but to try to think more carefully and inclusively about it. In each and every case, strategy requires the continuous and simultaneous evaluation of a complex set of variables. While this is no easy task, neither is it impossible.

There is never a point at which one strategic conception or route to victory can be depended on as decisive. What is decisive in one case may be irrelevant in another. While it is true that military strategists have met with disaster by substituting theory for reality on the battlefield, the red herring here is to suppose that the practice of nonviolent conflict must inevitably follow the least promising examples available. There are also many examples, in all types of struggles, in which strong, comprehensive reasoning combined with deep specific knowledge and insight lead to brilliant performance. A by-product of refining the strategic problematic for nonviolent conflict is to show the reader what excellent performance means.

Second, others find strategic nonviolent conflict an objectionable approach by virtue of its utilitarian thrust. True nonviolence, they will argue, lies in a commitment to transforming the process of conflict itself from a win-lose proposition into a win-win exercise. By enduring suffering rather than inflicting it, the nonviolent protagonists melt their opponents' hearts and lift the contest onto a completely different, and more human, level of interaction, where victory is less important than the quality of the process that produces it.

There can be no argument but that some nonviolent activists enter the arena of conflict with such motives. Our claim in this regard is a simple one: they are the exception and not the rule. No one takes their life in their hands in any form of conflict without some powerful motivation to drive them. Motivation, however, can take many forms, none of which enjoys an exclusive association with the use of nonviolent methods. Some of the cases discussed below will exhibit actors who espouse philosophies of principled nonviolence. Others will be driven by the coldest of calculations as to material interests. We noted this earlier as a simple observation of fact. Now we can go further and say that neither a principled nor a pragmatic orientation, in itself, constitutes a prior determinant of, or constraint on, overall strategic performance. We will simply leave it to the reader and to the analysis of particular cases to see whether the presence of specific motives bears significantly on the outcome.

It should go without saying that recognizing diverse motives for pursuing nonviolent struggle should not detract one iota from the courage and heroism, moral and physical, exhibited by hundreds of thousands of principled nonviolent actors over time.

Our third red herring asserts that two and only two factors determine the outcome of nonviolent struggles: the violent opponents' relative will to repress and the nonviolent protagonists' relative ability to endure. This argument surfaces, for example, when it is alleged that Gandhi and King "had it easy," in the sense that their opponents were liberal democrats, and that a regime's proclivity for extreme repression sets the outside limit on the potential of a nonviolent effort. All a dictator has to do is repress beyond the other side's capacity to endure, and the struggle is over.

This notion is persistent because it is half true. Repression and endurance are critically important in most contests, and the presence of a strong will to repress radically complicates the problem for the nonviolent strategists. Repression may constrain their ability to organize and communicate freely. It may change the cost structure for potential participants so drastically that mobilization becomes slower and more difficult. We have to confront, however, the fact that many nonviolent struggles against liberal and less violent opponents have failed, while many conflicts against decidedly brutal opponents have succeeded. There are, without question, other factors.

One key factor is that the skillful use of politics and diplomacy by the so-called easy opponent may be a greater threat to a nonviolent action movement than overt violence. It is harder to legitimize extra-constitutional measures to advance a cause when it can plausibly be argued that all avenues of recourse "within the system" have not been exhausted. In mass post-industrial societies, the effort to satisfy that requirement may be all-consuming. Such efforts as the U.S. civil rights movement, therefore, can spend as much time justifying their methods as they do contending with the adversary.

Conversely, the cases which follow will show several examples of regimes who were not afraid to use repression, who carefully calibrated it for a precise effect, and who nonetheless failed. Explanations for their defeat can be found in such areas as a noticeable deterioration of their expected sources of support, sometimes *because* of their violent methods and sometimes for wholly unrelated reasons. The minimum thing we can say at this point, however, is that the decision to repress nonviolent opponents violently is likely to involve far greater risks, uncertainties, and costs than is usually supposed.

Critics may nonetheless be tempted to argue an extreme case. Are potential costs, risks, and uncertainties likely to matter much to opponents who have an overwhelming preponderance of power, or who are irrational, or whose very objective may be the conduct of genocide? The hard truth is that such cases are all too real. Raymond Aron took exception to "passive resistance" because he saw people wrongfully assuming that "the age of massacres and exterminations is definitely over, and that a nation which puts down its arms will be neither deported nor reduced to slavery nor purely and simply exterminated."[16] "Passive resistance," as Aron thought of it, is a far cry from strategic nonviolent conflict. Still, he was right if we assume the effectiveness of either depends on the absence of genocidal behavior. Indeed, nonviolent conflict cannot require a kinder and gentler world in which to prevail, but it may offer (and has offered) a realistic alternative in the face of political violence as we know it.

The problem of extreme violence exists whether one adopts a violent or a nonviolent defense. If one has fewer resources than one's adversaries, inferior sanctions, fewer or less powerful allies, and no clear hope of success, it is obviously advisable to disengage as much as possible from overt conflict and adopt a strategy of withdrawal and survival, until a more advantageous situation can be developed. In such asymmetrical conflicts, nonviolent strategies may carry one advantage over violent ones: they can be inherently less escalatory or provocative, and may therefore be easier to disengage and retreat from *in extremis*. Another response to the problem, of course, is that the vast majority of conflicts are not so extreme.

Fourth, some critics argue that even in cases less extreme than the examples just discussed, it is such objective conditions as relative resources and authority, rather than the strategic performance of the protagonists, that determine the outcome of a struggle. In response, we argue that there are too many cases with outcomes that defy this expectation for it to be correct. Nonviolent mobilizations frequently have the initial impact of changing conditions in the environment in which they operate. Democratization efforts, for example, often begin with mass direct action in a previously harsh political environment, leading de facto to greater political tolerance and safe space in which to organize further efforts. Almost by definition, this dynamic takes place in contexts which were presumed to be intractable to nonviolent methods until the moment when those methods, in fact, come into play. Similarly, poor peoples' movements, whose comparative resources are often the very issue of the conflict itself, enhance their resource base through the process of conflict, rather than being constrained by it at the outset. We will say more about this in the next chapter under the principle relevant to material resources.

A summary argument to all of these objections is that no single-factor explanation for the outcome of any conflict is ever valid. This is true regardless of whether the weapons in a particular conflict happen to be predominantly violent or nonviolent. We intend to establish the relative importance of strategic performance, while not losing sight of other contributing factors.

The twelve principles presented in Chapter 2, therefore, are only useful to the extent that they address comprehensively all of the likely features of conflict that the nonviolent strategist must keep in full view. Only then will we be able to discuss meaningfully the prospects for widening the margin of victory.

NOTES

1. Based on data from the Minorities at Risk study, Ted Robert Gurr contends that the magnitude of "nonviolent protest by ethnopolitical groups" doubled from the late 1940s to the 1980s. Gurr, "Minorities at Risk: The Dynamics of Ethnopolitical Mobilization and Conflict, 1945–1990."

2. Gene Sharp has argued: "We are at the early stage of an expansion of historical significance" of the use of nonviolent weapons. While evidence for the claim is anecdotal, Sharp thinks a "major shift" away from violent means is in progress. Sharp, "Thinking About Nonviolent Struggle: Trends, Research, and Analysis."

3. See Table 1.1 and Gene Sharp, *The Politics of Nonviolent Action*, vol. 2, "The Methods of Nonviolent Action," for more extensive listings of methods which can be considered nonviolent sanctions.

4. For a full treatment of the varieties of principled nonviolence, see Gene Sharp, *Gandhi as a Political Strategist*, 201–34. *Satyagraha* is the term Gandhi originated for campaigns which would use nonviolent action but for which the primary motive would be the discovery of the truth of matters between the parties. Participants in the 1930–1931 independence campaign needed to subscribe only to nonviolent action as a method, and not to the principles of satyagraha.

5. It has been estimated that in 85 percent of all known cases of nonviolent action, the protagonists were not committed to nonviolence on grounds of principle. Peter Ackerman, "Strategic Aspects of Nonviolent Resistance Movements," 87.

6. For clarity's sake we must distinguish between the terms "technique," "method," and "maneuver" as they will be used in this text. "Technique" refers to the broad type of conflict under discussion, that is, the technique of strategic nonviolent conflict. This should be seen as a functional equivalent of other broad techniques of struggle, such as guerrilla warfare, conventional warfare, international terrorism, and so forth. "Method," which will be used interchangeably with "sanction," will refer to specific, discrete actions such as those shown in Table 1.1. Finally, "maneuver" will refer to a sequence of methods or sanctions designed to have a strategic impact on the opponents.

7. This brief sampling of discrete methods of nonviolent action, and its three-part classification, come from Sharp, *Politics*, vol. 2, which identifies and explains 198 such methods. The categories "noncooperation" and "intervention" can be further divided into economic, social, political, and psy-

chological examples. Sharp's classification scheme is original and illuminating, but it has some limitations and has been subject to misinterpretation. It does not, as some have supposed, represent an intensity scale, with noncooperation presumed to be more powerful than protest and persuasion, and intervention more powerful than either of those. Nor are the different classes of methods airtight compartments. A given act may be "protest" in one context and "intervention" in another, or acts from different classes may be nested within each other, as when civil disobedience occurs during a demonstration. Our concern here is simply to suggest that a significant range of optional methods exists.

8. See, for example, Johan Jørgen Holst, "Civilian-based Defense in a New Era," 11, 16.

9. Some will argue, correctly, that adversarial conflict may be destructive of all parties' interests, and that a sum-sum approach may be both morally and practically superior. In many cases they are right. Our contention is that the logic of strategy is simply not central in those cases, in the event that a process of conflict resolution, rather than prosecution, prevails.

10. While precise distinctions between these levels and their definitions vary from the ancient Greeks and Romans to the present, there is also a remarkable consistency over time with regard to such levels of strategic analysis and decision making, and their importance in being able to think clearly about the problem of conflict. See Edward N. Luttwak, *Strategy*, especially Appendix 1, for some comparative definitions. Our definitions of the levels are roughly compatible with the fairly standard ones put forward by Sir Basil Liddell Hart in *Strategy: The Indirect Approach*, Chapter 19, except that in the environment of nonviolent conflict we find "policy" a more useful concept than "grand strategy." In Chapter 2, principle 10, below, we will define and explore at some length the importance of these three levels for the conduct of conflict as well as two more: operational planning and logistics. Suffice it at this point to say that each level speaks to a fairly discrete set of problems, confusion among which can easily lead to erroneous analysis of relative power positions and tragically flawed decisions.

11. Sharp, *Politics*, 3:494.

12. In vol. 3 of *Politics*, "The Dynamics of Nonviolent Action," Sharp uses these and many more conventional sources on strategy to develop the claim that nonviolent weapons are subject to many of the same principles associated with strategic discourse. Liddell Hart's "indirect approach" and Clausewitz's "superiority of the defensive," for example, are not only found to be compatible with nonviolent strategy but are seen to find their ultimate expression in it.

13. Thomas C. Schelling, "Some Questions on Civilian Defence," in Adam Roberts, ed., *Civilian Resistance as a National Defence*, 351–52.

14. See, for example, Gandhi's "Open Letter to a British Viceroy," published in *Young India*, 12 March 1930.

15. The phrase "red herring" is used here to indicate something which misleads, consistent with contemporary usage. It is interesting to note, however, that the earliest known use of the phrase, in 1686, denoted a form of

nonviolent action, precisely as that term is used throughout this book. According to the *Oxford English Dictionary* (Compact Edition, Oxford University Press, 1985, vol. 2, p. 2454), a red herring (red, as a consequence of having been smoked) was dragged across the trail of a fox or some other quarry with a view to confusing the hounds and subverting the hunt. This practice, if it really happened, has all the features of a method of nonviolent action in our meaning. It does no bodily injury. It involves direct action (as opposed to simply asking the landed gentry not to stage a hunt). It requires no particular ideological commitment. (We do not know if the perpetrators were against blood sports in principle or just did not want their crops trampled by the hunt.) Finally, if successful, it would have constituted a sanction, by adding to the costs of pursuing prey in this manner.

16. Quoted in G. Mann, *The History of Germany Since 1789,* 434.

Chapter 2

The Principles of Strategic Nonviolent Conflict

We have argued that most mass nonviolent conflicts to date have been largely improvised. What would this form of conflict look like if that were not the case? Could strategic nonviolent conflict, fully prepared and premeditated, be waged with substantially greater skill, intelligence, and effect? Could the margin of success for the technique of nonviolent action or "people power" be deliberately widened? We believe there is reason to think that the answer is yes.

In this chapter we present twelve principles of strategic nonviolent conflict. They are designed to address the major factors that contribute to success or failure in nonviolent conflict and that may be subject to intentional human choices. We do not identify objective conditions for success. Maximizing, or at the very least assessing, opportunities embedded in those conditions is the job of the strategist.

Much of the conceptual content for these principles comes from the literature of military strategy, as well as from the theoretical literature on nonviolent action. We have found it useful to develop the framework of choice for nonviolent strategists in such familiar Clausewitzian terms as "the objective" or "offense" and "defense" because these concepts work. They go to the heart of the process of conflict.

An additional source of these principles is the history of nonviolent action, including case studies of the campaigns that follow. We ask the reader to bear them in mind when examining the cases, to see whether the principles are operative, either positively (the protagonists conform to the principle and do well, arguably as a result) or negatively (the protagonists fail to conform, with harmful consequences for their position in the conflict). We will argue at the end of each case the key ways in which we think the principles were at work.

Finally, before discussing the principles, it needs to be stressed that as concepts they are exploratory rather than definitive. The entire universe of relevant cases has barely begun to be understood by researchers of nonviolent conflict. Our assumption is that any formal model should be subject to refinement as the field develops and concepts are tested against a wider body of experience. It would be a mistake to imagine that there are no possible intervening variables, unexplored in this analysis, that could determine the outcome of a nonviolent struggle.

Not only do we think that all general principles are subject to constant refinement, but we also agree with those who take a more historical and interpretive approach to strategy: it is impossible to overestimate the importance of what can be learned from a particular case. For both students and practitioners of nonviolent conflict, there is no substitute for a deep grounding in the context and the unique circumstances of an individual case. Applying general principles in a naive, mechanistic, or formulaic way will lead to faulty interpretation by the academician and possible tragedy for the practitioner in the heat of battle.

We do claim, however, that these principles highlight the *salient features* of strategic nonviolent conflict, and that conformity with their broad recommendations will tend a nonviolent struggle toward success. While nothing can guarantee victory, we think the principles outlined below can be used to identify opportunities and pitfalls. We expect alert readers to become aware of the forms defeat has taken in the past, so that certain obvious blunders need not be repeated.

Three types of principles are offered: principles of development, principles of engagement, and principles of conception (see Table 2.1). This classification breaks down the myriad tasks of strategic nonviolent conflict and arranges them in an orderly fashion, so that strategists can analyze their situation, plan their approach, and pursue the conflict with greater clarity and precision.

Principles of development encourage the reader or practitioner to

Table 2.1
Principles of Strategic Nonviolent Conflict

Principles of Development

1. Formulate functional objectives.
2. Develop organizational strength.
3. Secure access to critical material resources.
4. Cultivate external assistance.
5. Expand the repertoire of sanctions.

Principles of Engagement

6. Attack the opponents' strategy for consolidating control.
7. Mute the impact of the opponents' violent weapons.
8. Alienate opponents from expected bases of support.
9. Maintain nonviolent discipline.

Principles of Conception

10. Assess events and options in light of levels of strategic decision making.
11. Adjust offensive and defensive operations according to the relative vulnerabilities of the protagonists.
12. Sustain continuity between sanctions, mechanisms, and objectives.

ask "What can be done to create the most advantageous environment for strategic nonviolent conflict?" The tasks suggested by these principles are seen as ongoing, but initial requirements should be emphasized prior to overt conflict with an opponent. Principles of engagement ask "Once the conflict is joined, how should we interact with the opponents so that nonviolent sanctions will have the maximum effect?" Conflict is fluid. The friction and chaos of opposing wills clashing require continuous fine tuning of strategic choices under the pressure of events. Principles of conception ask "How should we think about what we have already done to the opponents and what we are trying to do to them as the conflict continues?" The relationship between the remaining strategic options and the prospects for success need constant review.

The principles are not mutually exclusive or necessarily sequential (although focus on principles of development may precede emphasis on principles of engagement). Conformity to any one principle may be of decisive importance at any point in a given conflict, so that mastery and continuous use of all are essential to achieving a comprehensive strategic approach.

PRINCIPLES OF DEVELOPMENT

Principle 1: Formulate Functional Objectives

All competent strategy derives from objectives that are well chosen, defined, and understood. Yet it is surprising how many groups in conflict fail to articulate their objectives in anything but the most abstract terms. In each conflict there is an ultimate goal that, once attained, will constitute victory. That goal should be seen as the dependent variable toward which all levels of decision making are directed. Both for that goal, and for any subordinate objectives to be pursued along the way, precision is needed if strategy is to be coherent.

The concept of "freedom" is inspiring to millions. As an ultimate strategic objective, though, it is not highly functional because it lacks specificity. The legalization of independent trade unions (as in Poland in 1980), on the other hand, is the very model of a clear and functional objective. The clearer an objective is, the easier it is to assess its relative importance, and the less likely it will be to misjudge whether and when it has been accomplished.

Secondary objectives may also be critically important. Chosen well, they may decisively affect the ebb and flow of the fight. Chosen badly, they can create expensive distractions or unnecessary defeats. They may even be achieved, but with negligible effect on the opponents. To help formulate functional objectives, we suggest using the following five criteria.

First, objectives should be concrete and specific enough to be achievable within a reasonable time frame. Second, they should readily suggest the use of a diverse array of nonviolent sanctions. Third, the objectives should be seen to preserve the vital (as opposed to marginal) interests of the nonviolent protagonists, and, ideally, be of more compelling interest for them than for the adversary. Fourth, the goals must attract the widest possible support within the societies affected by the conflict. Fifth, objectives should resonate with the values or interests of external parties, in order to attract their support and potential assistance.

Most people will struggle and sacrifice only for goals that are concrete enough to be reasonably attainable. In some cases, clear, specific goals emerge easily. If the opponents are military occupiers, their simple expulsion becomes the ultimate objective. If that seems to require a long, sustained effort, then specific intermediate goals may be advisable. Concessions from the occupiers not to engage in specific repressive practices, such as capital punishment for resistance activities, may be a plausible intermediate step. Or the intervention of international observers may be attained for the duration of the occupation.

The point is that the resisting population will need progressive victories in order to grow in confidence, stay committed to the overall strategy, and measure its own performance. This is even more essential in cases where long-standing oppression is being challenged. The tendency to view the dominant power as omnipotent can best be undermined by a steady stream of modest, concrete achievements.

Some objectives are more readily suggestive of a specific repertoire of nonviolent sanctions than others. If opponents want to seize a specific resource, removing that resource or rendering it inoperable will have a direct impact on the outcome. Where economic objectives are at stake, raising the costs for opponents through economic actions such as strikes and boycotts may be useful. If national autonomy or independence is the objective, direct actions of all kinds by citizens may demonstrate their de facto independence, with both material and important symbolic consequences. The importance of having a diverse array of sanctions and linking them to specific outcomes is addressed in principles 5 and 12.

Nonviolent strategists have no control over how attached the opponents will be to their objectives, but an effort should be made to fight for things that are clearly of vital interest to the nonviolent protagonists. Generally, an objective has greater strategic utility if it is more important to the group pursuing it than to their adversaries. Claims involving cultural or national identity and survival, basic human rights, and closely held religious convictions often fall into this category. Contests over highly dubious territorial claims or marginal economic gain, on the other hand, may be less compelling to the nonviolent protagonists themselves and attract less sympathy and support from third parties.

In mass nonviolent conflict, objectives need to attract the widest possible base of support. This is not to equate success with sheer numbers but rather to suggest that unity, commitment, and the massed potential of nonviolent sanctions will be likely to diminish if some sectors stand more to gain than others, or if potentially key groups are left out entirely. Widely shared objectives also create the potential for more widely distributed risks and reduce the likelihood that any single party or circumstance can become a decisive target.

Finally, we have asserted that functional objectives tend to be ones that resonate with the values and interests of third parties to a conflict. This does not mean that some objectives are "right" and others "wrong" but simply that, in a given political or economic context or cultural milieu, some causes will earn more legitimacy or seem more compelling than others. It is hard to imagine broad international support, for example, for an economic embargo of Japan by jealous regional competitors. Broad external support for nonviolent struggles can develop, however, in those struggles that have at their core objectives that are of value beyond the fight itself.

Principle 2: Develop Organizational Strength

Occasionally, individual actions make a significant difference in large-scale social conflicts. Far more often, however, resistance is mounted and conflict is waged by groups. A key task for nonviolent strategists is to create new groups or turn preexisting groups and institutions into efficient fighting organizations.

To wage nonviolent conflict, fighting organizations must have or develop certain capabilities. They must be able to respond to the challenges and unique circumstances of an evolving situation. They need to be capable, at various points, of concealment (of persons, goods, information, money), dispersion (of critical resources and of nonviolent sanctions themselves), and surprise (by conducting operations that seize the initiative and throw the opponents off balance). Such organizations need to be able to make decisions under pressure, to translate their decisions into mobilization, and to motivate others to play various supporting parts.

There are obviously many ways to organize societies for conflict, and we do not want to suggest that there is a preferred model or ideal. In functional terms, however, we see three strata of organization at which strength and flexibility need to be developed, if the tasks of nonviolent struggle are to be performed well. They are the leadership, the operational corps, and the broad civilian population.[1]

The role of leadership in nonviolent conflict is twofold: to make the primary decisions that will shape the conflict, and to serve as a rallying point for inspiration, courage, and clarity of purpose. Just as there is no best model for organization in general, there is no formula for determining the ideal leadership structure in any given case.

It is widely assumed that charismatic individuals are necessary in the leadership of nonviolent struggle. But there are plenty of cases with no Mohandas Gandhi, Lech Walesa, or Corazon Aquino at their head. In cases where charismatic individuals rise or are thrust into leadership, they bring the advantages of the respect they command and the constituents they motivate. But allowed to function unchallenged, their personal weaknesses may unwittingly become the weaknesses of the movement itself.[2] It is inevitable that leadership roles will accrue to individuals. Individual leaders should be evaluated according to their performance as decision makers and motivators of people.

Probably the most common form of leadership in conflict is by a committee or other group empowered to make decisions for the wider organization. Such a decision-making body can be above or below ground, elected or appointed, in the theater of conflict or safely ensconced abroad. The critical requirement is that the group needs to be able to respond swiftly and intelligently to changing conditions and must have sufficient authority and credibility to make its decisions operational.

Nonviolent strategists often struggle in open defiance of their opponents, and leaders are vulnerable to repression. They can be killed, arrested, deported, or neutralized politically (as by scandal, real or manufactured, ridicule, or co-optation). To allay such threats, depth of leadership must be developed. Lines of succession should be clear. Knowledge of the basic strategy should extend well down through the organization. Above all, the success of the struggle should never be tied to the personal fortunes of the leadership.

Another way that "leadership" can be maintained is through conformity to a widely shared plan of operations by loosely connected or semi-autonomous units. Regional militia, cells, and so forth can carry on a struggle, as they typically do in guerrilla warfare, without regular contact with a central decision-making body, as long as the plan they follow is sufficiently comprehensive and yet flexible enough to allow them to adapt tactics to local circumstances. Whichever model or combination of models is chosen for the leadership of a conflict, the central tasks of leadership remain: to make strategic decisions and to motivate the whole fighting organization.

The next tier of organizational muscle is unique to nonviolent conflict. It is roughly analogous to the officer corps in military or paramilitary struggle. We will call it the operational corps. The people in this strata are really the organizational glue that holds a nonviolent movement or organization together.

The operational corps may be assembled and trained for the specific purposes of a conflict, or it may be co-opted from the middle leadership ranks of participating groups and sectors. The corps has four key functions. First, it must be able to communicate decisions and other basic information throughout its constituent population during the conflict. For example, the corps would communicate such leadership decisions as the day of a general strike or a change of behavior toward opponents or the decision that taxes and fines should be withheld and paid into escrow. The corps could also report to the leadership on such matters as the relative morale and likely behavior of enemy soldiers at any given moment.

The corps's task goes beyond simple communication. It must instruct, nurture, and support the general population in the performance of nonviolent conflict. Morale will need boosting. Potential defectors must be actively discouraged from leaving, while collaborators are identified and shamed. The nature of the technique of action and how it can lead the group to its objectives will need to be explained repeatedly.

The operations corps must also serve as the intelligence arm for the leadership. The corps needs to provide assessments of the stamina of the civilian population. As we will see, skillful pacing of engagements is critically important. The corps must seek out enemy movements well in advance so the nonviolent strategists can plan countermoves.

Finally, it is the operational corps that will perform highly specialized and sometimes particularly dangerous operations. Where the average citizen might be relied upon to stay at home in the event of a civic strike, confronting the adversaries' firepower in a roving street mobilization is another matter. The latter requires an extra measure of motivation and unique skills.[3] The precise tasks of the operational corps may vary widely depending on the objectives of a given fight. Who should perform them and how this tier should be organized will differ, but some such body will need to be ready to bear the brunt of conflict.

The third and final tier of nonviolent conflict organization is the civilian population in its entirety. As an amorphous mass, subject to competing pressures and influences, the population engaged in nonviolent struggle is less reliable than the foot soldiers of a typical national army. Frequently, though, the collective choices of masses of civilians become decisive. Military operations like coups d'etat and occupations are more easily completed in the absence of any manifestations of "people power." Both the leadership and the operational corps need to plan to utilize and extend existing social groups and institutions to engage the widest possible participation.

There is a historic debate as to the importance as well as the feasibility of organizing mass civilian struggle in a premeditated way. Some have argued that spontaneity is essential to the success of this technique of conflict, and that by definition it takes everyone by surprise, including anyone with pretensions to being a nonviolent strategist. It is argued that it is a fool's errand at best, and a positive harm at worst, to talk about mass mobilization in even slightly voluntaristic terms.[4]

The competing view, which we share, is that preexisting networks and organizations can be activated and harnessed in the service of particular objectives.[5] This view is supported by the fact that mass mobilization for civilian struggle happens, and it usually happens because identifiable parties do something to make it happen. Nonviolent strategists must think exhaustively and creatively about their relationship to their social surroundings, and the degree to which they or their operatives are likely to garner popular support, by virtue of the many groups and institutions they have access to or whose basic interests they are seeking to defend. It is obviously possible, and distinctly desirable for the performance of nonviolent sanctions, to think in advance about which groups have natural assets that can be brought to bear in an anticipated struggle. Trade unions usually have more than a passing familiarity with methods of noncooperation, such as the strike. Churches often have protected space in which resistance forces can mobilize. Professional groups may carry a certain level of legitimacy.

What are the threats to organizational strength? Students of social conflict will recognize them immediately: opportunists, free-riders, collaborators, misguided enthusiasts who break ranks with the dominant strategy, and would-be peacemakers who may press for premature accommodation.[6] Each of these may detract from morale, commitment, and the ultimate effectiveness of a nonviolent effort. Perhaps the most critical role for the operational corps to play is to deflect threats from these sources as they tend to occur when the stress of conflict is greatest. Known collaborators can be exposed and shunned. Black marketeers can be turned into social pariahs. Free-riders can be shamed into at least minimal participation, if a sufficiently tame role can be devised for them.

In the end, organizational strength at the levels of leadership, operational corps, and the general population translate into resiliency, responsiveness, and a proliferation of opportunities for the fighting organization.

Principle 3: Secure Access to Critical Material Resources

This principle is concerned with the material (as distinct from social, political, or psychological) resources needed to support the conduct of nonviolent struggle. Just as generals need adequate supplies of bullets, boots, and bandages, resources may prove to be decisive for practitioners of nonviolent conflict. Material resources play two pivotal roles. First, they contribute to the physical survival, well-being, and morale of the embattled population. Second, physical assets are part and parcel of the delivery and performance of certain nonviolent sanctions themselves.

This principle treats the resources in question as the means, not the ends, of conflict. Even if establishing control over some key resource were itself the contested objective, other "resources-as-means" would still need to be obtained.

During a conflict, the nonviolent protagonists will need to provide essential goods and services for themselves and their allies. If the fight is a long one, deprivation can easily take as great a toll as their opponents' attempts at repression. On the other hand, self-sufficiency with respect to food, clothing, energy, and medical supplies can contribute immeasurably to their ability to persevere. Relief efforts aimed at caring for the families of fallen resisters, or others placed at risk, heighten solidarity and hope. Access to negotiable currency or development of sophisticated barter schemes may reduce friction and spread the cost of resistance more evenly. A sense of fairness in burden sharing tends to mitigate inducements to surrender or to collaborate with the adversaries. This is the reason why, in the labor field, "strike funds" exist.

Thought should be given, at an early stage, to controlling sufficient reserves of essential materials to see the struggle through to a successful conclusion. While basic goods and services are used primarily for defensive purposes, such other assets as communications infrastructure and transportation equipment form the underpinnings of offensive operations. Deep redundancy of both quantity and type of communications gear is vital. A stockpile of quality fax machines, cellular phones, inexpensive shortwave radios, video and audio cassette players gives strategists the ability to make, disseminate, execute, and adjust their plans.

Swift and accurate communications are also necessary to authenticate instructions, to counter enemy propaganda, and generally to inform and bolster the fighting forces. Communications to the world outside the conflict are no less important, with images carried by print and broadcast media playing a key role in interpreting the conflict for outsiders and in motivating third party involvement.

Mobilization of mass defiance is obviously made easier by access to transportation, and, conversely, it is desirable to deny use of the transportation system to opponents. For example, alternative arrangements for one's own transportation requirements should precede embarking on a nationwide railway shutdown or a debilitating trucking and shipping boycott.

It is important to note that securing access to various categories of resources is not usually a zero-sum proposition, in the sense that if one side possesses something, the other cannot still take advantage of it somehow. The most efficient military occupation imaginable cannot monitor all the tangible assets of a society twenty-four hours a day. Even if one party controls a power station, for example, all parties will benefit from the free flow of energy as long as the station functions normally. Judgments need to be made whether exclusive control, or merely unchallenged access, to certain widely used facilities is best. Since material resources will affect both sides' endurance and capabilities, direct competition for exclusive control of material assets can be dangerously escalatory, unless gaining such control decides the conflict in and of itself.

Securing access to resources can be accomplished in several ways.

First, the source of necessary goods can be protected, such as by establishing safe havens or external staging grounds. If the source of the needed item is itself insecure, one can develop lines of action that depend on easily replaceable materials, perhaps ones that allies will be able to resupply at reasonable cost. Many important assets are portable and theoretically usable by either side. Then advance procurement and a system of dispersion into a large number of caches would be the best logistical solution.

The task for strategists, ultimately, is threefold. Material resources must be inventoried, prioritized, and then evaluated in terms of the risks and benefits of investing in the control of, or preservation of access to, each major type of resource. In evaluating alternatives as the conflict unfolds, it will be necessary to keep the relevant resources in continuous view and to assess whether they are creating opportunities or problems for the nonviolent forces.

Principle 4: Cultivate External Assistance

Critical help can come from outside the immediate arena of conflict. While the attitude of third parties can be potentially decisive, it cannot be counted on. Nonviolent strategists should cultivate external assistance as much as possible, at the very least seeking to neutralize outside support or sympathy for the adversary.

In defensive terms, the value of external support is that it reinforces principles 1 through 3 above, by enhancing the legitimacy of the objective, adding another dimension or depth to organizational strength, and, if the third parties are sufficiently motivated, providing an additional source of direct material aid. In offensive terms, third parties can add to the sanctions marshaled against the opponent.[7] Third parties can attack within the zone of conflict or punish the adversaries in outside areas where their vital interests lie.

Third parties are sometimes motivated by a direct material interest in the conflict, sometimes by a principled interest in the issues at stake, and often by a combination of the two. The amount of energy that should be invested in pursuing external support should be commensurate with the external parties' interests, of whatever kind, and their likely ability to provide the following specific forms of assistance.[8]

A willingness to replace vital resources that may be consumed in the course of the fight can be crucial, contributing to the endurance and unity of nonviolent struggle. Tolerating or encouraging safe bases of operation in the supporting party's territory can add immeasurably to the logistical capabilities of the nonviolent protagonists and, when appropriate,[9] the longevity of their leadership. Less risky for the supporting party than either of those options would be a simple agreement not to interfere with the performance of nonviolent sanctions by others, such as by honoring boycotts or not undermining economic sanctions by actively creating alternative markets for the target of those sanctions. Specific steps to enhance the legitimacy of the nonviolent protagonists can include conferring diplomatic recognition, multilateral initiatives on their behalf, possibly through the United Nations, and declarations reinforcing their views on the issues in contention.

The ultimate objective would be to have third parties launch sanctions of their own against the violent protagonists and, in effect, become direct parties to the struggle. But hopes in this regard have often been disappointed. Public attention to other peoples' conflicts and interests is fickle and fleeting. Willingness to risk costs on the behalf of others when one's own direct concerns are themselves pressing is not something to be expected.

Outside support need not come from the unanimous decision of an entire society or national government. Key sectors within societies or states may be just as important or even more so. Independent economic interests may align themselves against the adversary. In various situations, organized labor, ethnic or nationality groups, and social movements that identify with the issues of the conflict may seek to generate support. Established nongovernmental organizations in the fields of human rights, the environment, and international development assistance often have concerns and can play a role in the areas affected by nonviolent conflicts.

A strategist should try to undermine support that the opponent has come to expect and is counting on. An erstwhile ally's defection from the opponent's cause constitutes a significant sanction in itself. It may not always be possible, but allegiances can shift quickly in mass social conflict, and the momentum of the conflict itself may so change the configuration of interests that the unlikely becomes possible.

Principle 5: Expand the Repertoire of Sanctions

Scores of discrete nonviolent sanctions are available to strategists of nonviolent conflict. Sharp's list of 198 methods of nonviolent action—each of which, in its application, creates a distinct cost for its opponents—is the most extensive, and it is certainly not complete.[10] The ideal situation for strategists is one in which they can deliver on demand as many of these different sanctions as possible or desirable, in all kinds of creative combinations, and adapted to special circumstances.

A preliminary task for the strategist, therefore, is to create an inventory of the struggling population's general capabilities. What actions do they know how to take or are they practiced at taking? In the society at large, what forms of protest, noncooperation, and nonviolent intervention do people have images or memories of or experience with? What latent traditions of activism and direct social conflict can be tapped into?

Once it has been established that there is a general readiness to execute a variety of actions, the repertoire can be prioritized and eventually expanded. Strategists should ask themselves the following series of questions when developing or choosing sanctions. First, to what extent will the choice of particular sanctions enable us to seize and retain the initiative? This question implies an ability to do things that are not only unexpected but also imaginative, sometimes daring, and potentially motivating to others. Second, are some of the available sanctions easily replicable? If the adversary sees the threat of their use elsewhere, the impact is magnified. Third, can the sanctions be performed at different times and in diverse places without extensive special training and preparations by people imitating what they have seen or heard? Can available sanctions be dispersed or concentrated at will? Both are important. It will sometimes be necessary for crowds to mobilize in widely scattered areas to avoid the worst effects of repression, and at other times to mass opposition at key points of vulnerability.

Fourth, is the array of available sanctions relatively advantageous to use from the perspective of economy of force and risk versus return? Some sanctions can be very inexpensive to wield or can operate at very low risk. Unfortunately, such sanctions may have a correspondingly low impact. A minute of silence at work to display resolve is a case in point. Other sanctions are grand in design, costly, and replete with risk. They also may have the greatest impact. A sustained general strike is an example. Nonviolent strategists must order the desirability of the available sanctions according to the value of the likely trade-offs.

Fifth and finally is whether a group of sanctions to be used in a planned sequence are likely to build momentum and maximize the adverse impact on the opponents while preserving flexibility. The opponents may, for example, think that crushing a major demonstration with military force will take the life out of a movement. If, instead of quiescence, the violence triggers preplanned protest strikes in other locales, international protests, and attempts to induce mutiny among soldiers unhappy about what they have been asked to do, the nonviolent protagonists will have retained the initiative and imposed additional costs. This type of snowball effect should not be merely wished for or left to chance. Preparing in advance a wide repertoire of methods increases the likelihood that they can be brought into play to serve the ends of strategy.

There is no substitute for originality and creativity in adapting nonviolent sanctions to particular opportunities and in defending against particular threats. Suppose an occupying power decrees that it will kill one member of every tenth family in a town which proposes to launch a civic strike. Not wanting to bear this burden, the town might decide to reverse the tactic: workers might not go home at all, but stay at their jobs indefinitely and eventually pilfer, rather than enrich the occupying power with, the fruits of their additional labor.

Reducing the broad technique of nonviolent action to one or a few familiar methods of conflict is dangerous, but it is often the course that movements based on direct action take. The danger arises from the fact that if either or both parties perceive the conflict to hinge on the success or failure of a limited range of methods, then defeat on a limited front may be misconstrued as total defeat. Too often strategists overlook other promising options. This principle, then, recommends consideration of the greatest possible variety of nonviolent sanctions.

PRINCIPLES OF ENGAGEMENT

Principle 6: Attack the Opponents' Strategy for Consolidating Control

For the violent opponents, optimum control of the conflict situation derives from the presumed link between commands and the re-

sponses of those they seek to dominate. Whether the regime is repressing its own population or attacking another, it is in serious
trouble from the start if every action and outcome favorable to its
cause needs to be the product of direct coercion. It must seek to
establish and consolidate control by getting others to obey without
coercion. It is better still for the regime if it can get others to act in
anticipation of its commands so that the commands do not even need
to be issued. Obedience, then, is conditioned into conforming behavior.

Initially, commands are given and sanctions are threatened against
those who might disobey. For example, martial law may be declared,
and death or deportation might be announced as the penalty for
participating in resistance activities. The edicts of the regime combined with such threats might, in many cases, be sufficient to induce
the desired behavior. Peoples' habitual patterns of obedience, their
perceptions of the locus of law and order, their fear of retribution
(coupled, of course, with their estimation of the credibility of their
opponents' threats, the reliability of their soldiers, and so forth), all
may contribute to the consolidation of power that is the goal of the
repressor's strategy.

If commands and threats do not suffice, the punishing sanctions
themselves must be brought into play. This is less than ideal for the
violent protagonists, for whom the use of sanctions represents an
expenditure of energy, resources, and perhaps legitimacy. An opponent using violent sanctions becomes weaker, not stronger, unless
the targets of the repression misread the situation and assume they
are beaten or decide to acquiesce to avoid further punishment.

How the opponents seek to establish control will reveal a great
deal about objectives and strategy. The nonviolent strategist should
be analyzing the directions in which control is asserted from the outset of engagement. Is the resisting populace being told to carry on
with its normal range of activities, as is common after coups d'etat?
Or is it being pressured to desist from the specific behavior that
caused the conflict to be joined in the first place? Is overt compliance
with newly imposed expectations or regulations being sought? The
basic concept here is this: whatever the opponents want in terms of
control must be denied if denial can be achieved at an acceptable
price and the ability to fight on is preserved.

This principle recommends that the means of control be attacked
directly. If the opponents' troops are the principal means, efforts to

subvert those troops are essential. Providing incentives for mutiny or desertion, inducing role conflict by confronting the troops with the horrors of their actions, severing or interfering with their communications, demoralizing them by social isolation, or countermotivating them with attractive alternatives are all means by which this point of control can be weakened. Some of these things may seem like a tall order to perform, and, indeed, they are not all possible in many cases. In most cases of social conflict, however, including wars, there is some evidence of troop unreliability. Defections occur, orders are disobeyed or compromised, and control is thereby reduced. (See principle 8, below, "Alienate Opponents from Expected Bases of Support.")

The same logic applies to other means of control. Is an occupation government relying on a certain amount of collaboration from the host population? Sanctions can be designed specifically to deny the regime the needed help. Collaborators can be isolated, shunned, and targeted with economic sanctions themselves. They can be threatened a priori with legislation or with penalties for collaboration when the fight is over. If the opponents are trying to accomplish some objective with as few agents as possible, it is easily possible to force them to use more, simply by proliferating the incidents and dispersing the locations of nonviolent acts of defiance and disobedience.

In almost all cases, wide dispersion of nonviolent sanctions, both geographically and throughout the social and political environment, at least in the early phases of engagement, will compromise the opponents' ability to respond and diminish their overall control. If the opponents are operating on a precise schedule requiring quick responses, delaying tactics are in order. These are often the most easy to elicit from an embattled population. If strategies for control depend on complex orders which are clearly sent and understood, confusion and feigned incompetence may be the order of the day. All of the well-known methods of psychological warfare may be brought to bear in these situations. Direct confrontation may be unnecessarily dangerous and ultimately less effective. Again, the operations corps can be critical when it comes to coordinating opportunities to attack the adversaries' control in these indirect ways.

The net effect of a well-planned attack on the opponents' strategy for control should be severe disorientation and frustration. They should come to view their own repressive sanctions as unreliable, in the sense that, while they can do damage, they cannot elicit the desired results. When the violent protagonists come to see that success cannot be guaranteed by the material match-up of forces, they should be thrown significantly off balance. Weakening the opponents' self-confidence can be a significant milestone on the road to success for strategic nonviolent conflict.

Principle 7: Mute the Impact of the Opponents' Violent Weapons

The opponents' instruments of violence may still work, even if their strategy appears not to be working. Violent force can cause devastating damage and quickly diminish the material base from which nonviolent conflict is being waged. It can induce terror and demoralize people, reducing their willingness to take risks. Even more threatening may be the temptation to abandon one's nonviolent strategy and to lash out with a violence that is cathartic and vengeful yet void of strategic purpose. In the context of nonviolent conflict, violent retaliation is not likely to improve one's position and may elicit even harsher reprisals. (See principle 9, "Maintain Nonviolent Discipline.")

The task of anticipating and counteracting the effects of the opponents' violence falls largely to the operational corps. The corps cannot prevent the adversaries' deployment and use of violent methods, but it can implement a number of initiatives for muting their impact. We see several ways of doing this: get out of harm's way, take the sting out of the agents of violence, disable the weapons, prepare people for the worst effects of violence, and reduce the strategic importance of what may be lost to violence.

Getting out of harm's way requires good intelligence. Information on the intentions and movements of opponents is vital when conducting maneuvers of defensive dispersion. Some of the most successful actions detailed in the cases to follow, such as the rescue of the Danish Jews, turned on the ability to get accurate, timely information. People and things must be hidden or removed, preserving and denying resources in the same act. For all of this, preparation is key. It is obviously harder to design escape routes and establish supply caches once the defending area is occupied by enemy troops. Given a realistic appreciation of the opponents' potential for destructive repression, it should be easily possible to motivate the civilian population to conceive and plan for such evasive actions at an early stage.

The meaning of "taking the sting out of the agents of violence" has been alluded to elsewhere but needs emphasis in this context. The opponents are neither omniscient nor omnipotent. Their soldiers, collaborators, strategists, and allies will all be under pressure in the conflict, just as the nonviolent protagonists and their allies will be. The agents of violence can be blunted by confusion, fraternization in some cases, fear of being held personally responsible for atrocities, or fear of being isolated socially or physically. It is commonplace for troops under pressure to fire their weapons into the air, to disobey orders, and, less often, to change sides. The point is to induce or exploit these types of opportunities when they arise.

Disabling weapons through direct action, literally, "spiking the enemy's guns," requires careful consideration. So far, the literature in this field has largely confused or avoided the question of sabotage. Largely because of the dramatic and significant role of demolitions by partisan saboteurs during World War II, the concepts of sabotage and demolition have been used interchangeably in many discussions of the subject. Sharp, for example, itemizes eight reasons why sabotage is incompatible with the principle of nonviolent discipline. Virtually all of his arguments turn on the possibility of unintended violence to the opponents' agents or innocent bystanders. For example, a facility is blown up at the wrong time or with improper intelligence, causing casualties.[11]

Indeed, if sabotage and demolition were really equivalent, our recommmendation would be to avoid them altogether. Demolition, however, is a subset of sabotage, which should be defined as all acts which render inoperative the material resources of an opponent. Seen in this light, it is patently clear that there are both violent and nonviolent acts of sabotage. Demolition does have all the risks that Sharp contends, and it is not a useful tool in nonviolent conflict. The only plausible exception would be the one suggested by Liddell Hart, who envisioned army engineers controlling the risk of violent death by using explosives to create ditches and blow out bridges well in advance of attacking troops.[12]

What acts of sabotage can mute the impact of violent repression? Nonviolent sabotage, no longer a contradiction in terms, is essentially an economic sanction, to the extent that it renders resources for repression inoperative.

Many modern weapons are dependent on electronic support or computer control. Specially trained cadres can remove components, contaminate software, overload systems, and jam electronics. Guns, ammunition, and armored vehicles may be vulnerable to theft and tampering. Spiking the treads of tanks, for example, is a high-risk but tactically effective option. In the case of a long-term occupation or an entrenched oppressive regime, the manufacture of weapons may be disrupted at the factory level, if some resisters are in a position and willing to take such an aggressive step.

To deny that damage will be done by the opponents would be foolish and misleading. No objectives can be won in any form of acute conflict without significant human costs. Some measures can blunt the offending weapons, but even in the best circumstances that job will be incomplete. People must be prepared to expect the worst. It is vital that people learn not to equate casualties with defeat. Breaking down the false intuition that leads people to think "they shot us to pieces, so nonviolent action does not work" is vital to the success of strategic nonviolent conflict. The real issue is whether repression, which will almost certainly hold sway on the tactical and logistical levels, will prevail at the strategic and policy levels. If people have confidence in their basic strategy and fight on despite losses, their position may improve. Of course, a judgment must be made as to when repression has taken such a toll that retreat is advisable for a given population and for a specific period of time.

The final approach to muting the impact of violence is to negate the long-term significance of the actual losses. Deep redundancy and quick acquisition of replacement assets from alternative sources is ultimately desirable. The prospect of human losses requires support systems for victims and survivors. Medical, psychological, and financial support cannot eliminate but can mitigate suffering. Competent support distributed fairly may go a long way toward maintaining unity and resolve.

Principle 8: Alienate Opponents from Expected Bases of Support

The next best thing to muting the impact of a weapon is to increase the cost of using it. If violence is inevitable, nonviolent strategists should strive to see that it occurs in a way that harms the opponents' strategy. It is worse for the repressor if violent force is wielded in the open, under the glare of general scrutiny, and with public attention focused on the bloodthirsty and reprehensible acts. When the moment of confrontation comes, it must be clear to all watching that the violent outcome was the opponents' choice and was not forced by the actions of the nonviolent protagonists. A climate of revulsion for the adversaries' politics and strategy can be created which alienates the opponents from as many of their usual or expected sources of support as possible.

Their normal sources of support can be both internal and external. Internally, they will count on their own decision makers, agents, and supportive population. Externally, third party decision makers and their populations and agents are potential allies. Some may be traditional allies, while others are theoretically available to either side as the situation evolves. Within the camp of nonviolent participants, as we have noted earlier, there are the potential collaborators on whom the opponents' strategy may depend at some point. In the right circumstances collaborators can reverse their position and do considerable damage until the opponents become aware of the lost support.

All of these parties are subject to alienation from the violent protagonists' cause, and the revulsion alluded to above with respect to violent behavior is one of the primary ways by which this takes place. Commonly referred to as "political jujitsu,"[13] this dynamic takes the very force of the opponents' violence, manifested on the tactical level, and turns it to the nonviolent defenders' advantage on the strategic and policy levels by creating new and more negative perceptions of the adversaries' intent.

Another approach is to raise the costs of helping the opponents. Economic sanctions, for example, can be applied and, even if the would-be allies' decision makers are unmoved, their populations might react negatively to bearing hardships for a dubious cause. Those who help the aggressor can be isolated internationally and deflected from providing material support, and may even be, like the opponents' own troops, induced to change sides in some circumstances.

In the post–Cold War era, collective security may be gaining credibility and more widespread support. Without attempting to forecast the future, one can imagine how collective security and nonviolent strategy can be mutually enhancing. Parties who might have supported the violent protagonists may be disciplined into supporting

their targets instead, on the basis of treaty, law, or emerging norma-
tive standards, rather than being left to their own devices to see
which way their interests impel them. Potential allies of the violent
protagonists may be forced to assess their position in light of threats
to their standing in the international community. Then the task for
violent actors should be much harder than previously anticipated. As
adversaries become disoriented and are forced to look elsewhere for
reserves of strength in the conflict, they may begin to reevaluate
their readiness to continue fighting.

Principle 9: Maintain Nonviolent Discipline

In the previous chapter we distinguished between behavior which
is nonviolent—not directly resulting in overt physical injury to human subjects—and philosophies in which the rejection of violence is
a moral end in itself. Potential participants in a strategic nonviolent
conflict need to understand that they are not being invited to join a
new religion or change their basic world view. To participate in the
struggle, they must keep their behavior within a certain modus ope-
randi for the duration of the campaign. They need to know what
behavior is expected, in specific terms, and why it is essential to strategic success.

It is typical for groups engaged in nonviolent action to issue easily
understandable codes of conduct and to discipline their own members who stray. Instructions for remaining nonviolent might include
such things as injunctions against bringing weapons, alcohol, or
drugs to demonstrations or other actions; rules against taunting,
striking back, or otherwise compromising the safety of the opponents' agents; and advising people to withdraw if they feel their resolve to remain nonviolent giving way. Keeping nonviolent discipline
is neither an arbitrary nor primarily a moralistic choice. It advances
the conduct of strategy. The leadership and operational corps must
ensure that awareness of this fact permeates all levels of the nonviolent fighting organization.

Strategic nonviolent conflict is similar in many respects to violent
conflict, except when it comes to the individual actor's behavior.
Whereas soldiers are trained in the efficient use of their weapons,
nonviolent actors are expected to refrain from violence while still
actively resisting, in order to change the alignment of forces on the
strategic and policy levels. Nonviolent sanctions are capable of con-

fusing, frustrating, and embarrassing soldiers; diminishing the opponents' perceived legitimacy; turning others against the brutality of the violent strategy; and convincing the opponents that their own strongest weapons will not deliver the results, in terms of control, that they had hoped for.

Nonviolent discipline is, in one sense, like the "fire discipline" of the soldier, in that it is the ingredient that turns confrontations between adversaries into victories that serve the ends of strategy. When nonviolent protagonists maintain discipline, they not only delegitimize the opponents' violence, but they also gain credibility, stature, and, ultimately, power. On a more mundane level, they effectively remove fear of personal injury as a motive for the soldiers who might otherwise treat them even more harshly. Breakdowns in nonviolent discipline, on the other hand, will galvanize the opponents' forces and enable them to feel justified in obeying any orders given them. A few violent acts can snowball into conditions more typical of a riot, the functional equivalent of a rout in conventional battle.

The ultimate rewards of maintaining nonviolent discipline are both material and psychological. Specific encounters may be won, and objectives taken or successfully defended. More important, however, is the inducement of confusion and lack of resolve in the opposing strategists. Seeing nonviolent discipline acted out, they should come to a new appreciation of the forces at play, and see that the weapons on which they have relied may not, in fact, do the job this time.

None of these optimistic formulations, however, negates principle 7 in the slightest degree. The weapons of violence work and can wreak horrible destruction and suffering. The principle of nonviolent discipline recognizes that this fact can work against violent protagonists, and that one of the key ingredients in maximizing their losses is the way the nonviolent resisters comport themselves.

Individual nonviolent resisters need only account for their own and their immediate cohorts' behavior. Decision makers and strategists have another dimension of discipline to worry about. After a highly effective nonviolent campaign, they may be tempted to switch techniques of conflict altogether or to mix violent with nonviolent methods to bring about a speedy "final push" that spares a population unnecessary suffering. It is neither possible nor desirable, morally, politically, or strategically, to rule out, in an absolute sense, any use of violence. After seeing the dynamics of conflict once the choice for nonviolent struggle has been made, however, it would be a very rare case indeed in which the option for violence would be a help rather than a distinct hindrance.

Two tempting examples ought to be considered. The first is the case in which a violent *coup de main* seems desirable. If the opponents are led by a single dominant individual (as in some of our cases to follow), the assassination of that individual may seem to be the best solution. Even in highly personalized dictatorships, however, the structure of power is never simple. The chances of being able to prevent someone just as bad or worse from coming to power are remote, and the moral credit that has been amassed over the course of a hard struggle may be squandered in a single act.

A harder consideration arises when the opponent group has been isolated from all potential sources of support because principles 4 and 8 have been successfully pursued. There may appear to be no further marginal gain coming from the choice to remain nonviolent. This circumstance, if it truly exists, throws the choice out of the strategic realm and onto the level of policy. Is it really desirable, at this stage, to shift to violent action, with the costs to one's own side that attend such a choice, including the probable rise to greater political significance of one's own violent cadres as the conflict ends?

The choices of what to fight for, whether to fight at all, how to fight, and when to stop must all be taken at the level of policy. Such questions cannot be prejudged. If one is concerned with preserving the internal consistency of strategic nonviolent conflict, however, there is a final consideration that should be brought to bear against the violent option. Even contemplating a strategic shift to violence may seriously compromise the strategists' ability to optimize the complete range of available nonviolent alternatives. Stiehm makes this point well with regard to the strategist who entertains both sets of options simultaneously.

> because the possibility of using violence is always in such a person's mind, there is an inhibiting effect upon his ability to explore fully the possibilities of nonviolence or to take the risks inherent in serious struggle. His imagination, his persistence, and his capacity to accept suffering are likely to be so impaired as to prevent his utilization of nonviolence in any but its most obvious and safest form.[14]

While not wanting to push Stiehm's argument to extremes, it does seem likely that, given a general tendency to overestimate the effectiveness of violent action, it may well be worth bearing in mind.

Another problem is one of independent groups beyond the nonviolent strategists' control who may choose to "help" the effort by mounting violent campaigns of their own. In this case, one should follow Liddell Hart's advice to guarantee that the violent acts occur separately in time and space from the nonviolent campaign and that the two are clearly distinguishable to the opponents. If this is impossible, the only recourse would be to distance aggressively the nonviolent movement from those groups and make sure one's own supporters understand why that has been done.

PRINCIPLES OF CONCEPTION

Principle 10: Assess Events and Options in Light of Levels of Strategic Decision Making

In Chapter 1 we stressed the importance of a comprehensive view of strategy. We are now at the point where functional distinctions between the various levels of strategic decision making become relevant. These are the same for violent and nonviolent conflict. While different theorists have taken slightly different approaches, the broad outline here follows the conventions of classical military strategic thought. We see five levels on which decisions are taken. The distinctions between them have definite consequences for conceptualizing and executing a campaign. They are the levels of policy, operational planning, strategy, tactics, and logistics.

Policy, which in nonviolent conflict is similar to the notion of "grand strategy" in the military environment, is the level on which the most important decisions are taken.[15] What shall we fight for? Shall we fight at all? How will we know when we have won, or when we have been beaten? (What constitute acceptable terms for settlement of the conflict?) What costs are we willing to bear, and what costs are we willing to inflict, in order to obtain our objectives?

It is on the level of policy that the decision to engage in nonviolent conflict, as opposed to utilizing other techniques of conflict or the decision to stand down, is made. At points in the action where the immediate prospect of either victory or defeat is presented, it is a policy choice which determines whether to press on, advance, retreat, or withdraw. All other choices about how and when to wage conflict are subordinate to policy choices. If these are not clearly and well taken, the resulting strategy will be a muddle.

Coming next, between the setting of policy and the direct engagement of an opponent, is the level of operational planning. There is to our knowledge no case demonstrating an explicit operational plan for strategic nonviolent conflict, and the participants of many known cases have clearly suffered as a result. What happens on the level of operational planning, and what is it good for? Prior to engaging an opponent in an exchange of sanctions, a plan should be developed that specifies the following: which particular sanctions or methods (strikes, boycotts, mass defiance, parallel institutions, and so on) will be used initially, and how well are they matched to the resisting population; what tasks are likely to be important on the levels of strategy, tactics, and logistics, and who is to be responsible for them; a vision of the precise steps necessary to arrive at the stated objectives; and the mechanisms by which the desired outcome will be reached. In other words, the operational plan lays out, in concrete terms, how success is expected to occur.

An operational plan is static rather than dynamic. It gets spelled out before the fray and is based on assumptions about the opponents that may prove true or false once the fight is under way. It is therefore subject to modification, and maybe radical change, in response to circumstances as the fight unfolds. Nevertheless, it is vital to start from a plan that envisions how the desired outcomes might be achieved. A major fault of nonviolent struggles, historically, is that they make little or no provision for actually winning. They expect that actions will happen on the subordinate levels of strategy and tactics, and that following these actions, the opponents will capitulate. But why should they? What is the mechanism of their defeat? Will they be persuaded to view the contentious issues differently, or strike an opportunistic deal, or ultimately be coerced, in the sense that their peoples, armies, and resources will no longer perform well enough to keep them in power?

The mere existence of an operational plan cannot account for or control all of the harsh realities of conflict. It can, however, allow for contingency planning along many possible trajectories, and create a hedge against paralysis and inertia when the violent opponents perform competently.

Moving to the level of strategy, the task becomes much clearer if policies and operational planning are in order. Strategy determines how the group in conflict will think about and deploy all of its assets, human and material, in the context of an actual campaign of interaction with the opponents. The essence of strategy, focusing on how the opponents will behave, governs the ebb and flow of conflict. It is adjusted constantly in the light of real events and relative perceptions of strength. It is therefore as much a mode of analysis as it is a specific deployment of power potential.

Subordinate to strategy, then, are tactics, or the logic that informs individual encounters or confrontations with the opponents. If a factory is to be withheld from an occupier's use, what will the workers do to make that happen? Will they stay home, take over the facility, engage in nonviolent sabotage, or some combination of these or other options? Tactical decisions are ideally taken with local intelligence and skills, as well as with a view to serving the ends of strategy.

Logistics, finally, refers to a whole range of activities that support the conduct of strategy and tactics. If economic noncooperation figures largely in a strategy, logistical support may include moving or securing exclusive access to sources of revenue. The physical tasks related to marshaling resources for the conflict are part of logistics, as are the actual communications operations that bind the strategy and its supporters together.

Why is it important to keep these five distinct levels of decision making constantly in view? First, it allows nonviolent strategists to analyze fully the conflict and avoid overlooking important tasks that will strengthen their position in the fight. Within this framework, and at any time, strategists can decide if they are closer to, or farther from, their policy objectives; whether events are proving their operational plan to be sound; whether their strategies anticipate the adversaries' likely routes of attack; whether nonviolent sanctions are being selected wisely and executed effectively; and whether there are any major bottlenecks or shortages imposing significant restraints on the ability to win.

Second, the five levels of strategic decision making offer a framework in which to reduce misperceptions and to avoid missing the significance of particular events. Leaders who clearly see the difference between these levels will not be tempted to reason from tactical outcomes to strategic conclusions. That is, they will not be susceptible to misconstruing either a victory or a defeat on a limited front as having any more than its real, and limited, significance. The cases we will look at are replete with examples of confusion between tactical and strategic outcomes with sometimes disastrous consequences. The natural tendency to measure progress, and from this to derive a prognosis of likely outcomes, can create perceptual distortions. The time it takes to execute an operational plan is not the same as the time required to arrange the tactics of a particular encounter with an opponent. Those demanding to see progress too soon may quit before the real opportunities to win become clear. Lack of persistence, a major cause of failure in nonviolent conflict, is often the product of a short-term perspective. The impatient may also tend to respond to minor setbacks with the most powerful weapons. A general strike is not an appropriate response to a minor indignity inflicted by the opposition. An overused general strike becomes ineffective when most needed. Explaining to supporters that certain events have only tactical significance and that they must try to see the larger picture in terms of policy objectives and operations will help keep supporters informed, motivated, and patient.

Principle 11: Adjust Offensive and Defensive Operations According to the Relative Vulnerabilities of the Protagonists

There are two basic postures taken in conflict: offensive and defensive. These two modes are not as easily distinguishable in nonviolent conflict as they are in military conflict. Superficially, all nonviolent conflict appears to be defensive, when opposed by violent sanctions, since without the violent protagonists' aggression, conflict would never be joined. Yet we must make the distinction at the level of strategic interaction.

Is a strike offensive or defensive, for analytical purposes? The answer lies in its intent. If a strike is waged to cripple a country's economy and topple its government, it is offensive. If the same type of action is intended to galvanize the striking population and to protect their resources from predation, it is defensive. Once again, we are using a standard military concept. Attacks on the "center of gravity"—that is, the thing that keeps the opponents in the fight, be it their commitment to objectives, their resources, or whatever they hold dear—is offensive. No matter how aggressive, sanctions which protect one's own ability to stay in the fight and to prevail are defensive.[16]

Competent strategists simply should keep in mind where they are on the defense-offense continuum. They will need to communicate to the participants who follow their lead that a defensive stance is not tantamount to defeat but a legitimate response to current conditions of the fight. Indeed, there are many defensive operations that significantly diminish the opponents' relative power. It can be reasoned that the two modes are not mutually exclusive, and that, paraphrasing the popular dictum, the best offense is often, in fact, a good defense.

The relative mix of offense and defense is controlled by which side's center of gravity is more or less vulnerable at the time. Who has the greater freedom of action? In whose favor is momentum working? Who has the highest or lowest morale?[17] These indicators will allow strategists to choose between attack and retreat. The risk of too much offense is that it will make the group employing it vulnerable to a counterattack. Conversely, too much attention to defense will allow the attackers extra time to consolidate and entrench their position.

In the event that adjustments are called for, how are they made? Defensive course corrections include dispersion of sanctions, persons, and material resources; reduction of the number of tactical encounters; and the devotion of energy to constructive work rather than overt conflict behavior.[18] Another way to think about constructive work is that it contributes to the principles of development by enhancing the environment in preparation for waging conflict.

Offensive adjustments might involve, for example, increasing the sheer numbers of nonviolent actors that the opponents have to deal with in order to assert control. Or resistance and sanctions can be concentrated at specific points or on specific issues where the adversaries are weak. Or, as we have discussed above, new fronts can be opened by bringing in third parties or escalating demands when the opponents have few alternatives.

Principle 12: Sustain Continuity Between Sanctions, Mechanisms, and Objectives

The essence of strategic nonviolent conflict is that a specific set of weapons, an arsenal of nonviolent sanctions, is deployed to pursue agreed objectives. But what connects sanctions to outcomes? How does this technique of conflict finally attain objectives? The answer is through specific mechanisms of change. Sharp identifies four: conversion, accommodation, coercion, and disintegration.[19] Since the tides of fortune in conflict shift, one or more of these mechanisms may seem plausible at different points. It is important to be aware that all are possible ways a fight might end.

Conversion occurs when the opponents come to see the conflict differently. They change their minds about the merits of the struggle. This mechanism is rare but should not be discounted as a possibility. By far the most common outcomes are brought about by accommodation. Here the opponents decide that a settlement is preferable to a continued exchange of sanctions. The opponents are coerced, however, if their very ability to carry on the fight has been negated. This may result, for example, from wholesale mutiny of the opponents' forces when induced by nonviolent sanctions. Finally, there is disintegration, a process by which the opponents cease to exist as a political entity.[20] (Since this last mechanism strikes us as an extreme form of coercion, and therefore would appear to indicate little, if any, operational difference with respect to how strategy is waged, we will not refer to it beyond this point.)

Strategists must ask whether the mechanism of change toward which the strategy is working is the one best suited to achieving the ultimate goal. If the objective is to wrest from the opponents a limited, tangible resource over which the opponents' entire population feels it has a legitimate claim, conversion is unlikely but accommodation is possible. If an adversary is occupying one's homeland, on the other hand, there may be little basis for accommodation. It may be necessary to amass enough strength to pursue a coercive strategy.

Sanctions must also be matched with the desired mechanism of change. The easiest judgments to make are in relation to accommodation. If a sanction increases the marginal costs of fighting, it will tend to steer opponents in the direction of accommodation. The other mechanisms are harder to gauge, since conversion and coercion can take place relatively suddenly. In any case, it may be possible to induce more than one mechanism at the same time. The point is to deploy sanctions that have the greatest chance of producing a mechanism of change in the adversary that will lead to a desirable outcome.

A final consideration in this regard is about time. The interplay of forces at one juncture of a conflict may unfold very differently at another. By the same token, unanticipated opportunities may present themselves far into a struggle, and strategists will need to be alert for their emergence. Some mechanisms may simply take longer than others, either to work or to reveal themselves as possibilities.

While some of the preceding notions may seem obvious to the reader, the history of nonviolent conflict amply demonstrates that this is not necessarily so to the activist in the heat of conflict. Neither can nonviolent strategists be heartened by the fact that military commanders are rarely cognizant of mechanisms of change in their adversaries other than coercion. There are many examples to be found of sanctions chosen and strategies pursued with blind disregard for the probable effects, symbolic or material, on both parties in conflict as well as the bystanders. The attempt to sustain the connection between sanctions, mechanisms, and outcomes requires intelligence and an artistry that is at the heart of strategic nonviolent conflict.

CONCLUSION

These principles of development, engagement, and conception should be useful as reference points during consideration of individual cases. In the concluding analysis of each case covered in this work, we will be asking several questions. First, were the principles operative? That is, were the dynamics discussed in each principle observed either in the action or in the thinking of the participants? Second, how well did the nonviolent strategists conform to the principles? If they acted in accordance with a principle, did it do them any good? If they did not follow the principle, was their strategy arguably compromised as a result? If the principle was operative and the nonviolent protagonists acted at some times in accordance and at other times without adherence to the principle, do we see the expected mixed results?

In Chapter 9, "Strategy and the Margin of Victory," we will continue to explore the answers to these questions by comparing and contrasting the principles within each category (development, engagement, and conception). Additionally, we will seek to identify which principles are hardest to conform to and which are the hardest to exploit. We will then also identify ways in which principles within and between categories might be seen to reinforce each other.

Chapter 9, then, will allow us an opportunity to look again at these principles and ask again whether they are, in fact, comprehensive. That is, do they speak in an informed way to all of the problems, factors, and dilemmas that are likely to present themselves to the intentional practitioner of nonviolent conflict? The argument of this book, as we have said, is that the quality of strategic choice matters to the outcome of nonviolent conflict. We think the cases will show that it does. A further, compellingly interesting set of questions arises, however. Does strategy develop? Does the exercise of nonviolent conflict improve over time? Is the strategic problematic for this type of conflict subject to deliberate improvement and greater precision, such that the margin for success with this technique can be widened and performance with it improved? The degree to which an approach to nonviolent conflict is comprehensively strategic may well have an effect on the ultimate answers to those questions.

NOTES

1. External groups, third parties, and their relationship to strategy are addressed in principle 4.

2. In Chapter 5 we will argue that both the positive and negative aspects of highly personalized leadership were very much in evidence in the Indian case. The purpose of this discussion is not to detract from Gandhi's towering importance, but to be precise about the way leadership actually functions in different contexts.

3. First aid, self-defense, nonviolent discipline, the ability to establish rapport with troops, physical stamina, communications and language skills, and simple courage are all things that come to mind in this context. The point here is to recognize that these qualities and skills need to be accounted for somewhere in the fighting organization, and this function should not be left to chance.

4. See Johan Jørgen Holst, "Civilian-based Defense in a New Era," 16–22, for a recent iteration of this view. Rosa Luxemburg offers an older but consistent version in *Rosa Luxemburg Speaks,* ed. Mary Alice Waters, 198. Both commentators, and others who have taken this view, end up relieving themselves of the messy necessity of thinking about how to do that which they deem to be impossible.

5. See especially Theodor Ebert, in *Civilian Defence,* ed. T. K. Mahadevan, A. Roberts, and G. Sharp, 153, and Gene Sharp, *Civilian-Based Defense,* 31.

6. Ebert, 167, 180–85.

7. For a comprehensive overview of economic sanctions in particular and the situations in which they are likely to make the greatest contribution as supplemental support, see G. C. Hufbauer, J. J. Schott, and K. A. Elliot, *Economic Sanctions Reconsidered.*

8. We are dealing here with forms of support and assistance that are either nonviolent themselves or that support a nonviolent strategy. The possibility always exists that external support for a nonviolent strategy might

take a military form, and the issues attending that possibility require separate consideration.

9. A finely balanced choice is implied here: by choosing to repair to a safe base, leaders may end up playing their roles longer and more effectively. However, they may lose the benefits of courageous and open defiance of opponents, which might tend to confer legitimacy and authority on them and serve as a rallying point for others, even while exposing them to the very real risk of death or confinement. Ideally, both advantages can be seized if redundancy of leadership is developed.

10. Sharp, *Politics*, vol. 2.

11. Ibid., 2: 608–11.

12. Sir Basil Liddell Hart, "Lessons from Resistance Movements," in Adam Roberts, ed., *Civilian Resistance as a National Defence*, 244–45.

13. Sharp, *Politics*, 2:110–13.

14. Judith Stiehm, "Contemporary Theories of Non-violent Resistance," 17.

15. See, for example, Sir Basil Liddell Hart, *Strategy*, 321, for a fairly standard definition.

16. Karl von Clausewitz, *On War*, 128.

17. André Beaufre, *An Introduction to Strategy*.

18. Our use of the phrase "constructive work" is compatible, but not precisely synonymous with, Gandhi's usage. In his philosophy, a constructive program was a voluntary effort outside the aegis of the state, which had the dual purpose of redressing material inequalities and training the participants to be more competent and self-reliant. We refer to positive actions that can be taken primarily with a view to improving the material situation in which a conflict may be developed.

19. Sharp, *Politics*, 3:706.

20. Sharp, *Civilian-Based Defense*, 64.

Chapter 3

Nonviolent Sanctions in the First Russian Revolution, 1904–1906

The image of the first Russian revolution that is most deeply embedded in the popular mind is that of Bloody Sunday. On 9 January 1905 thousands of Russian workers and their families processed peacefully, in an atmosphere of reverence and loving devotion, to present a petition to the tsar, their "little father." Some of them carried his picture. By any standards other than those of tsarist Russia, the petition was modest in content and humble in spirit. Its purpose was to reach the tsar across the gulf of misunderstanding that had been created (so the workers thought) by the bureaucrats, bosses, and policemen who controlled their lives and made them wretched. Once he knew the truth, Nicholas Romanov II would surely put things right, they thought. Although the petition stated that they would rather die than have their claims denied, the workers could hardly believe that the tsar would refuse them a hearing or that his minions would open fire, killing hundreds, possibly thousands.[1] Nor could they know that their action, and the response to it, would spark a year of continual conflict with the autocracy, resulting in irrevocable changes in Russian life and politics.

The procession to the Winter Palace in St. Petersburg and the act of petitioning were nonviolent, and they worked the way subsequent theorists have supposed that such actions should work. Having failed in their initial objective of communicating with the tsar, these actions elicited such savage and senseless repression that the regime was permanently discredited. Those interested in change now had the perfect lever, and they began to use it with varying degrees of skill.

All this did not happen overnight. Social, economic, and political problems had been festering in Russia for a generation and more. These set the stage for a major struggle, and to some degree determined the shape that the struggle would take and the weapons that each side would use. The state had long been struggling under the strains of rapid industrial growth, an anachronistic and depressed agricultural system, and the government's need to integrate or control the diverse peoples of the Russian empire.

Russia's industrial base had been expanding rapidly since the 1860s, with the most dramatic growth occurring between 1890 and 1900. In a single generation the population of urban Russia doubled, while the industrial work force increased by at least 60 percent in the decade between 1887 and 1897 alone.[2] The new industrial proletariat was not homogeneous, by any means. Some workers maintained ties with the country villages of their origin, making enormous sacrifices to be able to send a little money back to wives, children, or parents. Some would return to the countryside for seasonal work. Others broke all traditional ties and gradually forged new identities in the city environment. A small group of these, perhaps 4 percent, became the "labor aristocracy," acquiring skills, literacy, and a margin of financial security not enjoyed by their fellow workers.[3]

What the workers did have in common, however, were the general conditions under which they toiled. A workday could be as long as sixteen hours, in a six- or seven-day week. The eleven-and-a-half-hour day decreed in 1897 was honored as much in the breach as in the observance. Subsistence wages, cramped accommodations (often rented from the employer, and on factory premises), and arbitrary treatment by foremen were the rule.[4] The workers enjoyed no political or civil rights. They could not legally meet to air grievances, bargain collectively, or petition their employers. Walter Sablinsky has observed that the Russian term for strike, *stachka*, was derived from a colloquial term meaning "to conspire for a criminal act."[5]

The strike, nonetheless, soon became part of the workers' repertoire of self-defense. Between 1895 and 1904, 1,765 separate strikes are reported to have taken place.[6] These were invariably motivated by specific economic grievances or issues associated with the governance of a particular workplace. Few of them succeeded, according to the criteria of Western labor movements with which we are familiar. Most strikes would end or be crushed before concessions were obtained from the employers, and strike agitators could expect imprisonment, fines, brutality, or all three. Only one major strike, the general strike in Baku in the summer of 1904, resulted in a contract between workers and employers. But strike activity would often lead to a visit from the factory inspectorate. This branch of the ministry of finance, until 1905, was responsible for the regulation of the workplace. Theoretically it could impose restrictions on employers, and often the abuses that had caused the unrest were, in fact, corrected.[7] Gradually, skill in using the strike weapon and confidence in its power grew. In 1905, when strikes would reach unprecedented scope and tenacity after Bloody Sunday, this economic weapon would be ready to turn to political purposes.

It is remarkable under these circumstances, but not uncharacteristic, that the government of Tsar Nicholas II did not have a labor policy. It chose instead to deny the existence of a dangerous situation. An 1895 ministry of finance circular declared: "In Russia, fortunately, there is no working class in the Western sense; therefore, there is no labor problem."[8] With few exceptions, this attitude persisted among Nicholas' top advisors until it was too late to address the problem effectively.[9] The notion that all workers were peasants-on-leave, and that peasants, by definition, were loyal Russians (except when subverted by radicals and foreigners) was never sound, but was disastrously misleading at the opening of the new century. Their grievances unredressed, the workers became the power base for the revolutions of both 1905 and 1917, and were ultimately the autocracy's undoing.

Rural Russia was suffering too, for different but related reasons. Since the abolition of serfdom in 1861, peasants had been coping with land scarcity, an inefficient system of communal farming, and crippling taxes which ultimately financed the burgeoning industrial infrastructure. Sergei Witte, one of Nicholas II's more enlightened ministers and advocate-architect of the trans-Siberian railway, acknowledged that "the Russian peasant paid for industrialization not from surplus but out of current necessities."[10]

The peasant masses, comprising five-sixths of the empire's total population,[11] were unorganized and were the last sector of Russian society to become politicized. They were, however, capable of outbursts of frightening violence. These were usually directed against the landed nobility, from whom most of their lands were leased or to whom they owed "redemption dues" for the land they worked. The attacks might range from the confiscation of goods such as timber or grain to the destruction of the local manor house. Such attacks came in waves throughout the latter half of the nineteenth and the early twentieth centuries. They were often aggravated by bad harvests, famine, and punitive raids by the government after the fact.

One particularly devastating famine occurred in 1898 and 1899. Historian Moissaye Olgin describes its effects:

> Famine meant hunger, disease and starvation in the literal sense of the words. Men, women and children lay under the low roofs of their cabins slowly dying. Their fields remained untilled, their horses or cows were sold for a trifle, their households were falling to ruin owing to their lack of physical strength to do work, and owing also to the lack of seeds (which shows that one year of famine had a fatal influence for many years to come).[12]

When thousands of peasants were forced off the little land they had, they might either swell the growing numbers looking for work in the cities or band together and maraud the countryside. The need to reform the land tenure system was acute, but efforts to do so were fiercely resisted by the landed nobility, which continued to control a vastly disproportionate share of the arable land. The agrarian problem was at least recognized as a threat by the regime, even if no acceptable solution to it was in sight. A series of government conferences on the subject was held between 1902 and 1905, but these were attended mainly by landowners. Not surprisingly, they failed to generate new policies that might offer relief to the masses of peasants. Complicating the industrial and agrarian problems was the fact that the Russian empire was grossly overextended. Fully half the 130 million people over whom Nicholas II was sovereign were not Russian, did not speak Russian, or were not of the Russian Orthodox faith. Poles, Finns, Armenians, Jews, and Letts comprised just some of the millions of members of national, ethnic, and religious minorities which existed in a state of complete political subordination. Attempts to "russify" these groups were sometimes met with resistance, as in Finland at the turn of the century.[13] At other times the autocracy either encouraged or tolerated pogroms against particular minorities, leaving a legacy of resentment and political instability.

THE AUTOCRACY AND ITS OPPONENTS

These problems would have tested the abilities of a capable and vigorous ruler. Nicholas II, as it happens, was incompetent, insecure, and petty.[14] To an impossible administrative task he brought an uncanny knack for making wrong-headed decisions and picking weak, sycophantic, or stupid advisors. The autocracy's gravest problem was the autocracy itself: its view of the world, its view of itself, and its inflexibility.

Theoretically, Nicholas was omnipotent. The Fundamental Laws of the Russian Empire proclaimed: "To the Emperor of all the Russians belongs the supreme autocratic and unlimited power. Not only fear, but also conscience commanded by God Himself, is the basis of obedience to this power."[15]

While it was subject to no constitutional constraints, practical limits were imposed on the tsar's effective power by the vast bureaucracy through which he acted. At the top, this bureaucracy was composed of ministers, heading the various departments of the government, and governors general, responsible for the administration of geographic areas. In the former group, the minister of the interior and the minister of finance were key figures in the struggle.

The ministry of the interior controlled domestic policy, including peasant affairs, postal and telegraph systems, censorship, and most important, the police. "There were political police and regular police, factory police and railroad police. Nowhere in Europe were the police as numerous, as venal, or as powerful as those of Russia."[16] Vyacheslav Plehve succeeded to the post of Minister of the Interior in 1902 when his predecessor, Dmitri Sipiagin, was assassinated. Plehve's repressive policies made him an odious figure in the eyes of moderates as well as liberals and revolutionaries. He took the view that any voice not in unison with the tsar's was seditious and had to be silenced. Leon Trotsky's description of Plehve's approach aptly depicts one of the regime's strongest impulses.

He loathed the revolution with the fierce loathing of a police detective grown old in his profession, threatened by a bomb from around every street corner; he pursued sedition with bloodshot eyes—but in vain. And so he found a substitute target for his rancor in professors, rural constitutionalists, journalists, in whom he pretended to see the legal "instigators" of the revolution. He drove the liberal press to the utmost limits of humiliation. He treated the journalists *en canaille:* not only exiling them and locking them up, but also wagging his finger at them as though they were schoolboys. He treated the moderate members of the agricultural committees organized on Witte's initiative as though they were mutinous students instead of "respectable" country gentlemen. And he got what he wanted: liberal society trembled before him and hated him with the inarticulate hatred of impotence.[17]

Sergei Witte, as minister of finance, typified a different impulse. His post made him responsible, among other things, for the capital development of Russia. Much of Russian industry was supported by foreign investment, a fact of crucial importance during the Russo-Japanese War of 1904. Witte was acutely aware that foreign confidence in Russian political stability was vital to the autocracy. His approach was to take a conciliatory posture toward the moderate and liberal opposition, and to design political concessions in the hope that they would be appeased, thus isolating the extreme left. Later on, as we shall see, Witte would become the chief advocate of strategic concessions, even though the government seemed bound to concede too little, too late.

These two impulses combined to make the autocracy resemble an automobile lurching along in the wrong gear. On the one hand, brutal and clumsy repression polarized the situation and alienated even potential supporters of the tsar. On the other hand, belated and half-hearted concessions raised expectations for change, which were invariably dashed when the reforms came to naught. Both methods, however, met with some tactical success at points in the struggle, even while they ultimately fueled the conflict in ways unfavorable for the regime.

Overarching the entire bureaucracy was an institution known as the State Council. The council's members were appointed by the tsar, and usually included ranking ministers and members of the nobility. Like a cabinet, this body was meant to advise the tsar on policy, but it tended to reflect his wishes rather than expose them to critical scrutiny. Unlike a cabinet, the council had no one to function as a prime minister, to coordinate the work of various ministries and to prevent inter-ministerial rivalries from reducing the effectiveness of national policy. In theory the tsar performed these functions himself. A prime minister would have been viewed as a threat to his singular authority. Other institutions, like the Russian Orthodox church and the nobility itself, bolstered the autocracy and reinforced the political premises on which it was founded. Nowhere was there an institution-alized voice for the critical evaluation of policy, and this fact crippled the government from the start.

Only in the provincial *zemstvos* and municipal *dumas* was there a suggestion of representative government. The zemstvos were elected councils which, subject to the oversight of the governors general, provided health and educational services in the countryside and were responsible for maintaining roads. The municipal dumas played a similar role in the cities. Harcave writes: "When Nicholas II, at the time of his accession, learned that the zemstvos were hopeful of ex-tending their jurisdiction, he labeled their optimism a 'senseless dream' and added: 'Let all know that, in devoting all My strength in behalf of the welfare of My people, I shall defend the principles of autocracy as unswervingly as My deceased father.' "[18]

The zemstvos and municipal dumas might have become allied to the tsar and worked as a modernizing force in Russia. On the whole they were composed of able, public-spirited men, not hostile by in-stinct to the government, but wanting to exercise their talents in pub-lic life like their counterparts throughout Europe. Instead these insti-tutions became the training ground for the liberal wing of the opposition movement, denied as they were any meaningful access to political power. The autocracy's failure to accommodate and utilize these potential leaders has been frequently pointed to as one of the regime's most catastrophic mistakes.[19] Witte observed in his memoirs that rulers "prepare revolution with their own hands" when they ig-nore or trample on the legitimate needs and aspirations of their peo-ple.[20] It was Nicholas II's habit to do exactly that. It only remained to be seen what form the revolution would take.

As the crisis of 1904–1906 approached, the final threat to the au-tocracy was, of course, the opposition movement itself. Most treat-ments of Russia during this period divide the opposition into two main camps, one favoring liberal reform, the other, socialist revolu-tion. Within each camp there were diverse organizations and groups exhibiting a wide variety of ideological and tactical orientations, yet united by a basically similar approach. These subgroups, and the two major camps themselves, were ultimately forced to make common cause by the intransigence and repression of the regime they op-posed. Together they formed a broad coalition, the common denominator of which was a desire to limit the power of the autocracy. That is about as far as their agreement went.

Liberal opposition to the government began to emanate from the zemstvos in the last decade of the nineteenth century. Under the leadership of Dmitri Shipov, Chairman of the Moscow Provincial Zemstvo Board, the opposition was moderate in tone. It sought, through legal methods, to persuade the tsar to allow reform as well as an elected national consultative assembly.[21] The zemstvos themselves provided the arena in which such proposals could be discussed, and attempts were made to coordinate and integrate the work of the zemstvos on a national basis. When these attempts were suppressed, Shipov and forty other moderate liberals formed a discussion circle called *Beseda,* or Conversation, that met privately on occasion in Moscow to address problems of gradual reform.[22]

In competition with the zemstvo-oriented moderates were the extreme liberals who organized in 1901 to found *Liberation,* an illegal newspaper which was smuggled into Russia from Germany. The paper served as an organizing point for the Union of Liberation, the first major liberal party to advocate illegal (though not violent or revolutionary) measures to advance its agenda. Formed on Russian soil in January 1904 after preliminary meetings abroad, the Union of Liberation stood for the establishment of a constituent assembly. This assembly would be charged with the responsibility of devising a democratic constitution for Russia. The constituent assembly would differ from the consultative assembly of the moderates in that it would be empowered to make laws to establish and protect the civil rights of all within the empire, rather than merely to proffer advice to the tsar, which he might then take or leave. It would be elected by what came to be known as four-tailed suffrage: universal, equal, secret, and direct.[23]

The revolutionary camp was also divided into two major parties. They were the Russian Socialist Revolutionary Party, or Social Revolutionaries for short, and the Russian Social Democratic Labor Party, or Social Democrats. The Social Revolutionaries expected the peasant masses to play a major role in the struggle and were committed to terror as a political weapon. Their famous "Fighting Organization" would later claim responsibility for most of the major assassinations of this period. The Social Democrats were committed to Marxism, and saw a leading role for the working class, by which they tended to mean the urban industrial workers. The Social Democrats further divided themselves, in 1903, into Bolshevik (majority) and Menshevik (minority) factions, after a series of bitter and seemingly petty doctrinal disputes.

Both Social Revolutionaries and Social Democrats were convinced that the autocracy had to be abolished outright and that it would be replaced temporarily by a bourgeois democracy, to be followed later by a socialist democracy. They were deeply suspicious of the liberals who (their doctrine informed them) would eventually reach a compromise with the autocracy and oppose genuine revolution. The radicals, therefore, vied with the liberals for the allegiance of the workers, intellectuals, professionals, students, and ethnic or nationalist groupings that might lend strength to the revolutionary cause.

The opposition movement encompassed a wide spectrum of different, and sometimes contradictory, goals and methods. Only a dissatisfaction with the regime and a belief in the necessity for change gave it the appearance of a movement at all. Its cohesion waxed and waned with the degree of pressure the government exerted against it at any given time.

1904: THE CRISIS OF LEGITIMACY

January 1904 was a critical month for the Russian autocracy. The First Congress of the Union of Liberation, in addition to articulating its political position, met to elect a council which immediately began to plan an action program designed to bring liberal opposition out of the shadows of Russian life. They proposed to hold a series of public banquets. It was not unusual for professional men to hold celebrations on dates of public significance. What would distinguish these banquets was that they would be used as pseudo-political forums. It was planned that petitions would emerge from them, addressed to various branches of the government, embodying the liberal agenda of four-tailed suffrage, a constituent assembly, and basic civil rights.[24]

The banquets were originally planned to be held on or around 19 February, the anniversary of the emancipation of the Russian serfs in 1861. At the outbreak of the Russo-Japanese War on 27 January, the banquets were postponed until the next likely date, 20 November, to commemorate the progressive (by Russian standards) judicial statutes of 1864.[25] In the end, thirty-eight such banquets were held between 5 November 1904 and 8 January 1905, the eve of Bloody Sunday.

The banquets, and the preparations for them, became focal points for the growth of liberal opposition throughout the year. They began as a conscious attempt to rally the liberal opposition movement around the radical constitutionalist banner. In the end, they functioned as a testing ground where moderate liberals (to the right of the Union of Liberation) and Social Democrats (to the left) would come to argue their own programs. The petitions and resolutions that finally emerged from the banquets were often products of compromise. The banquet campaign provided a venue for political dialogue as well as practical experience in the art of accommodation for a fairly wide section of the opposition movement. These experiences, and the primitive network of opposition elements created by them, contributed to the development of the revolutionary crisis of 1905.

The Russo-Japanese War contributed to the sense of crisis. Plehve is quoted as having said to the Minister of War, Aleksei Kuropatkin, late in 1903, that "What this country needs is a short victorious war to stem the tide of revolution."[26] It is not possible to determine just how widespread this opinion was or whether the autocracy deliberately provoked war in order to manipulate domestic politics. War came, though, and it was neither short nor victorious. What is certain is that it resulted in large part from the reckless expansion of Russian territorial holdings in Korea and Manchuria, and an attitude of contempt for Japanese claims in that region. These factors, combined with Russia's overconfidence in her own military power and gross underestimation of Japan's capabilities and determination, culminated in a disastrous confrontation.

The action began on 27 January 1904 when the Japanese launched a surprise attack on Port Arthur. It ended in humiliating defeat for Russia on 23 August 1905 with the signing of the Treaty of Portsmouth. During the nineteen months it took for the war to run its dismal course, it achieved an effect exactly opposite to the one envisioned by Plehve. At the outset there was, naturally, some degree of patriotic fervor, even among some of the moderate liberals.[27] As defeat followed defeat, however, the war became a symbol of all that was backward, inefficient, and corrupt in the autocracy and its methods. For the peasant masses, of course, the costs were less abstract. Increases in conscription, casualties, and taxes compounded their suffering and undermined the reliability of the troops who must, eventually, return disillusioned from the distant theater of war.

The opposition movement, of course, could exercise no control over the progress of the war, but if it had been able to, it could scarcely have improved on the schedule by which bad news arrived from the Far East. With uncanny timing, military disasters punctuated the unfolding revolution as if designed to wreck the credibility of the regime.

Just prior to the outbreak of war, the Russian labor movement took a strange and consequential turn. In another significant event of January 1904, a maverick priest named Georgii Gapon, who had been working among the poor of St. Petersburg for some time, founded, with police approval, the Assembly of Russian Factory and Mill Workers of the City of St. Petersburg. The Assembly was, in conception and purpose, a curious mixture of different approaches to the labor problem.

The tsar's eleventh-hour labor policy came in the form of a brainchild of one Sergei Zubatov. Zubatov had been an ardent socialist in his youth and was well versed in revolutionary writings and methods. He came to believe that only autocratic rule could work in Russia, but that it must be progressive and capable of directing positive change from above. As head of the Moscow Okhrana, or political police, he conceived of a scheme whereby labor unions would be allowed to organize legally. They would be subject to police oversight and direction, since their organizers would be Zubatov's specially trained agents. A pioneer in what is now call brainwashing, Zubatov was successful in recruiting many reliable agents from the ranks of the revolutionary movement itself.[28]

Zubatov was probably the autocracy's most profound strategist. He understood that the workers had significant grievances and that these would be exploited by the opposition movement unless something were done to alleviate them. Co-opting and directing the workers' movement would be far cheaper and more effective than repressing it, he reasoned. Some risks, however, attended this course. Any real improvement in the workers' lives would have to come at the short-term expense of their employers. The burden was on the Zubatovite activists to mediate with employers and to demonstrate that reforms would ultimately improve the entrepreneurial climate.

Partly out of genuine concern for progress and partly to retain credibility with their membership, the Zubatov unions found themselves organizing a number of strikes between 1901 and 1903. Some produced important concessions. The workers who participated in them gained a sense of their collective power and acquired valuable organizational skills.[29] It is ironic that the regime, at this juncture, was training its own opponents.[30] Eventually the business community reached the end of its patience with "police socialism." In the summer of 1903, a particularly militant general strike began in Odessa and swept through other major cities of the southern provinces. This served as a pretext for Plehve to repudiate Zubatov's policies and to send him into internal exile. Zubatov never held a government post again, though a few of the unions he spawned continued to function on a limited basis for a time.

During his time in St. Petersburg, Zubatov tried to recruit the priest Gapon. The self-styled worker-priest enjoyed wide popularity and seems to have been personally ambitious. While he associated with Zubatov and acknowledged him as a mentor, he waited until Zubatov was removed from the scene to found his own Assembly of St. Petersburg Workers, which nicely filled the vacuum left by Zubatov's demise.[31]

The Assembly was also sanctioned by the police. Any group planning to hold public meetings would have required police approval in order to operate. The Assembly, however, lacked the element of direct police control and manipulation that was essential to Zubatovism. From the outside the Assembly looked more like the mutual aid societies that were the only legal workers' organizations before Zubatov. These were apolitical and were concerned only with mutual relief and self-improvement activities. The Assembly's stated goals were similar. From the outset, however, Gapon planned to lead something much more akin to an independent trade union movement.[32]

In March, Gapon revealed his real agenda to four of his closest assistants, who were sworn to secrecy. The list of demands he showed them, which became known as "the program of the five," included such concrete goals as an eight-hour workday and the right to organize, as well as such far-reaching political goals as amnesty for all political prisoners, freedoms of speech, press, religion, and assembly, and promises that the government would "abide by law."[33] According to one of those present, the plan was to establish chapters of the Assembly throughout the major cities of the empire. Gapon is said to have stated: "then gradually we will cover all of Russia with a network. We will unite all the workers in Russia. There might be a crisis, general or economic, and then we will put forth our political demands."[34] The demands were not shared with the membership until the crisis that culminated in Bloody Sunday when they reappeared, practically unchanged, as the backbone of the workers' petition.

In the meantime, the Assembly experienced phenomenal growth, at least within the capital, St. Petersburg. The attempt to spread to other cities was made prematurely and nearly ruined the whole enterprise. In St. Petersburg, however, there were eleven branches functioning by the end of the year with over seventy-five hundred members.[35] The branch clubhouses became the sites for workshops, lectures, discussion groups, entertainment events, and cooperatives. Meetings would often include the members' singing "God Save the Tsar," and radical political agitators who approached them were usually met with hostility or derision. The program-of-the-five was such a well-kept secret that an Okhrana report on the organization in June referred to the Assembly clubrooms as "nests for the development of well-intentioned elements among the Russian workers who will strive to better their lot by legal means." These "nests" had in fact become the largest single independent organization in tsarist Russia, at a time when other forms of organization were becoming possible as well.[36]

On 15 July 1904, the hated Plehve was killed by a bomb. The assassination was carried out by the Fighting Organization of the Socialist Revolutionaries and was instigated by a double agent, Yevno Azev.[37] Plehve's repressive policies had been so widely loathed that the regime took a different tack when replacing him. A moderate, Sviatopolk-Mirsky, became minister of the interior and presided over several months of comparative liberalization. It was during this "Mirsky Spring" that the liberal opposition emerged and held its banquet campaign. Numerous organizations met for the first time and committed themselves publicly to the cause of political reform.

In a further gesture of conciliation, the tsar announced more concessions in an imperial *ukase,* or decree. Some minor restrictions on national and religious minorities and the press would be eased. A government insurance program for workers would be established. These measures were accompanied by a stern warning, however, that further illegal meetings for discussion of political topics would not be

tolerated. The meetings and banquets nonetheless continued. Leon
Trotsky wrote of this period that "the fate of concessions in a revolutionary epoch" is that they "fail to satisfy, but only give rise to more
stringent demands." Seeing this, the government once again "sought
aid in repression."[38]

On 5 and 6 December student demonstrations in Moscow were
attacked by cossacks and brutally dispersed. On the twentieth, Port
Arthur was surrendered to the Japanese after a costly struggle, in
what could be construed as a cowardly act by the Russian high command. It was in this highly charged and expectant atmosphere that
the drama of Bloody Sunday was about to take place.

1905: THE EXPLOSION

The opposition movement, as a whole, had no grand design to
guide its activities. It lacked both a capacity for comprehensive planning and a solid consensus on ultimate political objectives. At certain
points, however, the initiative of a single faction of the movement
became decisive in determining the future course of the whole.
Sometimes this would occur on the basis of explicit strategic reasoning, but more often it was a case of reacting to a particular crisis or
challenge in a way that produced unexpected results.

Gapon secured his place in the history of the Russian revolution
by converting a comparatively minor incident into a test of strength
between his Assembly and the owners of St. Petersburg's largest enterprise, the Putilov works, whose shipbuilding and arms production
were essential to the effort against Japan. The conflict escalated, finally involving the autocracy itself, and calling for a response from
the larger movement.

The spark was provided by a rumor in late December that four
workers had been dismissed at the Putilov works, purportedly on account of their activities in the Assembly. The factory was in the
Narva district of St. Petersburg, which boasted the largest Assembly
branch, with twelve thousand members from the Putilov works
alone. The factory owners, initially supportive of the Assembly, had
set up a rival mutual aid society utilizing remnants of Zubatov's defunct organization, once they began to perceive the Assembly as a
threat. The foreman responsible for the firing was active in the rival
society and openly hostile to the Assembly. While in fact only two

men had been fired and another two had possibly been threatened, the fact that all four were Assembly activists seemed to support the theory that an organized challenge was being mounted.[39]

When attempts to resolve the dispute by appeals to the plant management failed, Gapon began to see the episode as a test of his organization's ability and resolve to defend the rights of workers. On 27 December, at a meeting of delegates from the various Assembly branches, he gained support for a draft resolution to be presented to the city governor, General Fullon, and to the factory inspectorate of St. Petersburg. It called for the full reinstatement of the workers and the removal of the offending foreman, and was to be backed up by a strike if that were to become necessary. Gapon wrote in his memoirs that "if we abandoned them to their fate, the authority of the Assembly would be shaken . . . while, on the other hand, if we succeeded in obtaining their reinstatement, our prestige in the eyes of the laboring population would be tremendously increased."[40]

The authorities, who in turn saw these developments as a challenge, charged the Assembly with exceeding its authority and upheld the Putilov management's right to settle its own affairs. The workers struck in unison after a meeting on 2 January, the deadline for meeting their demands. Attempts by liberal activists to prevent further confrontation failed. Other enterprises came out in support of the Putilov workers, and additional demands were advanced. Most of the new demands had their origin in the program-of-the-five, which had been the hidden agenda of the Assembly for months.[41] Thus Gapon's own organization generated the crisis that he had imagined when the program was originally conceived and for which it was intended to be the antidote.

As the strike spread, Gapon decided it was time to unveil his idea of a petition to the tsar.[42] He believed, probably correctly, that after leading such a militant and widespread strike his personal fate was sealed.[43] His activities were not likely to be tolerated quietly much longer, so that he had little to lose and much to gain by raising the stakes. If the tsar received him as the representative of the workers and consented to intervene on their behalf, Gapon would become a national hero and savior overnight. If not, and the tsar's true colors were revealed, Gapon might then be in the best position of anyone to lead a radicalized popular movement.

The final days and hours before 9 January were devoted to two tasks throughout the Assembly branches. The first was the drafting, presentation to workers, and redrafting of the eventual petition. The second was the preparation of the procession itself and the organization of the thousands of new members that the strike and the petition attracted to the Assembly.

The petition was essentially the program-of-the-five with some significant additional demands, which were preceded and followed by impassioned pleas to the tsar to listen to his people and to give them justice. Among the new demands were a call for a constituent assembly, an end to the war with Japan, and the separation of church and state. Others arising from the Putilov strike included the immediate establishment of a state insurance program for workers, worker representation in decision making at the factory level, and the abolition of the factory inspectorate, which had proven itself unfriendly in the current dispute. The tone of the document would have been shamelessly melodramatic, if the visions of disaster it conjured up were not subsequently fulfilled.

> We are suffocating in despotism and lawlessness. O SIRE, we have no strength left, and our endurance is at an end. We have reached that frightful moment when death is better than the prolongation of our unbearable sufferings. . . . Issue Thy orders and swear to fulfill them, and Thou wilt make Russia happy and glorious. But if Thou withholdest Thy command and failest to respond to our supplications, we will die here on this square before Thy palace. There is no place for us to go, nor is there any reason for us to go any further.[44]

The demands of the petition were portrayed as the minimum without which life would be intolerable, with the constituent assembly being designated the "principal request, upon which everything else depends."[45] Such a stance did not leave much room for negotiation, even if the tsar or the government had been inclined to barter on such fundamental issues. It is entirely possible that Gapon, as spokesperson for the workers, might have shown some flexibility and acceded to some arrangement short of full implementation of the petition. No attempt was made by the government, however, to seek such a solution.

Many witnesses have described the repeated scenes in which the workers heard the petition read by Gapon or one of his lieutenants, signed it, and pledged themselves to die rather than be turned back. But a strange double-think was at work. There was a widespread feeling that the tsar could not possibly shoot his people, yet some precautions were taken for precisely that outcome. First aid supplies were acquired. Leading workers wrote farewell letters to their loved ones. Events were going to be fateful, in any case, and an atmosphere of frenzied expectation developed.[46]

The revolutionary workers, particularly the Social Democrats, were caught completely off guard by these developments. They had long since written off the Assembly as a vestige of the Zubatov program, and treated it with distrust and contempt. At first they opposed the petition and procession as being ephemeral and likely to provoke bloodshed. (In the latter judgment alone they were more prescient than their rivals.) As late as 8 January the Bolsheviks issued a pamphlet opposing the planned march. Already by the seventh, however, virtually the entire work force of St. Petersburg was on strike, and enthusiasm for the procession was rampant. Rather than be left out, many Social Democrats accommodated themselves to Gapon's line, and he cautiously accepted their help in organizing new members and making final preparations. "Gapon's greatest fear," writes Sablinsky, "was that the revolutionaries, whether maliciously or from sincere enthusiasm, would join the procession, carrying red flags and shouting revolutionary slogans. Mistaking the humble procession for a bloody rebellion, the government might then refuse to receive the workers' petition or even (but would they dare?) open fire."[47]

In an effort to avoid such a misunderstanding, Gapon sent copies of the petition to various government officials and to Tsar Nicholas II himself, with letters explaining the intent of Sunday's procession and guaranteeing the tsar's personal safety if he would consent to appear before them. The government, meanwhile, was making its own preparations. When the strike began General Fullon had taken the routine precaution of arranging for extra troops to be on call, in case they were needed in the capital. Plans for their deployment were worked out, and on 7 January they were brought into the city. If Gapon could not or would not restrain his own people, it was blithely assumed that the people would disperse when threatened with armed force. There is no indication that the government ever expected to participate in a massacre.

On the same day Fullon gave orders, to be posted publicly, that "no gatherings or processions on the streets will be tolerated, and that the most resolute measures prescribed by law will be used to avert mass disorders."[48] The orders were badly printed (because of the strike) and only appeared in the central city and in the official newspapers. They were also unsigned and were widely taken to be inauthentic.[49]

Sviatopolk-Mirsky, as minister of the interior, convened the relevant officials on the night before the march. Those present decided that a declaration of martial law was unnecessary and that two lesser measures would suffice. Gapon and his top aids were to be arrested. If the workers did march, they would not be allowed to reach the square in front of the Winter Palace but would be turned back at the outskirts of town. Late in the evening the tsar, at his favorite resort in Tsarskoe Selo, was informed by Mirsky that matters were under control and that he needn't appear in the capital the next day. Both sides, it seems, badly misunderstood each others' resolve at this point.

Gapon's arrest was never carried out. He was well protected by the workers, and his precise whereabouts went undetected on the eve of the confrontation. The procession began as planned, with an estimated 150,000 participants leaving from each of the Assembly branches, intending to converge on the Winter Palace square by different routes at two in the afternoon. The crowds were weaponless and reverential, as instructed. They carried icons, portraits of Nicholas II and his ancestors, and sang hymns. The various branches were all stopped by military contingents along the way and told to disperse. When the crowds pressed on, they were in several cases broken up by cavalry charges, using whips, clubs, and the flats of swords. Some gave up, frustrated, while others proceeded by smaller groups and circuitous routes to eventually reach the square itself.

The shooting began against branches that were stopped fairly close to the center of St. Petersburg, including the branch led by Gapon himself. Disbelief turned to horror and rage as workers, with wives and children among them, found themselves under armed attack by the tsar's own elite guard units. The commanders of the various city sectors were under orders only to break up the procession, and the orders to fire into the crowds were given independently in different areas, sometimes after warning shots were fired, sometimes not. Those who made it to the Winter Palace were attacked and driven out of the square in the late afternoon.

The question of total casualties has never been resolved. Government estimates in the days and weeks that followed ranged from 56 dead to 130 dead and 333 wounded. An independent group of journalists is supposed to have put the total wounded at 4,600, while some opposition sources and foreign news accounts inflated the figures considerably beyond that. It is probable that not more than 200 were required to make good on their promise to die for the cause if need be, while another 800 may have been wounded.[50] The problem of counting the victims was complicated by the facts that many casualties were removed privately during the day and that minor skirmishing with police and troops went on throughout the evening. The admonition to avoid violence was forgotten, as the now leaderless crowds began to vent their anger in rioting and street fighting.

The psychological and political consequences of Bloody Sunday can hardly be overstated. Up to this point, the vast majority of Russian workers had remained loyal to the tsar and viewed him as an ally in the fight to better their lot economically. Bloody Sunday confirmed the revolutionaries' worst charges about the insensitive and brutal nature of the autocracy, politicized the workers' struggle, and drove liberals, radicals, and workers together into an implacable attitude of opposition. Not reforms, but a dramatic alteration of the terms of political life, was now demanded.

Gapon, who survived the shooting and went into hiding, wrote: "And so there is no tsar! Between him and the people lies the blood of our comrades. Long live then the beginning of the popular struggle for freedom!"[51] Another participant reflected: "I paid dearly for Bloody Sunday. On that day I was born again—no longer an all-forgiving child but an embittered man ready to go into battle and win."[52]

If Nicholas II or any of his advisors had possessed even the slightest sense of occasion, they might have turned the procession into a public relations triumph. It would have cost the tsar nothing to receive the petition, bless his loyal subjects, and then either do nothing or circumvent the demands. Witte even reflected later that thirteen out of eighteen demands in the petition could have been granted immediately, without encroachments on the fundamental powers of the autocracy. As it was, the tsar earned his peoples' undying hatred. His insipid diary entry for the day reveals a failure even to grasp the fact that a turning point had been reached:

January 9, Sunday: A grievous day! Serious disorders occurred in St. Petersburg because workers sought to reach the Winter Palace. Troops were compelled to fire in several parts of the city; many were killed and wounded. God, how painful and heartbreaking! Mama came from the city straight to church. Had lunch with everyone. Went for a walk with Misha. Mama stayed overnight.[53]

THE OPPOSITION ADVANCES, THE REGIME RETREATS

Although the Assembly, as an organizing agent, disappeared after Bloody Sunday, the strike movement grew throughout the month of January, spreading to nearly all the major cities of the empire, to include a half-million workers. Demonstrations were held in many foreign capitals, where shock at the events in Russia was widespread.[54] The tsar was compelled to make some conciliatory gestures, all of which misfired.

The most transparent gesture was the summoning of a trumped-up delegation of workers to an audience with the tsar. Carefully selected by the police, the "delegates" were searched and brought, under guard, to the palace on 19 January. In a prepared speech, Nicholas II told these workers that they and their fellows had been misled by Russia's enemies, but that he still trusted in the basic loyalty of the people. He concluded that he was prepared to "forgive them their guilt" for what had happened.[55] His phrasing was incendiary, and opposition journalists used it to full advantage.

More significant, though equally futile, was the formation of a special commission to investigate the condition of workers and the validity of their grievances. The Shidlovsky Commission, named after the man appointed to convene it, was to consist of representatives of government and business, as well as genuine workers' deputies. The latter were to be elected at the factory level through a complicated balloting process. Each enterprise would vote for its electors, who in turn would select the representatives to the commission. Once the electors were chosen, they refused to send representatives to the commission until the Assembly branches were reopened and made immune from persecution.

The government disbanded the Shidlovsky Commission before its work began. Nonetheless, it served an important purpose. The experience of selecting factory representatives to participate in a quasi-democratic working group functioned as a model that was repeated throughout the remainder of 1905 and beyond. Many of the electors chosen at this juncture became the de facto spokesmen for the workers' movement, so the void left by the Assembly was soon filled. The same method was eventually used to construct soviets, or councils, and many of the Shidlovsky electors were active in those as well.[56]

Trotsky claimed that by February the strike involved a million men and women. He wrote: "Trade after trade, factory after factory, town after town are stopping work. The railway personnel act as the detonators of the strike; the railway lines are the channels along which the strike epidemic spreads."[57] He argued that the economic demands that were advanced and met at many of the striking enterprises were not of primary importance in themselves, but rather that demands were formulated because of the necessity felt by workers to stand up and be counted in the wake of the January crisis.

It was at this point that the liberal and intellectual opposition, until that point without a mass constituency, began to imitate the organizational pattern of the workers and to follow their example. Professionals, intellectuals, and students formed unions and "struck," that is, they ceased to perform their usual functions and joined in the revolutionary agitation. A catch phrase of the times was that it was "impossible to live thus any longer."[58] In other words, normal life was to be suspended until the struggle for freedom was completed.

On 4 February another critical assassination took place. Nicholas II's uncle, the Grand Duke Sergei, was killed by the Social Revolutionaries, once again at the instigation of the double agent Azev. Sergei was one of the few members of the nobility who had been able to exercise a genuine influence over the tsar. His death seems to have made a profound impression on Nicholas. It was followed by a series of real concessions which were designed to take the steam out of the burgeoning strike movement.

The February Acts, as they were called, unilaterally granted the right of petition (a right which had already been seized in practice) and announced plans for the convening of a consultative assembly. This would come to be called the Bulygin Duma, for Alexander Bulygin, who replaced Sviatopolk-Mirsky as minister of the interior. The composition and exact powers of the proposed duma were left to be worked out in subsequent legislation. The fate of the Bulygin Duma fits the pattern that has already been established. A few months earlier, it would have been viewed by opposition forces as a major achievement. A consultative duma was, after all, the original aspiration of the moderate liberals. Coming when it did, however, the proposal was viewed as a white flag and as a reason to press on for still more fundamental change.

The government's vulnerability was further underscored by the Russian retreat following the battle of Mukden which began on 22 February. Mukden had been the largest land engagement in the history of warfare until its time. The Russians had enjoyed a three-to-two advantage in numbers and a well-entrenched defensive position. Neither of these, however, proved enough to offset the skill and sheer audacity of the Japanese attackers. The retreat was orderly and well advised, and might have eventually led to a Japanese overextension of forces. The Russian forces, however, were dependent on a single, highly vulnerable supply line, had suffered extraordinary casualties, and were desperately demoralized. The time to sue for peace was drawing nearer.

THE PROLIFERATION OF RESISTANCE

As the "attrition of the emperor's prestige"[59] continued throughout the spring and summer of 1905, new opposition organizations emerged and more and more of society aligned itself against the government. The Union of Liberation held its second congress in March, and the Second Zemstvo Congress convened in April. Both groups agreed to press for a full constituent assembly, leaving moderates isolated and establishing radical constitutionalism as the new minimal norm.

In the wake of the Shidlovsky experience, many factories established permanent representative committees. Some of these, in turn, evolved into bona fide unions. Victoria Bonnell writes that "the eagerness for organization was one of the most distinctive features of workers' collective behavior in the 1905 revolution."[60] Sporadic strikes continued. Government figures show a quarter of a million workers participating in strike activity during this period, and that figure is almost certainly conservative.

By May there were enough unions (although these were still illegal) or proto-unions to form a national Union of Unions, made up primarily of professional and white collar organizations. The central bureau of the Union of Unions, directed by Pavel Milyukov of the Union of Liberation, would presumably be capable of coordinating strike activity in the pursuance of broad political objectives. In late

May it announced its support for "any and all means of struggle,"[61] further evidence of the galvanization of opposition around the extreme anti-government end of the spectrum. Unfortunately, the strategic advisability of "any and all means of struggle" was not subjected to analysis. The statement was rather intended as one of political solidarity with the revolutionaries, and as such it precluded certain kinds of choices, albeit strategically conservative ones, that might have been worthwhile to consider in the coming months.

Also in May the first citywide workers' council or soviet was formed in Ivanovo-Voznesensk, a short way from St. Petersburg. A unique feature of the soviets, as they developed here and elsewhere, was that as the new repositories of authority for the working class, they began to usurp and exercise some of the normal prerogatives of the government. By arrogating authority and exercising power, they began to provide a kind of parallel government during the latter stages of the conflict, fulfilling vital functions and setting policies for the areas under their control.[62] At their inception, the soviets had no exclusive ideological commitments and were genuinely democratic vehicles of worker self-organization.

The final disaster of the Russo-Japanese War occurred on 14 May. The last hope for the Russian war effort was that the Russian Baltic Fleet, tied up for several months in transit to the theater of war, might provide some belated relief. This hope was dashed when the fleet was surprised by a Japanese squadron in the Straits of Tsushima and completely destroyed within the space of a few hours. In the months that followed, the revolutionary tapestry was embroidered with a new and ominous thread: military units of both the navy and infantry, at different times and places throughout the empire, began to disobey orders and in some cases to mutiny.

The autocracy was already short-handed when it came to the task of repression. Workers were able to organize because of their sheer numbers. Police would complain that they could hardly keep track of, much less prevent or break up, all the meetings taking place in defiance of the law.[63] While the end of the war brought an opportunity to use more troops to suppress disorder, there was also a real possibility that some of them might actually be induced to join the opposition.

In July yet another specter appeared: that of organized peasant action. Events in the urban centers had of course resonated in the countryside. Rural uprisings were chaotic, undisciplined, and usually violent. As long as they remained unconnected, they could be put down with dispatch and with some justification. In July the All Russian Peasants Union was formed, similar in orientation to the Union of Unions. Its participants were mainly zemstvo activists rather than impoverished peasants. Should they be successful in forging links between city and country opposition elements, though, the government would hardly be able to cope. By late summer the Peasants Union had inspired a number of far-flung peasant groups to formulate their own petitions. These groups added themselves to the phalanx of organizations calling for a constituent assembly, even before they advanced their own special claims arising from the agrarian problem. As Harcave notes, "this was the first time that the peasantry had ever shown a readiness to act as an organized political force."[64]

But the final coalescence of all opposition elements was not about to occur. On 6 August the government announced its legislation for the new duma. As already noted, the Bulygin Duma was widely held to be inadequate when it was first proposed. The appearance of concrete legislation, however, still posed a classic strategic dilemma. Was it better to cooperate with the duma and use it as a forum from which to press the cause, or to boycott it in favor of a real constituent assembly?

The judgment of hindsight argues, in this case, for the latter. The terms of the legislation were so antithetical to the issues being advanced in the struggle that to go along with them would have been tantamount to capitulation. The members of the duma, to be elected by a highly restricted franchise by 15 January 1906, would be responsible only for "preliminary consideration" of legislative proposals.[65] The State Council would pass judgment on the duma's recommendations, after which the tsar, of course, would have the final say. The duma's business was to be conducted exclusively in Russian, effectively excluding whole national and ethnic populations from participation. Several nationalities were denied the franchise specifically by name, while much of the urban population was excluded by means of high property requirements for voting. In Harcave's words: "the intention of the tsar was clear: to have a Duma with the right to speak but not to act."[66]

By early September, three positions in relation to the Bulygin Duma emerged. At a third zemstvo congress, a majority of delegates voted to support the duma, which temporarily strengthened the position of moderate liberals. The Union of Unions, however, voted to boycott. The Social Democrats simultaneously agreed to boycott, to attempt to subvert the elections to the duma by means of a general strike, and ultimately to work toward an armed uprising to overthrow the regime. The tsar, no doubt, had hoped to mollify the opposition forces. While it failed to appease most of them, the proposed duma did divide them for a time along their natural lines of ideological cleavage.

THE DECISIVE STRUGGLE

Having made what must have looked like the ultimate concession, the government once again fell back on repressive measures. Illegal workers' meetings began to be broken up with increasing regularity. Under the direction of General Dmitri Trepov (governor general of St. Petersburg and assistant minister of the interior in charge of police), the widespread arrest and detention of opposition leaders was carried out.[67] Additional troops were stationed in restive cities, as well as in those rural provinces experiencing the most upheaval.

The incipient union movement continued to grow, however, as did the general atmosphere of militancy. This was in part due to the fact that the tsar, on 27 August, had restored legal autonomy to the universities, in an effort to conciliate the students and bring their strike to an end. Autonomy meant that meetings taking place on university premises would be immune from police interference and from prosecution. A student congress, meeting in Vyborg, Finland, voted to end the strike in order to take advantage of this new situation. It proved a wise decision. From this point onward, the universities served as a privileged sanctuary where not only students, but also workers, liberals, and radicals could meet to develop plans and debate perspectives. Witte, correctly, viewed the restoration of autonomy as a major tactical blunder on the government's part.[68] It virtually guaranteed that the different elements of the opposition would be forced to work together and would gravitate toward more radical proposals.

The idea of a general, empire-wide political strike had some currency by September 1905, although few would venture to guess when such a project might be possible or likely. In the end, events overtook abstract thinking. The last great strike wave of 1905 began on 19 September, when printers at the Sypin press struck for an increase in wages and were supported by the newly formed Moscow Printers Union, which called out the rest of the city's printers on the following day. Harcave writes that "within ten days they were joined by the city's bakers, wood workers, machine tool workers, textile workers, tobacco workers, and workers from the railroad shops."[69] On 2 October the Moscow Soviet, comprised of representatives of five trades, was formed. Its task would be to direct the strike, which by that time seemed to be losing energy in Moscow.

The impulse to strike had spread to St. Petersburg, however. Printers there had struck in sympathy with the Moscow printers, and a few large factories had joined them. The momentum proved sufficient to keep the strike movement going. On 4 October, the Central Bureau of the Union of Railroad Workers in Moscow called for a work stoppage, which did not take hold fully until the seventh. This proved to be the crucial step in extending the strike throughout the empire. Moscow was the hub of the entire Russian railway system. Its shutdown sent an irresistible message far and wide. By the next day the strike had spread to Nizhny-Novgorod, Riazansk, Yaroslavl, Kursk, and the Urals railway system.[70] It eventually included 26,000 miles of railway line and 750,000 workers.[71] Telegraph and telephone services shut down along with the trains, and by 10 October, when a general strike was declared in Moscow and the major cities of the Baltic region joined in the movement, all normal communication in the empire had ceased.[72]

The Great October Strike was the first of its kind and scale in history. Yet it lacked the benefit of any prior planning. Many authors have used the words "contagion" and "infection" to describe what happened, but the biological analogy is faulty in at least one respect. While germs travel from one individual to another, strikes spread by occupational groups. It is hard to imagine October 1905 without the preceding months of organization building and unionization. The St. Petersburg Soviet, convened on 13 October, was but a continuation of this trend. Everywhere members of society were exercising power collectively. Even the *corps de ballet* in the capital went on strike.[73] Finally, the government realized it was faced with a serious challenge to its existence.

Tsar Nicholas II consulted his chief ministers on 14 and 15 October. One by one, they acknowledged that the situation was beyond their control. General Trepov opined that the armed force at his command would be sufficient to put down an armed uprising in the capital but not enough to restore railroad traffic or to quell the wide-spread strike. Sergei Witte, recently returned from negotiating the treaty of Portsmouth, could see only two alternatives. Either the tsar could appoint a military dictator with unlimited power who would not hesitate to crush every sign of opposition, or he could announce the first really meaningful political reforms. Witte favored the latter, which could only amount, at this stage, to the summoning of a true constituent assembly.[74]

Grand Duke Nikolai, then commander in chief of the St. Petersburg Military District, confirmed Trepov's view and went further. The military strongman proposed as one alternative by Witte would be ineffectual, since there were insufficient numbers of reliable troops to neutralize resistance in all quarters of the empire at once.[75] The tsar paraphrased Witte in a letter to his mother a few days later: "there were only two ways open; to find an energetic soldier and crush the rebellion by sheer force . . . that would mean rivers of blood and in the end we should be where we had started. . . . The other way out would be to give the people their civil rights, freedom of speech and press—that of course, would be a constitution."[76]

The admission that "rivers of blood" might only lead to a repetition of the cycle of the previous year is a telling one. It shows that Nicholas II, in the face of widely dispersed resistance, finally accepted that there were limits to his repressive power. It is this realization that led him to order Witte to draft the imperial manifesto of 17 October. Taken at face value, the manifesto looked like a complete capitulation to the extreme liberal agenda. Its provisions were as follows:

> 1) to grant the people the unshakable foundations of civic freedom on the basis of genuine personal inviolability, freedom of conscience, speech, assembly, and association; 2) to admit immediately to participation in the State Duma, without suspending the scheduled elections and in so far as it is feasible in the brief period remaining before the convening of the Duma, those classes of the population that are now completely deprived of electoral rights, leaving the further development of the principle of universal suffrage to the new legislative order; and 3) to establish as an inviolable rule that no law may go into force without the consent of the State Duma and that the representatives of the people must be guaranteed the opportunity of effective participation in the supervision of the legality of the actions performed by Our appointed officials.[77]

If enforced, these measures ought to correct the major deficiencies of the Bulygin Duma and satisfy everyone but the revolutionaries, who would be happy only with the liquidation of the regime. It is debatable (and was hotly debated) whether the manifesto should be read as conferring a constitution and whether the revised terms of the duma would amount in practice to a constituent assembly. The third provision, especially, could be reasonably interpreted as fulfilling these objectives. It would subject the tsar's will to a veto by the genuine representatives of the people. This time the government really had gone as far as it could go to placate the opposition without dissolving itself, assuming, of course, that it meant to make good on its promises. The manifesto ended with a plea for a return to normalcy. It was not, however, to be taken at face value.

The opposition movement by this time had plenty of experience with disingenuous proposals from the government. Wasn't this just another temporizing measure? The movement had felt its own power in the October strike and was not about to demobilize itself on the strength of the manifesto. The newly formed Constitutional Democratic Party (Cadets), which included the Union of Unions, the Union of Liberation, and the zemstvo constitutionalists, closed its first congress on the very day the manifesto was issued by announcing that it would carry on the struggle until a constituent assembly was actually convened.[78] The radical parties, of course, dismissed the manifesto as meaningless and continued to press the notion that an armed uprising should develop out of the general strike.

The initial October strike was losing steam, though, at the time the manifesto was issued. A unified, confident movement might have recognized an opportunity at this critical moment and declared itself victorious. After all, the manifesto represented significant change, and it had been coerced out of the government by widespread popular noncooperation. If the tsar was going to play himself false, why not let him do it after the movement had time to recoup its resources and could thus repeat the October strike performance at full strength the moment the terms of the manifesto were threatened? But the movement was not united, and there is no evidence that anyone was reasoning along these lines.

THE BEGINNING OF THE END

The days between 17 October and the abortive Moscow uprising of 7 December have been called the "days of freedom." They were characterized by joyous public demonstrations throughout the empire and further extensions of de facto power by popular organizations. New unions and soviets proliferated rapidly, on the assumption that the civil liberties provisions of the manifesto could simply be acted on, without waiting for particular enforcing legislation. By the end of the year there were nearly fifty functioning soviets[79] and the number of active unions in Moscow and St. Petersburg had more than doubled, to ninety-one and seventy-four respectively.[80]

Many of the demonstrations focused on the question of amnesty for political prisoners. Witte, under enormous public pressure, declared a partial amnesty on 21 October, the day the general strike officially ended.[81] Many of the released prisoners, however, soon found themselves under attack by members of reactionary gangs known as the Black Hundreds. The tsar, the conservative nobility, and many of the clergy had for some time given tacit support and encouragement to this network of violence-prone monarchists, and were content to turn a blind eye when these groups went on the rampage during the "days of freedom." In the cities, liberal and radical activists were assassinated. In the rural areas, a wave of vicious anti-Jewish pogroms took thousands of lives. Frequently the funerals of the victims developed into mass demonstrations, which in turn were mirrored by much smaller counterdemonstrations. Petty street fighting with rival demonstrators and police was not uncommon.

It was in this tense atmosphere that Witte tried to reconstruct a functioning, authoritative government. He was charged with creating a new Council of Ministers, with himself as its chairman, which would be capable of implementing the October Manifesto. The enterprise was in trouble from the start, since the Council was meant to be responsible to the tsar and not to the projected duma. Witte could find no prominent liberals who would be willing to accept posts in the Council under these conditions. They were, for the moment, united under the Cadet banner and were withholding cooperation until a constituent assembly was convened. Witte was forced to utilize old guard bureaucrats who did not enjoy public confidence, lending further credibility to the radical perspective that the government was acting in bad faith.

A few additional measures had been taken to buy time and to appease certain sectors of society. On 22 October the autonomous constitutional rights of Finland, abrogated by Nicholas II in 1898, were restored. On 3 November, the government unilaterally issued a decree intended to ease the financial burden on peasants. It reduced land redemption payments by half and increased the amount of capital available to finance the ownership of their land.[82] Witte also promised to intervene personally on behalf of various occupational groups (most notably the railroad workers) to seek an improvement in their condition.[83] These maneuvers, however, failed to quell the unrest. Peasant rioting became serious in many provinces during late October and November, and twenty-six cases of mutiny or near mutiny in all branches of the military were counted in November alone.[84]

At this juncture, the leading opposition organ contending for power and legitimacy was the St. Petersburg Soviet. Having managed to perpetuate itself beyond the end of the strike, it took several initiatives in the final weeks of the revolution which forced the government's hand and impelled the crisis toward its conclusion. Shortly after the manifesto the Soviet declared an end to censorship. This was not an idle boast. Printers, responsive to the call, simply refused to print anything that had gone through the censors' hands. Less successful was the attempt to initiate the eight- hour day in the same manner. Workers who walked off the job after completing eight hours were subjected to lockouts and soon gave up the tactic. The defeat left the Soviet needing to prove its strength again.

The government, meanwhile, mounted a general counteroffensive in early November. This took the form of punitive expeditions into the most restive provinces and a crackdown on urban strike agitation. The former consisted of military detachments empowered to inflict summary punishment on rioting peasants, and were conducted in unusually ruthless fashion. The latter involved the arrest of union organizers, beginning in Moscow, where the First Congress of Postal and Telegraph Employees had called for a strike on 15 November. By the twenty-second, martial law had been declared in three Baltic provinces where new strike activity had occurred. Up until this point, the government had vacillated between two methods: repression and concession. The tsar and his ministers had tended to place equal faith in whichever methods they were using at any given time. Finally, however, they began to work out a mutually reinforcing combination of the two.

The St. Petersburg Soviet issued its response to these measures on 2 December. Its "Financial Manifesto" amounted to a declaration of economic warfare against the government, so long as it remained "in open war against the whole nation."[85] The manifesto called for mass refusal to pay taxes or government debts, insistence on gold as the medium for all major transactions, and the withdrawal (in gold) of all deposits in government banks. The government recognized this as the Soviets' most serious threat since mid-October and acted accordingly. The papers which had published the "Financial Manifesto" were forcibly closed and their editors arrested. The next day the Soviet's meeting place was surrounded by a massive armed force, and 250 arrests were made. These included all elected deputies to the Soviet and most of its executive committee.

Members of the committee who remained free called for a new empire-wide general strike to begin on 8 December. The Moscow Soviet followed suit with a call to strike on the seventh and accepted a Menshevik proposal that the strike would ultimately become an armed uprising. (The Bolsheviks had wanted to begin both simultaneously.) The strike took hold in all of the major cities of the empire within a week.[86] It was less comprehensive than the first general strike, but more bitter and militant in tone.

The violent uprising turned out to be quixotic in the extreme. It began when small groups of armed workers, incensed by attempts to arrest the Moscow Soviet on the eighth, erected barricades on the main streets of Moscow and began exchanging fire with the police. The violent uprising was consistent with Bolshevik theories of how change would come, but it never had popular support and did not spread to other cities. Although two-thirds of the troops garrisoned in Moscow were deemed unreliable,[87] those remaining, with some reinforcement, were sufficient to defeat the two thousand or so rebels in just over a week. With a thousand civilians dead and its stronghold in the Presnya district shelled nearly out of existence, the Moscow Soviet halted violent resistance and called off the strike on the nineteenth.

The radical wing of the movement was effectively decapitated by the suppression of the soviets and the decisive military defeat of the Moscow uprising. The strike abated throughout the empire while the government, its confidence restored, continued its punitive expeditions, repressing opposition on a piecemeal basis for months to come. It had survived a physical test of strength. The opposition had not coalesced in support of a paramilitary struggle, and both sides assumed that the existence of the regime was no longer in question.

THE STILLBIRTH OF RUSSIAN DEMOCRACY

On 17 October 1905, the autocracy of Nicholas II was clearly on
the defensive. When the first Russian State Duma was convened on
27 April 1906, the autocracy was just as clearly in command of the
situation. The events of the intervening months had reduced, rather
than increased, the government's incentive to act in accordance with
the spirit of the October Manifesto. The opposition movement had
spent its strength and was more fragmented than at any time in its
history. The Bolsheviks boycotted the Duma, calling it a "parliamentary comedy."[88] The Mensheviks, who chose to participate at the last
minute, acquired a few seats, but the vast majority of deputies were
Cadets (around 180) and peasant representatives of an anti-government persuasion (around 200).[89]

The elections occurred in March and early April, under rules that
were more liberal than those of the Bulygin project but much more
restrictive than the ideal of four-tailed suffrage. A series of imperial
conferences worked out the precise details according to which the
Duma would function, and its relation to the Fundamental Laws,
which would remain the tsar's prerogatives. The result was a highly
qualified and circumscribed Duma, but one which the liberal opposition had no choice but to live with, if it wanted to get a toehold on
governmental power.

The tsar imposed a number of serious limitations on the Duma.
The elected representatives would be balanced by a kind of upper
house, consisting of a reformed State Council. Half of the council's
members would be appointees of the tsar. The other half would be
elected by reliable groups including the Orthodox clergy and the nobility. As if that weren't enough, the tsar retained the right to replace
any member of the State Council at will. Not only the Duma's consent, but also that of the State Council would be required for any bill
to become law. The tsar also reserved a right of absolute veto over
both bodies, and certain matters were completly excluded from their
competence. The tsar would have autonomous command of the
armed forces, foreign policy, and state finance. He would have authority to declare martial law and to rule by decree between sessions
of the Duma. The Fundamental Laws, as redrafted, deleted the word
"unlimited" in relation to the tsar's power. Nonetheless, he would be
empowered to dismiss the Duma at any point, being required only
to specify a date for its resumption. Harcave summarizes aptly: "The

new political structure was, in fact, a hybrid, resulting from the efforts of the tsar and the bureaucracy to carry out the letter of the manifesto while preserving the spirit of the autocracy."[90]

When the Duma finally met, there was little pretense on either side that it was there to share in the work of governing the empire. Perhaps it is understandable that the Duma and the government each proceeded to confirm the other's worst suspicions by taking uncompromising stands and indulging in histrionic or high-handed rhetoric. One still wonders, though, why no members of the Cadet-led Duma understood the strategic imperative before them: to establish the principle of a working democracy, they would have to achieve something, however limited.

Instead the Duma agreed solidly to a maximalist agenda and offered no incentives for the tsar or the Council to respond favorably to any of it. The Cadets proposed a new political amnesty, a council of ministers accountable to the Duma rather than to the tsar, abolition of the present State Council, abolition of capital punishment, and revocation of special powers for the executive branch, as the autocracy was now euphemistically styled.[91] Most provocative, however, was the Duma's position on the land question. Land was to be forcibly seized from the large private estates, without compensation to its owners, and redistributed to the peasants. Ironically, it was the "unconstitutional" nature of this last proposal that provided Nicholas II with an excuse to dissolve the Duma after seventy-three days.

The Duma reconvened itself indignantly (and illegally) in Vyborg, and there issued a manifesto similar to that of the previous December, calling for economic resistance. There was little response to this gesture, and its primary result was to incur a three-month prison sentence for most of its signatories when they returned to Russia and their disqualification from running for elected office in the future. When the second Duma was summoned a few months later, its powers were further restricted, and the terms for its election were heavily skewed in favor of the landed nobility. The concerns of the extreme liberals and radicals in the opposition movement were once again outside the pale of legitimate politics.

In the interim between the two dumas, the regime retrenched and used an effective combination of harsh repression and concrete reforms designed to splinter the opposition further. Unions were legalized, and a workers' insurance law was finally implemented. Improvements were made in the legal status of certain minorities.

Significant improvements were made in the land tenure system without recourse to land expropriation. At the same time, punitive expeditions (now under the direction of Secretary of the Interior Stolypin) put down pockets of resistance throughout the empire, over one thousand executions for sedition were carried out,[92] and thousands of individuals were exiled to Siberia. These actions went unchallenged in any organized sense, although the terrorist elements of the opposition carried on a campaign of individual murder that lasted well into 1907. As a broad-based movement relying predominantly on nonviolent sanctions, the struggle of 1904–1906 was over.

ANALYSIS

Outcome of the Campaign

The 1904–1906 Russian revolution ended in a stalemate. Subsequent history shows that the events of 1905 left the autocracy irreparably damaged, and by the end of the campaign the opposition was in disarray. It failed to supplant the autocracy or even to influence its direction for several years to come.

PRINCIPLES OF DEVELOPMENT

Principle 1: Formulate Functional Objectives

The nonviolent protagonists failed to conform to this principle.

For the movement, with all its disparate elements, only opposition to the autocracy, in the broadest possible sense, emerged as an agreed objective. At the strategic level, a classic split developed between revolutionary and reformist factions diminishing the impact of the opposition. Much energy was expended in internal squabbles about the agenda, although there was some logistical coordination between groups at the height of the strike period.

In the summer of 1905, a consensus emerged briefly in favor of making the convening of a constituent assembly the minimal goal of all the various organizations, but this objective was quickly obscured in the controversy over the status of the Duma. Without agreement on specific policy objectives, the entire movement was stymied by a random selection of methods with no complementarity among them.

Principle 2: Develop Organizational Strength

The nonviolent protagonists only partially conformed to this principle.

The opposition organized a breadth and depth of structures which accommodated people with a wide array of skills. Even though the organizations failed to achieve concerted action, their evolution made the first Russian revolution unique.

Organizational strength proceeded apace early in 1904 and continued to develop throughout the conflict. First through the Zubatov unions and later through Gapon's Assembly, the workers of urban Russia adopted organizational concepts and habits that served them throughout the crisis and beyond. The creation of factory committees and conventional unions sprang directly from these early experiences. On the liberal side, the Union of Liberation's banquet campaign performed a similar role. The liberal forces grouped themselves around a clear agenda, and in the process they exhausted the limited opportunities to promote that agenda in a closed society.

The liberals failed to gain competence in one area essential to the successful conduct of democratic politics. They did not exploit opportunities presented to them in the First Duma because they had no sense of the need to compromise, to move slowly toward the fulfillment of their objectives. In short, they were prepared to oppose but not to govern.

It is regrettable that so novel and fragile a form of social and political organization as the soviets had to be improvised during the heat of the struggle. Their form and fate were determined by the haphazard evolution of the conflict rather than the other way around. It is not surprising that the radical parties, well organized and disciplined beforehand, were eventually able to gain a disproportionate share of influence in the soviets and to propel them toward precipitous action. The ascendancy of the radicals ensured a lack of unity. There was ample reason for the radicals and liberals to make common cause until the tsar fell, but it was part of the radicals' ideology that liberals would ultimately betray them.

Principle 3: Secure Access to Critical Material Resources

This principle was inoperative.

While conditions of economic strain helped to motivate and fuel the conflict, the presence or absence of material resources does not appear to have affected the ebb and flow of resistance activities. Autonomous universities and areas controlled by unions seemed to provide defensible space within which to organize, but there is no reason to think that these were decisive. Neither is there evidence that desirable tactics were closed off or endurance limited due to a paucity of resources.

Principle 4: Cultivate External Assistance

The nonviolent protagonists failed to conform to this principle.

Bloody Sunday and the pogroms of late 1905 caused a terrific stirring of public opinion abroad. It should have been possible to mobilize some external diplomatic, as well as financial, assistance.

For example, despite French sympathy for the insurrection and disgust with the regime's behavior, Witte was eventually able to secure a French loan which, in his view, was critical for the tsar's survival.

Witte was extremely worried about the image created abroad by Bloody Sunday and felt that such incidents undermined his attempts to finance the regime. Some Cadet representatives traveled to Paris in the hope of wrecking the deal between Witte and the French bankers. They failed, but the tactic might well have succeeded with perseverance. The autocracy was, in point of fact, a bad credit risk, and utterly dependent on the goodwill of foreigners for its continued existence.

Principle 5: Expand the Repertoire of Sanctions

The nonviolent protagonists conformed to this principle.

Although the opposition movement, with its various organizations, never focused on nonviolent methods as a specific category of weapons at their disposal, the repertoire of methods that came into play in this struggle was reasonably wide, diverse, and creatively adapted.

Building on the experience of waging different types of strikes for economic objectives, workers needed to take only a short step to adapt these methods for political purposes.

Some methods accomplished intermediate objectives. Printers' strikes ended censorship. Railway strikes carried across thousands of miles the message: "We're striking, and you should be too!" Also, banquets, petitions, demonstrations at funerals, political acts of non-cooperation, and mutinies show evidence of a wide tactical range. However, there was no consensus in prioritizing sanctions or selecting those which maximized initiative or economy of force or which risked the least for the most gain. With so much undisciplined raw energy, the first Russian revolution was a diamond in the rough.

PRINCIPLES OF ENGAGEMENT

Principle 6: Attack the Opponents' Strategy for Consolidating Control

The nonviolent protagonists only partially conformed to this principle.

The regime's strategy for control consisted of three elements, sporadically applied and vying for supremacy within the strategy: maintenance of the autocracy's legitimacy, both random and discriminate repression, and temporary concessions. The key to attacking this strategy was to keep the government behind the curve of changing demands so that all concessions remained inadequate and therefore unenforceable. This occurred with the Shidlovsky Commission and the Bulygin Duma, but not when the tsar called the first Russian State Duma into existence.

The tsar's strategy for maintaining legitimacy was undermined. Each false step by the regime highlighted peoples' misery. Bloody Sunday became a permanent symbol of the tsar's bad faith because of the startling contrast it presented between the regime's words and its deeds. It created an explosion of activity that made virtually all forms of repression irrelevant and exposed the tsar's ultimate vulnerability. At the same time, the opposition never properly weighed the significance of the October Manifesto, the tsar's major strategic concession. If they had, they might have concluded that the tsar could have tolerated the actual implementation of the manifesto, if he felt secure in the knowledge that things would go no further. Unquestionably the tsar saw the manifesto as a heavy price to pay for social peace. However, only when the opposition was in complete disarray did the tsar roll back and circumscribe the projected reforms and embark on punitive measures.

If the soviets had continued to proliferate, with one emerging in nearly every population center; if, without provoking the government to action, they had gradually extended their control to more and more areas of life; if they had developed redundancy of leadership, so that internment of soviet deputies did not automatically spell the end of their activities; the picture of events in late 1905 and early 1906 could have been completely different. A centralized network of soviets, working in coöperation (but not in lockstep) with liberal reformers, might well have done away with the regime or truncated its power so severely as to come to the same thing. Had the repressive component of the opponents' strategy been undermined in coordination with exploitation of the October Manifesto, the radical objective to overthrow the tsar might have been achieved in this campaign rather than twelve years later.

Principle 7: Mute the Impact of the Opponents' Violent Weapons

The nonviolent protagonists only partially conformed to this principle.

Insufficient advantage was taken of damage already inflicted upon the tsar's most repressive weapon, the military. The revolutionary potential of the military was much talked about, but a sensible strategy for exploiting it was never devised. By the start of 1905 Russian soldiers and sailors had been living with hardship and danger for months. Their efforts in Asia had ended in disgrace. Back in European Russia they were being asked to shoot at their countrymen on behalf of a regime that had disappointed them bitterly. They had been exposed to plenty of revolutionary propaganda, and the government was right to be nervous about their performance in skirmishes with the opposition. With some focus on appropriate nonviolent sanctions the opposition could have made the government still more anxious about its ability to use political violence at will. Heightened uncertainty about the military might have changed the entire dynamic of the conflict.

Geography and demographics more than anything else helped the opposition to conform to this principle. The vastness of the empire meant that repression, particularly in forms such as punitive expeditions in rural areas, was thinly stretched. Conscious steps by the opposition to blunt repression were left more to chance than design. There were important lapses. For example, as a result of ideological preoccupations, the opposition was ill-prepared for the November counteroffensive.

Principle 8: Alienate Opponents from Expected Bases of Support

The nonviolent protagonists only partially conformed to this principle.

There was considerable alienation of many elements of society that were formerly natural allies of the tsar. However, to the extent that there was conformity to this principle, it was accidental rather than a product of strategic choice. As already noted, one of the underexploited bases of support was the army, and there were others.

Governmental access to foreign financial support was another fertile area that was not systematically imperiled. Formerly moderate bureaucrats, a critical source of support, were alienated directly by the tsar himself during the heat of the conflict rather than by the designs of the opposition. The landed aristocracy might have been induced to split with the tsar, but they were not systematically courted by the opposition. Had that occurred, the tsar's view of the safety of his own position might have been severely shaken.

Principle 9: Maintain Nonviolent Discipline

The nonviolent protagonists failed to conform to this principle.

This is a clear case of the strategic dysfunction of violence. Clearly, the Russian revolution of 1904–1906 was not a pure exercise in nonviolent action. There was considerable violence in this struggle. At the same time Russians of all classes, in the millions, did participate in the application of nonviolent sanctions. In fact, the predominant methods used to challenge or reduce the autocracy's power, both in terms of numbers and strategic potency, were nonviolent ones. Strikes, general strikes, mass defiance of civil laws, mass demonstrations, economic noncooperation, and manifestations of parallel government were the methods which ultimately transformed Russia into a constitutional monarchy, however deeply flawed and unstable.

Nonviolent methods were severely compromised by the Bolsheviks' uncritical belief in the inevitable triumph of violence. The Moscow uprising made it impossible for the opposition to realize that a widespread, disciplined strike would be harder to suppress (as it had been in October) than a glorified street fight, in which they were certain to be outgunned.

The net effect of the December uprising was to galvanize the troops, incur severe costs for the opposition, and throw away the initiative by creating the false reality of a decisive struggle. In addition to the uprising, undisciplined peasant violence and assassinations triggered repression and clouded the issues for fence sitters within the regime that might have otherwise defected.

PRINCIPLES OF CONCEPTION

Principle 10: Assess Events and Options in Light of Levels of Strategic Decision Making

The nonviolent protagonists failed to conform to this principle.

There was no capacity, at the highest levels of the opposition, to conform to this or other principles of conception. The Radicals' decision to view the Duma as a policy defeat to be rejected, rather than a strategic victory to be exploited, became a self-fulfilling prophecy. By the end of the campaign the Duma was good for nothing. By pressing too soon for victories beyond the formation of the Duma, the movement was striving for the unattainable. Discontent led to preoccupation with tactical concerns and ideological squabbling. This myopia prevented any of the parties from seeing the policy implications of unfolding events.

Principle 11: Adjust Offensive and Defensive Operations According to the Relative Vulnerabilities of the Protagonists

The nonviolent protagonists only partially conformed to this principle.

Whether intentionally or not, opposition sanctions did frequently build on the tsar's vulnerabilities, especially those stemming from war damage and the regime's general loss of legitimacy. On the other hand, mishandling the opportunity inherent in the Duma meant that opposition leaders failed to see the need to widen their base for future confrontations. They missed making appropriate defensive adjustments when they had the chance.

Neither is there evidence that the opposition used feedback from the conflict to identify systematically the regime's vulnerabilities. The weakness of army loyalty and the crumbling financial structures, both easy targets, were never systematically attacked in an offensive mode. Indeed, it never occurred to the overwhelming majority of opposition leaders to do so. Since few concerned themselves with the preservation of the resistance per se, there were no conscious defensive adjustments to protect the opposition from having its weaknesses exploited by the regime, as they ultimately were.

Principle 12: Sustain Continuity Between Sanctions, Mechanisms, and Objectives

The nonviolent protagonists failed to conform to this principle.

Policy was never formulated at the highest strata of the movement. Examples of continuity of sanctions with mechanisms of coercion or accommodation worked on the strategic level, creating short-term quagmires for the tsar. However, the most vocal, radical elements clearly wanted the regime to disintegrate. While the strike movement sparked by Bloody Sunday was building momentum, it did not really matter whether everyone subscribed to a single mechanism. The opposition movement was too preoccupied with exploring and demonstrating its strength. Gapon's gambit, for example, was only the first to confront the regime with a lose-lose dilemma. Any response short of a wanton act of repression was necessarily viewed as a clear concession. But for much of 1905, increased levels of repression led to a loss of legitimacy and left the regime disoriented.

However, despite the professed desire to make the tsar's rule untenable, the unity of the movement became unhinged when the tsar tempted it with accommodation in the form of the October Manifesto. At this point, important strategic choices as to the appropriate ways to seek a victory needed to be made. They were not. The two critical mistakes of the movement, namely, the dysfunctional violent uprising and the failure to exploit the Duma, are the direct result of nonconformity to this as well as several other principles. Reversing these mistakes would have resulted in the kind of integration between methods, mechanisms, and objectives that is envisioned by this principle.

NOTES

1. See the discussion of estimated casualties, below.
2. Jeremiah Schneiderman, *Sergei Zubatov and Revolutionary Marxism*, 16–17.
3. Walter Sablinsky, *The Road to Bloody Sunday*, 10.
4. Victoria E. Bonnell, *Roots of Rebellion*, 62–68; Sidney Harcave, *First Blood*, 23. Harcave notes that the average wage was the lowest in Europe, and less than a third of that paid to German and British workers.
5. Sablinsky, *Bloody Sunday*, 20.
6. Moissaye Joseph Olgin, *The Soul of the Russian Revolution*, 23.
7. Schneiderman, *Zubatov*, 24.
8. Quoted in Sablinsky, *Bloody Sunday*, 3.
9. The belated and somewhat Byzantine solution of police-sponsored unions is discussed below. Prior to this experiment, only Sergei Witte favored the legalization of unions.
10. Sablinsky, *Bloody Sunday*, 6.
11. Richard Charques, *The Twilight of Imperial Russia*, 12.
12. Olgin, *Russian Revolution*, 42.
13. Toivo U. Raun, "The Revolution of 1905 in the Baltic Provinces and Finland," 459; Harcave, *First Blood*, 21–22.
14. This is hardly an original observation. For penetrating treatments of the character of the last tsar, see Charques, *Imperial Russia*, and Robert K. Massie, *Nicholas and Alexandra*.
15. Cited in Harcave, *First Blood*, 13.
16. Ibid., 14–15.
17. Leon Trotsky, *1905*, 59.
18. Harcave, *First Blood*, 17.
19. See, for example, George Kennan, "The Breakdown of the Tsarist Autocracy," 7; and Adam Ulam, *Russia's Failed Revolutions*, 135.
20. Sergei Witte, *The Memoirs of Count Witte*, 210.
21. Harcave, *First Blood*, 32.
22. Trans-zemstvo meetings were banned by Plehve in 1902. Harcave, *First Blood*, 32.
23. Program of the Union of Liberation, in Harcave, *First Blood*, appendix, 273–79.
24. Terence Emmons, "Russia's Banquet Campaign," provides a detailed analysis of these events.
25. Ibid., 51. Emmons notes that the selection of such dates would ensure that official permission would be granted for a public gathering, as well as provide a pretext for "congratulatory" telegrams to public officials with progressive political overtones.

26. David Walder, *The Short Victorious War*, 3; Witte, *Memoirs*, 250.

27. George Fischer, *Russian Liberalism*, 161.

28. Schneiderman, *Zubatov*, 78–82. This is the principal study of a fascinating character.

29. Bonnell, *Roots of Rebellion*, 102–3; Schneiderman, *Zubatov*, 191–92.

30. Ulam, *Russia's Failed Revolutions*, 151.

31. Sablinsky, *Bloody Sunday*, 80–81.

32. Ibid., 140.

33. Ibid., 102–3.

34. Ibid., 104.

35. Ibid., 121.

36. Ibid., 110, 142.

37. Charques, *Imperial Russia*, 83.

38. Trotsky, *1905*, 70.

39. Sablinsky, *Bloody Sunday*, 146–47. Sablinsky's study offers by far the most detailed and reliable account of this phase of the conflict.

40. Georgii Gapon, *The Story of My Life*, cited in Sablinsky, *Bloody Sunday*, 150.

41. See Sablinsky, *Bloody Sunday*, 184–91, for a detailed account of the evolution of the petition text.

42. Some scholars have questioned whether the petition was Gapon's idea at this juncture, but the history of the program-of-the-five, as treated by Sablinsky, reinforces the belief that he had planned some such action for some time.

43. Sablinsky, *Bloody Sunday*, 158.

44. The entire document is reproduced in Sablinsky, *Bloody Sunday*, 344–49.

45. Ibid.

46. Ibid., 220–25, 235.

47. Ibid., 197. Later, Social Democratic apologists tried to take credit for the radical content of the petition and for the militant spirit pervading these events.

48. In Sablinsky, *Bloody Sunday*, 205.

49. Ibid., 206.

50. Ibid., 266–67.

51. Cited in Sablinsky, *Bloody Sunday*, 269.

52. Bonnell, *Roots of Rebellion*, 106.

53. Sablinsky, *Bloody Sunday*, 278.

54. Harcave, *First Blood*, 116.

55. Sablinsky, *Bloody Sunday*, 280.

56. Bonnell, *Roots of Rebellion*, 175; Laura Engelstein, *Moscow, 1905*, 65–66.

57. Trotsky, *1905*, 81.

58. Harcave, *First Blood*, 98, 116–17.

59. This marvelously apt phrase appears in Ulam, *Russia's Failed Revolutions*, 136.

60. Bonnell, *Roots of Rebellion*, 149.

61. Engelstein, *Moscow, 1905*, 103.

62. Charques, *Imperial Russia*, 134. See also Gene Sharp, *The Politics of Nonviolent Action*, 2:430–31.

63. Engelstein, *Moscow, 1905*, 104.

64. Harcave, *First Blood*, 172.

65. Ibid., 162.

66. Ibid.

67. Ibid., 168.

68. Witte, *Memoirs*, 230.

69. Harcave, *First Blood*, 176.

70. Charques, *Imperial Russia*, 124.

71. James Malvour, *An Economic History of Russia*, 481.

72. Ibid.

73. Charques, *Imperial Russia*, 124.

74. Witte, *Memoirs*, 240–42.

75. Ibid.

76. Cited in Sir Bernard Pares, *The Fall of the Russian Monarchy*, 89.

77. Harcave, *First Blood*, 196.

78. Charques, *Imperial Russia*, 131.

79. Harcave, *First Blood*, 212.

80. Bonnell, *Roots of Rebellion*, 123, 134.

81. Vladimir Iosifovich Gurko, *Features and Figures of the Past*, 416.

82. H. D. Mehlinger and J. M. Thompson, *Count Witte and the Tsarist Government*, 68.

83. Ibid.

84. Harcave, *First Blood*, 222.

85. The manifesto is reproduced in R. W. Postgate, *Revolution from 1789 to 1906*, 385.

86. Harcave, *First Blood*, 232.

87. Ibid., 235.

88. Charques, *Imperial Russia*, 152.

89. Ibid., 151.

90. Harcave, *First Blood*, 246.

91. Charques, *Imperial Russia*, 154–55.

92. Ulam, *Russia's Failed Revolutions*, 196.

Chapter 4

The *Ruhrkampf:* Regional Defense Against Occupation, 1923

In post–World War I Europe, Germany's failure to pay reparations ungrudgingly was seen by those who had suffered under its military might as avoidance of a just debt. German pleas for more time or complaints that the burden was too great met with little sympathy from former enemies. In France the idea that German compliance could be forced rose to a pitch as politicians assured people that Germany would not escape its duty to pay.

To support the reparations policy, France and Belgium sent a joint military force to occupy Germany's economically vital Ruhr region early in 1923. A militarily weak Germany had two choices: either to accept the occupation of the Ruhr or find some nonmilitary means of resistance. Germany chose to confront France and Belgium with what it called "passive resistance" characterized by a stubborn refusal to assist the occupiers in getting what they had come for.

REPARATIONS IN THE AFTERMATH OF WORLD WAR I

When the Treaty of Versailles was completed and signed in June 1919, Germany accepted not only the title of aggressor but also

Prof. Ronald McCarthy served as a research consultant for this case study. Dr. McCarthy provided all the primary research from German sources and the initial descriptive historical copy. The modifications the authors have made to this material, including all the analytical judgments which follow, are their responsibility alone.

much of the cost of a devastating war. Among the burdens was a fifteen-year Allied occupation of the country west of the Rhine River and Allied control of major bridge crossing points plus a fifty-mile-deep demilitarized zone east of the river.[1] With the invasions of 1870 and 1914 very much on its mind, France in particular wanted every possible security from a powerful or rearmed Germany.

France and Belgium also wanted restoration of the lands and industry destroyed by war, help for those crippled in the fighting, and reparations. While the treaty outlined principles, it left the task of setting the total amount of reparations to a commission whose report was due in May 1921. Germany's first cash payment was also expected by that time. However, cash payments alone did not meet France and Belgium's needs because of the loss of productive capacity in the war and French dependence upon German coal and coke. From 1920 on, Germany was also required to make deliveries of coal, coke, wood, and industrial chemicals to help both countries rebuild.[2]

These payments in kind were the source of disputes from the beginning.[3] France suffered a severe coal shortage before German shipments officially began and arranged for early deliveries. A fraction of the promised amount was shipped, and the first reparations deliveries were short as well. While the German government explained that coal production was lower than expected, Ruhr coal magnate Hugo Stinnes broadcast his belief that exports to France jeopardized Germany's own recovery. His was a position that France was not to forget.[4]

When the total cash reparations claim was announced in May 1921, Germany had made less than half of the first installment. Nevertheless, the German government offered to fulfill all legitimate demands. It started to obtain needed foreign exchange and signed various agreements detailing how it would insure the payments. Despite this, government and financial circles in Germany believed that cash reparations in foreign currency could not possibly be financed for very long. The value of the mark was falling steadily, driven down by purchases of foreign exchange. As a result, the German government reversed its position and applied for a moratorium on cash payments at the turn of 1922, once again in July 1922, and yet again in November 1922.[5]

German failure to pay reparations in full did not stem solely from bad faith or even from the high cost of reparations. Loss of territory, economic disarray, and several years of political strife had taken their toll. The Weimar government enjoyed limited authority and its range of action was restricted by powerful domestic opponents. Neither the left nor the right accepted the republic, and for several years both sought its destruction either through revolution or overthrow. Besides, the German economy had produced, and the war had left intact, several industrial empires—including that of Stinnes—that wielded what Charles Maier has termed "enormous public influence."[6] When the industrialists refused to support policy, the government had great difficulty prevailing, especially where reparations were concerned.

FRANCE AND THE QUESTION OF SANCTIONS: 1919–1923

For those interested in strategic nonviolent conflict, two significant questions arise. First, what did France want from Germany that an occupation of the Ruhr might achieve? And second, why did France choose violent force—the physical seizure of German territory and assets—rather than diplomacy or some other course?

The Allied occupation of the Rhineland and the demilitarized zone did not calm French fears of German resurgence.[7] Although civil government remained intact during the occupation, the Inter-Allied Rhineland High Commission had broad powers to issue ordinances binding on the population. Allied officers could also requisition supplies and accommodations and give orders to transportation and communications workers.[8]

After great losses in war, the occupation was clearly not designed to cost but to benefit the Allies. To prevent a militarily or economically powerful Germany from reemerging, France and Belgium encouraged a drawn-out German reconstruction period. Both countries, to a greater extent than the English-speaking Allies, also used their temporary Rhineland holdings for economic advantage. France, for example, created a German market for its goods by breaking down tariff barriers, although not without German opposition.[9]

Local political unrest appeared to offer the possibility that the Rhineland might either split off from Prussia or perhaps secede from Germany altogether. Some French officials encouraged the local separatist movement that emerged early in the occupation. They saw an autonomous Rhineland as a kind of buffer state under French political and economic domination. The separatist group failed in a *Putsch* attempt in 1919, but the dream of an independent Rhine republic on France's borders remained alive in many circles.[10]

France expected a variety of benefits from the Treaty of Versailles, the occupation, and reparations, based on the expectation that Germany would live up fully to all aspects of the treaty. Germany, however, remained uncompliant, complained of the burden, and did not fulfill its stated obligations. The question for all the Allied governments became whether it was justified to punish Germany for failing to meet its obligations. Dissatisfaction soon led France to a broad interpretation of powers granted by the treaty to intervene with force if Germany balked.[11]

In January 1920 Premier Alexandre Millerand unsuccessfully proposed an Allied occupation of the Ruhr to force Germany to produce more coal. Millerand contended that the Versailles Treaty authorized unilateral action, implying that France could legally occupy German territory without the agreement of Great Britain or other Allies.[12]

Soon after, in response to the German government's repression of civil strife in the demilitarized zone, France briefly occupied four German communities east of the Rhine but agreed to withdraw after the British opposed the action.[13] Britain had joined in a Reparations Commission vote in the spring of 1920 to warn Germany that it ran the risk of an occupation of the Ruhr if coal reparations were not kept up.[14]

In early 1921 Prime Minister David Lloyd George concurred that Germany's increasingly numerous defaults warranted sanctions. French troops occupied Düsseldorf, Duisburg, and Ruhrort in the German Ruhr region on 8 March 1921. Although the German government agreed in May to meet Allied demands, French troops remained in the occupied communities.[15]

The British government was not happy with this operation and opposed the further use of sanctions. France, on the other hand, had at last been successful in introducing a sanctions policy.[16] For over a year, French policy moved toward further sanctions. In June 1922 Premier Raymond Poincaré laid the basis for the occupation of the Ruhr that followed months later. Germany, he claimed, was able to pay reparations but lacked the political will to do so.[17]

Poincaré believed that only a thorough revision of the reparations agreements and reform of German finances would allow France to receive any substantial payments. He and his advisors thought (with justification) that the Weimar government was powerless to force German heavy industry to bear part of the reparations sacrifice. Only force, economic as well as military, could break the industrialists' determination to lay the costs on others' shoulders.[18]

As Poincaré expressed it originally, an occupation of Germany's industrial region was not to be a punishment, but rather the enforcement of what he termed "pledges" or "productive guarantees." Since Germany was unable to guarantee French rights, France would seize the Ruhr in much the same way a sheriff with a court order takes away a debtor's property. France would in effect claim a lien on the German economy.[19]

But as Poincaré and his advisors drafted their plans in mid-1922, they began to see benefits in a Ruhr occupation. Sanctions would allow France to exploit the Rhineland's economy directly, force Ruhr industrialists to end their opposition to reparations payments, and permit direct access to the Ruhr's wealth.[20]

The questions—what France hoped to achieve and why it chose force—converge. France wanted its rights to reparations and security recognized, and saw coercive power over Germany as the most likely way to achieve its rights. As Artaud puts it, Poincaré saw Germany "not as a partner to negotiate with, but as an adversary to dictate your will to."[21]

GERMANY AND THE COMING OF THE RUHR OCCUPATION

The German government knew of French plans before the end of 1922 but did little to avert the danger or prepare for an occupation. Instead Germany developed yet another reparations formula to present to the Allies. Laid out in November 1922, it asked for a lengthy moratorium on cash reparations and extensive international loans, offering in return to try to balance Germany's inflation-ravaged budget.[22] A new German government soon took office, but incoming chancellor Wilhelm Cuno expressed his government's dedication to existing policy, a policy which Poincaré considered a sham.[23]

Cuno admitted the danger but trusted that the Allies would consider the new reparations plan, because of its "practical" content, at the Paris Conference in early January 1923. He counted not only on the willingness of U.S. bankers to make a large loan to his nearly bankrupt country but also on France agreeing to see the reparations question, so often discussed in the past, on the table once more. Cuno was wrong on both counts. The Paris Conference refused to consider anything the Germans had to offer, and Cuno remained in ignorance of his policy's flaws.[24]

Cuno tried to make Poincaré reconsider, warning that France would be the loser in any occupation of the Ruhr. In a speech on 31 December 1922, Cuno offered to enter into new security arrangements to calm French fears. He also pointed out that France's policy of "pledges" was not an economic arrangement to guarantee reparations but was "political" (meaning coercive). Cuno told France to choose between negotiation and coercion in the search for reparations payments because "the realization of the political guarantees means the death of all reparations."[25]

The German government made no preparations for an occupation of the Ruhr until after the Paris Conference. The government and industry clung to the expectation that France might reduce its zone of occupation,[26] while France was completing the final phase of its plan to occupy the Ruhr and increase its administrative and economic control of the Rhineland.[27]

Since the Treaty of Versailles allowed the use of sanctions under certain vague conditions, France sought a convincing justification for its actions. The German government remained behind in reparations shipments of wood and coal during 1922. The Reparations Commission voted unanimously on 26 December 1922 to find Germany in default in wood deliveries. A majority, with Great Britain opposed, also voted that Germany had defaulted deliberately, under the meaning of the sanctions clauses in the treaty. In early January the Reparations Commission majority of France, Belgium, and Italy also voted Germany in default on the much more significant item of coal.[28] The French justification had been provided.

As a final step, Poincaré enlisted Belgium and Italy to help carry out the occupation. Despite reservations about the use of force, the government of Belgium decided after the reparations conference in Paris that it would gain nothing without supporting France. Indeed, if France acted alone it might isolate Belgium further. Italy agreed to send a few engineers along. And although Great Britain disagreed that Germany's default warranted sanctions, its verbal opposition did nothing to halt French intentions.[29]

One key decision reflected the French view that it was not the German government but industry that held the key to reparations payments. If the magnates capitulated, an occupation of the Ruhr could easily be an economic success, and it was the assumption that the Krupps, Stinneses, and Thyssens had no stomach for resistance that pushed France to act. At heart the plan was an economic one, envisioning that a civilian occupation staff could oversee the economy of the Ruhr, identify where wealth could be extracted, and insure the compliance of industry. On 10 January 1923, France and its allies announced the occupation of the Ruhr and the troops marched the next day.[30]

OCCUPATION BEGINS

German policy turned to resistance only in the final days. Chancellor Cuno explained on 8 January 1923 that Germany fully intended to pay whatever reparations it could but would not "bend to violence of any sort." But Germany was not able to "meet violence with violence" and must instead "demonstrate to the world" French "lawlessness."[31]

On the next day, the German cabinet and President Friedrich Ebert held the first serious discussion of the coming occupation. They hoped to seize a wave of national indignation to unite the people behind the government but were unsure what to ask people to do. The government feared that nationalist feeling would lend support to the potential violence of the right wing and considered it vital to maintain an air of calm, public order, and mutual support. The first task was international protest, but the next step was not clear.

The ministers were aware of the difficulty resistance faced. France and Belgium could easily cordon off the Ruhr from unoccupied Germany, disrupting the flow of goods into and out of the region. The government budget depended heavily on the Ruhr coal tax, which France would probably seize. If economic dislocation caused unemployment and discontent among workers, it might drive them into the ranks of the Communist Party, far-right organizations, or the revived Rhineland separatists.[32]

The influential President Ebert agreed to a protest campaign aimed at foreign nations but insisted on avoiding any sort of pleas. Germany must instead impress the world with its ability to hold out in the face of injustice.[33] This was the basis for the government's first address to the nation, made as Franco-Belgian forces entered the Ruhr. This act of violence, the government declared, was "long foreseen and yet unexpected," because no one had believed such an economically irrational act would be taken. It appealed for unity, prudence, and "iron self-discipline," so that "no act may occur that damages our just cause." Except for a national day of protest on the following Sunday, the people were asked to hold out against, not to respond directly to, the occupation of their country.[34] What else Germany could do to make its resistance more effective was less clear, and would remain so for some weeks.

In the first days, France and Belgium were most concerned with establishing both military and legal-administrative bases of occupation. Announcements to the government and populace of Germany stressed the nonmilitary side of the occupation. The engineers' contingent was identified as a control commission, the *Mission Interalliée de Contrôle des Usines et des Mines,* or MICUM. The Reparations Commission and MICUM empowered the engineers to demand the cooperation of the German government, civil servants, and private industry in its work of ensuring future reparations deliveries.[35]

The occupation took approximately a week to complete. At first French and Belgian troops kept pressing on to reach larger communities such as Bochum and Dortmund, then began to settle in smaller communities as well. Infantry, cavalry, and artillery forces with transport and support of all kinds took part, occupying nearly the entire Ruhr region.[36]

Premier Poincaré announced to the German government that troops were accompanying the MICUM engineers only to protect them and that no "military operation" was intended. Commanding General Joseph Degoutte similarly tried to make an unthreatening impression. It was, he announced on 11 January, necessary to declare martial law, but only on a limited basis. German law would continue in force, officials would stay at their posts, and police could keep order unhindered. Civil freedoms were also guaranteed, at least "in principle." Public disturbances and possession of arms were forbidden, while the occupation reserved the right to punish those who disobeyed its commands.[37]

French and Belgian officers were conciliatory with Germans in the first days of occupation. Acts of protest by the German populace, such as mass meetings held on 14 January or the silent stares and empty streets that greeted marching troops, were ignored. At mid-month, officers contacting German officials for the first time promised that the occupation would try to avoid disrupting public life. The military received protests from mayors and other officials with equanimity. As long as Germans limited themselves to symbolic protest ànd, in Ludwig Zimmerman's words, "moral demonstrations," the occupation could proceed smoothly.[38]

PASSIVE RESISTANCE: A POLICY OF WAR BY OTHER MEANS

Resistance based on refusal to cooperate was termed "passive resistance" from the beginning.[39] The problem was that the term had no clear meaning. Passive resistance was contrasted with "active resistance," in other words, violent or military resistance. It was also associated with refusal to cooperate, such as with refusal by Germans to obey the occupation's commands. Passive resistance also suggested refusal to be provoked by declining to respond with violence to the occupation and its acts. Lastly, passive resistance was associated with a variety of lofty but vague terms: firmness, calm, prudence, avoidance of political passions, will, resolve, and self-possession. Chancellor Cuno saw it as the final phase of World War I, calling it "war by other, namely, by economic means."[40]

It took some weeks to translate concepts into clear actions. One of the few clear expressions of passive resistance as a policy was made by President Ebert in mid-February: "I believe we will win the war that much faster if no shot is fired on the German side, and while we do not abandon the line of moral resistance. That means, however, that no German hand may be lifted to ease the foes in their plans. We must do everything to make it more difficult for them."[41]

Ebert likened the "officials, the business administrators, the workers, the industrialists" to front-line troops. But unlike an ordinary war, "we cannot prescribe any fixed route of march," and resisters must bring "insight, their own intelligence, their knowledge of the details and facts" to bear.[42]

Resistance by means of noncooperation was devised and supported on pragmatic grounds. Violence was rejected because the "weaponless" German people had no chance against the occupying powers militarily. In addition, organized labor, whose participation was indispensable, associated violence with the right-wing politics it so distrusted. As Carl Severing, a prominent Social Democrat, later wrote: "To me, it was of essential importance from objective motives to hold to the line of passive resistance. It would not have succeeded if the mass of organized labor was disrupted in carrying on its struggle by imprudent acts of violence."[43]

Several crucial decisions waited until late January, suggesting that the German government was not entirely sure what it expected to accomplish and that it was having trouble satisfying conflicting viewpoints within the country. In parliamentary debate, Chancellor Cuno accused France of pursuing its old military aim of dominating the Rhine and preventing Germany from becoming an important power.[44] He spoke somewhat differently within his government, where, in effect, he accepted Poincaré's claim that France demanded productive guarantees toward fulfillment of Germany's reparations debt. That France would seize Ruhr coal or the proceeds of the coal tax was acknowledged. If stubborn resistance could hinder French aims, Cuno argued and President Ebert agreed, it would encourage Poincaré to accommodate.[45]

But many Germans saw the resistance differently. To them, France wanted to crush Germany by destroying its industry and separating the Rhineland and the Ruhr from the body of the German state. They agreed with the view Chancellor Cuno expressed in public. Resistance was, in Rupieper's words, "a fight for German existence."[46]

Once the central government adopted a policy of passive resistance, many decisions needed to be made. It was easy to decide that the people of the Rhineland and the Ruhr and the 1921 sanctions zone should resist,[47] but how and where were difficult to decide. Some members of Cuno's government wanted to exclude the railroads from the resistance campaign because of the economic effects of a French and Belgian takeover if the *Reichsbahn* refused to cooperate.[48] If the railroads were excluded, however, they would end up carrying foreign troops and seized coal, potentially devastating the coherence and morale of those who were expected or ordered to resist. It took nearly a week for the government to decide to declare noncooperation on the part of the railroads as well.[49]

Since the primary objective of the occupation was the seizure of coal and coke, the coal industry and its mostly unionized work force would necessarily bear much of the brunt of the struggle. Denial of coal to France was the key to any degree of German success. Toward that end, the Rhine-Westfall Coal Syndicate, at the suggestion of powerful member Hugo Stinnes, relocated its offices away from Essen to the north German city of Hamburg. By moving out of the occupied zone, the quasi-public syndicate could deny use of its records and expertise to the occupiers, and at the same time show its workers that the industrialists themselves were prepared to make some sacrifices. The records were shipped out during the night of 9–10 January. On the eleventh the government coal commissioner telegraphed all mines, suspending all shipments of, and payments for, reparations coal.

The occupying authorities attempted to ignore these maneuvers and to deal directly with syndicate members. In conversations with MICUM chief mining engineer Emile Coste, mine owner Fritz Thyssen spoke for his colleagues. He stressed that they would neither disobey any German laws nor obey any illegal commands from the occupiers. When Coste offered to pay for shipments of coal, Thyssen agreed in principle to sell it to him but declined to follow through when, on the fourteeth, he was expressly forbidden by the coal commissioner to deliver coal to the occupation for any reason.[50]

Civil servants would also be pivotal, and the necessity to instruct them on how to behave became acute on 18 January when the occupation declared the coal tax and other revenues in their care confiscated.[51] On the nineteenth, Cuno and his ministers ordered officials to "give no obedience whatsoever to directives of the occupying powers, but rely exclusively on the instructions of your own government." Special instructions were sent to railroad, postal, telephone, and telegraph personnel.[52] French prospects for a productive and trouble-free occupation were in a shambles.

FRENCH AND BELGIAN COUNTEROFFENSIVE, JANUARY–MARCH 1923

While the occupation proceeded without military opposition, it had not met its primary goal, economic control of the Ruhr. General Degoutte reported that his efforts encountered the "most serious resistance" mounted by the "civil service, industry, and the working class at once."[53] During the next eight weeks, the resistance forced France and Belgium to recast their Ruhr plans entirely. After lengthy reconsideration of their position, the Allies agreed to sweeping changes that, if successful, would result in Franco-Belgian direction of the Ruhr economy. Even these ambitious measures flagged before the tenacity of German resistance, eventually requiring that defeat of passive resistance itself become the overriding goal.[54]

A first task was to establish a defensible legal basis for further action. In late January the Reparations Commission declared Germany to be completely in default on coal reparations. Certain clauses of the Versailles Treaty were construed as granting the power to collect the defaulted in-kind reparations by military action and to demand cash payments in their place. On 3 February the French government also declared that no further German diplomatic protest notes would be accepted, since the legality of the occupation was now clear.[55]

With Poincaré personally directing the reconstruction of occupation policy, France and Belgium decided to concentrate on four major areas. First, resistance by individual Germans would be subject to punishment, while cooperation would be solicited and rewarded. Second, MICUM was instructed to continue its task of insuring access to Ruhr coal and coke. Third, a joint military-civil administration, the régie, would operate railroads and canals. Fourth, to insure maximum control within the zone, customs barriers would oversee the movement of people and goods between the rest of Germany and the Ruhr (and, when necessary, bring it to a halt).[56] Implementation of these measures would fall to the army, which would have command authority in the Ruhr over MICUM (on grounds that security was now a major concern), and to the International Rhineland High Commission, in which France and Belgium formed a majority over the United Kingdom.

Punishment of resisters began with the courts martial of Fritz Thyssen and five of his coal industry colleagues, initially on charges of failing to obey a direct military command, that is, to deliver coal. The charge subsequently was reduced to the much less serious failure to obey a requisition order. The defendants were found guilty and given moderate fines but no prison sentences. Their release occasioned exultant street demonstrations in an atmosphere described by defense attorney Friedrich Grimm as a "powderkeg."[57]

Government mining officials received somewhat harsher treatment in subsequent trials by the same court. Two senior administrators of the coal tax and state-owned mines were sentenced to one year's imprisonment, given no chance to appeal, and then simply expelled from the Ruhr region. In Duisberg (occupied by Belgium since 1921), Mayor Karl Jarres was expelled for his conduct as a witness at a similar trial. When he snuck back into the occupied zone, out of concern that his compliance with the sentence would be seen by ordinary people as avoidance of his share of the suffering, he was sentenced to a month's confinement, appealed that sentence, and received two month's imprisonment instead.[58]

These trials served to arouse intense national feeling among Germans, but they also allowed the occupiers to develop methods of division and punishment that could potentially break up the resistance front over time. If industrialists, civil servants, and workers were put at different levels of risk, their willingness to hang together might be broken.

Secure in their claim to authority under the Versailles Treaty, and confident that no other nation would intervene on Germany's side, occupation forces began to issue directive after directive to the German people.[59] The first, issued on 18 January, confiscated the German coal tax throughout the occupied zone in lieu of the reparations Germany now refused to pay.[60]

Subsequently, France and Belgium declared Germany's state-owned coal mines forfeit as a pledge for the unpaid reparations. Detachments of troops and engineers began to seize and carry off coal and coke from state-owned and private mines starting in late January.[61] The Allies also began to control transportation along the railroads and canals, communications, and the flow of people and goods across the edge of the zone.

THE CUNO GOVERNMENT AND THE ORGANIZATION OF RESISTANCE

Having opted for resistance, the German government now had no choice but to try to make its actions effective through organizing, planning, and communicating to the resisters a clear sense of what they were expected to do. The occupiers' change of tactics offered a brief respite in which to work. The goal of resistance remained unchanged: to deny forcible extraction of reparations long enough to bring about the possibility of negotiating a new international agreement. In the occupied zones, the ability to resist foreign control of government, industry, labor, transportation, and communication would be essential. All of this would require the cooperation of normally antagonistic elements of German society in an already depressed postwar environment. The prospect was sufficiently daunting for the Cuno government to arm itself with an emergency empowering act, which came into effect in late February.[62]

Recognizing the need for coordination among its own departments, the government organized the Rhine-Ruhr Central Office within the chancellory. Led by Karl Christian Schmid, the expelled mayor of Düsseldorf, the Rhine-Ruhr Central gathered together the various threads of resistance. It attempted not only to coordinate resistance as it developed and to bring together the expertise of civil servants from several departments, but also tried to anticipate the problems and tasks the unfolding campaign would encounter.[63]

While the Rhine-Ruhr Central coordinated the resistance policies and actions of the government itself, another layer of organization and leadership was needed for industrial action, where the interests of both management and labor, as well as country, were at stake. On 23 January Ernst Mehlich, commissioner for industry in the Ruhr, was delegated to take charge of this area.[64] Under his direction, joint labor-management defense committees were formed in Dortmund, Cologne, and Mannheim. The defense committees functioned as centers of communications and leadership, but their main activity was to secure and distribute wages to striking workers when the need arose.

All parties agreed that a general strike would hurt Germans more than their adversaries. Labor and management, therefore, would both work to keep operating until the occupation intervened. Work would then cease and resume only when the soldiers and MICUM engineers withdrew. Industry agreed to keep the work force active and at full pay wherever possible. Workers continued to receive full wages in a strike or shutdown caused by acts of the occupation and two-thirds pay if out of work as an indirect result of occupation. Employers agreed to pay wages from their own resources as long as possible and only then to draw on government funds. Despite industry's sacrifice, it was clear that these plans rested ultimately on the ability of the German government and people to support an expense whose extent could not be predicted.[65]

The Rhine-Ruhr Central and the industrial defense committees were not, in themselves, enough to deal with all problems arising from occupation. Each city government needed to establish its own occupation office *(Besatzungsamt)* to shield its citizens from the occupiers' demands.[66] Since the Cuno government did not produce precise guidelines for local officials until late February, the occupation offices often had to resolve conflicts between broad instructions to withhold cooperation and the acute local need to deal with practical matters, such as the quartering of soldiers or the handling of simple communications with the occupiers. At this early stage, the line between resistance and collaboration was by no means perfectly clear.

Financially, the Ruhr and the Rhineland should have been Germany's biggest assets in the postwar period. Instead the occupation turned them into huge liabilities for the Cuno government. The government had to finance such direct expenses of the resistance as the organizational infrastructure and communications. Wages of unemployed or striking workers had to be paid, at least in part by the state. Also, losses incurred by businesses and private citizens as a result of the occupation, such as damage to homes or the cost of goods requisitioned from shops, had to be covered. Finally, some direct relief to individuals and families was necessary for those who had no other source of aid. The worst aspect of these expenses was their total unpredictability.

Labor official Heinrich Meyer expressed the growing sense of the *Ruhrkampf* as a nonviolent, mainly economic struggle when he told Chancellor Cuno's cabinet on 23 January: "this war will be conducted with foodstuffs, not with cannon." The same lesson was learned more directly in the following days in Hattingen when the poor assembled to receive kitchen scraps from the French, a scene repeated in other communities.[67]

An ill-fated attempt to raise nongovernmental relief money was launched jointly by labor and industry, but it ultimately foundered on the habitual mistrust between the two sectors. Several labor organizations refused to pay into a joint fund, while industry groups held back money collected until labor delivered its share. By mid-year the union-management fund, a "fiasco" in the eyes of many, merged with the government's appeal organization, Rhine and Ruhr Aid.[68]

Technically a private but in fact a government-sponsored body, it acted in connection with the labor-industry defense committees.[69] Through it the government channeled billions of marks for aid, which it required the central bank or *Reichsbank* to advance on credit.[70] Most of the money did not go directly to the needy but to firms to be paid out as wages, on the theory that keeping unproductive workers on the payroll was ultimately less expensive than closing factories and turning workers out into the streets.[71]

This policy met with some success. In May 1923, only twelve thousand Ruhr workers were unemployed, a mere fraction of those out of work elsewhere in Germany. Of these, nearly three-quarters received compensation, at a higher rate than was paid in the rest of Germany.[72] Other fiscal realities, however, began to threaten financial support for the Ruhr struggle.

Inflation had been a serious problem in Germany since the war. Somewhat under control in 1922, it had again begun to climb after the murder by ultra-nationalists of Finance Minster Walter Rathenau in July. Early in 1923 the *Reichsbank* determined to combat the dangerous course of inflation by tightening credit. Its credit policy was impossible to achieve precisely because the bank was simultaneously expending much credit to prevent unemployment and loss of production in the Ruhr, as the bank itself recognized in late March 1923.[73]

Demand for credit to aid industry grew in the months following, accompanied by the need for credit to purchase foreign coal and food and by the as yet unmet calls for the government to begin compensating business for damage caused by the occupation. The coal and steel industries both demanded and received credit amounting to billions of marks during the spring of 1923. At the same time that Chancellor Cuno was asserting in early May that maintenance of the value of the mark was an essential element of the Ruhr struggle, its value was in fact falling and German inflation was threatening to race out of control.[74]

Having decided that resistance must be organized and directed from Berlin in conjunction with leadership in the occupied zone itself, and that resistance would be subsidized, Chancellor Cuno himself went to the Ruhr on 4 February. The trip involved his making speeches to meetings in several towns, where he also met with influential members of government and industry and tried in particular to gauge labor's support for resistance.

The chancellor found organized labor committed to resistance but concerned over its course. A miners' union officer in Bochum said workers feared food shortages, higher prices, and the effects of unemployment. He also asked a question that troubled many. What was the goal of the struggle? Labor was fearful that the wartime experience of a conflict stretched out to the bitter end might be repeated.

It was a lesson of the labor battles, Cuno was told, that no matter how hard the struggle was fought, in the end both sides must sit and talk. Organized labor urged the government to miss no chance to sit and reach an understanding with France and Belgium.[75]

Cuno reminded his listeners that Germany had tried many times to reach a "rational" conclusion to the reparations problem, and he accused the aggressors of tearing up the Versailles Treaty by their actions. Germany, he said, was conducting a "passive and practical resistance" and would avoid any hint whatever that violent or warlike measures were planned. He asserted that France and Belgium had neither won any coal for themselves nor halted supplying the rest of Germany from the Ruhr and could show no signs of success from their undertaking.

Unity, endurance, and preparation for a long struggle were the Chancellor's major themes. If Germany persists, he said, and if France and Belgium are denied the coal and coke they came for, the struggle will be a success. The defensive struggle must be one "in which each action of the other side shall produce a counter-action from us." On the issue of negotiation, Cuno expressed his own fear that at this early stage a desire to negotiate might be seen as a sign of weakness.[76]

Cuno's trip to the Ruhr was a great success, ensuring that the all-important united front of key Ruhr constituencies became a final reality.[77] With these long-delayed preliminaries accomplished, resistance entered a months-long phase characterized by dogged refusal on the German side and an equal determination to break that refusal on the French and Belgian side.

WEAPONLESS BUT NOT DEFENSELESS: THE POPULAR STRUGGLE, FEBRUARY–JULY 1923

Two competing images came to typify the *Ruhrkampf*. One was a French newspaper cartoon, often reprinted, showing the figure of Liberty gazing indifferently into the distance as she tightens a garotte around the neck of a struggling naked man. Its counterpart was a German poster depicting a wary and defiant man dressed in worker's clothing, surrounded and held at bayonet point by soldiers in French uniform. In these images, the occupying force's patient choking of the will to resist is contrasted with Germany's view of itself as, in the words of a Ruhr slogan, "weaponless but not defenseless."

After regrouping, France and Belgium spent many weeks preparing to tighten the noose. In the long run, they wanted access to coke and coal, control of transportation and communication, and creation of a frontier separating the Rhineland and the Ruhr from Germany. Resistance stood in the way. The occupation's next task, consequently, was to lay the groundwork for achieving its goals while working to punish, weaken, and break resistance.

Germany's response was to persevere. Although the resistance mounted by civil servants, industry, and labor held the key to success or failure, the entire population of the Ruhr and the Rhineland was involved.

After the first stalemated weeks, Ruhr communities searched for ways to broaden and maintain support for the cause. Public demonstrations were kept to a minimum for fear of violence. Despite this, some cities held demonstrations to protest the occupation's behavior. Hattingen townspeople, for example, protested arrests of civil servants in a brief demonstration on the morning of 15 February, followed by a day-long economic shutdown. After this, the occupation stopped the arrests for a time.[78]

Unlike the civil service and railroads, people in commerce did not get resistance instructions from the government. They became involved in the resistance in part because the people of the Ruhr feared that soldiers would buy all the food and consumer goods.[79] Labor unions called on merchants not to sell to the troops in order to forestall shortages. At the same time the feeling grew that Germans should not assist members of the occupation in any way.

Germans began to boycott troops. They deliberately snubbed soldiers on the street and vacated bars and restaurants when troops entered looking for service.[80] In some cities, organized sellers' boycotts developed. Shops, inns, and other businesses refused to serve occupation troops. When troops in Witten simply took the goods they wanted, shopkeepers shut their doors during the hours when soldiers were allowed out of their barracks.[81]

The occupation armies punished the boycott severely. Merchants in Bochum suffered an enforced six-week ban on retail sales. In Recklinghausen, miners fearful of food shortages helped organize a merchants' boycott. The regional commander threatened to bring the populace to heel, and on 7 and 8 February French troops took over the streets of the city, dealing out beatings and arrests. The military court also fined several shopkeepers.[82]

Without central organization, the boycotts were difficult to maintain.[83] Unlike most factory workers, the shopkeepers and innkeepers faced the occupation's pressure as individuals. While many kept up their resistance for some time, merchants' boycotts were among the first parts of the resistance to weaken.

Symbolic protest, propaganda, and the newspaper press also had a place in the *Ruhrkampf.* In the early months of the struggle, the German government, civil servants, and industry often protested the occupation and its actions. Any hope that the forces would act differently as a result was abandoned, but protests served to remind the people that Germany did not accept the occupation willingly. The Cuno government, for example, protested increasing violence by occupation troops in late February. The note said that the government did not expect any change but felt compelled to express its protest.[84]

Symbolic protest offered the Ruhr's people a chance to show their support for the German struggle. In Hattingen, schoolboys were forbidden to wear their cap bands (apparently because they were in patriotic colors). The boys instead went out with no cap bands or replaced them with a black mourning band. The occupation also banned the singing of patriotic songs, and doing so was enough to incur military punishment.[85]

Both sides carried on the propaganda struggle as well. France and Belgium distributed numerous placards, broadsides, pamphlets, and newspapers throughout the Ruhr, stating their case to the populace.[86] For example, a French poster distributed in late January, entitled "Why the Excitement?" tried to prove that the Ruhr occupation and its measures were entirely justified. It placed responsibility for the occupation at the door of the government and heavy industry, a common theme in the occupation's propaganda.[87]

France and Belgium tried to drive a wedge between labor and industry, splitting the united front. In one placard, Allied propaganda tried to convince communist workers that an ultra-nationalist group, the Young German Order, was trying to stir up discontent for its own, and the government's, purposes.[88]

Germans responded with protest posters of their own. Propagandists distributed the image of France strangling a naked figure, mentioned above, with added text calling on Ruhr citizens to "be brave and hold out."[89] Both sides pasted their broadsides onto walls and buildings, tarring over the posters put up by the other side.[90]

German resistance was aided by the newspapers' efforts to keep the resistance spirit alive. While the press seldom agreed to publish the occupation's directives, it did print communications from local governments informing the people of the occupation's measures. This, Petras writes, helped people respond, orienting them "in the often confusing and despairing situations of the *Ruhrkampf*." Consequently, the occupation undertook to censor and control the press where possible and to ban uncooperative newspapers for periods of time.[91]

In encouraging the resistance, the press walked a narrow line between stirring up nationalism and maintaining the spirit of opposition. German identity and national feeling were an important basis of support for the resistance. The Hattingen local newspaper, for example, wanted people to "think German, feel German, and act German."[92] The problem with this was that German nationalism was identified not only with support for government and one's country but also with the strain of violence in the far-right groups. Thus the Hattingen newspaper included among its nationalist themes the reminder that resistance demanded not a "hurrah mood" but "serious and prudent decisiveness."[93]

Resistance became part of everyday existence in the Ruhr communities. While the occupation often tried to keep soldiers out of the public eye, their impact was unavoidable. The army requisitioned private and public space ranging from single rooms to entire buildings to be used as quarters, casinos, watch rooms, horse stalls, hospitals, kitchens, and jails. Schools were especially attractive as quarters, forcing the community to find other places to educate children.[94]

THE STRUGGLE FOR COAL

Control of coal and coke was clearly seen as the center of gravity by both the occupier and the occupied. By obtaining coal, France and Belgium could resupply their own economy, control that of the Ruhr, and establish a concrete symbol of their operation's success. By denying access to coal and coke, Germany could achieve just the opposite on all counts. After failing to induce cooperation by means of the Thyssen group's and others' trials in January, the occupiers set about to seize the materials directly.

Occupation troops began seizing coal in January from coal trains, barges, and mine stockpiles, but their confiscation system developed slowly and a good deal of coal was transferred out of the zone to unoccupied Germany.[95] In the meantime, the German government released a series of instructions forbidding any sort of cooperation with the occupation's efforts to get coal for its own use or for shipment home.[96]

The occupation, by then engaged in setting up barriers on the borders of the Ruhr, responded by forbidding the export of Ruhr coal, soon followed by a list of other industrial products as well.[97] The occupation also seized coal intended for domestic use. For some weeks, it concentrated on household and community stores and the workers' share or *Deputatkohle,* which was traditional in Ruhr mining. These seizures were designed to punish and intimidate rather than yield useful amounts of coal.[98]

Mine owners hoped that the railway resistance would prevent most of the seized coal from being transported to France and Belgium. Except for scattered cases, the occupation did not take very much coal from mines or factories at first. Industry tried to keep the mines operating by piling up heaps of coal and coke in the yards and moving the excess onto sidings in loaded coal cars.[99]

As the occupation's methods of carrying off coal became more sophisticated, this practice backfired. By mid-March, the occupation was able to locate loaded coal cars by airplane. It was then a simple matter to haul them away. The army found it more difficult to move piled coal and coke, but as the months went on had greater success.[100]

The occupation was slow to seize Ruhr coal in quantity partly because it was engaged in strengthening the legal basis for its actions. Shortly after the occupation began, France and Belgium declared their intention to seize the German coal tax in lieu of cash reparations. This was undercut by the German government, which simply collected the tax from mine bank accounts outside the Ruhr. In response, the occupation declared that any mine refusing to pay the coal tax to MICUM would be liable to seizures of coal and other property in like amount.

MICUM officials then informed each mine of its share of the tax, giving it until mid-April to comply. When a mine did not comply, as indeed none did, further measures were taken such as forbidding the mine to load or transport coal and confiscation of vehicles. Although the occupation was still shipping relatively little coal, by late April it had effectively halted the commerce in coal within the Ruhr itself.[101]

At this point, the occupation began to seize and remove coal in much larger amounts. According to German government figures published at the time, coal shipments to France and Belgium through March 1923 were but a small proportion, perhaps 10 percent, of the amounts supplied the previous year as reparations. By June 1923 export of seized production (especially of coke, which the occupation desired most) amounted to nearly half of the same month's shipments in 1922.[102]

The German coal industry tried to counter this modest success, somewhat too late, by producing only enough coke for immediate use, hiding stocks within the shafts, and adulterating or breaking up unneeded coke in order to make it useless to French and Belgium industry. Nearly all coke plants shut down, except those producing gas or electricity for Ruhr communities.[103]

Two MICUM actions in March give a flavor of the occupation's methods. On 11 March, a Sunday, MICUM announced its decision to seize the coking furnaces at the state-owned Westerhof Mine. Soldiers immediately took over the coking plant and associated rail lines. In its announcement, MICUM reminded the management that mine owners and operators had been given several chances to cooperate (including the January meetings with the Thyssen group) and had refused.

The occupation engineer in charge offered weekly receipts for the coke he removed, but within a few days the director of the mine said that all the high-quality coke had been taken. The engineer asked the director to supply more coke, hoping, in Spethmann's words, "to enter into a connection of some sort with the Germans and thus drive holes in the passive resistance in the mines." When the manager refused, French troops ringed the plant with barbed wire and brought in workers to carry off a further 2,200 tons of coke.[104]

Five days after the Westerhof occupation began, French troops arrived at a section of the vast Concordia mine to seize coke and rail connections. The engineer demanded 700 tons of coke per day, which MICUM would pay for (minus the coal tax). This was quickly refused. As the troops carried out the seizures, the entire work force went out on strike.

Five MICUM officials went to the home of a mining official to work out a deal for reopening the mine. They pledged not to interfere with work or storage of further coal production and to move troops out of the plant to a surveillance point. The factory council hesitated to produce coal likely to be seized later, despite French promises to the contrary. In any case, the work force refused to return while the French were present and stayed on strike for many weeks.[105]

Before April, occupation presence at a mine or factory on a given occasion was brief, though long enough to make a point and carry off some coal. Workers struck immediately when troops or engineers entered a plant or mine and refused to operate in the presence of the occupation. As time went on, however, the occupation granted the army and MICUM sweeping powers to take over the property of uncooperative German firms, which in the summer of 1923 they began to use. In July a local Belgian commander offered certain mines a chance to operate on their own if they would transfer a third of their production to him. MICUM imported French and Polish miners and took over a small number of mines and coke plants, making some efforts to get production going without German help. While the occupation itself lacked the resources to carry on mining on any scale, importing workers represented a threat to the effectiveness of passive resistance. Removal of coal and coke to France and Belgium did fall after June 1923, but the fact that some had been seized represented a crack in the noncooperation policy and, in that sense, a victory for the occupation in an area considered vital by the Germans.[106]

TRANSPORTATION AND THE RAILROAD RÉGIE

As with the struggle for coal, the occupation wanted to control transportation for two reasons. They wanted the material advantages, to be sure, but the secondary objective of using the railroads to break passive resistance soon became paramount.

The German government came uncomfortably close to losing the railroad struggle in the first week of occupation by allowing service to operate as usual, even when used by the occupying forces. But the government, after a brief delay, decided to continue service to the German populace while simultaneously withholding assistance from the occupation. Railway workers responded with a unity which completely denied effective use of the Ruhr's transportation system to Belgium and France for many weeks.[107]

Troops began to seize certain trains and occupy stations in late January and early February. They were confronted at once with strikes and in some cases withdrew.[108] While regrouping, the occupation laid comprehensive plans for the takeover of Ruhr rail and canal traffic under a single military-dominated administration, the régie.[109]

The first step in forming the régie was to identify and militarize key rail lines running through the Ruhr toward France and Belgium. By early March, the occupation held the northern and southern main lines and had begun to put the régie into place.[110] In response, the German government instructed railroad workers not to follow any orders of the régie or even to appear in their workplaces as long as régie personnel were present.[111] The occupation retaliated by expelling workers on a mass basis. In some cases up to four hundred workers and their families were expelled simultaneously. By the end of the *Ruhrkampf* some tens of thousands of rail workers and managers had been expelled.[112]

While the German government encouraged the populace at large to boycott the régie, the occupation took steps to enforce its use. It established control points at sites on the border between the Ruhr and the rest of Germany from which traffic could be monitored and controlled, and it progressively restricted all alternatives to the régie trains. In late March the occupation began to require passes for travel and the export of goods outside the zone. A month later a new ordinance required that the driver of any automobile or truck conveying goods within the Ruhr must have permission issued by the occupation or would face confiscation of the goods.

A mid-May 1923 report by General Degoutte indicated that by forbidding mass transportation by bus or truck he thought people could be forced to use the régie trains.[113] The next step in this campaign was to stop the use of streetcars as a substitute for train travel. For Germans avoiding the régie, the streetcars served to transport people as well as all kinds of goods including food. In the summer of 1923, occupation authorities restricted the number of streetcars and ordered reductions in schedules and occasional halts.[114]

The resistance found substitute means for getting people and goods in and out of the Ruhr. Some used established smugglers' routes, including paths over the hills and shallow places in the Ruhr River. In one case, the dense network of rail lines serving mines and factories was used to smuggle tank cars of benzene to a place where the benzene could be transferred out of the zone by pipeline. In Hattingen, an action committee took on the job of finding other options. It convinced the government railroad to set up a temporary station at the very edge of the zone that became a favored point for the transit of people and goods away from French eyes (the famous *Gruner Weg* station).[115]

As the occupation gradually reduced the options for people who had to travel, more were forced to use the régie, to accept the need to apply for passes, and to seek permission to use cars and trucks on the roads.[116] The German government condemned restrictions on transportation on non-régie trains as a "hunger blockade" intended to starve the Ruhr into submission.[117] The highly organized railroad workers remained firm in the face of mass expulsions, with no more than two hundred of their number agreeing to work for the régie.[118]

TIGHTENING CONTROLS AND "ELASTIC RESISTANCE"

Unable to induce the German populace to cooperate, the system of military and civil control established within the zone ultimately depended on force. The occupation authorized itself to punish individuals as well as communities for breaches of its ordinances and commands. The sanctions employed against individuals included expulsion from the zone, fines, and imprisonment, all of which were used from the beginning of the occupation.

The Belgian and French armies established military police courts and courts martial in several cities in addition to those already active in the previously occupied zone. These courts recognized only French or Belgian military law and the ordinances of the occupation, never German law. Defendants were allowed to defend themselves and generally allowed counsel, but conviction and punishment were undoubtedly the rule.[119]

The Hattingen military court, as an example, expelled at least ten people (in addition to those expelled without trial) and condemned over two hundred others to prison. As Petras shows, the largest number of these cases stemmed from the conduct of passive resistance, while many others involved actions taken either in the so-called active resistance or from hostility toward the occupation. Resisters were imprisoned for refusing to obey commands, refusing to sell goods to occupying forces, singing forbidden patriotic songs, distributing or smuggling leaflets, and insulting the French. In addition, thirty-three members of the Hattingen community were held as hostages over the course of the year. Many others were fined, generally for the same sorts of offenses.[120]

Conditions in French and Belgian prisons were poor enough that the German government in February considered allowing the political prisoners to serve their time in German jails, but decided that there was no way to make this work.[121] In one prison, officials kept up their spirits by organizing a society of "prisoners of honor." People in the same community did everything they could to lighten the burden of imprisoned resisters, leading one source to call that prison a "sanatorium for passive resistance." This was not possible in other prisons, which Grimm condemns as "primitive."[122]

Expulsions, like imprisonments, were not only a hardship for the individual but also threatened the resistance as well. Over the course of months, the upper levels of administrators in many communities and industries were either expelled or imprisoned. Filling their posts was imperative but not easy. Where possible, expelled officials stayed in touch from outside the zone. As one official was expelled, the next most qualified person stepped into the role, sometimes only to be expelled in turn. Dortmund, for example, had had five police chiefs by the end of March and four mayors by early July.[123]

As control became more sophisticated, the occupation began to punish activities that had been tolerated previously or that it had been unable to stop. One example took place in Hattingen at the Henrichshutte factory. The factory had been supplying itself with coal from outside the occupied Ruhr zone, but only with difficulty. With almost constant protests, including a one-day economic shutdown in the city, enough fuel arrived to keep the plant going through March. Some of this coal came across the Ruhr in aging cable cars.

At the end of March, French MICUM engineers guarded by troops occupied the Henrichshutte without warning. The workers struck at once, gathering in the yard to the sound of factory whistles blowing. The engineers halted and disabled the railway. Members of the plant's management were arrested and tried for disobeying various ordinances.

The success of military control, however, ultimately did not depend on such refinements as courts and prisons. It depended on the ability of the soldier with the bayonet to keep the populace in line. Troops were used for a variety of tasks over the months of the Ruhr occupation, from patrolling and setting up control barriers in the streets, to guarding engineers as they entered factories and mines, to enforcing curfews and travel bans. Not surprisingly, confrontations between the citizenry and the troops occurred, leading to a number of German deaths.

Eighty-five had died at the time the German government collected statistics at the end of July. Of these, fifty-five were killed by sentries or patrols, almost half of them in the neighborhood of railroads and canals. Fifteen were killed in connection with the occupation of factories, mines, and railroads. Smaller numbers died in border incidents and street demonstrations, in confrontations between German and occupation police forces, and in revenge slayings.[124]

In several cases troops were used to inflict collective punishments on the Ruhr population. The February effort by miners to organize a boycott in Recklinghausen, and the abusive French reaction, was dubbed the "terror regiment" by Germans. In another incident in June, civilians coming into the city of Buer, ignorant of a curfew declared in their absence, were fired on by Belgian patrols. Several soldiers were killed.[125]

Collective punishment was more evident in later months of the resistance. For example, in Dortmund someone shot two French soldiers in the street. During a quickly declared curfew, patrols swept the streets, driving passersby into groups. Many were beaten by the troops, and six were shot and killed.[126]

Harsh treatment did little to dampen the resistance. The German government published many accounts of these horrors. They often stressed the most enraging aspects, such as the needless deaths of civilians, accusations of sexual misconduct by soldiers, or the practice of beating people with officers' riding whips.[127]

On 14 March, General Degoutte ordered the dissolution of the German security police apparatus in the Ruhr and expulsion of its members. The occupying troops viewed the armed, state-run force charged particularly with guarding against threats to public peace as a direct threat to their safety.[128]

The impact of disbanding the security police was slight in the early months of resistance. In May clashes between the discontented unemployed of the Ruhr and government forces broke out into open street fighting (see below). Before this time, the greatest threat to public order was clashes between troops and the Ruhr people who refused to obey their commands.

The greatest loss of life in a single clash occurred at Essen's giant Krupp factory on 31 March. Accounts of the Krupp confrontation vary, and several points are disputed between French and German sources. On that morning, a small French unit took over a vehicle garage in the factory as if to confiscate trucks and automobiles for the occupation's use. The management tried to convince the patrol to leave, without success. At that point, about nine in the morning, the plant's steam whistles blew as a signal that an occupation was in progress.

Hundreds of employees stopped work at once and crowded into a courtyard near the garages. Feeling threatened, the patrol kept the crowd from coming too close. The French officer said that agitators, some armed with pistols, stirred up the crowd while unknown persons sprayed steam into the area. At last the sirens fell silent, but the demonstration in front of the garages continued. Shortly after 11:00 A.M., apparently provoked by movement in the crowd, the patrol fired. Thirteen workers were killed on the spot and many injured. As the crowd fell back, the patrol left the grounds.[129]

The French immediately arrested Krupp managers, later including the owner of the immense firm, the forbidding Gustav Krupp von Bohlen und Halbach. Tried in May for conspiracy and threatening the peace, the convicted Krupp people were sentenced to prison terms up to twenty years and hundred-million-mark fines.[130] The victims' funeral, meanwhile, became the focus of an immense outpouring of national sympathy and determination to continue to resist the occupation.

General Degoutte took the measure of the Ruhr occupation in two reports to his superiors, one in mid-April, the other five weeks later. In both, he admitted that resistance, thought lagging in March, was strong once more. While pleased at the progress in seizing coal, he was troubled by Germany's rekindling of the resistance spirit, particularly among the hard-pressed railroad workers. Degoutte recognized that he did not have enough technical personnel to operate mines and factories without German cooperation. The five thousand people already at work in the régie, he thought, were not half the number needed to operate on a regular basis.

Degoutte asked his superiors for permission to increase the pressure on the Ruhr's population. He recommended taking over mines, making greater efforts to seize the flow of funds the resistance needed, banning all transportation options that allowed people to do without the railroad, and extending the program of mass expulsion of railroaders. People would begin to accustom themselves to occupation soon, he thought, but in the meantime France and Belgium must continue to act "without quarter and without weakness."[131]

Meanwhile, the Cuno government was compelled, in the face of inroads already made into the resistance front, to consider anew what form resistance should take. The optimistic view that France and Belgium could actually be forced to withdraw had given way to the realization that the struggle would be lengthy and had to be oriented toward achieving international negotiations over the Ruhr's fate. As early as mid-February, two officials active in the resistance suggested that gritty persistence, admirable as it was, was an insufficient basis for a policy of extended resistance. One suggested a policy that met small issues with "elasticity and prudence" so that it could better be "firm and strong" in great issues.[132]

Labor leaders once again raised this question of "elastic" or "flexible" resistance in March. There was widespread belief in union, professional, and local government circles that the resistance was at its height in March and April 1923 and that the government must get negotiations under way to end it and prepare for the time when a lower level of intensity was needed. This was especially true in the Rhineland, now occupied since 1918 and the site of many of the occupation's first experiments in repression.[133]

It was very difficult to agree on what constituted flexible tactics or which might be employed. For example, several advisors suggested that people should comply with the ever-growing system of passes needed to transport goods into and through the Ruhr, for personal travel, and in crossing border points. In this way, they argued, people could gain access to needed goods, including some already waiting to be off-loaded from docked barges, and avoid the exhaustion of travel.[134]

But how could this be done without undermining the railroaders who were making real sacrifices?[135] While real interest was shown in the concept of elastic resistance, no plan developed for putting it into effect. To the extent that resistance did become more flexible, it was on a piecemeal basis. Nevertheless, starting in early May, the absolute strictness of German resistance in the first months declined in the face of the losses in resources and energy the campaign had suffered.[136]

"ACTIVE RESISTANCE": SABOTAGE AND VIOLENCE

To some in Germany, "passive resistance" was not enough. They believed that it must be accompanied and supplemented by "active resistance," by which they meant sabotage, threats against occupation troops, and perhaps more. Near the end of January, volunteers arrived in Berlin from all over Germany, hoping to be taken into the army for a campaign against the French. During the Thyssen group's trial in Mainz, groups of youths beat up French soldiers and interfered with railroad watchmen, and took to the streets until late into the night to sing provocative patriotic songs.[137] Volunteers were sent home and crowds dispersed and discouraged, but the impulse they represented was more difficult to channel.

Ex-soldiers, ex-Free Corps fighters, and members of secret nationalist defense organizations formed the core of those committed to methods of sabotage and violence. Assembling at cities such as Hagen, on the borders of the Ruhr, "demolition columns" infiltrated into the zone to blow up bridges, canals, and to hinder the occupation's efforts to ship coal and coke home.[138] Most acted on their own, but many believed that they had the secret sympathy of government and the covert support of the *Reichswehr* on their side. One of the most prominent examples of their activities was a series of attacks on the Rhine-Herne Canal. These were carried out in part by the Free Corps unit *Bund Oberland,* banned but nonetheless active in the *Ruhrkampf* underground.[139]

Occupation troops took over the locks on the strategically vital Rhine-Herne Canal, running east to west through the heart of the Ruhr, in late January. Shippers and dock hands stopped work at once, but French engineers managed to put a stretch back into operation. In February, German sabotage teams sank barges in the canal to block vital points. The French retaliated by seizing canal ports and rail facilities, as well as issuing an order warning Germans not to come near canal harbors or locks, linger on bridges, or use canal waters or their banks in any way, subject not only to punishment but also to the possibility that sentries would fire at once. The local commander in Recklinghausen also named a list of civil servants from communities along the canal who would be held personally responsible for future acts of sabotage if the perpetrators were not caught.[140]

With the canal system a key link in the plan to transport coal and coke back to their homeland, the French labored successfully to clear the obstructions. In early April a German demolition squad blew a hole in a major branch canal, allowing long stretches of the canals to run dry and leaving barges scattered on the empty bed. The French quickly cordoned off the area and made a number of arrests. The sabotage of the Rhine-Herne Canal was a sensation throughout the area and considered quite a success in hindering the transport of coke and coal to France.[141]

Demolition and destruction of physical structures used by the occupation, such as bridges, telephone lines, or the coal and coke piles themselves, constituted most of the sabotage. French and Belgian soldiers were occasional victims of the violent resistance as well. Snipers fired on sentries on several occasions, usually doing no harm, but occasionally sentries and other soldiers were killed. When the victims were found dead in the morning, their comrades reacted harshly, often to the point of terrorizing German civilians.[142]

Support for so-called active resistance grew, and it tested the Cuno government's commitment to a strategy of passive resistance. In late January army commander Hans von Seeckt began organizing a sabotage center at Munster near the Ruhr.[143] The center's response to requests for help were unsettling to some of those that received it. On Easter night, for example, railroaders smuggled several loaded trains into unoccupied territory. They asked for a lightly armed escort to meet them but instead encountered over three hundred heavily armed men. That this unit was recruited from rightist organizations only added to the railroaders' concern.[144]

In March and April 1923 scattered acts of sabotage were common. Trying to interfere with the occupation's seizure of coal and coke, sabotage concentrated particularly on transportation and communications equipment. Sabotage groups damaged tracks and equipment on the rail lines taken over by the occupation. In April a sabotage group attacked the Ruhr Valley line, blowing up tracks, telephone lines, and a major railroad bridge.[145] Some circles were well pleased with the results. At the end of May, representatives of Ruhr coal mines encouraged continued small acts of sabotage not because they accomplished a great deal in themselves, but for the psychological impact on the foe. They called for greater protection for the "brave people" engaged in sabotage, accusing some public officials of having actually cooperated with the occupation in pursuing and arresting activists.[146]

The mine owners were not entirely wrong about the attitude of officials and union leaders who judged the sabotage campaign not on the basis of its limited effect on the French and Belgians but on its impact on the resistance campaign as a whole. In March some mine owners and mine workers argued for setting sabotage aside in favor of "peaceful" resistance. Sabotage did not significantly hinder the transport of coal, they argued, but justified harsher French sanctions.[147] The reprisal they feared most was the taking of hostages, which France and Belgium soon put into effect.

The occupation declared that officials and communities also were themselves responsible for sabotage when those who actually carried it out escaped. The French and Belgian forces divided rail and telephone lines into sections and named a specific official responsible for each one. Communities also were told that they would suffer reprisals for sabotage, such as fines levied against the whole city or a ban on travel, telephones, and telegraph.[148] For both punishment and deterrence of sabotage, civil servants and prominent citizens in some cities were forced to ride on trains in dangerous areas.

The sabotage campaign's future was thrown into doubt by a series of events in the spring of 1923. The first involved Albert Leo Schlageter, whose execution made him a martyr to the rightist cause. Schlageter, a Nazi, joined a sabotage and espionage group organized by Heinz Hauenstein, who claimed to have the support of the *Reichswehr*. Schlageter's group demolished a railroad bridge in mid-March, and several members were later captured, tried, and condemned to death. Despite a strong protest from the German government, Schlageter was executed at the end of May.[149]

In the meantime, Hauenstein and several others, one of whom

claimed to be an army lieutenant, were arrested by German officials outside the occupied zone. Adam Remmeling, prime minister of Baden, and Prussian interior minister Carl Severing both wrote angry letters to the Cuno government demanding a halt to support for the demolition groups. Remmeling insisted that the burden of French reprisals, such as arrest of officials and fines, fell on the Ruhr's people without sabotage actually aiding the German cause.[150]

When yet another saboteur was arrested and sentenced to death, the Cuno government sprang into action again to ward off his execution, successfully this time. Once more Cuno was told that the people of the occupied area were angry about his government's tolerance of sabotage, feeling that they alone suffered when the occupation punished an entire city with a curfew on travel between 9 P.M. and 5 A.M.[151]

Cuno's rather bland response to Remmeling's challenge was to deny that the government supported sabotage, claiming that actions of this sort were a natural and unavoidable result of the anger of the Ruhr people. Remmeling was definitely not mollified by such an answer, accusing the government of harboring a secret unofficial policy of sabotage alongside its public support for passive resistance.[152]

On the last day of June, saboteurs exploded a bomb in a troop train crossing the Rhine River bridge at Duisburg, killing nine Belgians and injuring many others. The Belgians captured seven members of the sabotage group, whom a military court condemned to death, although the sentence was later commuted. The Belgian army also punished the city severely. They forced hostages to ride on trains crossing the bridges and curfewed travel within the zone. The occupation closed the Ruhr border posts in early July, isolating the zone from the rest of the country.[153] Protests against the sabotage campaign continued. Germany's diplomats abroad warned that these events threatened foreign approval of the resistance. Labor union leaders told one of Cuno's contacts that sabotage was a "heavy burden" to them and that the government was not responding strongly enough.[154]

Some government leaders in the occupied zone tried to counter the violence. After French soldiers were fired upon in separate incidents in Duisburg, Essen, and Hattingen, the mayors offered rewards for finding the culprits. The Hattingen mayor was denounced outside the Ruhr as a collaborator. He defended himself by showing that he intended to gain the release of hostages by giving evidence that local government did not protect saboteurs.[155]

In face of foreign protests and disgust at home, Cuno's administration abandoned support for sabotage and "active resistance." Twenty French and Belgian soldiers died during the Ruhr conflict, many in acts of sabotage and violence.[156] These acts did little to hinder the occupation, although they perhaps restrained some Germans from collaboration. On the other hand, harsh occupation sanctions in the wake of sabotage weakened passive resistance by absorbing vital resources and weakening commitment. German resistance was based in part on the belief that other powers would eventually intervene if the nation pursued a nonviolent campaign. Outside support for Germany was clearly weakened by the destruction and death that violent resistance caused.[157]

STRAINS ON THE UNITY OF RESISTANCE

The divisive debate over violence was just one of several strains working negatively against Germany's will to resist during the spring and summer of 1923. Others included a raging inflationary trend, the reassertion of internal political divisions, and a relative absence of meaningful international support for the German cause.

Inflation took hold of Germany's economy in the wake of financing World War I, and turned into hyperinflation by the latter half of 1922. The mark's loss of value against foreign currency was both a major measure of inflation's course and a direct contributing factor. At par with the dollar in 1913, the rate of exchange was 1.57 marks per dollar at the end of 1918. In mid-1922, the rate was 75.6 and at the end of the year, 1,801 marks to the dollar. In mid-1923, the rate was 26,200 to one; in September, 23.5 million to one; in November, 522 billion to one; and at year's end, one trillion marks to the dollar.[158] While the occupation and resistance did not cause hyperinflation, the need to finance the resistance, primarily by printing new currency, certainly worsened the trend.

Hyperinflation took an unmistakable toll on German unity. Farmers, for example, refused to sell their 1923 harvest for paper money, even to their German customers. Labor became more than usually suspicious of management and government when efforts to keep wages in line with prices failed. Real and potential food shortages, the decline in the buying power of wages, and the shift in public attention to the task of maintaining a decent life absorbed enormous energy. The approach of autumn heightened people's fear of food and money shortages during the coming winter. Government and banking authorities were constantly concerned about the adequacy of the currency supply, which in itself consumed officials' time, attention, and productivity.

After the first blush of national unity in the face of a threat, traditional political orientations began to reassert themselves, with a deleterious effect on the resistance. Right-wing nationalists tended either to opt out of the struggle (the Nazis, for instance, forbade involvement and used the period to build their power base) or to force the pace of the violent struggle and provide the primary recruitment pool for sabotage activities. The left and organized labor, meanwhile, were deeply suspicious of the nationalists' motives and actions. While they supported passive resistance, they had urged negotiation from the beginning, and felt that it was they who paid the highest price until some kind of accommodation was reached.

After weeks of agitation for increased wages and lower unemployment, communist-led workers declared a general strike in the mines and factories near several major cities in the Ruhr in late May 1923. Bands of strikers marched from mine to mine to call out the work force by persuasion or drive it out by force. In the cities, groups tried to force shop owners to cut prices, burned newspaper offices, and attacked police headquarters.[159] General Degoutte had dissolved the German security police in March, so Cuno had to suppress the strikes with what local police force was left. The job took nearly a week and left dead and wounded on both sides.

A final line of political cleavage formed along the west bank of the Rhine. Rhinelanders who hoped to break away from Germany had been active in the years following World War I. Separatist activity was limited during the early months of passive resistance, but it increased sharply thereafter, hampering efforts to consolidate any gains from the struggle. Encouraged by French Rhineland Commissioner Jacques Tirard, the scattered and competitive Rhenish separatist groups put together an umbrella organization during the summer of 1923.[160]

The separatist movement, profiting from the inability of the German government to stop it, began in earnest with mass meetings and demonstrations in the summer. *Putsch* attempts by separatists erected several short-lived "republics" in the Rhineland and Palatinate in late 1923. Taking power by terror, the regimes lasted until they collapsed or were suppressed by police. The last Rhineland republics fell under the bullets of nationalist gangs in early 1924.[161] France and Belgium supported Rhenish separatism because it served more to strengthen their control in the region than to create actual new states. In addition, the possible loss of the Rhineland kept the German government off balance.

Tangible help from the outside was not forthcoming. Both the United States and Britain looked askance at the occupation from the beginning but had no incentive to break with France and Belgium to stop it. Britain initially denied France use of its Cologne occupation zone for increased rail traffic when German transport workers struck, but relented in time, so that resistance to coal and coke removal was somewhat outflanked.

Swedish Prime Minister Karl Branting tried to encourage neutral nations to refer the dispute to the League of Nations tribunal in Geneva. Poincaré outmaneuvered Branting by having the tribunal moved to Paris and letting it be known that France would quit the League of Nations rather than submit to scrutiny. Branting relented and agreed to view the conflict as a reparations issue, something outside the League's responsibilities.[162]

International labor organizations were ineffective in their effort to mount an international protest. German labor unions appealed for help to the International League of Labor Unions, based in Amsterdam. The labor international suggested an elaborate plan for coordinated international general strikes as a demonstration against the occupation and in favor of a world boycott of French goods. For various reasons, not the least of which was the presence of French and Belgian workers in the organization, nothing came of these schemes.[163]

The Cuno government now faced a dilemma. With no help in sight, and a deteriorating economic and political situation, the chancellor could ask his country neither to give up resisting the occupation nor to sustain that resistance indefinitely. As a feeble alternative, the German government came up with a reparations proposal that reflected as much the desire to placate right-wing parties in Germany as any wish to start negotiations, as advocated by the left. Cuno's cabinet realized that Poincaré had to reject the German proposal but hoped that Britain would take the opportunity to come to Germany's aid.[164]

The reparations proposal was sent to all the major powers in a diplomatic note on 2 May 1923. From a diplomatic viewpoint, the note was a serious error. Not only was it vague, but also Germany again assumed that the allies would grant it large loans and a moratorium period. It also requested that the London Schedule of Payments be dropped in favor of the intervention of economic experts. The note was rejected out of hand by France, as expected. Worse, it failed to impress the U.S. government or the British cabinet, which dismissed the note as a "great disappointment."[165]

The 2 May note was a disaster for the future of passive resistance in the Ruhr. It began with a lengthy preamble justifying resistance, written to placate anti-negotiation sentiment in Germany. Since the note concerned the reparations issue, there was no need to refer to passive resistance. Instead, the government defensively insisted that its diplomatic overtures did not imply "abandoning its legal standpoint or giving up passive resistance." The note vowed that passive resistance would not end until the Ruhr was evacuated and the Rhineland restored to a condition acceptable under the Versailles Treaty.[166]

Until this time, the *Ruhrkampf* had continued under the fiction that it was completely spontaneous on the people's part, even though all parties knew that the government played an important role. Poincaré seized on the contradiction immediately. If the government could keep resistance going, he implied, it could call it off. Poincaré declared that France and Belgium were "determined to evacuate the newly occupied territories only in proportion to and in relation to the fulfillment of payments."[167] From that time forward, France insisted that a genuine and final halt to German resistance was a precondition to any discussion of the status of the Rhineland and the Ruhr.

Chastened by the May note's reception, Cuno ordered a thorough restudy of the German position. Although again hampered by domestic politics, the government managed to extract promises from various groups in several economic sectors to support specific reparations guarantees. The government sent a new note to the Allies containing its proposals on 7 June.[168] Unlike the earlier note, it was silent on the question of resistance and took a moderate and practical tone.

At this juncture, the significance of the unfortunate May note became clear. Great Britain and even Belgium responded positively, Britain in particular maintaining that here was a basis for future discussion. Yet Poincaré refused to discuss any of the issues involved until passive resistance ceased. He would not discuss calling a conference nor would he hold talks with Britain. Britain was forced either to turn against France, which it would not do, or be silent. Cuno had unwittingly maneuvered Germany into a situation where it must either capitulate or continue resistance to the end.[169]

THE COLLAPSE OF PASSIVE RESISTANCE

Continual domestic unrest, financial collapse, and diplomatic failure brought down Chancellor Cuno's government. He stepped aside to be replaced by the parliamentary activist of the German People's Party, Gustav Stresemann. Stresemann's "grand coalition" cabinet raised the ministry for the occupied regions to cabinet rank, and with it the hope of a settlement in the Rhineland and the Ruhr.[170]

The Stresemann cabinet spent the last two weeks of August taking the measure of the Ruhr question. The facts were alarming and pointed to the conclusion that resistance in the occupied regions was inextricably linked to the rapidly depreciating mark. The key problems of resistance were identified at a cabinet discussion on 23 August and in reports from various economic and defense committees of the occupied regions in subsequent days.[171]

Stresemann hoped that continuing to resist might fulfill the dream of bringing the United Kingdom to Germany's side. In his view, France had not really changed its policy. Britain, tiring of the Ruhr occupation, showed signs of interest in luring Belgium from Poincaré's side. Combined with intimations to France that both security and economic guarantees could be forthcoming if German sovereignty were respected, Stresemann believed that British pressure might bring France into negotiations.[172] All serious discussion within the German government after that time started with the assumption that France could be induced to talk, despite more than eight months of French refusal to do anything of the kind.

Some of Stresemann's advisors assured him that resistance could be maintained at least until cold weather began. The will to resist appeared strong among the people of the Ruhr, especially organized labor and railroaders. The occupied zone could be supplied with food and fuel, some claimed, and truly heroic efforts were under way to smuggle enough funds into the region to meet payrolls. Besides, as some argued, the populace would feel abandoned if resistance were called off now after their months of bravery and sacrifice.[173]

But warning voices on the other side could not be ignored. Passive resistance was now shot through with near-fatal flaws, they contended, which made its continuation impossible. Their objections broke down essentially into three parts: the problem of continued finance, the growing ability of France and Belgium to control the Rhineland and the Ruhr, and the decline of the organizational and psychological infrastructure of resistance.

Although the government's intention from January on had been to finance the Ruhr struggle as much as possible with credits, industry and wage earners alike demanded cash. Wages, cash seized by the occupation, and unemployment compensation in the Ruhr cost trillions of marks per month. Keeping workers at their jobs without having them produce anything the occupation could seize was enormously costly. In addition, wage and price adjustments forced by steady inflation drove expenditures beyond control.[174]

Prussian Prime Minister Braun warned at the August cabinet meeting that if economic collapse ensued, "Germany would no longer be a factor in negotiations, but only an object of the policies of foreign states." This viewpoint gained more support when financial officials finally reported that Ruhr aid was so expensive that it could no longer be supported. Unless the constant drain on funds ended, they reported, financial collapse was imminent.[175]

At the same time, France and Belgium were beginning to enjoy the kinds of results from their long months of occupation that they had once expected. Although still lacking the hoped-for cooperation from the Ruhr and Rhineland work force, they had dampened the intensity of the resistance by their repressive measures. The railroad régie was operating the most vital rail lines with a growing German ridership. France had also begun to make noises about international operation and financial control of the Rhine Valley rail lines on a long-term basis.

Occupation troops confiscated cash needed for Rhine-Ruhr aid regularly, sometimes before it left the printer. Shipments of coal and coke to France and Belgium had declined briefly, largely because

Ruhr industry stopped producing anything the troops could seize. By summer's end, MICUM engineers had begun to operate cokeries on their own and plans were in the works to bring miners from Poland to reopen the Ruhr coal mines. Using their place on the International Rhineland Commission, France and Belgium were also capitalizing on Germany's currency crisis. Several Rhine region cities wanted to issue emergency banknotes of their own. Holding out the threat of preventing them from circulating or, worse, taking the occasion to issue a Rhineland currency of its own, the Rhineland Commission invited municipal officials to a conference on this question. Talks of this kind fed the German government's secret fear that the occupation might deal with communities, industry, and labor directly and cut out the central government. Efforts to insert a government commissioner, Duisburg's expelled mayor Karl Jarres, were not successful.[176]

Finally, the organizational fabric of resistance was unraveling. The number of expelled civil servants and railroad workers approached one hundred thousand by the end of August. Railroaders and their families were sometimes expelled by the hundreds or simply turned out of their dwellings to be supported by the local government. Many suffered greatly because of this. Resistance leaders were forced to hesitate before refusing an occupation command for fear that no one would be left to replace those expelled. For example, when occupation forces ordered German officials to ride on régie trains as hostages to ward off sabotage, union leaders debated whether they could afford the luxury of refusing lest the last few of them be expelled.[177]

There were other signs of social disorganization as well. During a brief interruption in the flow of money into the Ruhr, unpaid coal miners assembled in gangs to plunder crops in the countryside and loot food stores. Farmers, as has been mentioned, refused to sell produce for inflated currency, and small businesses and shop owners simply could no longer find the will to resist. The pessimistic Carl Severing said that government could no longer speak of passive resistance at a time when the railroads carried coal and coke in abundance to France and Belgium and "the business world has made its peace with the French." The Coal Syndicate increased its demands for government credits used to pay unproductive workers kept on the payroll. Indeed, business and industry had begun to make their own contacts with French and Belgian officials. Magnate Otto Wolff took it upon himself to put out feelers to the French army by holding discussions with Generals Denvignes and Degoutte.[178]

Beyond this, the general conditions of life under the occupation demoralized and depressed people, especially as its methods reached ever deeper into daily life. Unemployment increased despite government efforts to keep the Ruhr population at work. Inflation was so rampant that wages barely sufficed to buy the essentials of life. Accusations flew that Ruhr aid funds were being misused and squandered, sometimes by labor, sometimes by industry. By September, occupation regulations had brought all public transportation to a halt except for the régie trains. Customs barriers between the occupied and unoccupied zones, accompanied by continual changes in the regulations an individual must comply with in order to pass, had tightened the occupation's grip. In addition, the occupation punished acts of sabotage by declaring periods of curfew, border closings, transportation bans, and halting the flow of mail, as well as taking hostages.[179]

What was to be done? Some few suggested that passive resistance ought to be kept up, even reinvigorated. Consensus was firm in late August, however, that the cost had become too great and that passive resistance must be called off before cold weather came. But when and how? Chancellor Stresemann hoped that government or labor in the occupied regions could be induced to request an end to passive resistance, but they refused.[180] He would have to accept the responsibility and find his own way.

The complexities were great, not the least of which was to avoid the feeling among the Rhineland and Ruhr population that their struggle had been for nothing. The foreign connection, however, was equally difficult. If France and Belgium came to believe that passive resistance was abandoned because of German weakness, they might increase their exploitation of the Ruhr. With this in mind, Stresemann began discussions with the ambassadors of France, Belgium, the United Kingdom, the United States, and Italy, and with the papal nuncio.[181]

When Stresemann came into office, he recognized Cuno's error in taking the position that no negotiation was possible until France and Belgium evacuated the Ruhr. Poincaré simply replied that no negotiations were possible until passive resistance ended.[182] Nevertheless, Stresemann hoped to exploit continued passive resistance in order to

gain some sort of advantage in beginning talks with the Allies, even
though he knew by this time that it could not last too much
longer.[183] He appeared to believe that with Great Britain's help passive resistance could be given up at the same time as negotiations
began.

Stresemann was pleased with the outcome of his few quasi-official
conversations with the French and Belgian ambassadors and briefly
believed that an accommodation could be reached. The cabinet
worked on a reparations proposal that would offer the Allies revenue
from direct exploitation of the economy of western Germany, but
without occupation. In fact, it offered concessions so sweeping as to
raise the question of whether or not they were compatible with German sovereignty.[184]

On 9 September, Commissioner Ernst Mehlich of the Rhine-Ruhr
Central proposed a fresh way of conceiving the link between breaking off passive resistance and starting talks. Since Poincaré claims
that resistance is the bar to negotiation, Mehlich suggested, Germany
must call his bluff by halting passive resistance while simultaneously
calling for changes in the status quo. Mehlich assumed that French
failure to comply would signal a rededication to resistance on a limited basis, but he was nevertheless the first major German official to
state that passive resistance might cease before negotiations began.
During the middle of September, Stresemann continued to assert
that retaining passive resistance, if only for two weeks, could somehow bring about talks.[185]

The *Ruhrkampf* and the financial crisis were not the only issues
Stresemann had to address. He was concerned that the nationalist
parties, enraged by a halt to resistance, would revolt. Indeed, nationalists in the occupied region were already prepared to denounce
Stresemann as a traitor after hearing rumors that resistance would
end. And the conservative government of Bavaria was protesting
nearly every decisive government measure, while refusing to suppress Nazis and other ultra-nationalists. There was even talk of a
military dictatorship in some circles.[186]

It was not until 20 September that the decision to "demobilize"
in the Rhineland and the Ruhr was finally taken. Once convinced,
Stresemann made every effort to build a consensus around his decision. He chaired meetings of every Rhine-Ruhr constituency on 24
and 25 September, forging agreement with his position among all

elements except the angry nationalists. Significantly, the terms Stresemann's government was seeking from the Allies shifted subtly over these few days. Military evacuation of the Ruhr no longer appeared on the list of demands, which were now limited to return of expellees, amnesty for prisoners, and promises of German sovereignty over its own territory. Indeed, French intransigence led the German government to accept that passive resistance must be given up without negotiations being promised. Of the two options available, allowing passive resistance to collapse in confusion as a result of its internal problems or organizing the most orderly retreat possible, the Stresemann government had chosen the latter.[187]

President Ebert delivered the government's decision to the German people the next day, 26 September, proclaiming the end of passive resistance. Ebert reviewed how France and Belgium had illegally entered the Ruhr, the resistance Germany had mounted, and its human and financial costs. Passive resistance, he said, must now be ended to maintain the nation's integrity. The government canceled all directives to its officials mandating resistance and, on the next day, announced to its foes that resistance had ceased. This done, Stresemann waited for France and Belgium to respond.[188]

Perhaps the German government knew how slender the possibility was of reconciliation. Poincaré was as unyielding as ever in his speeches. Rhineland Commission head Paul Tirard pointed out the flaw in German reasoning during a talk with Cologne mayor Adenauer. Germany must realize, Tirard said, that France would not agree to any settlement that did not preserve its position in western Germany. Nor would France give up the position it now held in the Rhineland and the Ruhr for mere promises. When passive resistance ended, Poincaré acted as if nothing had actually changed. On 1 October, Stresemann was forced to announce to his cabinet that "the negotiations with France have failed."[189]

KILLING THE GOOSE: OCCUPIERS' OBJECTIVES AFTER THE COLLAPSE OF RESISTANCE

It should be remembered that when France and Belgium began occupying the Ruhr region of Germany nine months earlier, it was primarily to secure reparations payments, in cash or in kind, and to enhance their own future security by hedging against the reemergence of Germany as an economic and military power. To gain these objectives, the focus of their activities devolved into the struggle to break passive resistance. As we can now see, this secondary objective was achieved in its entirety. Under pressure from all quarters, Germany gave up its only means of self-defense without even a reasonable hope of moving toward a settlement that it could live with. The occupiers would seem to have been completely victorious.

The primary objectives, however, depended at least on a minimally functioning German economy, and the occupiers had, to put it crudely, helped to kill the goose that might have laid the golden egg. Germany was so completely debilitated at this point that the United States and Britain finally felt compelled to intervene and propose a framework for negotiations which included internationalizing the whole question of reparations. In practice this meant that an independent commission of financial experts, led by American financier Charles Dawes, would investigate Germany's ability to pay and revise the reparations schedule accordingly.

The results were twofold: France and Belgium never got the payments they were awarded at Versailles, and they temporarily traded places with Germany as the ones to be isolated in world opinion. The Dawes Commission focused international attention on the financial plight of Germany, and was the first step toward the Locarno Treaty and the inclusion of Germany in the League of Nations.

ANALYSIS

Outcome of the Campaign

The outcome of this contest was a stalemate. Germany failed to expel its invaders and paid dearly in blood and treasure, but managed in the end to get international relief and a start on the road to recovery. France and Belgium controlled the situation for nine months and forced an end to resistance, but saw their economic and security objectives compromised immediately after "winning" the fight. In fact, the single most lasting result of the operation was the refueling of German resentment, for which the *Ruhrkampf* would stand as a continuing justification. The Dawes Commission, which

followed the inconclusive campaign, led to the end of the occupation
and a modification of reparation demands on Germany. The resistance and its aftermath were not disconnected from the events surrounding the Dawes Commission.

PRINCIPLES OF DEVELOPMENT

Principle 1: Formulate Functional Objectives

The nonviolent protagonists conformed to this principle.

The German objectives were to reopen the reparations question
and to prevent the forcible extraction of resources in place of reparations. Both objectives were clearly vital to all Germans, as they
touched the very heart of sovereignty and national interest. But the
second objective was more important to citizens of the Ruhr.

Given the economic realities of the early 1920s, forced reparations
could be seen by third parties as harsh and counterproductive, if not
illegitimate or immoral. Pursuit of the German objectives, though
not fully realized, ultimately led to an international reexamination of
the reparations question.

The objectives developed for the campaign were functional, within
the definition of this principle. They suggested the use of a ready
repertoire of nonviolent sanctions. The effectiveness of these sanctions was directly related to, and dependent upon, the resisting population's degree of noncooperation. Forced reparations required the
cooperation, or at least the noninterference, of the German people
of the Ruhr. The success of direct economic and political noncooperation became a key variable of the outcome. There were plenty of
points of contact with which to develop a variety of related nonviolent methods.

Principle 2: Develop Organizational Strength

The nonviolent protagonists conformed to this principle.

The organizational structure of the resistance was complex and
strong. Each of the preferred three tiers of organization came into
being. The Cuno government took over leadership, while the most
active industrial and political groups functioning as an operations
corps worked in close contact with the general population. Occupa-

tional and civil service groups provided the desirable depth of organization, with transport workers, munitions workers, and merchants playing key roles.

A central problem faced by this de facto three-tiered organization was communication, especially from the "external" Cuno government to the population "inside" the occupied zone. The Ruhr-Rhine Central was obviously intended to address this problem, but it was never wholly adequate to the task.

Principle 3: Secure Access to Critical Material Resources

The nonviolent protagonists failed to conform to this principle.

This is a case in which resources constituted a large part of the reason for the contest. In this principle, however, we are concerned with the material resources needed to wage the campaign, both offensively and defensively. As a consequence of not being clearly focused on the requirements of nonviolent struggle, the Germans were poorly prepared to counter the Franco-Belgian invasion. Even if they had taken prior measures to protect their resources, the material constraints of the immediate postwar period might well have prevented optimal performance.

The Germans over the course of the conflict could not protect access to certain critical assets, especially roads and railroads. As a result, freedom of movement was progressively curtailed, which meant foodstuffs and other necessities could not be efficiently distributed. Another hardship peculiar to this conflict was inflation, which severely depreciated the value of the currency. Government efforts to subsidize unemployment stemming from the resistance exacerbated inflation. Hyperinflation led, among other things, to the collapse of the merchant class's endurance. The government failed to find ways to bolster the resources available to various groups put under extreme pressure. Consequently, by the latter stages of the campaign, the government no longer believed "passive resistance" could be sustained indefinitely.

Principle 4: Cultivate External Assistance

The nonviolent protagonists only partially conformed to this principle.

The contest took place in the aftermath of a war in which a defeated Germany was the aggressor. Garnering international support on the basis of a moral agenda was bound to be an uphill battle. That fact was compounded when Germany defaulted on reparations agreements which, however unfair or unrealistic, had behind them the force of international law. Germany was dependent on demonstrably bad behavior by the French and Belgians for the dynamic of this principle to take hold.

Britain was the most likely party to see the reparations issue Germany's way, and not enough was done to develop this potential. Instead, during the early and middle parts of the conflict, the English viewed the Germans as being evasive and stalling on reparations and thus were unwilling to help. Creative and energetic measures were overlooked to portray the French and Belgians as both cruel and unwise in their policies. For example, mass disobedience of the curfew could have highlighted the level of intrusion imposed on the Germans. It was only when the British and then the Americans came independently to conclude that the French and Belgian approach was wrong that they intervened to end the contest as a draw rather than an outright defeat for Germany.

Principle 5: Expand the Repertoire of Sanctions

The nonviolent protagonists only partially conformed to this principle.

"Passive resistance," in general, and in its use in this instance, is a term that does not tell us much about what anyone was expected to do or about their vision of how the campaign might develop. However, there was a progression of specific sanctions, flowing directly from the nature of the occupation and its objectives. For example, everything the occupiers intended to seize became a point of resistance. While this pattern created lots of opportunities, it also meant that the German resistance was essentially reactive. The Germans never developed an ability to shift the ground of conflict according to their will and initiative.

Overall, the sanctions deployed did not show much ingenuity or creative adaptation, nor did they begin to include the full range of possibilities. The sanctions also exhibited poor economy of force because they tended to be costlier to implement than the damage inflicted. The Germans failed to catch their opponents off guard with an unexpected variety and sequence of nonviolent methods. Consequently, they were met with related sets of countermeasures.

PRINCIPLES OF ENGAGEMENT

Principle 6: Attack the Opponents' Strategy for Consolidating Control

The nonviolent protagonists failed to conform to this principle.

The Franco-Belgian strategy was very focused. Control would be established by cordoning off targeted mines and proceeding to remove whatever coal was required to meet reparations payments. Support services necessary for this task or to support the invading forces would be secured as well. Transport services were the most vital support services, and access was vigorously contested by both sides. Though a temptation, the desire by the French to control the entire economy of the Rhine and to create a security buffer was kept secondary.

Germany's adversaries were prepared to turn up the pressure to whatever level they thought would succeed. Repression was sufficient to dissuade and demoralize but not enough to evoke immediate and wholesale international condemnation. The Germans were never capable of putting boundaries around that increasing pressure. Despite successes in denying the occupying forces certain objectives for a time, they could not be stymied, and eventually wore down the resistance. A strategy designed for the longer term might have modulated resistance in the mines and at the trains to force the occupation forces to be gradually more responsible for the entire effort. The more occupying forces were required to extract and transport coal, the more vulnerable they would have become to periodic nonviolent intervention to impede their work.

Principle 7: Mute the Impact of the Opponents' Violent Weapons

The nonviolent protagonists partially conformed to this principle.

"Muting the impact" in this case takes the form of avoiding the occasion of violence and of rendering it less important to the ultimate outcome. For a case on this scale, overt violence by the occupation was fairly low. Violent reprisals by the occupiers against German resistance was on balance unsuccessful and turned costly and counterproductive. The outrage and determination created among the German citizenry outweighed the negative impact of the violence. However, the hardships and dislocation created by occupying soldiers, premised on the threat of violence, were cumulatively quite effective. As previously noted, they helped debase the currency and reduced economic activity.

The German population incurred serious losses in the Ruhr, and these losses were compounded by mistakes of the leadership working outside the region. The burden of nonviolent action was born unevenly. Shopkeepers suffered when they went on a sellers' boycott. Union members suffered when they went on strike, while outside a few targeted industries, management was not perceived to be bearing an equivalent hardship. Events like the Union-Management fundraising fiasco led to disunity.

Principle 8: Alienate Opponents from Expected Bases of Support

The nonviolent protagonists failed to conform to this principle.

The principal bases of support for the occupiers would be the other Allied powers and the occupiers' domestic populations. Neither was ever effectively attacked. Nor was the individual French or Belgian soldier ever seriously induced to defect. Most probably, the social and political distance created by the recent war made it unlikely that this principle could have worked positively for the Germans, and it certainly meant that divisions between and among the occupiers themselves would have been extremely hard to create.

The Allied powers ultimately drew their own conclusions about this struggle, but not because of anything the Germans did to shift their support.

Principle 9: Maintain Nonviolent Discipline

The nonviolent protagonists failed to conform to this principle.

Violent sabotage, when seriously contemplated and carried out, had predictably bad consequences. To some Germans sabotage represented either a reasonable complement or a critical backstop to "passive resistance." The potential effectiveness of sabotage was initially overestimated. Debate over the role of sabotage caused tension and dissension among the right-wing participants in the struggle. Cuno's early hesitancy to renounce sabotage alienated the left who believed that business leaders wanted to use sabotage to protect their own assets and not necessarily to defeat the occupation.

Sabotage created electrifying moments of apparent success. Eventually, though, it increased the severity of reprisals. Many Germans considered giving up violent sabotage to be an important defeat. In fact, violent tactics were never in Germany's interest. They dissipated energy and led to confusion and demoralization. Worse still, the controversy over sabotage made it more difficult to explore defensive nonviolent strategies.

PRINCIPLES OF CONCEPTION

Principle 10: Assess Events and Options in Light of Levels of Strategic Decision Making

The nonviolent protagonists failed to conform to this principle.

Conformity with this principle would imply that the Cuno government had an overall vision of what it was trying to do or how the struggle should evolve. As with the Russian case, there were many logistical and tactical successes. The premise of resistance was that enough tactical victories would eventually add up to policy success.

Unfortunately, there is no evidence that, on the tactical and logistical levels, serious thought was given to the day-to-day requirements of the struggle and the need to provide time and places of protection and rest for the resisters. There were tactical options, if exploited with sufficient vigor, that could have widened the strategic options and even led to the occupiers rethinking their policy. These included protecting unlimited access to "free Germany" for the resisters in the Ruhr, long-term economic support for the hardest hit sectors, and continuous international exposure of the occupiers' repression.

Principle 11: Adjust Offensive and Defensive Operations According to the Relative Vulnerabilities of the Protagonists

The nonviolent protagonists failed to conform to this principle.

Lack of endurance is key to the collapse of nonviolent resistance in this case. Failure to moderate the pace of confrontations was a contributing factor. From start to finish, the campaign was waged as if the operative command was "damn the torpedoes, full speed ahead!" It was considered traitorous to slow down and prop up the German center of gravity. There was little appreciation of the importance of constructive work away from the fray to maintain the population's strength and to slow down the effects of the opponents' repression. More could have been done to ensure the geographic dispersion of the "passive resistance" in order to provide aid, shelter, and rest to key combatants.

Somehow the Germans managed throughout this contest to be overengaged and overcommitted to the most aggressive sanctions, while at the same time failing to take the initiative. The Germans were unable to shift momentum in the conflict. While a measured response to the invasion might have worked against the Germans in the short and intermediate term, it could have worked in their favor over the long term. No one considered making the supply of coal vulnerable to interruption rather than bearing the immediate cost of shutting down the flow entirely.

Principle 12: Sustain Continuity Between Sanctions, Mechanisms, and Objectives

The nonviolent protagonists failed to conform to this principle.

The Germans never properly analyzed the various routes open to them for victory. Fierce noncooperation may have been successful for a time with respect to the invaders' determined efforts to extract coal. What, though, would make them rethink their goals and withdraw? If the Germans were seeking conversion, sanctions should have been designed to change either the French and Belgian or the international community's stance on reparations.

If conversion was not a possibility, the German option was to coerce the occupying forces to leave or to seek an acceptable accommodation with them, such as revised reparations schedules. The Germans did not give themselves enough time to accomplish either.

The decision to give up "passive resistance" before the occupying forces had, in fact, withdrawn meant that the outcome was simply left in the hands of others to decide.

Ultimately, there was no coordination between the strategy to resist occupation and the strategy to reopen the reparations question.

Efforts to pursue the two main objectives became divorced from each other. Cuno's note of 2 May wrecked his credibility with the Allies by demonstrating how implausible his proposals were rather than convincing them in time to preempt the defeat of passive resistance.

NOTES

1. Erich Eyck, *A History of the Weimar Republic,* 1:83–86.
2. Carl Bergmann, *The History of Reparations,* 8–22; Guy Greer, *The Ruhr-Lorraine Industrial Problem,* 92–102.
3. Bergmann, *Reparations,* 26–29, 30–31, 85–89.
4. Greer, *Ruhr-Lorraine Problem,* 118–29; Walter A. McDougall, *France's Rhineland Diplomacy,* 105–6; Charles S. Maier, *Recasting Bourgeois Europe,* 194–205.
5. Gordon A. Craig, *Germany,* 440; Bergmann, *Reparations,* 81–84, 92–96, 99–103, 139–54.
6. Maier, *Bourgeois Europe,* 210.
7. McDougall, *Rhineland Diplomacy,* 37; Ludwig Zimmerman, *Frankreichs Ruhrpolitik,* 32; Eyck, *Weimar Republic,* 83–85.
8. Text of Rhineland Agreement in Ernst Fraenkel, *Military Occupation,* 233–36.
9. Fraenkel, *Military Occupation,* 4–6, 18–21, 40; Royal Jae Schmidt, *Versailles and the Ruhr,* 68–80; McDougall, *Rhineland Diplomacy,* 42–67, 89–93, 130.
10. Klaus Reimer, *Rheinlandfrage,* 28–91, 100–102, 137–62; McDougall, *Rhineland Diplomacy,* 46–51, 70–71.
11. McDougall, *Rhineland Diplomacy,* 4–9.
12. Greer, *Ruhr-Lorraine Problem,* 120–26; McDougall, *Rhineland Diplomacy,* 108–9.
13. George Eliasberg, *Der Ruhrkrieg von 1923,* 209–17; Horst Lademacher, "Nördlichen Rheinlande," 2:692–93.
14. McDougall, *Rhineland Diplomacy,* 110–13; Greer, *Ruhr-Lorraine Problem,* 126–35.
15. Fraenkel, *Military Occupation,* 99–100; McDougall, *Rhineland Diplomacy,* 139–55; John W. Wheeler-Bennett and Hugh Latimer, *Information on the Reparation Settlement,* 30.
16. McDougall, *Rhineland Diplomacy,* 148, 155, 158–59.
17. Denise Artaud, "A propos de l'occupation de la Ruhr," 4–5.
18. H.-J. Rupieper, "Politics and Economics," 184–85; McDougall, *Rhineland Diplomacy,* 244–49; Schmidt, *Versailles and the Ruhr,* 35, 37.
19. Bergmann, *Reparations,* 92–93, 115–16, 118, 148–69.
20. See McDougall, *Rhineland Diplomacy,* 200–226; Zimmermann, *Frankreichs Ruhrpolitik,* 50–59, 78–86; Rupieper, "Politics and Economics," 184–89.
21. Artaud, "Occupation de la Ruhr," 14.
22. Bergmann, *Reparations,* 139–54.
23. K.-H. Harbeck, ed., *Das Kabinett Cuno,* xxvii.

24. Ibid., 20–21, 37–38; Rupieper, "Politics and Economics," 143, 147–50; Bergmann, *Reparations,* 157–69.

25. Harbeck, ed., *Kabinett Cuno,* 108.

26. Ibid., 69–70, 108; Rupieper, "Politics and Economics," 155–60, 169, 210.

27. Harbeck, ed., *Kabinett Cuno,* 20.

28. Greer, *Ruhr-Lorraine Problem,* 173–76, 292–301; Herbert Michaelis and Ernst Schraepler, eds., *Ursachen,* 5:12, 16–18; Rupieper, "Politics and Economics," 178–79, 181.

29. McDougall, *Rhineland Diplomacy,* 235–43.

30. Ibid., 208–51; Rupieper, "Politics and Economics," 194–95, 205–6.

31. Michaelis and Schraepler, eds., *Ursachen,* 5:12–13.

32. Harbeck, ed., *Kabinett Cuno,* 37–38, 122–25, 126–27, 142–43.

33. Ibid., 124.

34. Michaelis and Schraepler, eds., *Ursachen,* 5:21–22.

35. Rupieper, "Politics and Economics," 210; Michaelis and Schraepler, eds., *Ursachen,* 16–18, 20–21.

36. Hans Spethmann, *Zwölf Jahre Ruhrbergbau,* 4:49–52; Harri Petras, *Hattinger Raum,* 25–27, 31, 33–34; Carl Severing, *Mein Lebensweg,* 1:370.

37. Michaelis and Schraepler, eds., *Ursachen,* 16–20.

38. Petras, *Hattinger Raum,* 27–28; Thilo Gante, *Die Besetzung der Stadt Dortmund,* 31–32; Zimmermann, *Frankreichs Ruhrpolitik,* 100.

39. A. E. Cornebise, "Some Aspects of the German Response," 9, 42.

40. Harbeck, ed., *Kabinett Cuno,* 140, 192; Severing, *Mein Lebensweg,* 1:375; Michaelis and Schraepler, eds., *Ursachen,* 5:29–30; Cornebise, "Aspects," 14.

41. Michaelis and Schraepler, eds., *Ursachen,* 5:68–69.

42. Ibid.

43. Severing, *Mein Lebensweg,* 1:375.

44. Michaelis and Schraepler, eds., *Ursachen,* 5:29–30.

45. Harbeck, ed., *Kabinett Cuno,* 138, 148–49.

46. Rupieper, "Politics and Economics," 219.

47. Lademacher, "Nördlichen Rheinlande," 2:704.

48. Harbeck, ed., *Kabinett Cuno,* 126–27, 129–30; Rupieper, "Politics and Economics," 214.

49. Harbeck, ed., *Kabinett Cuno,* 142–43, 146, 149–50; Rupieper, "Politics and Economics," 215.

50. Harbeck, ed., *Kabinett Cuno,* 144–45.

51. Spethmann, *Ruhrbergbau,* 3:324–25.

52. Harbeck, ed., *Kabinett Cuno,* 176–77, 183; Michaelis and Schraepler, eds., *Ursachen,* 5:42, 47–48.

53. Zimmermann, *Frankreichs Ruhrpolitik,* 103.

54. See ibid., 103–19.

55. Michaelis and Schraepler, eds., *Ursachen,* 5:57, 61–62.

56. Zimmermann, *Frankreichs Ruhrpolitik,* 104–7.

57. Friedrich Grimm, *Vom Ruhrkrieg zur Rheinlandräumung,* 31–42.

58. Ibid., 51–58.

59. Grimm, *Ruhrkrieg,* 105.

60. Harbeck, ed., *Kabinett Cuno*, 159.

61. Spethmann, *Ruhrbergbau*, 4:14.

62. Harbeck, ed., *Kabinett Cuno*, 183, 195–96.

63. Ibid., 309–12, 754.

64. Ibid., 210–11.

65. Ibid., 175, 190, 236–37, 285–86; Lothar Erdmann, *Die Gewerkschaften im Ruhrkampfe*, 140–41; Spethmann, *Ruhrbergbau*, 4:119.

66. Petras, *Hattinger Raum*, 68, 77–78.

67. Harbeck, ed., *Kabinett Cuno*, 188; Petras, *Hattinger Raum*, 152, 154.

68. Erdmann, *Gewerkschaften*, 109–18; Harbeck, ed., *Kabinett Cuno*, 185–86.

69. Harbeck, ed., *Kabinett Cuno*, 236–37; McDougall, *Rhineland Diplomacy*, 271.

70. Rupieper, "Politics and Economics," 220, 223–24.

71. Harbeck, ed., *Kabinett Cuno*, 452; Rupieper, "Politics and Economics," 221.

72. Harbeck, ed., *Kabinett Cuno*, 457–58.

73. Ibid., 320; Erdmann, *Gewerkschaften*, 141–42.

74. Harbeck, ed., *Kabinett Cuno*, 452–54, 457–58; Rupieper, "Politics and Economics," 221–25; McDougall, *Rhineland Diplomacy*, 271–72.

75. Grimm, *Ruhrkrieg*, 58–59; Spethmann, *Ruhrbergbau*, 4:117–22; Harbeck, ed., *Kabinett Cuno*, 217–18.

76. Spethmann, *Ruhrbergbau*, 4:122–31.

77. See reports by Hans Redlhammer of the Rhine-Ruhr Central in Harbeck, ed., *Kabinett Cuno*, 218.

78. Petras, *Hattinger Raum*, 76.

79. Spethmann, *Ruhrbergbau*, 3:124–25.

80. Petras, *Hattinger Raum*, 175; Grimm, *Ruhrkrieg*, 86–87.

81. Ibid., 88; Cornebise, "Aspects," 84–85.

82. Grimm, *Ruhrkrieg*, 88–89; *Zum Ruhreinbruch*, 23–25.

83. Spethmann, *Ruhrbergbau*, 3:124–25.

84. Michaelis and Schraepler, eds., *Ursachen*, 5:79.

85. Petras, *Hattinger Raum*, 175, 54–55.

86. Ibid., 149–51.

87. Spethmann, *Ruhrbergbau*, 3:110–11.

88. Petras, *Hattinger Raum*, 150–51.

89. Spethmann, *Ruhrbergbau*, 3:113–14.

90. Cornebise, "Aspects," 159; Petras, *Hattinger Raum*, 149–51.

91. Petras, *Hattinger Raum*, 95–98, 177.

92. Ibid., 97–98.

93. Ibid., 175–76.

94. Ibid., 36–39, 44–45.

95. Spethmann, *Ruhrbergbau*, 4:14; Harbeck, ed., *Kabinett Cuno*, 187.

96. Ibid., 212; Spethmann, *Ruhrbergbau*, 3:115.

97. Ibid., 117, 119; Spethmann, *Ruhrbergbau*, 3:116, 119–20; 4:14–15; Michaelis and Schraepler, eds., *Ursachen*, 5:64–65.

98. Spethmann, *Ruhrbergbau*, 4:15–18.

99. Ibid., 5–61.

100. Ibid., 26–27; Harbeck, ed., *Kabinett Cuno,* 303–4.

101. Spethmann, *Ruhrbergbau,* 4:125, 129–31.

102. Harbeck, ed., *Kabinett Cuno,* 484, 501–3; *Zum Ruhreinbruch,* 8.

103. Harbeck, ed., *Kabinett Cuno,* 501–2; Spethmann, *Ruhrbergbau,* 4:27–28, 59–61.

104. Ibid., 20–23.

105. Ibid., 24–26.

106. Spethmann, *Ruhrbergbau,* 3:141–43; 4:64, 67–71; *Zum Ruhreinbruch,* 8.

107. Harbeck, ed., *Kabinett Cuno,* 176.

108. Ibid., 192, 303.

109. Zimmermann, *Frankreichs Ruhrpolitik,* 104–6, 116.

110. Harbeck, ed., *Kabinett Cuno,* 303.

111. Ibid., 304–5; Michaelis and Schraepler, eds., *Ursachen,* 5:93–94.

112. *Zum Ruhreinbruch,* 47–48.

113. Zimmerman, *Frankreichs Ruhrpolitik,* 120.

114. Gante, *Dortmund,* 55–56; Petras, *Hattinger Raum,* 129–30.

115. Grimm, *Ruhrkrieg,* 60, 130–31; Petras, *Hattinger Raum,* 178–80.

116. Harbeck, ed., *Kabinett Cuno,* 467–68, 493, 516.

117. Ibid., 585–86.

118. Zimmerman, *Frankreichs Ruhrpolitik,* 120.

119. Gante, *Dortmund,* 78–79; Petras, *Hattinger Raum,* 46–51; Grimm, *Ruhrkrieg.*

120. Petras, *Hattinger Raum,* 58–62.

121. Harbeck, ed., *Kabinett Cuno,* 214, 219, 242.

122. Petras, *Hattinger Raum,* 64–67, 183–85; Grimm, *Ruhrkrieg,* 105–7.

123. Severing, *Lebensweg,* 1:380; Gante, *Dortmund,* 34–35.

124. *Zum Ruhreinbruch,* 9–22.

125. Ibid., 23–26.

126. Ibid., 26–27; Gante, *Dortmund,* 90–91.

127. E.g., *Zum Ruhreinbruch,* 28–47.

128. E. Poupard, *L'occupation de la Ruhr,* 175–77; Gante, *Dortmund,* 22, 42; Grimm, *Ruhrkrieg,* 75–76.

129. See German and French official accounts in Michaelis and Schraepler, eds., *Ursachen,* 5:95–100; Grimm, *Ruhrkrieg,* 113–18; Spethmann, *Ruhrbergbau,* 4:265–66.

130. Michaelis and Schraepler, eds., *Ursachen,* 132–33; Grimm, *Ruhrkrieg,* 118–23.

131. Zimmermann, *Frankreichs Ruhrpolitik,* 118–21.

132. Harbeck, ed., *Kabinett Cuno,* 241, 260–62; 270–71.

133. Ibid., 348–49, 376–77, 352–56, 415–18, 471, 493; see also 534–37, in which the feeling that "Berlin is defending the Rhineland to the last Rhinelander" is reported.

134. Ibid., 350, 352–56, 493.

135. Ibid., 427.

136. Grimm, *Ruhrkrieg,* 124–38.

137. Michaelis and Schraepler, eds., *Ursachen*, 5:48; Harbeck, ed., *Kabinett Cuno*, 194.

138. Severing, *Mein Lebensweg*, 1:383–84; Böhnke, *Die NSDAP*, 25, 32.

139. Ibid., 32.

140. Michaelis and Schraepler, eds., *Ursachen*, 5:81; Spethmann, *Ruhrbergbau*, 4:16–17.

141. Ibid., 24, 31–36; Böhnke, *NSDAP*, 32.

142. Grimm, *Ruhrkrieg*, 157–62, 168–70.

143. Cornebise, "Aspects," 71–72.

144. Harbeck, ed., *Kabinett Cuno*, 453.

145. Ibid., 303–4; Petras, *Hattinger Raum*, 187–88; Cornebise, "Aspects," 136.

146. Spethmann, *Ruhrbergbau*, 4:61.

147. Harbeck, ed., *Kabinett Cuno*, 304.

148. Michaelis and Schraepler, eds., *Ursachen*, 5:69, 91.

149. Böhnke, *NSDAP*, 54; Robert Waite, *Vanguard of Nazism*, 236–37; Severing, *Mein Lebensweg*, 1:404–5; Michaelis and Schraepler, eds., *Ursachen*, 5:137.

150. Harbeck, ed., *Kabinett Cuno*, 550–51, 568–69.

151. Ibid., 584–86.

152. Ibid., 593–95; see also 198–99, 596 for a letter from the Hesse president challenging Cuno to dissociate himself from "irresponsible elements."

153. Severing, *Mein Lebensweg*, 1:412; Cornebise, "Aspects," 149–50.

154. Ibid., 151; Harbeck, ed., *Kabinett Cuno*, 650–51.

155. Severing, *Mein Lebensweg*, 1:393; Petras, *Hattinger Raum*, 182–83; cf. the mine owners' accusations of collaboration reported above.

156. Cornebise, "Aspects," 152–53, 26.

157. Lademacher, "Nördlichen Rheinlande," 705; Waite, *Vanguard of Nazism*, 235; Petras, *Hattinger Raum*, 187.

158. Otto Pfleiderer, "Die Reichsbank," 172.

159. Lademacher, "Nördlichen Rheinlande," 706.

160. Reimer, *Rheinlandfrage*, 272–88.

161. Ibid., 306–23, 328–31, 345–56, 368–77.

162. Hermann Graml, *Europa*, 329–30.

163. Erdmann, *Gewerkschaften*, 68–83.

164. Rupieper, "Politics and Economics," 287–93.

165. Bergmann, *Reparations*, 191–93; Michaelis and Schraepler, eds., *Ursachen*, 5:121–32; Rupieper, "Politics and Economics," 293–96; McDougall, *Rhineland Diplomacy*, 273–74.

166. Michaelis and Schraepler, eds., *Ursachen*, 5:121–22.

167. Ibid., 126–29.

168. Rupieper, "Politics and Economics," 298–309.

169. Ibid., 309–10.

170. Ibid., 394–404; Harbeck, ed., *Kabinett Cuno*, 733–52; K. D. Erdmann and Martin Vogt, eds., *Das Kabinett Stresemann*, 1:xxi–xxxi; Gustav Stresemann, *Vermächtnis*, 1:87–89.

171. Erdmann and Vogt, eds., *Das Kabinett Stresemann,* 1:75–83, 132–34, 181–83.

172. Ibid., 1:59, 75–79, 83; Stresemann, *Vermächtnis,* 1:98–99.

173. Erdmann and Vogt, eds., *Das Kabinett Stresemann,* 1:7, 79–81, 134–35, 181–83, 193–96.

174. Ibid., 1:57–58, 189–90; see report, p. 134, showing that 54 trillion marks were authorized for Ruhr aid from 7–18 August and 180 trillion actually drawn.

175. Ibid., 163–65, 187, 189–91.

176. Ibid., 142–44, 153, 188–89, 195–96, 207–8; Spethmann, *Zum Ruhrbergbau,* 4:67–76; *Zum Ruhreinbruch,* 8, 48–49.

177. The number of expulsions reached 140,000–180,000; Erdmann and Vogt, eds., *Das Kabinett Stresemann,* 1:80, 134, 153, 183; *Zum Ruhreinbruch,* 47–48.

178. Erdmann and Vogt, eds., *Das Kabinett Stresemann,* 6–7, 79–80, 132, 142–44, 191, 198–200; Stresemann, *Vermächtnis,* 1:94–95.

179. Erdmann and Vogt, eds., *Das Kabinett Stresemann,* 1:150–55, 194–95, 265–66.

180. Ibid., 1:197.

181. Ibid., 1:204–5, 290–95, 312–13; Stresemann, *Vermächtnis,* 1:101–6, 121–23, 127–28.

182. Ibid., 108.

183. Erdmann and Vogt, eds., *Das Kabinett Stresemann,* 1:349.

184. Ibid., 204–7; McDougall, *Rhineland Diplomacy,* 291–92; Rupieper, "Politics and Economics," 454–56.

185. Erdmann and Vogt, eds., *Das Kabinett Stresemann,* 1:217–20, 222–23, 278–80.

186. Ibid., 1:44–45, 135–37, 214–17, 248–50, 284–85, 387–89, 393–96; see also General Seeckt's sketches for reordering government, 2:1203–10; Stresemann, *Vermächtnis,* 1:114.

187. Erdmann and Vogt, eds., *Das Kabinett Stresemann,* 1:299–302, 320–22, 334–45, 349–71.

188. Ibid., 374, 378–79; Michaelis and Schraepler, eds., *Ursachen,* 5:203–4.

189. Erdmann and Vogt, eds., *Das Kabinett Stresemann,* 1:271, 418.

Chapter 5

The Indian Independence Movement, 1930–1931

The movement to achieve an independent India spanned the years 1919 to 1947. One campaign in that protracted struggle, the 1930 to 1931 civil disobedience campaign, is of particular interest to those interested in strategic nonviolent conflict. It constituted a clear-cut sequence of strategic maneuvers in the service of clearly defined objectives on both sides. This was the first campaign in which immediate and unconditional independence for India emerged as the explicit objective, and it mobilized more Indians for direct action in the service of that objective than any other single campaign.

The Indian movement generally, and the 1930–1931 campaign specifically, contains some of the best-known yet least understood examples of the use of nonviolent sanctions in history. Popular fallacies abound concerning the nature and quality of Mohandas Karamchand Gandhi's leadership, the supposed predisposition of Indian culture to nonviolent action, the extent and effects of British repression, and the meaning of the term "success" in a struggle of this kind.[1]

Although Gandhi functioned as a charismatic leader for one side in this fight, he was still only one actor in a very complex situation. His undisputed position at the top of the leadership structure helped provide unity of command. But those who assert that "nonviolent action only works when you have a leader like Gandhi, with unquestioned moral authority" tend to overlook the disadvantages. Although at times a brilliant strategist, Gandhi was many other things as well. On occasion, his activities as a social philosopher and activist obscured his strategic vision and caused the national movement to lose direction and initiative. At other times, when Gandhi was empowered to negotiate on behalf of the whole movement, his personal limitations circumscribed the independence struggle itself. His leadership, in short, was a mixed blessing. It should not be the yardstick by which the ultimate potential of this form of struggle is measured.

The stereotype of the "mild Hindu" is persistent but utterly misleading. A common misperception is that "successful nonviolent action must be culturally specific, since only people with a predisposition to submissive behavior could face guns and abuse without retaliating, as the Indians did." The nonviolent movement in India was by no means exclusively Hindu. Those Muslims who participated most actively came from a tradition which glorified personal and collective violence. Whatever Indian submissiveness may have been observed by European commentators is far more likely to have arisen from prolonged conquest and colonization rather than from anything endemic in Hindu or any other Indian culture. The subsequent history of the Asian subcontinent has shown, if anything, a marked propensity for violent conflict. Most important, there is nothing submissive about militant nonviolent action when its intent and effect is to tear the political ground out from under an opponent's feet. Finally, similar behavior has been observed in many other cultural contexts, even if it has not been consciously labeled as nonviolent action. It is wrong to dismiss, as some do, the Indian case as being unique and therefore irrelevant in analysis that includes comparison with other cases.[2]

Another misconception stems from the notion that British restraint from violent repression was the key to Indian success. In contrast, Sharp writes:

> Admittedly, the British were not nearly so ruthless as Hitler or Stalin would have been, but they were far more brutal in repression than is today remembered. People not only suffered in foul prisons and prison camps, but literally had their skulls cracked in beatings with steel-shod bamboo rods *(lathis)* and were shot while demonstrating. . . . If the British exercised some restraint in dealing with the nonviolent rebellion, this may be related more to the peculiar problems posed by a nonviolent resistance movement and to the kinds of forces the nonviolent action set in motion, than to the opponent being "British." The same people showed little restraint in dealing with the Mau Mau in Kenya, or in the saturation bombing of German cities.[3]

Whatever degree of restraint was practiced by the British, it would not necessarily have improved the Indian strategic position. A liberal environment in which some constitutional constraints are operating is certainly more conducive to resistance, but it can also help the opponents retain legitimacy. It is possible that if the British had killed more rather than fewer Indians, they would have lost India sooner. In fact, it is precisely due to diplomatic skill and an aura of civility at the bargaining table, combined with carefully measured repression, that the Raj was able to continue for as long as it did.[4]

INDIAN REALITIES AND THE BRITISH RAJ

One hundred years passed between the final consolidation of British rule in India and the end of the First World War in 1918. Britain maintained her position throughout those hundred years by means of extremely skillful diplomacy, efficient administration, and the application of superior armed force when threatened. The Raj was among the most sophisticated and enlightened of the classical colonial regimes, but like all the others, it was bound to face a challenge in the new century.

British India watched while the imperial powers decimated themselves in World War I, while the last Russian dynasty finally bowed to revolution, and while the language of self-determination was bandied about in the vacuum created by the fall of the Hapsburg and Ottoman empires. Like many other colonies, British India nurtured expectations of change, feelings of self-respect, and a conscious desire for independence. Unlike many other colonies, India had a fairly well-institutionalized nationalist movement and a government that was, at least technically, committed to progressive political development.

Like tsarist Russia, India was enormous and diverse. It was comprised of 319 million people,[5] approximately 750,000 villages, dozens of semi-autonomous princely kingdoms, two dominant cultural groupings,[6] and a large handful of significant religious and ethnic minorities. India could never have been run by a foreign power incapable of motivating and using local talent. So, like the Muslim invaders two centuries before them, the British set about to construct an integrated regime, one which interfered as little as possible with local norms but which left themselves firmly in control.

As early as 1833 Queen Victoria had declared that there should be no racial bar to office in the governance of the colony,[7] but in practice few Indians got top civil service jobs. In 1885, though, Indian judges were formally pronounced to be the equals of their British counterparts, in the face of strong conservative resistance within Britain. In two Indian Councils Acts (1892, 1909), steps were taken to enlarge the provincial councils which governed purely local affairs and to provide for the election of additional Indians to those councils.

Indian nationalists were quick to point out that the councils controlled nothing important. Tax collection, economic policy, military and foreign affairs, and educational policy were all in the hands of the British crown and parliament, through the agency of the Viceroy for India and his executive council. Moreover, the doctrine of "trusteeship," which provided the rationale for the whole arrangement, was inherently offensive to the nationalists. It maintained that the colonized needed to be weaned gradually from their barbarous past and schooled in the ways of Western civilization by their tutors, the colonizers. Some features of India's barbarous past were still in evidence, to be sure,[8] but for the nationalists this was not the point.

Colonization had stifled India's economic, social, and intellectual development, they argued. If India was not ready for self-rule, whose fault was that, when Indians were denied avenues of responsible growth?[9] Britain might preach the values of democracy, hard work, science, and Christian morality. In practice, though, Britain established monopolies in key goods such as salt, cloth, and alcohol, and wrecked all local incentive. The British abetted superstition or sectarian strife when it suited their interests. They may have brought the blessings of technology, but always in a way that tightened their grip on political power. And Britain was not afraid to employ brutality to enforce its will, despite a veneer of civilization. Jawaharlal Nehru, who became a major nationalist leader while still a young man, reflected on the Raj in later life with bitter eloquence:

> I wondered how it was that British people who strain at a gnat in England could swallow a camel in India without turning a hair. Indeed I have always wondered at and admired the astonishing knack of the British people for making their moral standards correspond with their material interests and for seeing virtue in everything that advances their imperial designs. Mussolini and Hitler are condemned by them

in perfect good faith and with righteous indignation for their attacks on liberty and democracy; and, in equal good faith, similar attacks and deprivation of liberty in India seem to them as necessary, and the highest moral reasons are advanced to show that true disinterested behavior on their part demands them.[10]

Whether sincerely paternalistic or cynically exploitative, the very existence of the Raj was a standing insult to the sensitive, literate class of which young Nehru was a prime example. Educated at Harrow and Cambridge, only son in a family of Indian politicians, he could see no meaningful place for himself in his own country's affairs. Nehru became a great leader in part because he articulated the aspirations of a growing middle class whose members could see their future clearly circumscribed if the Raj did not change course.

How would change come, and at whose behest and convenience? At the height of the Great War, on 20 August 1917, the British government announced its commitment to a new bipartisan policy. Henceforth the goal of its Indian policy would be the gradual establishment of responsible self-governing institutions, to be run by and for Indians. Without being too specific, the government clearly intended to suggest evolution toward something like dominion status within the British Commonwealth, similar to the position then enjoyed by Australia, Canada, New Zealand, and South Africa. Could Britain be trusted to honor its own stated intentions, or was this a sop thrown out by a besieged nation in need of continued support from its dependencies?

This was the question facing the national movement at the end of the war. The Indian National Congress (INC), the principal organ of that movement, had been founded in 1885. By the turn of the century, clearly discernible moderate and radical trends within the party, led by Gopal Krishna Gokhale and Bal Gangadhar Tilak respectively, had emerged. The moderates naturally argued that Indians must prove themselves worthy of self-rule by responding energetically to each new constitutional reform as it came and using it to justify more progress. The radicals maintained that nothing short of complete independence would do. The tension between these two basic points of view continued throughout the campaign of 1930–1931 and greatly influenced the formulation of strategic objectives.

The two factions did stand together and fight during an earlier episode, which sheds some light on the more famous Independence Movement of the interwar period. Lord Curzon, who was Viceroy in 1905, launched an ill-conceived plan to partition Bengal, an enormous province of great religious diversity. Both Gokhale and Tilak threw their support into a campaign of defiance which included a boycott of British goods and public burnings of Lancashire cotton. Britain reversed the partition policy in 1911.

This brief flare-up of nationalist action shows that the methods of noncooperation were known and used in India before Gandhi, soon to be a disciple of Gokhale's, arrived on the scene. It also demonstrated that a clumsy British maneuver might potentially unite diverse groups of Indians at any time, and this unity would be the necessary ingredient in any serious challenge to the British. It is also clear that the potential for violence in Indian politics was not far below the surface. After 1905 there was a revival in Bengal of quasi-religious terrorist organizations. While they were marginal, their existence in future years provided the pretext for some very unpopular, and therefore catalytic, British measures.

It was in the later war years that Gandhi made his appearance as a political entity in India. The early part of his adult life had been spent in legal training in Britain and practicing law among the Indian community of South Africa. There he built a reputation as a tough and shrewd defender of Indian interests, by leading resistance activities against anti-Indian policies. His unique contribution was the concept or process of *satyagraha*, which translates roughly as "adherence to truth."[11] Satyagraha is both a form of principled nonviolence and a technique of political action. In Gandhi's formulation, its practitioners *(satyagrahis)* must combine *ahimsa* (noninjury to living beings) with an unconditional effort to seek the truth of a situation with and for their opponents. In the Indian context, this would mean struggling to show the British that colonialism brutalized all parties to it and that they would be better off without its burdens.

On Gokhale's advice, Gandhi kept quiet and studied the Indian scene for a year after his return from South Africa. Meanwhile, his little book *Hind Swaraj* (Home Self-Rule) helped to popularize his ideas. In 1917 he led India's first satyagraha campaign in Champaran, on behalf of exploited peasants. The first outing for the new weapon in India was a complete success, and Gandhi's stature rose. Until this point he was just another interesting nationalist voice. It was just in time for him and for India, because events were about to force the pace of change.

THE END OF TRUST: THE CRISIS OF 1919
AND AFTER

The new British policy announced in 1917 was described in the Montagu-Chelmsford Report, which might have been seen, in a better climate, as offering real progress toward "self-governing institutions." Its central feature was *dyarchy,* or the exercise of dual authority in the provinces by both government appointees and locally elected ministers. More authority would be allowed to devolve to the provinces under this arrangement, and the way was opened for Indians to serve at the ministerial level. Embodied in the 1919 Government of India Act, the report's recommendations would become law in March 1921. The debate over the merits of the proposal, however, was eclipsed by events.

In late 1918 the Rowlatt Bills were promulgated. Their intent was to control a few wartime manifestations of terrorism and to prevent their recurrence during the postwar period. The two bills were never invoked, but they were the political equivalent of the Stamp Act in American colonial history. They incensed Indians and provided a focal point for resistance.

The bills made trial without jury permissible for political offenses and extended to the provincial authorities the right to intern suspected terrorists without trial. On the day they were to become law, Gandhi, fresh from a victorious campaign in Champaran on behalf of sharecroppers' rights, proposed a nationwide *hartal.* (The hartal was a traditional Indian form of protest in which all normal activity ceased in response to some moral outrage.) Millions of Indians understood and honored the hartal, but not all saw it as part and parcel of satyagraha requiring nonviolent discipline. Riots followed the hartal in many cities, and set the stage for the infamous shooting at Amritsar.

There a General Reginald E. H. Dyer, ostensibly fearful of losing control of a tense situation, ordered his troops to fire without warning on an illegal but nonviolent meeting in an enclosed courtyard called Jallianwala Bagh. It was an especially cold-blooded act, taking

379 lives by official count and leaving over 1,200 wounded. As the facts trickled out, it became evident that Dyer had planned to shoot civilians as a lesson for all of India but had made no provisions whatever for medical care of the wounded. With its usual magnanimity the government investigated the shooting and censured Dyer, but his supporters in Britain raised a substantial retirement chest for him and treated him as a national hero. Most shocking for Indians, the House of Lords voted to support his action.

Gandhi found the House of Lords' action appalling. Along with some humiliating orders that had accompanied the establishment of martial law in Amritsar, he considered it a more treacherous act than the shooting itself. From then on he viewed the Raj as "satanic" and cooperation with it as "sinful."[12] Erstwhile reformists like Motilal Nehru, Jawaharlal's esteemed father, swung into the radical independence camp, never to go back. In short, India had experienced its "Bloody Sunday."

The following summer Gandhi persuaded the INC to inaugurate a campaign of political noncooperation, but despite the provocation of Amritsar, it fizzled out after a few years. To withdraw cooperation at the precise moment when the Montagu-Chelmsford proposals for self-governing institutions were to become law was too much to ask of many Indians. Opportunities for progress seemed great, and the tangible fruits of noncooperation were unclear. Nonetheless, Gandhi's personal prestige rose throughout this period. He was arrested and sentenced to six years' imprisonment (of which two were served) for sedition in 1922. When he emerged in 1924, Gokhale was dead and Gandhi was the undisputed leader of the INC. He began to develop its fighting potential for the next round.

PRELUDE TO THE 1930–1931 CAMPAIGN

The next opportunity came in November 1927 with the arrival in India of the Simon Commission.[13] The Government of India Act of 1919 had mandated a ten-year review to consider progress in implementing the reforms. The commission was appointed two years earlier than necessary by a Conservative government in London, probably to prevent its being convened and filled by the Labor Party, which might win the next general election and eventually did in May 1929. Some have suggested that the early appointment was a gesture of goodwill,[14] but that seems hardly credible, since its convener, Lord Birkenhead, had been the only lord to oppose the Montagu-Chelmsford Report when it first appeared.[15]

The Simon Commission did not include a single Indian representative. The vehicle for judging political progress in India and the political maturity of Indians was to be entirely British! The official rationale was that the commission needed to be made up of members of Parliament, and that while two Indians currently held seats in that body, they could hardly be chosen purely on account of their race.[16] Lord Irwin, as British Viceroy in India, was fully aware of the reaction it might provoke, but acquiesced in the makeup of the commission. He judged that the risk of an Indian boycott of commission hearings was outweighed by the risk that a "mixed" commission might concede too much to the nationalist point of view. He later acknowledged the seriousness of this error.[17]

The commission was a perfect foil for nonviolent action. Demonstrators appeared wherever hearings were held. Crowds waved black banners and shouted "Simon go back!" the only words some participants could speak in English.[18] Indians refused to testify before the commission. The Muslim League supported the boycott, in a rare gesture of unity with the INC. The league's founder and leader, Mohammed Ali Jinnah, announced that "Jallianwala Bagh [Amritsar] was physical butchery. The Simon Commission is the butchery of our souls."[19] Though it eventually produced a comprehensive and largely balanced report, the Simon Commission's work was overshadowed by the boycott and by the parallel work of Motilal Nehru.

Nehru managed to have an alternative report accepted, both by an All-parties Conference in the spring of 1928 and by the INC at its annual meeting in Calcutta in December. The "Nehru Report" found that full responsible self-government for India was the only legitimate basis for further constitutional discussions, and it proposed a draft dominion constitution as a basis for such discussions.[20] The language was intended to allow both dominion status and full independence as possibilities, and was thus much too conciliatory for Congress militants.[21] A portentous compromise was reached at Calcutta, and the Nehru Report became the INC's working position for one year. If its detailed proposals for dominion status within the Commonwealth were not executed within that year, by means of a government round table conference, open struggle for full independence would ensue. The younger Nehru accepted this arrangement only to avert an open split on the question, and because he felt certain the year would pass without change, leaving the Congress united for the inevitable struggle.[22] The end of December 1929 became the deadline for acceptable progress.

Violent acts by either side were few during the period of the Simon boycott, but two incidents took on great symbolic importance. The first was the death of Lala Lajpat Rai, a widely revered congressman from the Punjab, as the presumed result of a beating he sustained during an anti-Simon demonstration. Rai was struck down in a *lathi* charge, an operation in which police used steel-tipped clubs to strike demonstrators. The lathi charge would become the dominant, but not exclusive, form of repression during the 1930–1931 campaign.

The second incident was possibly a direct response to Rai's death, minimally evoking more sympathy because of it. This was the bombing of the Legislative Assembly of the central government by Bhagat Singh and Batukeshwera K. Dutt.[23] One person was injured. Sir John Simon himself witnessed the event, after having completed the thankless task of guiding the commission to its conclusion. The resulting trial became a political cause célèbre.

Both events reminded each side of the violence of which the other was capable. Singh and Dutt kept the specter of terrorism alive for the British. Rai's death assured Indians that resistance for them, nonviolent or otherwise, would entail some serious risks.

Since the riots at Amritsar, Gandhi had been acutely aware of the need for training and discipline for satyagraha. Violent provocations by police and soldiers were to be expected and were no excuse for violence and chaos among Indian resisters. Gandhi was empowered by the Congress to act as commander in chief for the coming struggle, and at the behest of the Congress Working Committee he conducted in 1928 what amounted to both a training exercise and a preliminary skirmish.

He commissioned Vallabhbhai Patel, the mayor of Ahmedabad and a Congress activist, to lead a local satyagraha movement in the district of Bardoli.[24] The farmers and peasants of Bardoli were being asked to pay a 22 percent land tax increase after a particularly bad agricultural year. Patel led them in withholding all taxes until the increase was rescinded. Solidarity was enforced in part through a social boycott of nonresisters. The movement lasted from 12 February until 6 August, and ended with the resisters paying the tax into a government escrow account, pending an investigation of the fairness of the tax. The investigation found that the tax was not justified, and it was withdrawn.[25]

The Bardoli experiment demonstrated the power of disciplined collective action. Nonpayment of taxes was an extremely aggressive act and subject to harsh penalties. When a whole population did it, however, the government was at a loss even to confiscate their goods and land and to sell them fast enough to stop the movement. The provincial Bombay government reacted slowly and apparently missed the wider implications of the exercise. Lord Irwin did not. The movement had paralyzed Bombay, and there was no good reason why the same technique, applied on a national scale, could not do the same to the whole imperial apparatus in India.

Biding his political time, Irwin waited until the Labor Party formed a government (with a minority in the House of Commons, however), and in the summer of 1929 he began to float the idea of holding a round table conference to discuss the constitutional makeup of India. Finding guarded approval for the idea within the new government, he announced on 31 October that dominion status was indeed to be the avowed goal and that a round table conference would be organized to discuss the "next step" toward achieving it.[26]

It was a bold initiative, and there is no reason to think that it was not sincerely meant. If only Irwin and Gandhi counted, they might have solved their countries' problems on that basis. Each leader, though, was responsible to a much broader constituency. Each had hardliners to placate and an unproven ability to get results. Only two months remained before the Congress' waiting period would expire and make direct action inevitable, and extreme pressures were brought to bear on both leaders.

On 2 November the Indian "Leaders' Manifesto" was issued. Drafted by a collection of leaders including but not limited to INC members, it asked for amnesty for all political prisoners, an explicitly dominant role for the INC at any round table meeting, and the drafting of a constitution at that meeting rather than a discussion of "next steps." British diehards, led by Winston Churchill, were furious about Irwin's overture and would not allow INC terms to be accepted.

A futile meeting between Irwin and the Indian leaders was held at Irwin's home on 23 December, in an atmosphere made tense by an attempt on Irwin's life that same morning. No understanding was reached concerning the mandate of the round table conference or the precise definition of "dominion status," a definition that would be evaded from this point onward. Congress went to its annual meeting, this time in Lahore, to declare that independence from Britain was to be the ultimate objective and to sanction a nationwide civil disobedience campaign toward that end. Congress members who served in the Legislative Assembly were advised to withdraw, and most did, signaling a new wave of political noncooperation. Jawaharlal Nehru, then forty years old, moved the independence resolution and assumed the presidency of the Congress on the eve of battle.

THE "FINAL STRUGGLE FOR FREEDOM": 1930–1931

Final Preparations

As a campaign, the 1930–1931 phase of India's independence movement is unique in several respects, although not in ways usually attributed to it.[27] First, unlike any other case examined in this work, it was inaugurated and directed by a preexisting above-ground organization, the INC. Other parties, such as the Muslim League or the semi-autonomous princes, and minority leaders of various communities, might make important contributions or cause serious difficulties depending on how they acted, but there was no doubt that the national leadership and initiative resided in the INC. The Congress functioned as if it were the alternative government for a free India, acting decisively and authoritatively during the early phases of the struggle.

The case is unusual in a second respect. The nonviolent protagonists announced at the start their intention to win. (Perhaps surprisingly, such an intention is not always explicit in nonviolent struggles.) "To win" could only mean the attainment of independence, or *swaraj*. The campaign was repeatedly described as the "final struggle for freedom."[28] Gandhi cautioned his closest followers that "not a single believer in nonviolence . . . should find himself free or alive at the end of the effort to submit any longer [*sic*] to the existing slavery."[29]

The strategic objective could not have been clearer after this point. If Gandhi or other top leaders had in mind an objective short of independence which, if achieved, would end the struggle, they did not make it public at the outset. The time for dominion status as an acceptable solution had passed. Only later did Gandhi equivocate on the exact meaning of independence. To the annoyance of his younger and more militant followers, he would occasionally imply that it was not independence that mattered, but making the Indian people worthy and powerful enough to attain it.[30]

A third striking feature of the campaign was the degree to which the mechanisms for strategic decision making were thought out in advance. Since Congress was directing the campaign, the Congress Working Committee was appointed as the official strategy-making body, and Gandhi was its general. In the event that the entire Working Committee, Gandhi, and all of the leading Congress activists were arrested or killed, the local Congress organizations throughout India would assume authority to direct the struggle.

As a final galvanizing exercise, 26 January was declared to be *Purna Swaraj* (Complete Independence) Day, and nationwide celebrations were planned at which community after community pledged itself to support the independence declaration. The day was seen explicitly as a means of self-purification and dedication rather than as the opening "shot" in the struggle. Scores of thousands recited at public gatherings:

> We believe that it is the inalienable right of the Indian people, as of any other people, to have freedom and to enjoy the fruits of their toil and have the necessities of life so that they may have full opportunities of growth. We believe also that if any government deprives a people of these rights and oppresses them, the people have a further right to alter or abolish it. The British government in India has not only deprived the Indian people of their freedom but has based itself on the exploitation of the masses, and has ruined India economically, politically, culturally and spiritually. We believe, therefore, that India must sever the British connection and attain Purna Swaraj, or complete independence.[31]

On 15 February Gandhi was authorized by the Working Committee to begin conducting civil disobedience at his own discretion and with followers of his own choosing.

It must be said that while nonviolent direct action (including civil disobedience, political and economic noncooperation, and nonviolent intervention) was the chosen technique of struggle, it did not follow that all agreed with Gandhi on his concept of satyagraha, the necessity to eschew violence, or his broader social philosophy. His critics within the Congress, however, recognized the expediency of his methods in confonting the British Raj and were willing to reap the benefits of Gandhi's popularity. Practical benefits derived from a clear chain of command.

The militants were also mollified by Gandhi's assertion that the campaign would not be called off this time in the event that outbursts of violence occurred. He had learned bitter lessons from such outbursts in 1919 and 1922. If absolute nonviolent discipline by all Indians were the condition for carrying on the fight, opponents would be able to derail the struggle by provoking violent incidents. But Gandhi did intend to complement the efforts of the committed satyagrahis with disciplined mass noncooperation by the whole society. He wanted the Indian people to follow the strictures of satyagraha; but he finally conceded that those people would serve the movement too who saw their civil resistance as the most expedient path to independence.

The risk that some violent action might occur could not be avoided when the alternative was not to lead a struggle at all, and thus to leave the field open to the avowedly violent nationalists or to the perpetuation of a violent status quo. Steps were taken to keep the movement under control. Two articles by Gandhi appeared in the 27 February issue of *Young India*, the principle organizing tool of the movement. One article spelled out the "rules of conduct" for satyagrahis. It was later simplified by the Working Committee into a five-point pledge to be taken by all civil resisters. It went:

> 1. I desire to join the civil resistance campaign for the independence of India undertaken by the National Congress.
>
> 2. I accept the creed of the National Congress, that is, "The attainment of *Purna Swaraj* (complete independence) by the people of India by all peaceful and legitimate means."
>
> 3. I am ready and willing to go to jail and undergo all other sufferings and penalties that may be inflicted on me in this campaign.
>
> 4. In case I am sent to jail I shall not seek any monetary help for my family from Congress funds.
>
> 5. I shall implicitly obey the orders of those who are in charge of the campaign.[32]

The second article, "When I Am Arrested," explained for the masses (and, for that matter, to the government) how the fight was to be conducted, in the broadest terms, after Gandhi's inevitable arrest. It would be "the duty of everyone to take up such civil disobedience or civil resistance as may be advised and conducted by my successor, or as might be taken up by Congress . . . civil disobedience, once begun this time, cannot be stopped and must not be stopped as long as there is a single civil resister left free or alive."[33] Still, if they wanted to help the cause, patriotic Indians were admonished to obey the next echelon of leaders, to refrain from violence, and to bear hardship cheerfully.

So the objective, the leadership structure, and the weapons were selected consciously in advance. As in war, such strategic decisions as to timing, fronts on which to fight, and choice of troops were left to the commander-in-chief and his staff. It took Gandhi until March to announce a course of action, but when it came it was brilliantly conceived and worth the wait.

The Action Begins

The opening gambit of the conflict is usually identified as Gandhi's 241-mile march to the sea, where he would proceed to collect salt illegally on the beach at Dandi and invite others to do the same. The fight was really begun, however, with his letter to Lord Irwin of 2 March 1930, which began "Dear Friend." In addition to announcing how and when he intended to break the salt laws, signaling the beginning of widespread civil disobedience, Gandhi's most famous missive to Irwin accomplished several other things. It reviewed the grievances that were the basis of the Indian claim to independence and itemized specific areas of oppression where direct resistance could be the only remedy (land revenue, the salt tax, cloth and liquor monopolies). It also justified direct action by arguing that reasonable discussion had broken down from the British side, and it explained for Irwin's benefit exactly how nonviolent resistance and civil disobedience were supposed to work. It pleaded with the viceroy to help find a way out of the impasse through negotiation.[34]

Gandhi did have a preference for conciliation and compromise when either was possible, and his appeal to Irwin to find a positive way out of open struggle was no doubt genuine. As a satyagrahi, indeed, Gandhi held himself obligated to make such a late appeal before taking action. Beyond that, however, the letter had other purposes to serve. When Irwin's secretary replied merely with a terse acknowledgment of receipt and a statement of regret at the course of action contemplated, Gandhi made both his letter and the reply public. That put the ball squarely in Irwin's court. Wasn't he the one turning matters into a contest of strength by his apparent rigidity? Moreover, he was faced (and everyone knew it) with a choice. Either he could have Gandhi arrested immediately for sedition or he could let Gandhi openly and willfully break the law. Neither choice was palatable. Finally, all of the instructional material in Gandhi's letter, which explained in an unassuming tone how defeat would come to the British, was there as much for the Indian public's benefit as it was for Irwin's. The grand strategy was now an open book. Anyone could read about it in the pages of *Young India* and follow it, even if all the leaders died or went to prison.

When the march to the sea itself began, all eyes were focused on Gandhi. The action has been described often, and provides one of the most enduring images of the man and the movement he led. Press dispatches from the scene, and (much later) Richard Attenborough's film *Gandhi,* portray the affair in sumptuous, spine-tingling detail. Subhas Chandra Bose, an advocate of revolutionary violence and no supporter of Gandhi's, found himself comparing the march to Napoleon's triumphant return to Paris. Another observer compared it to the exodus of the Israelites under Moses.[35] Virtually anyone lucky enough to be present for any part of the event, and to have subsequently written about it, acknowledges it as a formative personal experience.

The Salt March opened up new tactical possibilities for the movement and imposed yet another set of difficult choices on the opponents. The dietary need for salt was a daily fact of life for every person and animal in India. The substance itself was everywhere but could not be processed into usable form by unauthorized persons. The existence of a government monopoly on salt, resulting from the 1836 Salt Act, perfectly exemplified the perceived evils of colonial rule. Paying the tax on salt (and thereby providing much of the revenue to run the colonial regime) was more a mild irritant than a desperate hardship for most.[36] But why pay the bill for their own subjugation? Why should one of their own natural resources be turned into a weapon against them?

The current prime minister of Great Britain, Ramsay MacDonald, had opposed the Salt Act publicly before taking office. He was now in the unfortunate position of having to enforce a law that he himself had denounced.

The decision whether to arrest Gandhi would eventually apply to every Indian who followed him as well. In his letter to Irwin, Gandhi also spoke to every Indian. We are men and women, he was saying. We are courageous, smart, and deadly serious. If you arrest us, more will follow until you can't arrest us all. If you fail to arrest us, then you will be forced to stand by helplessly while we kick out one of the main supports of your regime. Either way, we do not fear you.

Irwin chose to let the action go ahead rather than to make Gandhi into a martyr at this juncture. It is hard to say whether it was the better choice. There was some chance that the public imagination would not be captured, that Gandhi would look silly rather than heroic, and that the movement would simply peter out. As it happened, the response was worse than Irwin feared and better than Gandhi hoped for. The Salt March ended with a dramatic scene at Dandi with some four thousand spectators and participants. A few days later "permission was given to all Congress organizations to do likewise and begin civil disobedience in their own areas."[37] Jawaharlal Nehru describes the popular reaction:

> It seemed as though a spring had been suddenly released; all over the country, in town and village, salt manufacture was the topic of the day, and many curious expedients were adopted to produce salt. We knew precious little about it, and so we read it up where we could and issued leaflets giving directions; we collected pots and pans and ultimately succeeded in producing some unwholesome stuff, which we waved about in triumph and often auctioned for fancy prices. It was really immaterial whether the stuff was good or bad; the main thing was to commit a breach of the obnoxious salt law, and we were successful in that, even though the quality of our salt was poor. As we saw the abounding enthusiasm of the people and the way salt-making was spreading like prairie fire, we felt a little abashed and ashamed for having questioned the efficacy of this method when it was first proposed by Gandhiji. And we marveled at the amazing knack of the man to impress the multitude and make it act in an organized way.[38]

Gopal estimates that at least five million Indians broke the Salt Act in some five thousand different locations during the year that followed.[39] At first the government instructed provincial authorities to confiscate contraband salt and to avoid mass arrests. The action was too widely dispersed to repress in a consistent, even-handed manner, and Irwin was still cultivating his image as a restrained, responsible leader.

In addition to providing drama and helping the Congress to seize the initiative, salt law violation was an easily repeatable action. It could be performed with comparatively little risk. And it set the pattern for the rest of the campaign. Whenever a new method of resistance was developed, it could be duplicated ad infinitum by the local Congress branches. Later, when the government began to enact special ordinances to curtail such activities, the ordinances themselves would become the targets. For example, when the young Nehru was arrested later in the month under a new ordinance for a seditious speech, public readings of the offending speech were held throughout the country on the prisoner's birthday!

The Cloth and Liquor Fronts

Gandhi was spoiled for opportunities after Irwin's failure to have him arrested. Arrest would come sooner or later, but what to do in the meantime? On 13 April (still in Dandi) he addressed a large meeting of women. They could do their part, he told them, by spearheading campaigns against the textile and liquor monopolies. These would be tougher fronts to work on than the Salt Act. To be effective, many more people would have to be persuaded to boycott textiles and liquor and picket lines would have to be organized and sustained.

Theoretically, a boycott of foreign cloth had been in effect since February 1929, and indigenous production of homespun cloth had been part of the Gandhi/Congress constructive program for some time. Their view was that by legislating a comparative advantage for cloth manufactured in Britain, the government, over a long period of time, had virtually destroyed a local cottage industry while cornering for themselves yet another market. The situation could not be reversed until there was an alternative source of supply.

The spinning and weaving of Indian cotton became a patriotic activity of which everyone was capable, with a little effort. The spinning wheel took a proud place as the symbol of independence on the Indian flag. Like the illegal manufacture of salt, the making and wearing of *kahdi,* as it was called, had several tactical advantages. It resurrected an indigenous craft and it made an effective boycott thinkable. It also provided a symbol through which its wearers could publicly proclaim their allegiance, and it generated feelings of self-sufficiency. For many people, it was a first point of contact with the nationalist cause.

Although men and women alike were expected to spin or weave, Indian women in particular took up the challenge. All over India, they denied the government still more revenue by picketing liquor stores and drug dens, enforcing a kind of patriotic prohibition. The energy and tenacity of women in the textile and liquor boycotts surprised many observers and has undoubtedly had a long-term effect on the role of women in Indian politics.

All of the components of mass civil disobedience and noncooperation were now in place and could be carried on regardless of what might happen to the leaders. Gandhi announced that "now is the time for everyone to be both chief and follower."[40] The trained satyagrahis were now free to escalate the conflict through direct interventionist tactics and test the government's restraint.

Resistance Leads to Repression

There was one area of the country where Congress' organizations had a particularly strong hold, where preparations for concerted civil resistance were under way, and where the requirements of satyagraha were well understood, at least by those about to put it to the test. That was the North West Frontier province, populated primarily by Muslim Pathans. The Pathans lived in a bleak environment that tested survival regularly. They were renowned for physical bravery and for being adept in the ways of violence, both in their private and public lives. The Raj had always imposed more severe restrictions on the frontier than elsewhere, in anticipation of the fiercest resistance from its inhabitants. It is remarkable, but not inexplicable, that the Gandhian technique of conflict should have taken root in such a culture.

Several Muslim Congress activists, but most notably Khan Abdul Ghaffer Khan, had instilled the new ideas in a group of followers known as the Khudai Khidmatgar, or Servants of God. (They were called "red shirts" by the British because of their chosen mode of dress.) By blending the notion of absolute nonviolent discipline with the traditional value of personal courage, the Pathans laid the groundwork for some of the most profound confrontations of the independence campaign. The most famous occurred on 23 April, just seventeen days after the inaugural action at Dandi.

On that day, local Congress leaders planned to begin picketing five liquor stores in the town of Peshawar. As a preventive measure, the government had several key leaders arrested. (Ghaffer Khan himself was arrested on the twenty-fourth.) It also barred the arrival of an All-India Congress Committee delegation that had planned to arrive on the twenty-second to investigate conditions in the province, which were known to be more repressive than elsewhere. The large crowd that would have welcomed the delegation marched in a spontaneous procession and held a mass meeting in support of the arrested leaders. By all reports these events were entirely peaceful. Two leaders who had not been rounded up were escorted, during the procession, to the police station, where they voluntarily offered themselves for arrest.

The rather benign scene turned grim when troops were called into Peshawar to quell the unrest. A confusing series of events followed. Accounts differ widely, but the most widely believed sequence of events is as follows. As the crowd was returning from the police station, two armored cars carrying soldiers careened without warning into pedestrians lining a narrow street. Three people were killed immediately and several more were injured. As the casualties were being seen to, an English officer on a motorcycle appeared and was killed in an altercation that began either with him firing at the crowd or when his vehicle collided with one of the armored cars. In any case, the armored car caught fire. Next, another body of English soldiers arrived and began to fire without warning into the crowd. Eyewitness accounts say that some people, including women and children, deliberately exposed themselves to the fire, died, and were pulled away and replaced by others. There were sixty-five known dead, but the total was widely believed to be much higher, as the troops took a number of bodies away and burned them.[41]

Remarkably, orderly picketing went on at the five chosen locations throughout the twenty-third, despite the day's chaos and carnage. During the night the provincial government produced an ordinance forbidding groups larger than five to meet in public, but this was universally defied despite the danger of violent repression. When peaceful picketing continued on the twenty-fourth, the government ordered the liquor stores of Peshawar closed for two months.

Profoundly disturbing to the government must have been the action taken by two platoons of the Royal Garhwal Rifles who were ordered to reinforce Peshawar. They refused to go on the grounds that their role was to defend India from attack, not to shoot their countrymen.[42] The mutineers each received long sentences of hard labor.

The North West Frontier province had troubles other than those directly inspired by the independence movement. Incursions by border tribes to the north threatened to wrest away control of the province. Martial law was declared, and for most of the rest of the campaign, the province was isolated and travel to it was severely restricted.

Activity was beginning to heat up in other parts of India as well. Sporadic violence against picketers and demonstrators occurred in many places, and the authorities conducted mass arrests of persons making illicit salt. Special ordinances were used widely in the attempt to halt specific activities. The Press Ordinance, for example, required newspapers and journals to place a security deposit with the government. They would forfeit their money and be closed down if found printing anything the government deemed subversive.[43] The ordinance was highly effective in curbing the major mainstream papers. *Young India*, and the Navajivan Press which produced it, were simply forced underground, and *Young India* began to appear in mimeographed form. A new form of sabotage emerged in late April. Palm trees, from which alcohol was extracted for toddy, were surreptitiously cut down. Over eleven thousand trees were destroyed by 1 May, and the Congress endorsed such breaches of the "forest laws" after the fact in a Working Committee resolution.[44] The government's hope that civil disobedience might run out of steam faded, and new consideration was given to the possible arrest of Gandhi.

The Arrest and Its Effects

The British authorities knew at an early stage that they faced a dilemma where Gandhi was concerned. On 7 April, the day after the Salt March, Irwin wrote to his direct superior, Wedgewood Benn, secretary of state for India. He noted the religious aura that was beginning to surround the leader and cautioned that "while . . . we must be careful to avoid the foundation of a 'Gandhi legend', we should also be clumsy-footed if we thought that the law could successfully treat him as it treats any other mundane and immoral law-breaker."[45] The dilemma had paralyzed Irwin for nearly a month. It now appeared that Irwin's delay in arresting Gandhi would accomplish both of the things he had sought to avoid.

After consultation with the heads of all the provincial governments, Irwin decided on 29 April to make the arrest. The timing was carefully thought out. It needed to be after May Day but before 10 May, the date of the Moslem *Id* festival and the anniversary of the Mutiny of 1857.[46] The fourth of May was fixed as the arrest date, and the decision was justified in this way to Benn:

> Our conclusion is based on the following grounds and has been reached only after most anxious consideration of the various factors for and against. We are convinced, so far as the general political situation is concerned that we must arrest him sooner or later and any further delay is likely to damage the prestige of Government which has already suffered through the Chittagong incident and events at Peshawar. We believe that delay is likely to increase rather than reduce the risks of disorder in various towns following on his arrest.[47]

The next day Ramsay MacDonald announced his unconditional support for any "decisive action he [Lord Irwin] might consider necessary to take against Gandhi and the civil disobedience campaigners,"[48] indicating that a broad consensus on this point had, at last, been reached.

The evening of 4 May found Gandhi busy at work on a second letter to his "Dear Friend," outlining for Irwin's benefit the next maneuver of the campaign. It was to be a nonviolent assault on a government sanctioned salt works at Dharasana. Irwin was already aware of the intended action in broad outline. Gandhi's draft letter elaborated:

> God willing, it is my intention on . . . to set out for Dharasana and reach there with my companions on . . . and demand possession of the salt works. The public have been told that Dharasana is private property. This is mere camouflage. It is as effectively under Government control as the Viceroy's House. . . . But I would fain avoid the further step. I would, therefore, ask you to remove the tax which many of your illustrious countrymen have condemned in unmeasured terms and which, as you could not have failed to observe, has evoked universal protest and resentment expressed in civil disobedience.[49]

Most of the balance of the letter was devoted to two themes: the unnecessary violence Gandhi saw the government using, particularly the shootings, and the necessity for satyagrahis to court suffering, if all this were to be changed. Gandhi expressed dismay at being left alone while his countrymen suffered, showing that he intended to push until the government reacted to him in one way or another.

The arresting officers treated Gandhi with respect when they arrived on the night of 4–5 April, allowing him time to wash, pack his things, and pray with his followers who were present. Biographer Louis Fischer notes that "there was no trial, no sentence, and no fixed term of imprisonment. The arrest took place under an ordinance, passed before a British Government existed in India, which regulates relations between the East India Company and the Indian potentates."[50]

Irwin's hopes of minimal reaction to the arrest were ill-founded. Spontaneous mass demonstrations and hartals occurred throughout the country. About half of the country's textile mills shut down in protest. In at least two locations, crowds were dispersed with gunfire. In Solapur twenty-five were killed and around a hundred persons were wounded. Messages of support for Gandhi began arriving from around the world, and in several countries Indian communities staged sympathy strikes and demonstrations.[51]

The Congress Working Committee used the occasion of Gandhi's arrest to issue fifteen resolutions, some intended to bolster existing measures of resistance, others outlining escalatory new steps. One resolution called on students and professionals to come forth and "make all sacrifices they are capable of" in the hour of crisis. Provincial Congress Committees were instructed to begin no-tax campaigns in selected provinces. The Congress requested a complete boycott of any publication that was in compliance with the Press Ordinance (i.e., anything still legally in print) and ex post facto endorsed deliberate Forest Law violation.[52]

In a conference held on 10 May, 128 villages in the Bardoli district declared that they would pay no land taxes until ordered to by either Gandhi or S. V. Patel. Dozens of other villages around Jambusar and Borsad also began no-tax campaigns, and in Borsad *taluka* fifty village headmen resigned their posts in noncooperation with the government.[53]

To describe all the actions that were initiated or renewed as a direct result of Gandhi's arrest would be impossible. Suffice it to say that though Gandhi was in fact treated well as a political prisoner, the movement now had a "martyr." Congress retained the initiative, and continued to make the most of its opportunities. In addition to all this, if Lord Irwin had thought to avoid a spectacular and aggressive action at Dharasana, he was about to be disappointed on that count as well.

Escalation at Dharasana

> They are deliberately attempting to present us with the alternative of using what they will represent to be unjustifiable and tyrannical repression or conceding their demands. If that is what they are aiming at, the real defeat for them is to prevent them creating such a state of feeling. Unfortunately it is impossible to achieve this merely by leaving them alone. They won't let us leave them alone. On the other hand, if we treat it as a war, then, whatever the immediate material gain in high spirits for our supporters and so on may be, the Congress has really won because a war spirit on our side means a war spirit on theirs. It is to avoid this dilemma that we should chiefly endeavour.[54]

This communication from Benn to Irwin on 28 April reveals an exact appreciation of the strategic situation. Irwin now had to make another unpalatable choice. He literally could not leave the Congress activists alone. He was being drawn consciously, but against his will, into a posture of open warfare with them.

Irwin's opposing general would now be Abbas Tyabji, seventy-six years old and a retired High Court judge of the Princely State of Baroda. He was next after Gandhi to lead the Dharasana salt action, which now took on the character of a national focal point and test of resolve. On 10 May Tyabji announced that he and three hundred volunteers would March to the salt depot on 12 May and attempt to take it over. An Indian district magistrate warned him that the proposed action would be met with force, and begged him to reconsider. Tyabji responded by attempting to convert to the nationalist cause the policeman carrying the magistrate's message.[55]

Beginning on the twelfth, a national melodrama lasting twenty-six days unfolded in three distinct phases. First, Tyabji led a solemn procession of satyagrahis toward Dharasana. He insisted on making the journey on foot, despite his age, with Gandhi's wife Kasturbai at his side, "like the incarnation of Mother India."[56] Tyabji and fifty-nine volunteers were arrested without violence en route. Those who were not minors were sentenced to three months imprisonment. The leader's message to the country upon entering prison stated that "there can now be no peace in India till freedom is won."[57]

Next, Sarojini Naidu, a revered poetess and prominent Working Committee member, rushed to the scene from Allahabad to assume the leadership, saying "I go to victory or death."[58]

> We ask no quarter, [Mrs. Naidu said] and we shall give none. I shall march ahead of the Satyagrahis . . . when they endeavour to break through the military guards at the salt depot. I shall cut the barbed wire with pliers and seize the salt with my own hands. I am a woman but I shall actively participate in this campaign for liberty as though I were a man. I realize the tremendous responsibility entrusted to me by the Mahatma and the nation, but in making the most of this heaven-sent opportunity neither jail nor death shall hold any terrors for me.[59]

For several days Mrs. Naidu led the volunteers in tactical skirmishing with the guards. They tried approaching the facility, and when blocked, sitting down. One sit-down lasted twenty-eight hours. They tried dashing toward the barbed-wire enclosed salt pans, reaching through and grabbing the salt earth before being beaten back. Around four hundred volunteers were arrested without violence during this phase. Some were released and rejoined the action.

The third phase of the action began on 21 May when the more intense confrontation anticipated in Naidu's rhetoric began. She exhorted twenty-five hundred demonstrators, who were about to approach the salt works in columns carrying ropes and wire cutters: "You must not use any violence under any circumstances. You will be beaten but you must not resist: you must not even raise a hand to ward off blows."[60] One eyewitness, a foreign journalist, reported what happened when the columns advanced and attempted to use their ropes to pull down the barbed wire supports, ignoring police orders to disperse:

> Suddenly, at a word of command, scores of native police rushed upon the advancing marchers and rained blows on their heads with their steel-shod lathis. Not one of the marchers even raised an arm to fend off the blows. They went down like ten-pins. From where I stood I heard the sickening whacks of the clubs on unprotected skulls. The

waiting crowd of watchers groaned and sucked in their breaths in sympathetic pain at every blow. Those struck down fell sprawling, unconscious or writhing with pain with fractured skulls or broken shoulders. In two or three minutes the ground was quilted with bodies. Great patches of blood widened on their white clothes. The survivors without breaking ranks silently and doggedly marched on until struck down. When every one of the first column had been knocked down, stretcher-bearers rushed up unmolested by the police and carried off the injured to a thatched hut which had been arranged as a temporary hospital.[61]

While the demonstrators themselves posed no threat of violence to anyone, the distraught spectators had to be held in check by the leaders, who undoubtedly prevented a great disaster. Twenty-five police riflemen were deployed on a hill near the crowd, and the foreign journalist was asked to move out of the line of fire. The demonstrators then altered their approach, advancing in groups of twenty-five at a time and sitting down calmly until they were beaten and removed. The eyewitness continues:

> Finally the police became enraged by the non-resistance, sharing, I suppose, the helpless rage I had already felt at the demonstrators for not fighting back. They commenced savagely kicking the seated men in the abdomen and testicles. The injured men writhed and squealed in agony, which seemed to inflame the fury of the police, and the crowd again almost broke away from its leaders. The police then began dragging the sitting men by their arms or feet, sometimes for a hundred yards, and then throwing them into ditches. One was dragged into the ditch where I stood: the splash of his body doused me with muddy water. Another policeman dragged a Gandhi man to the ditch, threw him in, then belaboured him over the head with his lathi. Hour after hour stretcher bearers carried back a stream of inert, bleeding bodies.[62]

Naidu was arrested, though not beaten, and V. J. Patel took over the command later in the morning. The harrowing scene continued throughout most of the day and evening, with approximately seven hundred individuals hurt. There were reports that some policemen seemed reluctant to be brutal unless their officers were nearby. During the following days there were reports of Sikh policemen weeping as they struck the satyagrahis to the ground.[63]

The scenario was to be repeated six or seven times while the resistance forces camped around the Dharasana salt works. On 6 June they finally withdrew. Hundreds had been bloodied in the nationalist cause. And petty, harassing violence had been heaped on the encampment throughout the twenty-six days.

No salt was ever confiscated nor was the Dharasana facility appropriated by the resisters. There were other raids on other salt works which did, in fact, end with the taking of illicit salt, but the image of scores of satyagrahis falling "like ten-pins" at Dharasana captured the attention of millions of people in India and throughout the world.

A Congress spokesman at the time stated that "our primary object was to show the world at large the fangs and claws of the Government in all its ugliness and ferocity. In this we have succeeded beyond measure."[64] They also succeeded in creating a lasting source of national pride and a tangible feeling of moral superiority over the opponents. Just how important these factors were throughout the remainder of the struggle is hard to determine.

It can be determined, however, that the Dharasana affair was infused with, and largely motivated by, a keenly religious sense of personal sacrifice that for a time seemed an end in itself. This may have sent the wrong signal to many Indians who were not prepared to have their skulls cracked open. In the long run, winning the objective of complete independence would not depend on whether a few thousand individuals bravely withstood intense suffering, but on whether the overwhelming majority of Indians, millions of them, could see the necessity to tolerate major inconveniences and perhaps moderate suffering. Could they be motivated, for example, to sustain the various campaigns which strained the government's sources of revenue?

Lord Irwin met the escalation at Dharasana by supporting the local authorities in their enforcement of the letter of the law. Private property was not compromised, and the bad public image was simply taken on the chin.

Steady Pressure

The rest of India was not quiescent while the Dharasana episode was unfolding. From diverse provinces reports came in to the Working Committee of the following: large demonstrations, and occasion-

ally random gunfire to disperse them; the destruction of palm trees
(2,500 in Surat, 10,000 in Karnatak); wholesale beatings of men,
women, and children engaged in salt manufacture or the destruction
of foreign cloth; continued repressive violence in Peshawar; the establishment of civil disobedience encampments and harassment of
same by police; a student strike in Gujarat College, Ahmedabad;
scores of additional villages joining the no-tax effort; and continued
resignations from local government and civil service posts.[65]

On the whole, local authorities (if they were not part of the general
rebellion) were left to deal with protest activities on their own. Lord
Irwin confined himself in late May and early June to the promulga-
tion and extension of ordinances designed to suppress sedition anywhere in the country. Ordinances called for the arrest of those advocating nonpayment of taxes, the picketing of shops, and social
boycotts of public officials. They went into effect throughout the
country, "regardless whether the laws [prohibiting them] applied in
both of the respective provinces or not."[66] The infamous Press Ordinance was extended by government interpretation to apply to mimeographed communications, since these had begun to appear with
greater frequency. The ordinance was then selectively applied
against pro-Congress literature.

Irwin seemed to be following the advice he had received from one
of his provincial governors in early May, "to avoid the use of any
method, or the occurrence of any such incident, as may prevent
emotion becoming subject to that normal decline which always follows when it has once reached its peak."[67] In other words, he was
seeking to keep the appearance of being in control without giving
cause for still greater animosity from the Indian masses. If he could
keep the lid on, the cauldron might return to a simmer.

It was a difficult balancing act. Irwin admitted to Benn on 2 June:
"All thinking Indians passionately want substantial advance which
will give them power to manage their own affairs. However much
they may deplore the civil disobedience movement, they feel at heart
that it is likely to make British opinion more elastic by exposing the
various disadvantages of a system which does not carry consent."[68]

The next concentrated wave of action came in Gandhi's home
province of Bombay. It began with a mile-long night procession
made up entirely of Muslims. At the end of the procession, the participants adopted a popular resolution that the Muslim community of
Bombay should wholeheartedly support the civil disobedience move-

ment, and that Muslims should honor the boycott of the proposed Round Table Conference. The gesture was of great significance. It demonstrated that Muslim sentiment beyond the North West Frontier province did not necessarily follow the lead of Jinnah and other national leaders, who had shunned the nonviolent movement as Hindu-dominated.

A week later the Simon Commission Report was finally issued in London. Gopal writes, "never did so massive a document cause so slight a ripple."[69] Its chief effect was to convince many Indians of the government's bad intentions. The document never mentioned the phrase dominion status, even in summarizing Indian feelings on the issue. The report was completely overshadowed, in any case, by the active struggle and the possibility of a round table conference.

On 19 June, Motilal Nehru, now acting president of the Congress, addressed a demonstration of 150,000 in Bombay. The demonstration had been going on for four days, despite police efforts to disperse it with force. Between the twentieth and twenty-fourth, a critical exchange of views occurred between Lord Irwin and the governor of Bombay, Sir Frederick Sykes.

Sykes took a position reminiscent of Sergei Witte's in October 1905. He argued that Irwin's policy of minimal force to control the movement, combined with advancing the round table process, was short-sighted. The movement was growing, and either real concessions on the constitutional issue would have to be made or repression would have to be thorough and massive enough to crush the movement, regardless of the political consequences. The course of repression, which he favored, would set back the cause of gradual political reform in favor of unambiguous control by the government.

Irwin sent a general telegram to all of his governors on the twenty-second, followed by a specific reply to Sykes on the twenty-fourth. They contain the overarching British perspective that would prevail to the struggle's conclusion.

> There are three ways in which, as it appears to me, the civil disobedience movement might end — (a) It might be called off as the result of negotiation with Government in the course of which Government would make certain concessions as to the future constitution or as to the purpose or composition of the Round Table Conference which it would not have been prepared to make before the movement was started. (b) It might be called off without any such conditions, but doubtless on the implied understanding that special powers would be

withdrawn and prisoners for the most part released. (c) It might gradually peter out through exhaustion, or disintegration, or the development of communal antagonisms.[70]

Irwin rules out "a," calls "b" improbable, and designates "c" as the
most likely alternative. He answered Sykes:

> In this argument I think you underrate the value of steady pressure
> steadily applied. It need not necessarily be dramatic so long as it is
> persistent. I cannot think that the present state of feeling will last in-
> definitely or that those who are at present financing the movement
> will not gradually get both tired and frightened. . . .
>   . . . I believe it to be out of the question to expect to crush the
> whole movement in any dramatic fashion, but I do not believe that
> this is really the alternative to the policy, in which you say you have
> hitherto acquiesced, of using the minimum force necessary to meet the
> situation from day to day. I again prefer the policy of steady pressure.
> We have, in my view, got to use whatever force is necessary to keep
> the movement under control. The ultimate settlement must be dealt
> with independently.[71]

On the twenty-third, a mass parade in Bombay ensued in defiance
of a magistrate's order prohibiting it. The parade turned into a six-
day demonstration which mounted police with lathis were determined, finally, to break up. Participating in the demonstration was a
contingent of Sikhs who, like the Pathans, came from a culture devoted to bravery and the martial arts. With their imposing beards,
turbans, and *kirpans* or sacred swords, they confronted the police,
promising never to draw their swords in self-defense or to leave the
field. They were beaten senseless in a scene as blood-curdling to witnesses as it was demoralizing for the police. The Sikhs accepted
blows with utter composure, repeatedly grinning and standing for
more until unconscious. One policeman is supposed to have re-
marked, "You can't go on hitting a blighter when he stands up to
you like that."[72]
Motilal Nehru boasted that for every volunteer jailed in this period, twenty more joined the movement. He himself was jailed in late
June and sentenced to six months in prison.
The Bombay movement next declared a cloth boycott week, in
which cloth merchants would be encouraged to honor the Working
Committee resolutions banning the sale of any foreign cloth. Most

agreed, but a few did not. The effort culminated in the death of Babu Ganu, a young satyagrahi who was deliberately run over by an English lorry driver when he tried to block the man's truck with his body. The driver worked for one of the hold-out merchants, who later joined the movement.[73] Ganu's death sparked new demonstrations and its commemoration became a focal point for the local movement from then on.

A bewildered Sykes reported to Irwin on 4 July that he feared "chaos resulting from a breakdown of the whole economic fabric of society," noting that even moderate Indian and European sentiment had swung behind the Congress objectives, if not methods. The real alternatives, he continued to assert, were either genuine conciliation or decisive repression. Unfortunately, he complained, he lacked the power to offer the first, and in Bombay in particular, repression would have to extend well beyond the Congress activists in order to be decisive, given the way things had developed. Irwin's concept of "steady pressure" seemed ineffective in Bombay.[74]

On 10 July, *Young India* began appearing in mimeographed form, although its press and assets had been seized. At around the same time, the Working Committee was outlawed, and its replacement members began to meet underground. This obviously required clandestine communications, so runners were employed to coordinate meetings and exchange information. When they could, the British apprehended and tortured these runners to discover where and when Congressmen were meeting.[75]

Irwin was acutely aware of the political liabilities of repression. He told Sykes on one occasion: "I am sure these lathi charges are exactly what our enemies want, and we ought to be constantly racking our brains for a substitute which would deny them the advantage they at present derive from them."[76]

He was anxious to justify the repressive measures he did sanction. In a 9 July speech before Parliament, concerned mainly with the special powers and ordinances he had invoked, he described the independence movement as "a deliberate attempt to coerce established authority by mass action . . . the application of force under another form" with "the avowed object the making of Government impossible." Under these circumstances, he said, "a Government is bound either to resist or abdicate."[77]

> I fully realize that in normal times such frequent resort by the Governor-General to the use of his special powers would be indefensible.

But the times are not normal, and, if the only alternative is acquiescence in the result of efforts openly directed against the constituted Government of the King-Emperor, I cannot for the moment doubt on which side my duty lies.[78]

The number of civil resisters arrested at this point in the conflict was estimated at 16,738.[79]

The struggle had now gone on for just over three months. Vallabhhbhai Patel, arrested near the beginning, was released and went straight to Bombay to help keep up the momentum. On 13 July, he issued a rejoinder to Irwin's speech of the ninth. He noted that since the Congress was now forced to operate underground, "every home must be a Congress office, and every soul a Congress organization."[80] Behind the brave words, there must have been a sense that the three months' all-out struggle, and Irwin's steady pressure, had taken a toll.

It was now within bounds to at least talk about the circumstances under which civil disobedience might end and the Congress might be induced to participate in the round table conference, short of immediate and full independence.

A process of shuttle diplomacy had been set in motion by a reporter, George Slocombe, in late June, which culminated on 15 August. Slocombe, who had interviewed Gandhi in jail in May, approached Motilal Nehru and moderate leaders, M. R. Jayakar and Sir T. B. Sapru. The plan was that if this group could agree on terms for ending civil disobedience, the moderates could act as intermediaries with the viceroy, while Nehru could approach Gandhi and his son, Jawaharlal. The chief condition specified by Motilal Nehru was that the government should give a private understanding to the leaders that it would support the concept of full, responsible government by and for Indians, subject to conditions arrived at through the round table process and the British parliamentary process.

Irwin, reacting to this formula, offered a more restricted view of what government would promise: "to assist the people of India to as large a degree of management of their own affairs as can be shown to be consistent with the making of provision for those matters in regard to which they are not in a position to assume responsibility."[81]

By this time Motilal Nehru was in jail with his son in Allahabad. Via Sapru and Jayakar, Gandhi conveyed his view to them that any restrictions or safeguards such as those outlined by Irwin should apply only to the transition period leading to self-government. Gandhi further stipulated that the conference makeup would have to be acceptable. The cloth, liquor, and salt campaigns would not be suspended. Political prisoners would have to be released. Those who had resigned posts in protest should be reappointed. Attached properties, fines, and so on should be returned. And the government's new ordinances would have to be repealed.

The Nehrus, in turn, expressed pessimism that anything could be achieved by a round table conference unless prior agreement was achieved on the most basic issues. Jawaharlal, neither for the first nor last time, cautioned Gandhi that his apparent softening on the constitutional question (i.e., admitting the legitimacy of any safeguards) was inconsistent with the Congress' objective of complete independence. Gandhi replied that any arrangement whatsoever would have to include a provision for Indian secession from the British Empire.

The viceroy expressed guarded hope that the Sapru-Jayakar effort might lead to moderation among Indian opinion leaders. To further the process, the members of the Working Committee were allowed to meet with Gandhi in jail. But when the leaders got together, their position hardened.

Before civil disobedience could end, they agreed, the government would have to concede India's right to secede at will from any dominion arrangement, to control defense and finance, and to review the public debt situation.

On suspension of civil disobedience, the leaders demanded release of all satyagrahi prisoners, restoration of all confiscated properties and fines, and the repeal of all repressive ordinances. The liberals conveyed these conditions to Irwin on 15 August, and he replied that there was no longer any basis for discussion. The struggle would go on a while longer, and the conference, if it occurred, would do so without Congress' participation.

The Revenue Front

By early September, *Young India* was claiming that the movement had inflicted substantial revenue losses on the government of Bombay, and had redirected the money to serve the long-ignored human needs of that province. Irwin complained to Benn at this time that business in Bombay was at a standstill, and that "sober and sensible businessmen seem quite prepared to continue the movement, even though ruin is staring them in the face," a disposition he viewed as "far from being a good augury of peace."[82] The businesses that were at a standstill of course, were the ones specifically affected by the Congress program: boycotts of liquor, foreign cloth, importation of anything British, and, of course, the salt trade.

These, along with the burgeoning no-tax campaign, became the dominant focus of the movement throughout the fall and early winter. The need to harvest before the seasonal monsoons prevented people from demonstrating, and other forms of direct confrontation had to take a back seat. But thousands of people in southern India refused to pay land revenues and lost their homes, crops, and possessions as a result. Property was attached by the government in lieu of payments, and then sold at auction. Seized crops were often harvested by laborers from outside the immediate community. In some cases, people fasted in protest against those who had purchased their goods from the state.

The secretary of state confessed to being depressed in September that the movement was still so lively. He cited particularly the note of pride and defiance in the personal correspondence of Jawaharlal Nehru, complaining that it "did not show the spirit of a beaten man."[83] But Irwin was still cautiously optimistic. He observed that at least there had been no major problems with police or army disaffection. In fact, he claimed, morale had never been higher, and the ranks were full, despite Congress propaganda aimed specifically at police and military troops.[84] Both men were now hoping that the First Round Table Conference, scheduled to begin on 12 November, would capture the attention of moderates, especially among the businessmen, and cause them to back away from the Congress and the civil disobedience movement.

The start of the conference came and went, however, with no discernible let-up in the revenue-oriented resistance activities. By late December the effects were measurable. Indian imports of British cotton piece goods, primarily from the Lancashire cotton mills, had plummeted, from 1.25 million yards in 1924 and 1.07 million yards in 1929 to a mere 0.72 million yards in 1930.[85] Importation of items for personal consumption, such as cigarettes, drugs and medicines, and toiletries decreased by 30 percent, 19 percent, and 18 percent respectively during the campaign.[86] In the Central Provinces, 75 percent of all foreign cloth shops were closed outright, and the government's revenue from the liquor tax was reduced by 40 percent as a result of continuous picketing. In Bengal the government faced a total deficit of Rs. 9,482,000.[87] The secretary of state summarized the situation before Parliament, citing an overall 25 percent reduction in trade with India, of which 18 percent was directly attributable to Congress activities, and only 7 percent to the worldwide depression.[88]

As the no-tax movement spread, the government began sending armed squads of tax collectors into villages, particularly in Gandhi's home province of Gujarat. Tax collectors quickly earned a reputation for unnecessary harassment and brutality toward tax resisters.[89] In response, whole communities practiced *hijrat*, or protest evacuation of their own lands. Eighty thousand *hijratis* left Gujarat and went to the princely state of Baroda. They left the local authorities without sufficient manpower to harvest the crops. The authorities had to sell the abandoned land very cheaply, or derive no benefit at all from the situation.

On 31 December, Irwin communicated to Benn that the situation was deteriorating and that the no-tax agitation alone warranted the extension or renewal of all special ordinances. He noted that "events have proved that the movement has still a great deal of vigour and that relaxation of counter-measures or the abrogation of special powers is soon followed by unfortunate developments."[90]

At year's end, the total number of resisters imprisoned was estimated at 60,140.[91] The First Round Table Conference came to a close on 19 January, a week before the first anniversary of Purna Swaraj Day, having produced nothing of benefit for either side. The British government stood by the principle that there should be extensive safeguards, guarantees, and reserved powers which would protect India's minority communities, British commercial interests, and the security of the subcontinent during any transition, all of which added up to something less than either dominion status or independence. The Indian delegates who participated, particularly the Liberals, came away from the conference sensing that nothing had been accomplished except quibbling over narrow interest-group issues. The Liberals formally appealed to Gandhi and the Congress to come forward and join the proposed Second Round Table Conference.

Ramsay MacDonald also called for Gandhi's participation and declared the Congress once again to be a legal organization on 25 January. He released Gandhi, the Working Committee members, and their wives from jail on Purna Swaraj Day, 26 January, so that they could confer to consider this offer. On his release Gandhi insisted that, whatever else happened, the cloth boycott and Salt Act resistance should continue, since the objectives of these methods were legitimate ends in themselves and could not be denied. The Working Committee met 31 January–1 February and resolved to continue civil disobedience for the time being. They modified this position slightly on 6 February, by instructing local Congress organizations to keep on fighting but not to develop any new tactical situations.

Shortly thereafter, Motilal Nehru died, uttering the memorable last words: "Let me die, if die I must, in the lap of a free India. Let me sleep my last sleep, not in a subject country but in a free one."[92]

The situation had changed significantly in the direction of a free India since August, when Motilal was jailed. Both parties to the conflict, having agreed at that time to fight it out rather than give anything up in an accommodation, were again flirting with the possibility of serious negotiations. It should be recognized, however, that the government at this point was more anxious for the dialogue to begin than was the movement. Irwin's policy of steady pressure had clearly not exhausted the movement, and the highly touted conference had not convinced anyone that mattered to leave the nationalist standard. After a year of struggle, the Congress retained the initiative.

THE STRUGGLE ENDS: THE GANDHI-IRWIN TRUCE

The movement is still dangerous both because of the mischief it is actually doing and because of the far greater mischief it is capable of doing, if given favourable conditions. The boycott is effective, and although it is less general than a few months ago, defiance of it has not been on a sufficiently large scale to justify any assumption that the movement in this respect is anywhere near disintegration. Its continued strength is explained by two causes, firstly, the wide sympathy which the general objects of the civil disobedience movement command, and secondly, the great efficacy of the weapon of social pressure and boycott . . . Having found a powerful weapon in the civil disobedience movement and particularly in the boycott there is a real danger that they will prefer to rely on these rather than on discussion and

argument and will proceed on the assumption that there is no safe-
guard or reservation which agitation cannot eliminate.[93]

These two messages from Irwin to Benn, on 17 and 31 January,
respectively, summarize the viceroy's views as he moved into the negotiation period that would turn out to be decisive. As usual, his
perceptions were astute. They led him to conceive of a negotiation
strategy that was far more focused and deliberate than the one that
the Congress would pursue. He knew he would have to give up
something in order to avert the dangers of a continued nonviolent
movement, but what?

He outlined the issues that were likely to be at stake in a cable to
Benn on 2 February, twelve days before Gandhi approached him
with a request for face-to-face talks. He saw three broad groups of
issues.

The first group included practical matters related to the cessation
of hostilities, such as the repeal of ordinances, return of property
taken from resisters, and release of political prisoners. These were of
no importance to the British except to the extent that they created
leverage to negotiate a favorable settlement on the larger questions.
Acceding to Congress' demands in this category merely meant returning to the status quo ante and would cost nothing, especially
since measures could be reinvoked and persons rearrested if the settlement broke down. The British preference was for civil disobedience to be suspended before the punitive measures were revoked, on
the grounds that the Congress had to prove its ability to control its
followers while the government did not.

The second group of issues involved what Irwin referred to as
Gandhi's "social interests": salt, picketing of liquor, and swadeshi
leading to the rejection of foreign cloth.[94] Although Gandhi personally viewed these as ends in themselves, for the movement they functioned as limited focal points for nonviolent maneuvers during the
conflict, which were supposed to lead to complete independence.
While more substantive than the first group, concessions on these
issues did not really threaten British interests either, because they
did not erode the basic elements of British control.

Finally, there were the "constitutional group of difficulties," including "safeguards, right of secession, examination of debts, pay of
security services and the Army."[95] These were the difficult issues,
because their resolution was directly related to the ultimate definition
of dominion status or independence, whichever it was to be, if either.

Irwin's best possible course would be to appear very stingy over issues in the first two groups and then gradually give ground on them in exchange for what he really wanted—the cessation of civil disobedience and the Congress participating in and, therefore, legitimizing the round table process. If the constitutional questions could be relegated to the round table process, the British government would have emerged from a sticky mess without having given up anything important. This is exactly what happened.

The talks between Gandhi and Irwin began in Delhi on 17 February, in closed session, with Gandhi empowered to act for the Working Committee, which would ultimately have to ratify the results. Over a period of two weeks, with some short interruptions, the two men met and grappled with the whole range of issues. During this time, they both testified later, they came to respect and even to like each other. Irwin admired Gandhi's tenacity and sense of humor, although he found him somewhat vain, and saw this as a weak spot. Gandhi credited Irwin with sincerity and diplomatic skill, and felt proud that the viceroy now appeared to be dealing with at least one Indian as an equal. (Repeatedly in later years Gandhi argued that this represented a victory in itself.)

During the talks Gandhi exhorted his followers to continue the fight but to preserve their nonviolence. Of late, some rioting had begun to mar the overwhelmingly nonviolent movement. He insisted that true satyagrahis could not give up or change objectives in midcourse but should hold out for an honorable settlement. On 25 February, in the middle of the talks, Gandhi gave a speech at Hindu College, Delhi, that disturbed some of his followers. He told his audience that the most important tasks ahead were the creation of Hindu-Muslim unity, the elimination of untouchability, and the making and wearing of homespun cloth. Gandhi had always thought that India would be free only when it made itself worthy of freedom. In his mind, the social agenda was part and parcel of freedom. But the younger leaders felt that this approach devalued and jeopardized the all-important strategic objective, independence.[96] It would prove to be hard to counter their argument.

The document which came to be known variously as the Delhi Pact, the Delhi Truce, and the Gandhi-Irwin Truce was completed on 27 February and ratified, with great reservations, by the Working Committee on 5 March. Jawaharlal Nehru was deeply discouraged by it, but thought that an open break with Gandhi would be more destructive than the agreement itself, and so did not press his own strategic viewpoint.[97]

The truce contained twenty-one provisions, of which the most critical were: civil disobedience would be effectively suspended; the Congress would participate in the next round table conference; all constitutional questions would be deferred to the conference but with a priori limitations, such as that the principle of "safeguards in the interests of India" was acknowledged. The government would withdraw its repressive ordinances and measures, again with limitations. It would remit all fines or property which had not yet been collected or were still in government hands. But seized property sold to third parties was permanently forfeited. Prosecution for civil disobedience would cease, except for police officers and civil servants induced by the movement to collaborate with it. Picketing of foreign cloth could continue, as long as it was motivated by a desire for self-sufficiency, but could not be used for political coercion. Furthermore, picketing must be demonstrably nonaggressive in style, or else it could be stopped by the local authorities, at their own discretion. The Salt Act as such would not be repealed, but, for humanitarian relief, poor people with direct access to salt earth would be allowed to process and use it for themselves.

A major sticking point had been the issue of whether there would or would not be a public inquiry into police conduct throughout the campaign. The text of the truce gave Gandhi credit for pushing hard on this issue (a face-saver for him) but announced that the government would simply not conduct such an investigation. Gandhi gave up the point, it turns out, when Lord Irwin told him flatly that he wanted to keep police morale high in case the conflict erupted again, and Gandhi accepted this as a moral victory, having gotten Irwin to reveal his true motives.[98]

Finally, the last provision was a blanket concession that the government could adopt any measures it deemed necessary to protect public order, in the event that the Congress did not adequately enforce its side of the agreement. No reciprocal clause enabled the Congress to resort to its own methods of struggle if the government reneged.

A generous interpretation might be that Gandhi, eager to give his forces a rest and to prove that the Congress could produce a settlement, however limited, did so with the hope of fighting another day if the Second Round Table Conference was unsuccessful. A less generous view would be that Gandhi "gave away the store" because he was desperate for an agreement and grossly underestimated his own side's real strength. In either case, it is hard to avoid the conclusion that this accommodation, admittedly only a truce and not a final settlement, was unenforceable and one-sided. Moreover, it contained only two out of five of the provisions identified by the Working Committee as essential prior to the suspension of civil disobedience the previous August, when the movement's position was materially weaker![99]

Gandhi himself was not sanguine about the terms of the truce. In a press conference on the day after their publication, though, he argued that: "It would be folly to go on suffering when the opponent makes it easy for you to enter into a discussion with him upon your longings. If a real opening is made, it is one's duty to take advantage of it, and in my humble opinion, the settlement has made a real opening."[100] Yet, a few days later, he cautioned that "the settlement is provisional and the negotiations may break down at any stage. Let us therefore keep our powder dry and our armour ever bright. Failure should not find us napping but ready to mobilize at the first command."[101]

In the months that followed, Congress activists scrupulously implemented their side of the bargain. A fighting organization became, in effect, a peacekeeping force. New orders were issued to picketers, emphasizing courtesy and personal discipline in public. It was better to let foreign cloth be sold, Gandhi argued, than to break the spirit of the agreement with any behavior that could be construed as coercive.

No such attitude applied on the British side. The viceroy's office was given to quibbling over the terms of the truce, while local bureaucrats and police officers actively circumvented its provisions, often violently harassing peasants who had withheld taxes before the truce. Local Congress organizations had to divide their energies between restraining their followers' enthusiasm for battle and remonstrating with the authorities over these excesses.

The situation was compounded by the fact that agriculture was definitely feeling the effects of the Great Depression by this time. Payment of even current land revenues, whether taxes or rents, was extraordinarily difficult. Gandhi spent most of his time during the months leading up to the Second Round Table Conference arguing the peasants' case before a new viceroy, Lord Willingdon, who had replaced Lord Irwin.

On 14 June Gandhi wrote to Willingdon requesting the establishment of an arbitration board to decide questions of interpretation
related to the truce. Willingdon refused but invited Gandhi to list his
specific grievances for review. Gandhi prepared a list of seventy-nine
violations, and the two men met to discuss these on 21 July. Willingdon would not budge on the question of establishing a tribunal, and
insisted on the government's right to use all its resources to force
payment of revenues. A discouraged Gandhi, with the Congress
backing him, threatened to boycott the Round Table Conference on
13 August. In the absence of civil disobedience, this was the Congress' most powerful threat. The government wanted Congress participation, at least to the extent that it hastily set up talks leading to
a second settlement, as it came to be called, at Simla in late August.
Here Willingdon's government agreed to look into the land revenue
situation in Bardoli, where it was most extreme, but nowhere else.
Arbitration of grievances was again turned down, and Gandhi went
along with the continued truce under protest. In a dissenting letter
attached to the new agreement he wrote: "We feel that, where in the
opinion of Congress a grievance arising out of the working of the
Settlement is not redressed an inquiry is a necessity of the case, because of the fact that Civil Disobedience remains under suspension
during the pendency of the Delhi Pact." [102]

Gandhi obviously wanted the round table process to work, but he
no longer expected it to. Just before sailing to London as the Congress' sole delegate and spokesperson he said, "My expectations of
the Conference are zero if I am to base them on a survey of the
horizon." He warned the nation not to "look to England or Simla or
Delhi for Swaraj," but to expect to win it "through our own strength
and in the meaning of our own strength." [103]

Gandhi had helped to construct a state of affairs, however, in
which the nation's strength, expressed in civil disobedience, was restrained until the round table process was completed. Meanwhile,
the government had free rein to reassert its strength, and nothing in
the terms of the truce prevented it from doing so.

Gandhi went off to the conference, which proved to be a monumental distraction. The government successfully circumvented any
serious discussion of constitution building for a free India by focusing attention on two unresolvable questions, and by insisting that
these must in fact be resolved before the constitutional questions
could be addressed. These were the communal question and the

question of federation. The first referred to the optimum relationship between India's ethnic and religious minorities and the dominant Hindu population. Would there be special voting constituencies
for the minorities, to guarantee them a proportional number of seats
in a hypothetical parliament? How would such constituencies be con-
structed? What precise safeguards would protect minorities from a
tyranny of the majority, or were safeguards, in themselves, a form of
discrimination? The federal question was nearly as thorny. If self-
governing institutions were to be developed in India, what would be
the status of the princely kingdoms? Would they share power in a
federation of Indian states? Would a central federal authority have
more or less power over their affairs than the British government
currently had?

Gandhi was representing the Congress, and the Congress was
speaking for the nation on the question of independence. Dozens of
other representatives were present and participating in factions and
groupings that the foregoing questions were designed to draw into
conflict. Not surprisingly, these questions were not resolved, and
Ramsay MacDonald was able to announce, in the closing session of
the conference on 1 December, that further "reconciliation of different interests" would need to take place before any commitments
could be made concerning India's future.[104]

Gandhi returned to India to find that Willingdon had tightened
his grip on the situation considerably. He had artfully reneged on
the Simla agreement to investigate land revenue practices in Bardoli
by establishing a commission of inquiry which refused to hear any
testimony from the Indian side. In the United Provinces the local
Congress Committee advised peasants to withhold land payments
until some sort of relief could be negotiated. The government refused to discuss the matter without the committee's first reversing
itself, which it would not do. The national leadership began to prepare for a resumption of civil disobedience, and many of them, including Jawaharlal Nehru, had been arrested and jailed on arbitrary
pretexts by the time Gandhi arrived.

After surveying the situation, Gandhi sent a telegram to the new
viceroy. He noted in his message that there were now additional repressive ordinances in several provinces, that many of his colleagues
were in jail, and that there were reports of violence against Congressmen in the Frontier Provinces. Requesting an interview to discuss
these matters, Gandhi received a reply from one of Willingdon's sub-

ordinates, agreeing to see him but declining to discuss any of the issues referred to.[105] The reply came on 31 December. The next day Gandhi and members of the Working Committee still at large published a resolution which said, in effect, that if the viceroy did not reconsider his reply to Gandhi, and agree to speak with Congress representatives as the legitimate voice of the nation, the truce would be over and civil disobedience would resume.[106]

Willingdon was in a much stronger position than his predecessor. For several months Indians had been instructed to hold back, to trust Gandhi to bring back something of worth from the Second Round Table Conference, and not to embarrass the movement. Now they were being actively repressed, they had suffered a disastrous agricultural year, and those who had taken part in the movement had little or nothing to show for it. When Willingdon refused to discuss anything at all under the threat of resumed struggle, he took a calculated risk that paid off. Local Congress organizations were unprepared to go back onto a war footing, and the popular response to the Working Committee's call was sluggish. Continued appeals for a new wave of resistance were issued throughout 1932, but the energy and expectations of 1930–1931 were not recaptured for many years to come.

ANALYSIS

Outcome of the Campaign

The Indian campaign for independence in 1930–1931 was defeated because it fell short of its stated goal. However, strategic nonviolent conflict mounted a significant challenge to the British Raj and did lay the groundwork for subsequent struggles for independence that ended in success.

Finally, a word about success is in order. Many people are inclined to think of the Indian independence movement as the one great shining success for nonviolent methods in international conflict. These methods were most actively applied in India during 1930–1931, therefore, the campaign must have been at least something of a success, or so it is generally supposed. For strategic discourse to be meaningful, success can only be measured by whether stated objectives in a conflict are won or lost. Independence did not

come until 1947, and, therefore, the campaign was a failure. It is
true that, by the end of it, British statesmen were dealing with Gandhi as something of an equal. It is also probably true that the
1930–1931 campaign put the writing on the wall for them, in the
sense that most rational observers from this point onward considered
eventual independence inevitable. When we look at the distribution
of power and the status of interests at the end of the campaign, however, they add up to a British victory, and it is important for us to
understand why.

PRINCIPLES OF DEVELOPMENT

Principle 1: Formulate Functional Objectives

The nonviolent protagonists only partially conformed to this principle.

At the outset, tension existed between reformers and radical advocates of independence. The decision to set a deadline for dominion
status resolved the tension. Either it would achieve an interim objective or remove the final obstacle to participation in the struggle for
the moderates. Once the deadline passed unmet, the declared objective of independence was the very model of a functional objective.
There could be no ambiguity about whether it had or had not been
achieved. It was clear, compelling for all Indians, and progress toward it was easily measurable.

Independence also suggested specific sanctions. Anywhere that the
Raj exercised its prerogatives was a front for nonviolent action. The
Salt March and cloth boycotts are perfect examples. Subordinate objectives, such as the removal of the Salt Laws, contributed to the
ultimate objective and were inherently valuable and compelling in
their own right. On the other hand, Gandhi's focus on social issues
tended to blur the focus of the independence campaign and to distress the younger, more politically oriented leaders. Although the
stated objective was crystal clear, Gandhi temporized in an unhelpful
way. By suggesting a distinction between "winning" and "earning"
independence, he prepared the ground psychologically for failure.
Goals such as Hindu-Muslim unity, ending untouchability, and wearing homespun cloth were represented to be as important as ejecting
the British. Through his philosophical approach and actions, Gandhi

reinforced the view that if the British didn't leave it would be because the Indians were somehow deficient.

Principle 2: Develop Organizational Strength

The nonviolent protagonists conformed to this principle.

For a full decade before the campaign, the INC, under Gandhi's leadership, was preparing itself as a fighting organization and building on a long tradition of articulate nationalist sentiment. The Bardoli campaign, intrinsically valuable, was also seen as a training exercise for future nonviolent resisters at all levels of Indian society. Other organizations were recruited, such as the Muslim League, and networks were developed, which easily and naturally joined the campaign. Local chapters of the INC, throughout India, were developed so that there was depth of leadership and an ability to act locally in accordance with a broad program of action. Congress' Working Committee amounts to what we call the operational corps, turning broad policy into stratagems and local issue-oriented tactical encounters.

In terms of the leadership model, the decision to make Gandhi the commanding general was a mixed blessing. It did give the Indian movement a capacity to react quickly and decisively to its Imperial opponents—a luxury rare to such movements. Also, it made good use of Gandhi's strengths, especially his tactical brilliance. It is hard to imagine the Salt Campaign unfolding the way it did in the absence of his particularly inspired leadership.

But Gandhi's personal foibles burdened the movement. Irwin, we are told, saw Gandhi as somewhat vain. Gandhi's pride in dealing with the viceroy on equal terms seemed to have led him to seek reconciliation prematurely. It can also be argued that Gandhi's preference for compromise over coercion, as well as his underestimation of Congress' power, made the ultimate objective in this campaign impossible to achieve.

The model of leadership chosen in this struggle is atypical, despite the popular assumption that strategic nonviolent conflict is only viable with a charismatic leader on center stage.

Principle 3: Secure Access to Critical Material Resources

This principle was inoperative.

It is possible that traditional economies, and in particular ones in which the repressive force is vastly outnumbered, are better able to absorb punishment in a way that makes material resources less decisive. If millions of people require comparatively little to subsist, then as long as they are not paralyzed or disempowered by repression, their best option may be to struggle on no matter what resources are at their disposal.

Lost access to resources was critical only for highly targeted areas of repression. For example, families who participated in revenue actions, especially tax withholding, lost everything they had, sometimes permanently. If the conflict had gone on for another six months, however, it is by no means clear which side would have collapsed first due to economic distress. The agricultural sector was severely affected, but this also came very late in the fight, and it might have been possible to shift the focus away from this sector if the struggle had continued.

Principle 4: Cultivate External Assistance

This principle was inoperative.

Both the Salt March and the raid at Dharasana were covered by the international media as defining events for the conflict, and this undoubtedly created a great deal of third-party sympathy, including within Great Britain itself. However, sympathy was never converted into the forms of overt support that were envisioned if this principle were to be decisive.

Gandhi's open letters to Irwin were successful, at least rhetorically, as propaganda exercises, but they did not result in specific types of aid from outside parties. Given geography and the demographics of the period, it is not at all certain that external assistance would have had a major impact on the case even if it had been forthcoming.

Principle 5: Expand the Repertoire of Sanctions

The nonviolent protagonists conformed to this principle.

This is an ideal case to exhibit this principle. Continued British rule depended directly on the cooperation of Indians. Stability and legitimacy for the Raj required the maintenance of normalcy in everyday affairs. Often these were the easiest things to deny through nonviolent action. Daily routines presented myriad opportunities for resistance. The variety and depth of methods used is staggering.

There were boycotts, civil disobedience, hartals, mass demonstrations, revenue actions, tree cutting, salt actions, "ordinance actions," many varieties of political noncooperation, and more.

Nearly all of the sanctions could be used widely and were easily replicable. Most had good "risk-return characteristics" and had the desired multiplier effect as Irwin could not avoid seeing the unused potential for parallel sanctions in other places. The sanctions potentially most damaging to the opponents were those that constrained tax revenue.

PRINCIPLES OF ENGAGEMENT

Principle 6: Attack the Opponents' Strategy for Consolidating Control

The nonviolent protagonists only partially conformed to this principle.

The opening thrust, the attack on government manufactured salt, struck directly at the strategy for control, by challenging the legitimacy of the colonial system. With every act of defiance on the salt front, British legitimacy deteriorated. One aspect of Gandhi's genius was his ability to attack along lines which offered multiple objectives. His actions also presented his adversaries with unpalatable choices. The best of many examples was the question of Gandhi's arrest. Did British control depend on neutralizing Gandhi? Did that mean arresting him or leaving him free? One alternative would create a wave of resentment and fuel the struggle. The other alternative would make the regime look weak and indecisive, while allowing Gandhi the freedom to work further mischief. Either way, subversion of the regime's control was likely to increase.

British strategy for control, however, rested on pillars other than legitimacy and an ability to extract minimal compliance to laws. The Irwin strategy of "steady pressure" was intended to cow the movement. The movement responded with steady escalation, making the British doubt their strategy at various points.

In two other respects, however, the Indians did not conform to this principle, and their cause suffered as a result. First, the Round Table gambit was not recognized for what it was—a means of stalling and conquering by division. It opened up several opportunities. The

INC could have countered by agreeing only to direct talks with the British government. Or the INC could have gone to London only after a consensus position had been agreed upon among the Indian representatives. The INC could also have refused to stand down from direct action during the talks. Or it could have rejected the proposed conference outright.

The other major source of control that was never decisively attacked was the reliability of the army and police, which were made up of predominantly Indian officers. The security forces occasionally wavered, but if their loyalty had been undermined it would have wreaked havoc for the British.

Principle 7: Mute the Impact of the Opponents' Violent Weapons

The nonviolent protagonists conformed to this principle.

Two methods of muting the impact of violence were operative here. Dispersion was used with most of the sanctions deployed, with the desired effect of overstretching the opponents' repressive resources. Only a small fraction of the Indians who produced illicit salt were punished. The same was true for participation in boycotts. The regime could not shoot people for not buying foreign cloth.

With the more concentrated actions, the process of political jujitsu was successfully brought into play. Especially at Dharasana and Peshawar, the deaths and serious injuries were turned to the maximum disadvantage of the perpetrators, fueling the movement and creating symbols to rally around. Wounds that were not lethal came to function as badges of honor rather than as symbols of intimidation. In support of those victimized, Gandhi often complained to the viceroy about police brutality and confiscation. This seemed to create some hesitancy to continue with similar forms of repression. And, of course, the Congress was quick to care for the wounded and dispossessed.

Principle 8: Alienate Opponents from Expected Bases of Support

The nonviolent protagonists only partially conformed to this principle.

Moderate Indian politicians, of which Motilal Nehru was the premier example, were needed by the Raj for its very existence. When moderates went over to the independence movement en masse, one entire and expected base of support was captured for good. Soldiers and police, on the other hand, as we noted above, were hardly touched, and were a source of great unexploited potential in this case. The refusal of two platoons of Royal Garhwal Rifles to reinforce Peshawar indicates what may have been possible. Another indication is Irwin's resistance to enquiries about police brutality, fearing police alienation. Gandhi's willingness to drop this request unilaterally is a puzzlement, and again illustrates the weakness of one-man charismatic leadership during the conflict's concluding stages.

The British home front was addressed, but not well enough to make a difference. There is no evidence, for example, that the people the INC and Gandhi appealed to in England were critical constituencies for Irwin.

British allies were never likely to play a major role. In this late colonial period, allies supported one another's colonial policies directly or at least stayed out of the way. It would have been hard to persuade third parties to oppose Britain's policy in India.

Principle 9: Maintain Nonviolent Discipline

The nonviolent protagonists conformed to this principle.

The use of an explicit pledge of nonviolent conduct at the outset of the campaign was excellent preparation for the steadfast discipline that followed. The basis for the pledge was embedded, at least in part, in the moral aspects of satyagraha. For example, behavior at Peshawar conformed to the pledge, but it also transcended the boundaries of pure calculation. Strategic commitment alone cannot explain this willful offering of the ultimate sacrifice, especially by people who were familiar with the uses of violence. Nonviolent discipline had the intended effect throughout the campaign. It shamed the violent opponents, impressed third parties, and prevented the characterization of the movement as anything less than heroically nonviolent.

Nonviolent discipline made what seemed to be the failed raid on the Dharasana Salt Works a success. In that series of encounters, however, a point of diminishing returns was probably reached early on. Additional discipline and sacrifice probably did not garner much extra credit for self-control. The point of the confrontation having been made early, perhaps it would have been better to withdraw sooner.

There were instances of violent sabotage, but they were marginal and did not taint the overall campaign. Even Irwin, after the attempt on his life, could distinguish between Gandhi's forces and those using the methods of violence.

PRINCIPLES OF CONCEPTION

Principle 10: Assess Events and Options in Light of Levels of Strategic Decision Making

The nonviolent protagonists only partially conformed to this principle.

Unlike the Ruhr, the nonviolent protagonists were able to make decisions with respect to logistics and tactics in the light of an overall strategic conception. Encounters were well planned and the significance of one engagement for another was understood. Gandhi was exceptional in his ability to think at the strategic and operational levels by seeing the interrelationship between nonviolent sanctions, society building (constructive work), and independence.

However, performance on the policy level was not up to this standard. The "freedom or death" mindset limited choice too narrowly on the policy level, because it allowed only two alternatives, neither of which was in the sole capacity of the INC to deliver. The Round Table brought neither freedom nor death. Negotiations compromised independence. A more flexible and realistic view on the policy level might have led to clearer thinking on the strategic level as to how to avoid such negative outcomes as the paralysis of civil disobedience. There were no real contingency plans if the talks went badly. The opposition anticipated this weakness and exploited it.

Principle 11: Adjust Offensive and Defensive Operations According to the Relative Vulnerabilities of the Protagonists

The nonviolent protagonists only partially conformed to this principle.

Some adjustments hit squarely at British vulnerabilities, and others failed to do so. The results were predictable and followed the principle. For example, British forces were vulnerable, along cultural lines, to the aggressive use of women as nonviolent resisters. This was exploited well. In the cloth and alcohol boycotts in particular, women leaders and activists were used to great advantage and with limited risk.

Dharasana is a classic example of an offensive adjustment, indeed, a highly provocative escalation, developed to exploit and follow on from Gandhi's arrest.

Since revenue was the "oil" that "greased" the Raj's "wheels," tax actions probed this vulnerability directly. The failure to exploit fully this line of attack was a negative. Dispersed tax avoidance could have been a perfect technique to use as pressure in coordination with round table discussions.

As already noted, the Gandhi-Irwin truce was a flawed defensive adjustment. The movement retreated precisely when it should have continued to attack. If the movement was momentarily spent, a defensive slowdown would have made much more sense.

Perhaps not enough was done to exploit Irwin's reluctance to use violent reprisals. His correspondence on the problem of civil disobedience shows that he was sensitive to the claims of immoral behavior that his opponents could muster.

Principle 12: Sustain Continuity Between Sanctions, Mechanisms, and Objectives

The nonviolent protagonists only partially conformed to this principle.

On the positive side, there was nearly perfect continuity between tactical deployments and strategic objectives. No cloth, no salt, no taxes, equaled no British control. Direct correspondence existed between actions and consequences.

The easy replicability of the most important types of actions with their cumulative effect also ensured that the mechanisms of change—in this case both accommodation and coercion—could be pursued widely throughout Indian society. The revenue actions, though incomplete, had real coercive potential and were in harmony with the ultimate objective.

Friction between mechanisms and objectives came late in the contest. Failure to appreciate the true relative power positions of the main parties, combined with a premature shift to conversion, or at least accommodation as the preferred mechanism of closure, led the movement, at Gandhi's insistence, to demobilize its best sanctions. This was done before the objective of independence was secured or even significantly advanced.

Gandhi's unwillingness to incorporate the views of others in the Congress insulated him, allowing him to imagine that personal "undertakings" and "back door" assurances by the viceroy would lead to independence. It almost seems as though Gandhi became impatient and forgot that Irwin was not England. Thus the Round Table became a disorienting event, rather than a sustaining one, in the strategy for Indian independence. The next viceroy, Willingdon, sensed the lack of integration between sanctions, mechanisms, and objectives and exploited this weakness easily with sharp repression that ended the campaign.

NOTES

1. For the specialist, the most persistent myths about nonviolent action in India should have been laid to rest by Gene Sharp's incisive treatment of them in *Gandhi as a Political Strategist*, 2–13. We follow his reasoning extensively below.

2. There are, in fact, some ways in which the case is unique, primarily in relation to the degree of conscious strategy it exhibits. A sheer display of nonviolent bravery under fire, however, is not one of them.

3. Sharp, *Gandhi*, 12.

4. "Raj," literally, means "rule."

5. Percival Spear, *A History of India*, 2:212, 249. This figure is for 1921. It rose to 389 million by 1941 and has risen continually since.

6. Hindu and Muslim, with the Muslim community by far the smaller, and yet more prominent than the other minorities.

7. Spear, *History*, 173.

8. The occasional practice of suttee and thugee, for example, is often mentioned by British apologists. The former refers to the burning of widows on the funeral pyres of their husbands; the latter involved robbery and ritualized murder in the service of the goddess Kali.

9. See Jawaharlal Nehru, *Toward Freedom*, 275–85, for a fine rendering of this argument.

10. Ibid., 225.

11. Sharp, *Gandhi*, 219–20.

12. Spear, *History*, 191.

13. The commission was named for Sir John Simon, its appointed chairman.

14. Spear, *History*, 201.

15. S. Gopal, *The Viceroyalty of Lord Irwin 1926–1931*, 19.

16. Ibid.

17. The Earl of Halifax [Lord Irwin], *Fullness of Days*, 115.

18. Nehru, *Toward Freedom*, 131.

19. Cited in Gopal, *Lord Irwin*, 23.

20. C. H. Philips, ed., *The Evolution of India and Pakistan*, 228–33.

21. Subhas Chandra Bose, for example, wanted to begin direct struggle for full independence right away, to take advantage of considerable student and labor unrest that had developed. Bose, *Indian Struggle 1920–1942*, 164–65.

22. Nehru, *Toward Freedom*, 140. Gandhi wanted a two-year trial period, so the compromise was mutual.

23. Tariq Ali quotes Singh as saying that the bombing was meant to "wake up India and to avenge the death of Lajpat Rai," in Ali, *The Nehrus and the Gandhis*, 34.

24. Bardoli had been the planned site of a no-tax campaign in 1922, which was called off because of violence breaking out elsewhere in the non-cooperation movement.

25. Gopal, *Lord Irwin*, 29–34.

26. Lord Irwin's Statement on Dominion Status, 31 October 1929, in Philips, *India and Pakistan*, 286–87.

27. See introductory section, above.

28. B. Pattabhi Sitaramayya, *The History of the Indian National Congress*, 1:654, citing Gandhi in an Associated Press interview, 5 April 1930.

29. Mohandas K. Gandhi, "When I Am Arrested," *Young India*, 27 February 1930.

30. See, for example, his statements in *Young India* of 24 April 1930, cited in Gene Sharp, *Gandhi Wields the Weapon of Moral Power*, 100.

31. See *Congress Bulletin*, 17 January 1930, no. 2, for the entire text.

32. *Congress Bulletin*, 27 March 1930, no. 6.

33. Gandhi, "When I Am Arrested."

34. The entire letter can be found in Sharp, *Weapon of Moral Power*, 61–66.

35. Pattabhi Sitaramayya, *History*, 650.

36. Gopal, *Lord Irwin*, 56. He points out that the average individual spent only three *annas* per year on this tax, and that illicit manufacture was almost completely unknown, indicating that the hardship it caused was probably marginal.

37. Nehru, *Toward Freedom*, 160.

38. Ibid.

39. Gopal, *Lord Irwin*, 61.

40. Quoted in Sharp, *Weapon of Moral Power*, 91.

41. This version of events can be found in more detail in Sharp, *Weapon of Moral Power*, 107–12. It was compiled by M. Abdul Qadir Kasure from eyewitness accounts and appeared in *Young India* on 8 May 1930.

42. Gopal, *Lord Irwin*, 69.

43. Sharp, *Weapon of Moral Power*, 113.

44. Ibid., 112, 127.

45. Halifax Papers, British Library, India Collection (hereafter Halifax Papers), shelf mark Mss.EUR.C.152/6, p. 73.

46. Gopal, *Lord Irwin*, 70.

47. Halifax Papers, shelf mark Mss.EUR.C.152/16, p. 81.

48. Sharp, *Weapon of Moral Power*, 118.

49. Gandhi to Irwin, 4 May 1930, cited in Sharp, *Weapon of Moral Power*, 114–18.

50. Louis Fischer, *The Life of Mahatma Gandhi*, 271.

51. Sharp, *Weapon of Moral Power*, 121.

52. Ibid., 125–27.

53. Ibid.

54. Halifax Papers, shelf mark Mss.EUR.C.152/6, p. 195.

55. Sharp, *Weapon of Moral Power*, 132.

56. Ibid., 133.

57. Ibid., 135.

58. Ibid.

59. Ibid., citing the *Chicago Daily News*, 14 May 1930.

60. *Chicago Daily News*, 22 May 1930, cited in Sharp, *Weapon of Moral Power*, 139–41.

61. Ibid.

62. Ibid.

63. Sharp, *Weapon of Moral Power*, 146–56.

64. J. C. Kumarappa, *Young India*, 29 May 1930, cited in Sharp, *Weapon of Moral Power*, 151.

65. Sharp, *Weapon of Moral Power*, 151–61.

66. Ibid., 158.

67. From Malcolm Harley, 13 May 1930. Halifax Papers, shelf mark Mss.EUR.C.152/24, p. 361N.

68. Halifax Papers, shelf mark Mss.EUR.C.152/16, p. 89.

69. Gopal, *Lord Irwin*, 90.

70. Halifax Papers, shelf mark Mss.EUR.C.152/24, p. 251.

71. Ibid.

72. Cited in Sharp, *Weapon of Moral Power*, 165.

73. Krishnalal Shridharani, *War Without Violence*, 21.

74. Halifax Papers, shelf mark Mss.EUR.C.152/25, p. 577.

75. Ram Gopal, *How India Struggled for Freedom*, 397.

76. 29 December 1930. Halifax Papers, shelf mark Mss.EUR.C.152/25, p. 511.

77. Cited in Sharp, *Weapon of Moral Power*, 169.

78. Ibid.

79. Ibid., 172.

80. Ibid.

81. Pattabhi Sitaramayya, *History*, 711.

82. Referring to a firsthand account from Bombay. Halifax Papers, shelf mark Mss.EUR.C.152/16, p. 142.

83. Ibid.

84. Ibid.
85. Sharp, *Weapon of Moral Power*, 185–86.
86. Gopal, *Lord Irwin*, 97.
87. Sharp, *Weapon of Moral Power*, 189.
88. Ibid., 185.
89. See especially the report of British journalist H. M. Brailsford, cited in full in Pattabhi Sitaramayya's *History*, 706, for documentation of this trend.
90. Halifax Papers, shelf mark Mss.EUR.C.152/16, p. 215J and p. 243.
91. *Young India*, 11 December 1930, no. 50.
92. Cited in Sharp, *Weapon of Moral Power*, 205.
93. *Conversations*, 17 and 31 January, respectively.
94. Ibid., 2 February 1931.
95. Ibid.
96. Bose, *Indian Struggle*, 281.
97. Nehru, *Toward Freedom*, 193–94.
98. Halifax, *Fullness of Days*, 149.
99. These were the release of political prisoners and the repeal of repressive ordinances.
100. In Pattabhi Sitaramayya, *History*, 747.
101. *Young India*, 19 March 1931, p. 40.
102. Cited in Tagdish Saran Sharma, ed., *India's Struggle for Freedom*, 106.
103. Mohandas K. Gandhi, *Collected Works of M. K. Gandhi*, vol. 46.
104. Sharma, *India's Struggle*, 471.
105. *Collected Works of M. K. Gandhi*, vol. 47, 502.
106. Ibid., 269–70.

Chapter 6

Denmark: Occupation and Resistance, 1940–1945

The case of Danish resistance to German occupation in the 1940s is unlike any other case examined in this book, and most cases involving nonviolent action in history, in that it occurred as a subordinate conflict within a world war. The story of Danish resistance is largely one of nonviolent sanctions as improvised instruments of social and political defense against the backdrop of World War II. The course and outcome of the wider war obviously must have had a huge bearing on what transpired in Denmark. Our purpose is to identify the role and contribution of nonviolent action in that context.

Precisely because of the complexities inherent in the war setting, the Danish struggle offers rich insights, as long as certain pitfalls are avoided. We must not imagine that "nonviolent action" was a self-conscious category of resistance for Danes who engaged in it. The choice between "resistance" (violent *or* nonviolent) and "diplomacy" (meaning minimal cooperation with the invaders) was the focus of most discussions, as we will see shortly. When resistance was chosen, violent and nonviolent methods were frequently employed side by

Dr. Lennart Bergfeldt served as a research consultant for this case study. Dr. Bergfeldt provided all the primary research from Danish sources and the initial descriptive historical copy. The modifications the authors have made to this material, including all analytical judgments which follow, are their responsibility alone. For a more detailed treatment of these events, please refer to Dr. Bergfeldt's dissertation, "Experiences of Civilian Resistance—The Case of Denmark 1940–1945" (University of Uppsala, Sweden, 1992).

side. Occasionally, when particular means were being debated, such as strikes versus factory demolitions, the merits of nonviolent options were recognized and chosen. Most often, though, the relationship between the two types of methods was more complex. They were mutually reinforcing at some points and not at others. As we go through the case, then, we must not casually attribute consequences to either set of methods without reference to the possible effects of the other.

The evolution of resistance organization and strategy may seem to the reader to be just as haphazard as the selection of means in this case. As a neutral country, Denmark did not expect to be invaded. Danes were forced to devise, debate, and execute strategy while under extreme pressure as the conflict unfolded and in response to a changing international situation. The reader expecting to find a single, coherent fighting organization like the Indian National Congress or Poland's Solidarity in charge of an easily identifiable strategy will be disappointed. But as the case unfolds, what we will see is an increasingly clear picture of how the performance of nonviolent action, while not solely determinative of Denmark's fate, was nonetheless crucial to its relative security and ultimately to its restored status as a sovereign nation.

INVASION: ITS OBJECTIVES AND INITIAL RESULTS

Most Danes awoke on 9 April 1940 to find the invasion and occupation of their country by German forces a fait accompli. The main action had taken place in the predawn hours as part of a simultaneous takeover of Norway and Denmark. Naval authorities in both Britain and Germany had been urging just such an action since October 1939. Whoever accomplished it first would control the Baltic Sea and key Norwegian ports, especially Narvik, through which Swedish iron ore had to pass on its way to the war. Hitler learned of a British plan to move in this direction, and preempted it.[1] For Denmark, this meant that German troops crossed the southern border while naval forces entered its ports and bombers approached the cities. The operation was swift, precise, and virtually irresistible, making a military response futile, though some skirmishing went on for a few hours.

In the hierarchy of German strategic objectives, the military-economic one was no doubt most important. Control of Scandinavian strategic locations and resources was both a positive boon for Germany and a serious blow to its adversaries. A second broad objective would affect the tone and terms of the occupation. That was the desire on Germany's part to create an appearance of normalcy. Politically, Danish cooperation, or at least peaceful acquiescence, would help to limit the damage done to Germany's foreign policy efforts by its invasion of a historically neutral country, one with whom it had only recently signed a mutual nonaggression treaty.[2] Economically, business-as-usual would mean Germany's benefitting from Danish productivity, especially in the area of foodstuffs, which became increasingly important as the war went on. Socially, the longer-term objective of the Nazi theorists, that of an Aryan kinship in an integrated Europe dominated by them, would obviously be advanced if the Danes accepted or endorsed the fact of German control.[3]

As the military invasion was being carried out, the German minister to Denmark, Cecil von Renthe-Fink, presented a memorandum to Danish Minister of Foreign Affairs, Peter Munch. The memorandum blamed Britain and France for the invasion, declaring that Germany had entered Denmark only to protect that country's neutrality. There was no hostile intent, nor were Denmark's territorial integrity or political independence at risk, it said. The German government expected a cooperative response from the Danish government, but in any case would tolerate no resistance, which, it was stated, would lead to unnecessary bloodshed. Along with the memorandum came a list of instructions designed to facilitate the military occupation.[4] A prompt response was demanded. German bombers were in the air over Copenhagen.

Despite the invaders' blandishments to the contrary, Danish territorial integrity had obviously been breached, and there was nothing to be done about it without horrendous cost and the certainty of eventual military defeat. The choice was clear to those members of the government and armed forces who assembled in the king's residence on the morning of the ninth. At six o'clock, less than two hours after the attack had begun, they decided to accede to the German demand for a Danish surrender.

Once the decision was ratified by the entire government, the people of Denmark were informed that: "Under protest the Danish Government has decided to arrange the conditions of the country with regard to the occupation."[5] They were instructed to remain calm, loyal, self-restrained, and not to provoke confrontations with the foreign troops. The objective of this stance would be to " try to secure the Danish people and our country against the disasters of war."[6] The king's personal message to his subjects stated: "During these circumstances, so serious to our country, I urge everyone in town and country to behave in a fully correct and dignified manner, while any rash action or expression can lead to the most serious consequences. God save all of you. God Save Denmark. Amalienborg, on 9th of April. Christian R."[7]

Munch's immediate reply to von Renthe-Fink had been a verbal protest. This was reiterated as a "serious protest" against the attack on a neutral country in an official reply to the German memorandum. The reply indicated that the Danish government "in the given situation decided to arrange the conditions within the country in consideration of the just occurred occupation."[8]

The tone and content of these initial statements were very important, both as a base position from which to negotiate the conditions of occupation and from the perspective of how Denmark's actions would be perceived by others during and after the war, not to mention its eventual status in international law. It was important to establish that the decision to yield was a pragmatic accommodation and was not prompted by ideological sympathy. If the Danish government, in some form, continued to exist, it would do so only to protect its people from the rigors of war and occupation and to continue to assert its own ultimate sovereignty and neutrality.

Both parties in the Danish government at the time of the invasion were vociferously anti-Nazi. During the first day of occupation, a larger provisional coalition government was formed, including all of the principal political parties. The chairman of the new *Rigsdag* (parliament) closed its first day's business with the warning: "Unity must come. Dissension must disappear. Now it is a matter of Denmark, and Denmark alone."[9]

THE EMERGENCE OF A DANISH STRATEGY

The events of 9 April provide a preview of the direction the Danish occupation-defense would take for at least the next three and a half years. With the territorial and military questions having been decided by the invaders' force of arms, a policy evolved for the protection of Danish society and culture. Initially, it was not based on planned resistance of any direct sort, either nonviolent or violent. Rather, it began as a strategy of diplomatic and political maneuvering to limit the damage that might arise from many possible contingencies. Only when adequate and defensible accommodations were not reached with the occupiers would nonviolent obstruction and eventually open resistance come into play.

Peter Munch offered his resignation shortly after the invasion, since neutrality, under his tenure, had not kept the country inviolate. When his continued service was requested, he became the architect and chief executor of the new policy of negotiation-under-protest. Under his guidance, for the first several months of occupation, Danish policy was driven by three objectives: the continued material welfare of Danes, the preservation in principle and restoration in fact of Danish sovereignty, and the ultimate social and cultural survival of Denmark. These objectives required Munch and his government to maintain as strong as possible a bargaining position vis-à-vis the occupiers, to consider carefully how Denmark's actions might be interpreted in international law, and to foster and maintain a united national front to reject Nazism. In attempting to achieve these aims, Munch repeatedly emphasized and exploited the following points:

1. Since Denmark had not fought Germany, it was not a conquered country.

2. The stance of official protest must be maintained to show that the occupation was a breach of neutrality and that German "protection" was a fiction.

3. Anything like a final political settlement between the two countries must therefore be avoided.

4. Negotiations "to arrange the conditions" of occupation must occur out of sheer practical necessity and imply no rapprochement between the adversaries.

5. The very fact of negotiations taking place signified a relationship between sovereign equals.

6. German statements, such as the opening memorandum and the subsequent leaflet, "Roll-call to the Soldiers and People of Denmark," while disingenuous, should be referred to and exploited, to the extent that they paid lip service to Danish independence.

7. Denmark should strive to run its own foreign policy, which
meant refusal to join the war on either side.

In practice, negotiating on this basis was a very precarious business. The Germans would make demands; the Danes would have to
respond. To the extent that the demands were unimportant or
strictly practical, concessions would be made. If the demands seemed
to threaten any of the core objectives, a different pattern emerged.
Munch would play for time, drag out the talks as long as possible,
and obstruct the process, even while maintaining an outward attitude
of cooperation.

Realistically, Denmark was at Germany's mercy in many respects
but still held a few cards of its own. It served the occupiers' propaganda interests to be able to portray Denmark as free. It served their
material interests to control a placid society. Munch's negotiating
policy and style might be a nuisance to the Germans but one that
could be endured if it reaped the desired benefits. For his part,
Munch knew that if he ever pushed too hard, Germany could opt
for alternatives that would be much worse for his country. Either
direct rule or a puppet government, perhaps utilizing the DNSAP
(Denmark's National Socialist Workers' Party), were obvious choices.

The initial Danish approach struck a delicate balance between national self-assertion and subordination. Explaining it to the Danish
population and preserving social and political unity at the same time
was no easy task. While most Danes united behind their government
and king in the face of a common external threat, some, notably of
the extreme right and left, took the crisis as a signal to attack. The
more internal a matter was, the more vulnerable the government's
position, as was the case when in May it came under sharp attack
over its economic policies. By June France had fallen, leaving only
Britain to stand against Germany in the military conflict. Denmark's
position had become even more precarious.

In light of the new situation, under diverse threats and pressures,
the Danish government restructured itself. On 2 July a "parliamentary cooperation committee," later known as the "nine men's committee," was formed. The committee functioned as a parliament-
within-a-parliament, providing a safe forum for difficult internal discussions and an alternative center of power, where the actual parliamentary work was often done and real decisions taken.

The declaration which created the cooperation committee stated that its purpose was to "secure the independence and integrity which have been assured our country and which is the utmost desire of our people." It would produce parliamentary solutions, especially to economic problems, "under the changed conditions," and "secure the best possible cooperation with the nations with which relations are possible, and whose understanding we seek."[10] In keeping with the basic strategy, the declaration mixed a rational adaptability to circumstance with an ultimate sense of national identity, and made deliberate appeals to the occupiers' better instincts and stated intentions.

Shortly after the formation of the committee, the coalition government restructured itself. It was limited to twelve ministers, of whom three were nonpolitical departmental experts. (This was a concession to those who wanted a stronger, technocratic central government.) Munch, who had been heavily criticized by the far right, was replaced as minister of foreign affairs by Erik Scavenius, who had served in that post during the First World War. The whole restructuring effort was designed to create a small, unassailably united government with as wide a popular mandate as possible. This was thought to be the best defense against Nazification of the government or the installation of a puppet government, as well as a hedge against internal dissension, which could only serve the opponents' interests.

Like Munch, Scavenius was a Liberal. He was a career diplomat and a recognized expert on German affairs. His particular addition to the Danish strategy was the notion that the Germans had their own internal contradictions that might be exploited. Not every German was a Nazi. Maybe the best way ultimately to prevent a pro-Nazi solution was to cultivate moderate Germans and to gain their sympathy and confidence. Under his direction, the policy of negotiation-under-protest began to look more conciliatory. It was marked by more verbal accommodation (the inaugural statements of the new government were widely seen as submissive) and more cooperation along economic lines.

The policy came to be called "Scavenian," and it drew considerable criticism as time went by. Still, Scavenius made himself indispensable to both sides, to the extent that he could sometimes get things done by threatening to quit to either. Sometimes, however, his concessions would go too far and provoke demonstrations by outraged Danes. Despite an apparent consensus that getting through hard times with as little damage as possible was the right course, there might well be a point at which the risks of resistance would begin to look attractive next to the exigencies of life under occupation.

INITIAL DANISH MANEUVERS, DEFENSIVE AND OFFENSIVE

While most of the Danish population was shocked into complacency by the invasion, or heard the king's appeal for calm and dignity as a signal to let the government take care of things, there were nonetheless some early manifestations of direct resistance. In their defensive aspects, acts of resistance had the effect of galvanizing the all-important national unity front. In its offensive mode, resistance tended to polarize the situation and challenge not only the occupiers but the Danish government itself and its delicately balanced position. The developing resistance, the changing character of the occupation, and the shifting external tides of the war became the forces shaping official Danish strategy.

The first significant direct action was taken on the day of the invasion itself. Henrik Kaufman, Danish ambassador to the United States, declared himself to be a "free" Danish ambassador and coined the term "Free Denmark," which became both a resistance slogan and the title of an underground newspaper.[11] The phrase also neatly described a significant pattern of action. Two-thirds of the Danish merchant fleet (230 ships) found themselves abroad when the crisis occurred and responded to a BBC appeal to take refuge in Allied ports. Some fifty-six thousand Danish seamen thus came to sail under the Allied flag.[12]

Also at the outset, illicit leaflets began to appear and circulate. Some of these described acts of heroism on the morning of 9 April. One of the more telling documents that surfaced contained the following text:

Ten Commandments for Danes:
1. You must not go to work in Germany or Norway.
2. You shall do a bad job for the Germans.
3. You shall work slowly for the Germans.
4. You shall destroy important machines and tools.

5. You shall destroy everything which benefits the Germans.
6. You shall delay all transports.
7. You shall boycott German and Italian films and papers.
8. You must not shop at Nazis' stores.
9. You shall treat traitors for what they are worth.
10. You shall protect anyone chased by the Germans.
   Take part in the struggle for the freedom of Denmark![13]

Leaflets could be produced by just a few people and yet have a widespread effect on attitudes and morale. The "ten commandments" were reprinted later in the conflict, at times reinforcing official policy.

Some of the most important defensive maneuvers of this early period were the ones which built pro-Danish and anti-German solidarity. There were traditions to build on in this regard. The southern part of Jutland had retained its ethnic identity through cultural resistance and some nonviolent protests despite a period of German rule (1864–1920). Now a latent anti-German sentiment could become a strenuous rejection of Nazism cloaked by a rebirth of Danish values and heritage. The new national feeling manifested itself in some potent symbolic ways. Public songfests featuring traditional Danish music were encouraged, and German cultural events boycotted. Tributes to the king became expressions of national unity, and his birthday in September 1940 became a national festival, with hundreds of thousands of people demonstrating in the streets of Copenhagen.[14] A general attitude of "freezing out" the occupiers took hold, and people wore a variety of small national symbols to show what side they were on.

Attesting to peoples' need to comfort each other in difficult times, the organizational life of the country took an upturn under occupation. The membership of existing groups increased, and new organizations were formed. Notably, the *Dansk Ungdomssamvirke* (Danish Youth Cooperation Movement) was founded as an umbrella organization for the nation's many small youth groups. Along with *De aeldres Råd* (the Council of Elders), it used its activities and organizational resources to develop national cultural resistance to the German presence and ideology.

A more offensive tack was taken in collaboration with Great Britain during the summer and autumn of 1940. In July, Britain's Special Operations Executive (SOE) was founded, with a view to establishing and abetting underground resistance movements in the occupied countries. A Danish section was set up, in the hopes of pursuing intelligence work, sabotage, and eventually serving as an internal front against the Germans in an Allied counterattack. A prominent Danish journalist, Ebbe Munch, managed to be stationed in Stockholm, where he functioned as an SOE agent, passing information from Danish intelligence sources to the British Legation.

By late September, Danish émigrés in Britain had set up *Det danske Råd* (The Danish Council) with the express purpose of assisting England's efforts against Germany. The British also encouraged the idea of a prominent Dane coming to London to promote more active resistance within Denmark. This eventually came to pass when John Christmas Möller, former leader of the Conservative Party, arrived in London in May 1942.

A year earlier, on 22 June 1941, a turning point came in the war. Hitler's forces attacked the Soviet Union. The immediate consequence for Denmark was a new and invasive German demand: that Danish authorities round up and incarcerate all leading members of the Danish Communist Party (DKP).[15] Compliance would mean a serious compromise of Danish constitutional principles. The alternative, however, that the German authorities would do the job themselves, was considered a greater evil. Within a few days the DKP was declared illegal, and some three hundred of its members placed under arrest. Most were later released, but one hundred or so were kept interned in a camp. Two months later, the government banned communist associations and their activities. These measures were more than token concessions. Ostensibly, however, they were carried out to protect Danish communists from direct exposure to the occupiers and were thus arguably consistent with the national strategy.

The DKP moved underground, where it was not without prior experience and resources. There were prearranged hiding places, and some printing equipment was waiting to be used. The latter half of 1941 showed an increase in the number and circulation of clandestine newspapers, for which the DKP was primarily responsible. A principal theme in the new underground press was that the government line of negotiation-under-protest should be dropped in favor of active, offensive resistance. Along with the "free Danes" abroad, especially the Danish section of the SOE, the illegal press was a voice in favor of joining the Allied effort against Germany.

November 1941 saw the first mass demonstrations by Danes against the Scavenian policy. The proximate cause was Denmark's endorsement of the Anti-Comintern Pact, the war alliance binding Germany, Italy, and Japan. This move was seen at home and abroad as another major concession. This was preceded by the delivery of Danish military equipment to the Germans and the sanctioning of a Frikorps Danmark (Danish Free Corps) to aid the Axis effort directly. A five-day-long demonstration in Copenhagen was a bellwether of public sentiment that sooner or later a line would have to be drawn. Following the demonstrations, the cabinet decided where that line would be. If the occupiers demanded anti-Jewish legislation, if they insisted on strict compliance with the Anti-Comintern Pact, or if they tried to enlist Danish troops as belligerents, they would be unequivocally turned down, at whatever risk.[16]

On the other side, German Foreign Minister Ribbentrop gave orders to limit German demands on Denmark to those deemed absolutely necessary. With the Danish Nazis politically isolated and the two-front war going badly, this must be seen as a choice to avoid further confrontation with a resistant population. Pressure for confrontation was building, however, within the growing Danish underground. The first issue of *Frit Danmark* in April 1942 called for an end to the negotiating policy and appealed to the government to take the initiative in open resistance. Since the government still needed more justification to take such a consequential step, the underground had its own two-front situation, resisting an occupier and influencing the Danish authorities to do the same.

In the midst of this tension, the first sabotage groups emerged. In Ålborg a group of youths calling themselves the Churchill Club managed twenty-five acts of sabotage against German materials in a single month. Another group, KOPA (Communist Partisans), began attacking small factories in the Copenhagen area, usually where work for the Germans was being done. In November 1942 the first major sabotage against German supply lines was conducted when a train was derailed between Copenhagen and Elsinore. These actions did little damage to the German effort. It was only much later that sabotage became an important military factor. In 1942, though, it served to force the Danish government to choose between placating its own patriotic underground or the forces of occupation.

In August Germany made two new demands: the death penalty for resistance fighters and greater press censorship. There was no way to square the death penalty, or any threat to Danish jurisdiction in criminal matters, with the avowed objective of protecting society from the occupiers. The government rejected the demand and newly elected Prime Minister Buhl gave a radio address condemning the sabotage campaign. The underground was not impressed. A few days later Christmas Möller, Denmark's most prominent exile, responded on the BBC. He called for more open resistance, including sabotage.

The occupiers now faced a unified popular front, an underground with growing resources and capabilities, and a Danish government which, when forced to choose, had shown itself less rather than more accommodating.

THE GERMAN RESPONSE TO RESISTANCE

These new developments might well have produced an open breach between Germany and the Danish government. There was serious pressure to force a breach, from the German side, in the persons of a newly arrived Chief of Staff, General von Hanneken and Ribbentrop himself. Von Hanneken, arriving on 2 October, advocated direct military rule, repressively enforced. This approach is said to have been rejected by Berlin as too inflammatory, however, in light of the growing resistance.[17] Ribbentrop, after an icy month of no official contacts, summoned Scavenius to Berlin for a stern lecture, blaming his government for the new resistant attitude and demanding changes.

This discussion was then superseded by the appointment of Dr. Werner Best as *Reichsbevollmächtigte* in Copenhagen. Best, an intellectual and an SS[18] officer who had already served in occupied France, was committed to flexibility, pragmatism, and, above all, order, until the military conflict was won. He breathed new life into the precarious Scavenian policy. He believed that this course, and not repression, would most effectively keep resistance, and especially sabotage, to a minimum.

The German ambivalence continued to be mirrored on the Danish side. The latter half of 1942 saw further encroachments on Danish judicial autonomy. Germany persisted in claiming the right to try resistance suspects in German courts martial, threatening a fundamental objective of the negotiations policy. At the same time, the Axis powers suffered military setbacks and began to appear more vulnerable. Both trends argued for a break. The *Rigsdag* and the cooperation committee wished to maintain themselves, nonetheless, as an extra institutional buffer, and so called for parliamentary elections in the spring to reiterate their constitutional authority.

Best chose to support these elections and secured permission from Berlin for them to be held in March. The election campaign was not to be a divisive one over parties, candidates, and issues. It was about the principle of national unity itself, with the mainstream parties wishing to assert their legitimacy by turning out a large vote and further isolating the DNSAP, the Danish fascists. The parliamentarians also sought to distance themselves from the Scavenian executive branch, by insisting that "the election concerns only the parliament which now and in the future shall represent the will of the people."[19]

While the DKP and underground press urged people to spoil their ballots in protest, and the DNSAP and the right-wing Danish Rally contested the election (with pathetically meager results), the Danish Youth Cooperation Movement supported the cooperating parties and worked to turn out the vote. The mainstream parties won 141 out of 149 seats and 94.5 percent of the votes cast in a record 89.5 percent turnout. Best, for his part, experienced a small triumph by having engineered an event which corroborated his view that the Danish Nazis were an embarrassment. He proposed formal withdrawal of German support for the DNSAP, which must also be seen as a victory for Danish cultural resistance.

The inherent tensions in each side's position increased throughout the spring of 1943. The number of sabotage actions steadily increased,[20] encouraged by the still-growing underground press, and supported logistically by the SOE, which by now had established direct contact and cooperation with the DKP. More sabotage meant more trials, which in turn meant more pressure on Danish courts to assert their jurisdiction. The accumulated frustration of three years' occupation, plus the growing perception that the Allies might win the war, added momentum to the cry for creating "Norwegian conditions," that is, conditions of all-out resistance. A British bombing attack on Copenhagen, accompanied by propaganda suggesting that domestic sabotage would best eliminate the need for more of the same, gave the resistance a practical argument as well.

TACTICAL INNOVATIONS LEAD TO A
STRATEGIC SHIFT

Strikes, which usually constitute one of the nonviolent arsenal's more potent weapons, had been notably absent for the first half of

the occupation of Denmark. While the working classes suffered economically during this time, they nonetheless seemed to have judged
direct economic combat unwise. Like the government, they took a
wait-and-see, play-it-safe stance. That stance began to change in the
winter of 1942–1943. When workers struck in the spring and summer of 1943, they did so as part and parcel of the new fighting
mood, in support of political as well as economic objectives.

Strikers' demands in this period included such items as: air raid
warning systems and shelters in the workplace, removal of German
or Nazi sabotage guards from the workplace, and higher wages to
compensate for wartime risks in facilities such as shipyards. At first
the official voice of the trade unions, the Social Democratic Danish
Confederation of Trade Unions, wanted to husband its resources
and move cautiously. The growing influence of the DKP within
unions, and the argument for more direct resistance, however, prevailed, and more strikes ensued.

By July strikes were the focal point of resistance. Along with the
DKP, the Danish section of the SOE broadcast appeals from London
aimed at reducing economic collaboration. In addition to strikes,
workers whose product helped the occupiers were encouraged to
work slowly, badly, or to engage in passive resistance. Sabotage was
also on the increase, and in late July one such act set off a major
political strike in Odense. The same occurred in Ålborg and Esbjerg
a few days later.

The Esbjerg strike set off a fateful wave of strikes known as "the
August insurrection." This lasted some three weeks and involved
thirty-three out of Denmark's eighty-six major towns. The strikes
usually began with a quasi-political labor grievance, spread into more
general "peoples' strikes" or economic shutdowns, and were accompanied by a certain amount of random street rioting. The town-level
strikes came in fits and starts and were never quite total. Communications and transportation systems continued to function.

In response to the August strikes and increased sabotage activity,
Best demanded that convicted saboteurs be sent to prison in Germany. Scavenius flatly refused and countered with a proposal to return to full parliamentary rule. His idea was that a more apparently
legitimate Danish government would be better able to enforce existing laws and control the situation without German interference.[21]
As the two parties reached a stalemate, the German military reasserted itself. Von Hanneken asked the German High Command for
permission to intervene on 22 August.

In a final effort to prevent losing control to the military, Best asked the Danish government for a clear statement of its intent to keep order, "if necessary also by the use of force."[22] The reply reiterated the point that that should be possible if only the occupiers would desist from interfering with the legitimate authorities' efforts.

By the twenty-eighth von Hanneken had taken over. He presented the Danes with a much harsher ultimatum, which required an answer the same day. Von Hanneken demanded that the Danes declare a state of emergency, prohibit meetings and strikes, impose a nightly curfew, censor the press, and impose the death penalty for sabotage.

The Ministry and the Parliamentary Cooperation Committee replied: "An implementation of the German demands will ruin the possibilities of the government to keep the population calm, and the government, therefore, regrets that it cannot consider it defensible to take part in the implementation of such arrangements."[23]

The Danish government had abandoned the policy of negotiations and effectively decommissioned itself. The German military was now in control. It attacked what was left of the Danish military infrastructure. Garrisons and naval bases were assaulted on the morning of the twenty-ninth. War materials were seized, except for some ships that were scuttled by their Danish crews or escaped to Sweden. Twenty-three Danes were killed and nineteen wounded.[24]

For the resistance the situation was largely, but not entirely, simplified. On the one hand, a clear breach had finally occurred, and the underground needn't compete with a constituted government for peoples' loyalty. Efforts could be focused on the external enemy, supported by the growing view that Germany was faring badly in the wider war. The events of August had shown that more people were ready to fight, and in part those events created the situation in which they could do so. But all complications were not resolved. The apparatus of the Danish government did not disappear completely, and a confused state of affairs regarding it persisted throughout the war.

The military state of emergency was predicated on the Hague Convention of 1907, which was not technically applicable since there was no state of war between the two countries. Von Hanneken was in control of policy, but Best was still legally responsible for the occupation. On the Danish side, the king received, but pocketed, his government's official request to resign. So, while neither the king nor his government were functioning, they also continued legally to exist.

A military solution was not an administrative solution. Who would run the country? Best tried to establish a new, more cooperative

Danish government and threatened direct German rule as the alternative. The Danes refused. After all, they had been looking for and
had finally received an out from the negotiations policy. The ministry, as an organ of their government, was now defunct. However,
individual ministers and department heads remained in place, and
requested their civil servants to do so as well. The net result was an
unofficial ministerial network which retained the capacity to resist,
obstruct, and quibble over particular German directives. Foreign
Minister Nils Svenningsen emerged as the chief go-between for the
ministerial group, which later in the new year established a cooperative relationship with the underground, allowing for the state's resources to be channeled directly to resistance efforts and for relief
work.[25]

DECISIVE BATTLE: THE RESCUE OF THE DANISH JEWS

The German authorities in Denmark, up to this point, had been
ambivalent about a possible assault on the Danish Jews, viewing it as
too provocative. By September 1943, however, they had little left to
lose as the situation became polarized. They could probably not have
foreseen, though, the costs of bungling the operation.

At least one informant from within their ranks, G. F. Duckwitz, a
shipping expert stationed in the German Embassy, warned the Swedish government, two Danish Social Democrats, and the Danish ministry of foreign affairs about the impending action. The message was
spread via synagogues and many Jews went underground. By the
time the roundup began on the first and second of October, only a
few hundred Jews were left to be apprehended. The rest, some seven
thousand persons, were in the process of being secreted away to Sweden by means of an improvised illegal transport network.

The scope and complexity of this operation were nothing short of
astounding. The evacuees were taken by boats of all description, but
most commonly fishing boats, across the sound to Sweden. While
existing resistance groups participated, many new ones were formed
for the task, and these typically continued until the end of the war.
It is widely recognized that the threat to the Danish Jews galvanized
the public more than any other single threat and set many Danes on
the path of open and illegal resistance.

There were many related tasks, involving different risks, that contributed to the effort. Temporary hiding places had to be found, ground transport provided to the coast, and contacts had to be made on the Swedish side. Sea transport was crucial, and to this the Danish Coastal Police either turned a blind eye or gave clandestine support. Legal and open protests of the roundup were important too, as they created a diversionary distraction for the German authorities. Virtually all civic organizations and voluntary associations lodged some form of protest, and students struck and participated in all types of activity.

In the end only 472 Danish Jews were taken to be interned on the continent. All but 25 of these survived the war.[26] The now-unofficial Danish authorities maintained contact with these internees and negotiated with the Germans for the right to send them food and medicine. Apart from the value of saving over seven thousand lives, the rescue operation represented a major defeat for the occupiers. Human and material resources shifted to resistance work and remained at the disposal of the underground for the duration of the conflict.

THE ASCENDANCY OF THE FREEDOM COUNCIL

Denmark's Freedom Council was created on 16 September 1943 to fill the vacuum left by the government's withdrawal and to coordinate the new groundswell of resistance actions. It was made up of only seven persons, six of whom represented particular underground organizations. The Freedom Council asserted leadership mainly through the underground press. Despite the fact that no one knew who its members were, its instructions were widely followed. Although it viewed itself as a fighting organization and claimed no political mandate, the Freedom Council did come to fill somewhat the political void created by the government's resignation in August.

In November 1943 the Council issued a pamphlet, "When Denmark is Free Again," which announced the basic resistance program and helped to gain both internal and external recognition. Disavowing all party-political objectives, it called for united action toward a national independence consistent with Denmark's democratic ideals. Furthermore, it called for a postwar judicial regime in which collaborators would be tried and sentenced according to the full rigor of the law.

During late 1943 and early 1944 committees of the Council were formed to oversee and coordinate the key functions of the resistance, including sabotage, the underground press, a judicial committee, and a committee to prepare for the apprehension of traitors. The Freedom Council also came to fulfill a military function. Small armed units had begun to form, and Danish officers released after October went underground to join them. The military committee of the Council became the high command for the emerging resistance army, and in the summer of 1944 changed the long-standing policy of neutrality by placing the resistance army at the disposal of the Allied military chiefs.

The outside world soon accepted the Freedom Council as the official leadership of Danish resistance. Officials in the United States and Great Britain declared the new Danish effort a valuable contribution to the Allied cause, while the Soviet Union received a diplomatic representative of the Council, stressing that it would only deal with "Fighting Denmark."[27] The ultimate recognition came in August 1944, when the Contact Committee was formed to coordinate with the party politicians. An agreement in principle was reached by the turn of the year for the establishment of a liberation government at the end of the occupation, which would be made up half from the resistance leadership and half from the politicians. A joint agreement was also reached to ask Washington, London, and Moscow to recognize Denmark formally as an Ally.[28]

A pattern emerged in which, for the latter half of the war, structure followed function in the Danish resistance under the broad leadership and direction of the Freedom Council. Society itself went progressively underground and reorganized its resources around particular needs.

In the area of underground publishing, some 250 separate papers produced 11 million copies in 1944 and another 10 million in the first four months of 1945; an underground news agency was established; an estimated 3 million copies of three hundred illegal book titles were circulated; and much of this activity was pursued by previously above-ground publishers who had joined the resistance. Printing was frequently done in Sweden and smuggled back into Denmark.

The scope and effectiveness of sabotage groups grew steadily in the last years of the war. Their primary aim was the denial of Danish industrial resources to Germany in its hour of need. Derailment of railway traffic to Germany increased and was simultaneously effective and provocative. Sabotage also came to take on a secondary, defensive aspect. It damaged air facilities, releasing Allied planes from the need to bomb them, sparing Danes the collateral effects of bombing. But the main significance of sabotage was that it moved Denmark credibly and unmistakably into the Allied camp.[29]

While there were plenty of clandestine methods of communication, including special couriers and memorized, coded messages, the normal channels such as telegraph, telephone, and postal services were, by this time, mostly co-opted for resistance purposes. The nationwide escape network, which coalesced at the time of the threat to the Danish Jews, remained active, aiding some twenty thousand refugees during the second half of the war.

Finally, in a complete inversion of the original arrangement, what was left of the ministerial apparatus remained to function as a minimal shield for the population against rough treatment by the occupiers. With the Freedom Council now in charge, government officials played a subordinate, though not negligible, role protesting on behalf of Danish internees and monitoring their well-being. The officials were also able, by their nominal control of various departments, to mislead the Germans as to the real state of Danish productivity in various sectors and limit German exploitation of their society in the waning months of the war.

THE ISSUE OF VIOLENCE

Violence versus nonviolence was never a primary focus of the Danish struggle. The original strategic debate centered on a choice between the negotiations policy of Scavenius and a condition of overt rebellion against the occupation. As the negotiations policy became increasingly untenable, and the policy of overt resistance came to dominate, direct action of all sorts increased, both violent and nonviolent. The complexity of the relationship between these modes of action cannot be avoided. There can be no doubt that both types of methods increased the costs of occupation for the Germans and that both stimulated repressive counteraction, which in turn provoked more resistance of all types.

In the fall of 1943, however, we can see a marked and reciprocal escalation of violent acts on both sides. Sabotage, particularly demolitions, was on the rise, with nearly 100 episodes in October and 151 actions in November.[30] Sabotage groups are particularly vulnerable to penetration and betrayal by paid informants. The resistance in Denmark was no exception. Under the aegis of the Freedom Council, sabotage groups began trying suspected traitors or *stikkere*, and eleven were convicted and executed in December. A total of 350 "liquidations" took place before the end of the war, carried out by special execution squads.

The Freedom Council was well aware that violence could get out of hand. Its directives in late October warned that random sabotage and the shooting of German soldiers could provoke reprisals for no tangible gain. Instead, for the general population, nonviolent obstruction was urged: "all of us must purposefully and untiringly . . . put obstacles in the way . . . deny, delay, and diminish." Violent sabotage was to be reserved for those "who have the courage and the means" and was to be directed "against points of vital importance for the occupation power."[31]

The Germans were not without the resources or the will to fight fire with fire. In addition to some 350 Gestapo officers in Denmark at the height of the conflict, they maintained their own regular police force and about 700 plainclothesmen. Beyond these and the German armed forces themselves, several voluntary organizations carried out repressive action. The most famous of these was the Schalburgkorpset (Schalburg Corps). This group was made up primarily of former members of the Frikorps Danmark and was named for a member who had died on the Eastern front. The Schalburgkorpset included both paramilitary and political operatives, the former numbering 500 to 600. Smaller groups also operated under German direction to conduct terroristic retaliation for Danish sabotage.[32]

The occupiers and their collaborators carried out a variety of repressive measures, including executions, hostage-taking, countersabotage, torture, searches and roundups, and random terror, to counter the escalation of violent action on the Danish side.

From August 1943 until the end of the occupation in May 1945, there were 193 formal executions of Danish citizens. In late 1944, formal executions were replaced by Hitler's orders to shoot to kill saboteurs in action and carry out "clearing murders" in retaliation for the executions of *stikkere* by the resistance movement. Approximately 125 prominent Danes met this fate before the war ended. Although there was less hostage-taking for German security purposes than in many other occupied countries, those who were sentenced to die, but had not yet been executed, often functioned as hostages.

Countersabotage appeared as a major weapon in January 1944 and persisted until the end of the war. As it was often carried out by the Schalburgkorpset, it came to be called *schalburgtage*. Just as sabotage attacked the vital material resources of the Germans, *schalburgtage* attacked the valued public resources of the Danes: theaters, club offices, student facilities, media offices, civic buildings, public monuments, department stores, and dance halls.

In addition to countersabotage, special guards were employed to fight sabotage directly. The Danish authorities, in a 1942 concession, had required certain factories to employ guards. As Danish guards were of dubious reliability, German guard units, often made up of soldiers who had returned from the front, protected air fields, naval facilities, and factories producing war materials. They substantially heightened the risks for the would-be saboteurs.

Gestapo-led searches and torture over the winter of 1943–1944 produced some 600 arrests of resistance fighters and many self-imposed exiles. Some of those arrested were executed, while roughly a third were sent to concentration camps in Germany. About a fourth had played some part in sabotage. Eight saboteurs were shot on sight.

This mutual escalation of activity was matched by a similar escalation of rhetoric. On 4 December 1943, Best announced a policy of "very ruthless counteractions."[33] The Freedom Council replied in an open letter that this course would only strengthen Danish resolve: "Our answer to the German declaration of a ruthless fight therefore is: a ruthless fight."[34] On 30 December Hitler personally ordered a ratio of five clearing-murders for each German or German collaborator killed in occupied countries, although this order was not carried out in Denmark.[35]

In January the politicians judged that things had gone too far. The ministerial department heads met and discussed the possibility of contacting the underground and asking for a cessation of sabotage. No such communication seems to have occurred. The parliamentary cooperation committee did, however, issue a statement condemning the widespread use of political violence, saying that Danes generally did not support it.[36] The Freedom Council rejected this appeal, but there was, nonetheless, a temporary lull in both sabotage and countersabotage from January to April, while the underground invested more energy in building up its army.[37]

In April sabotage occurred at power supply facilities and at factories making engines and other mechanical equipment. Given the increased defenses surrounding such targets, including barbed wire, electrified fences, and armed guards, sabotage groups came to resemble commando units. In June audacious strikes were conducted against an arms factory in Copenhagen and a nearby aircraft components factory. The Germans invoked their whole repertoire of repressive measures in response.

On 24 April, Best had met with Danish newspaper editors to announce that each Danish act of sabotage or murder would result in the execution of an imprisoned resistance fighter. The Freedom Council again replied in an open letter that this attempt to drive a wedge between the public and its resistance leadership could only fail. Danish traditions, they stated, were "diametrically opposed to the Nazi ideology. . . . You can have people to burn, harry and murder. You can imprison and execute. You can try charm or threats. But you will never be able to shatter our will and ability to fight against the power that has plunged the world into war and deprived Denmark of its freedom."[38]

STRIKES AGAIN

In the summer of 1944, the same broad chain of events repeated itself. Intensified sabotage met with intensified repression, which in turn provoked protest strikes. Those strikes cost the occupiers more than the sabotage that was their original concern. Best responded to sabotage actions in Copenhagen in June with a series of restrictive measures that directly impinged on its citizens. The worst was a nightly curfew from 8 P.M. to 5 A.M., beginning on 25 June.

The famous Copenhagen strike began on the twenty-sixth when workers, starting at the Burmeister and Wain shipyard (one of Copenhagen's biggest employers) defied the curfew in a novel way. They left work at 1 P.M., for the purpose of tending their allotment gardens. The garden produce was vital to their families, and as long as the curfew persisted, so did the go-home-early campaign.

As the campaign spread and more people were out on the streets early, skirmishing with patrolling *Wehrmacht* groups ensued. Barricades and bonfires appeared, some arson occurred, and Danish Nazis were harassed. Danish casualties from random shootings began to mount. In their usual role as protective screen, Danish officials who were able to make themselves heard pointed out that the curfew was the cause of the unrest. On the twenty-ninth it was put back to 11 P.M, but the mood of insubordination continued to spread.

No doubt a wave of intensified Allied radio broadcasts, which had accompanied the invasion of Normandy and a new Russian offensive earlier in the month, reinforced the will to fight. By the last day of June, Copenhagen was in a state of general people's strike. The central tramway system shut down; commuter trains went out; telephone workers struck; businesses, workshops, and stores all began to close. Only public utilities, providing water, gas, and electricity continued in operation, along with the dairies.

Best, von Hanneken, and their senior police officer, G. Pancke, now agreed that the harshest measures were called for. Best told Svenningsen, unofficial leader of the department heads, that "German honor had been drawn into the mire, and this would have to be suffered for. . . . The Copenhagen riff-raff would have to taste the whip."[39] On 1 July military reinforcements were brought in, and that evening they took over the utilities and shut them down. The next day a state of emergency was declared. Military units were sent out with orders to fire on any group of more than five persons, and the city was effectively blockaded.

On the morning of Saturday the second, before the last of these actions was completed, the Freedom Council came out in favor of continuing the strike, and unilaterally escalated the demands. The council's leaflet noted that this was the most widespread and widely supported action so far. It had already forced a tactical concession in the reduction of the curfew. Now, the council argued, the struggle should be pressed until the Schalburgkorpset was removed from the country and the state of emergency ended. It appealed for discipline. "Until these demands have been met the strike must continue as before, with determination and solidarity."[40]

The strike did continue, with the population inventing clever ways to circumvent some of the German measures. Alternate supply networks for perishable items and fuel were quickly developed. When gas, electricity, and water were stopped, people obtained water from lakes and cooked on open fires. The blockade was not perfectly effective, so some Copenhageners simply went on holiday in the countryside for the duration. Sympathy strikes in eighteen Zealand and eight Jutland towns also erupted.[41]

The heads of the ministerial departments were the first to understand that the situation could not last indefinitely. They were getting signals that the Germans were ready to mete out heavy punishments. There were even intimations that some sections of the city might be bombed. Whether or not that was true, great hardships were in store as soon as the already limited food supplies ran down. In an attempt to avoid an arduous and bloody confrontation, the officials tried to negotiate a settlement, starting Friday, 1 July. This meant, of course, that they and the Freedom Council were moving in exactly opposite directions.

The Germans were at first unwilling to negotiate, but they too knew that the situation was precarious. Losses in the wider war meant that this was no time to be waging active warfare on civilian populations, and repression seemed to be making the Danes only more militant. On Sunday they agreed to lift the blockade and re-open the utilities. The department heads urged people to go back to work and employers to reopen their businesses, an unlikely development without the active support of the Freedom Council. But the council opted to hold out for all their demands, and on Monday the strike continued at almost full strength.

The Germans retreated on Monday. Implicitly acknowledging that armed force could not control the whole city, they ordered the military patrols and the Schalburgkorpset off the streets. The department heads went back to the Freedom Council later in the day and found them ready to accept a settlement. In a bulletin in which they declared victory, the Freedom Council pointed out that several repressive measures had already been lifted and that fulfillment of their key demand, an end to the curfew, was imminent. Furthermore, the people's strike had proven the effectiveness of popular struggle against violent repression, they claimed, and it should be viewed as "a prelude only to the final fight," for which strength must now be mustered.[42] Within a week the curfew was lifted and the Schalburgkorpset was relocated, not out of the country, but to a small town in Zealand.

The Danish victory in Copenhagen in 1944 restored the status quo ante with respect to the norms of the occupation. It gave the Danes self-confidence, international prestige, and solidarity. It revitalized the strike weapon and made an excellent school for its future use. It was not a cost-free operation for either side. About 100 people died and 600 were severely wounded.

The Freedom Council, in analyzing the outcome, found the people's strike to be a better weapon than sabotage. They also found it "a much more effective weapon than widespread disturbances. The people's strike was decisive—not the barricades or the unrest in the streets."[43] The council now foresaw the possibility of more effective and deliberate use of this weapon.

> As the situation now stands, there can be no doubt that, partly through the Freedom Council and partly, and not the least, through the Trades Unions, we can bring a general strike into force at very few hour's notice, from public offices and departments down to modest messengers. The whole country will come to a standstill when we wish it, and not only that, we can order a general strike in branches of work in the population where it is expedient, and let other branches work normally.[44]

The Freedom Council's new-found control and flexibility were demonstrated in strikes during the balance of the fight and in a new method—premeditated, time-restricted public demonstrations. On 12 July there was a two-minute silence at noon in memory of those who had died most recently in Copenhagen. The same method was employed on 29 August, accompanied by instructions not to provoke street confrontations but to remain dignified while honoring the demonstration. Later in the year, important dates such as the anniversary of the invasion were similarly recognized. Nearly universal compliance with the calls for such displays served mainly to demonstrate that the council commanded the people's loyalty.[45]

When a spontaneous strike began on 14 August in response to the execution of eleven young Danes, the Freedom Council stepped in and declared a one-day strike for the following day. This call resulted in thirty-four towns going out on strike for brief periods over the next ten days.[46] A month later, on 15 September, a strike developed when the Germans broke a critical promise. The Danish authorities had agreed to operate a camp on Danish soil (at Fröslev) on condition that its prisoners would not be removed to Germany. When Danish railway personnel became aware of transfers from this camp to one near Hamburg, they shut down the railway lines near the border and the action soon spread throughout Jutland.

Sensitive to rail transport reliability, the Germans threatened to kill hostages and deport 500 more prisoners if the action did not cease. The Freedom Council responded with a call for a nationwide protest strike which would specifically exclude railways, communications, and public works. Monday the eighteenth saw a strike bigger than that staged by the railway men but averting the dire consequences promised.

The occupation provoked the last and largest strike of 1944 by trying to round up and deport the Danish police force. The police, who had stayed in place throughout the occupation, had dragged their heels when investigating sabotage and other resistance offenses and had frequently ignored or actively abetted the underground movement. They were a major thorn in the occupiers' side, and in September von Hanneken and Pancke, without Best's knowledge, decided to act against them. They succeeded in rounding up only about two thousand police and two hundred and fifty border guards. The remaining seven thousand police went underground. They formed an underground police force and joined groups preparing to arrest collaborators when liberation came.

The resulting strike was the biggest in the history of the struggle. It was centered in Copenhagen but affected all parts of the country. Combined with the earlier action in response to the deportation of prisoners, it affected fifty-eight towns and all of Jutland. Danish Radio News was forced to relocate to Sweden when it refused to broadcast anti-strike propaganda. In comparison to the earlier general strike, in Copenhagen in particular, there was very little street fighting, in accordance with the council's instructions.

This last big strike raised again the question of whether the department heads could serve any further purpose or whether they should resign their positions. Despite pressure from the Freedom Council, Svenningsen and the others decided to issue protests but stay at their posts.

THE LAST LAP

The summer's action took place in anticipation of imminent liberation. But events did not unfold as quickly as people expected. There would be another winter of occupation in store. But it turned out to be relatively quiet, with few mass protests and a general defensiveness and caution prevailing.

There was some hardship. The occupiers appropriated fuel for military purposes. There was also a large influx of refugees and wounded German soldiers, putting a further strain on the system. In terms of food and other amenities, however, Denmark was in better shape than most counties. There was relatively little unemployment, and the black market did not take hold in Denmark as it did in many parts of Europe.

The Allied Command ordered the organized underground to take a defensive stance. The command did not want an open fight in Denmark. Military supplies, dropped by air in significant quantities, were stockpiled, and operations for the final winter were mostly confined to protecting certain resources and key facilities from German exploitation.[47] For example, naval and merchant shipping vessels were sometimes sequestered and brought to Sweden, which prevented both their destruction and their use by the Germans. Such sabotage as was practiced in the final winter was concentrated in Jutland, which was perceived to have increased in strategic value as the war drew to a close.

The department heads became more intransigent with the German authorities and more cooperative with the underground. One of their most important achievements was the complete withholding of labor consignments for the purpose of building fortifications in Jutland.[48] They also continued to work tirelessly on behalf of Danish prisoners abroad, who almost certainly fared better than they would have without these efforts.[49]

The Gestapo's work during this final phase was so effective, including the arrests of some Freedom Council members, that the underground asked for and received British Air Force bombing raids against three key Gestapo headquarters. The raids destroyed archives and impaired further investigation of the underground as well as provided opportunities for some prisoners of the Gestapo to escape. But they also produced casualties in the hundreds.[50]

Liberation came abruptly in the spring. Hitler committed suicide on 1 May and Germany capitulated in Denmark, Holland, and northwest Germany on the fourth.

In Denmark, church bells rang and flags flew, while the underground police units began rounding up collaborators and German henchmen. They interned approximately twenty-one thousand persons, some of them for their own protection against lynching.[51] Talks began between the old ministerial government operatives and the Freedom Council about the new government. After long negotiations, and in accordance with their previous agreement, an interim government was formed consisting of nine representatives of the mainstream political parties and nine participants in the resistance movement, all former Freedom Council members. A Social Democrat, Vilhelm Buhl, became prime minister.

There were some diehard occupation forces who fought in the streets against the Danish units charged with their apprehension, and some regular German military units would not surrender to their Danish counterparts but awaited the arrival of British troops. On the whole, however, the transition to peacetime was remarkably smooth.

The tensions between those Danes who had supported the negotiations policy and those who had resisted at an early stage began to work themselves out in predictable ways. People who felt unjustly treated by the judicial system and the retroactive laws against treason portrayed themselves as having followed the demands of the Scavenian line. The hard-line resistance types, on the other hand, quickly became disillusioned with the return to normal politics, having hoped for some radical changes in Danish political life.

When elections were held in the fall, broad questions of social and economic policy dominated the agenda, and the resistance movement did not have a major influence on the outcome. The communists won 15 additional seats in the *Rigsdag* (totaling 18 out of 149 seats), but the traditional politicians quickly regained control of the government, and Denmark began in earnest to put the war in the past. The most significant long-term change resulting from occupation by Nazi Germany was the reversal of Denmark's historic policy of neutrality.

ANALYSIS

Outcome of the Campaign

The Danish campaign of resistance to German occupation ended in victory. Though crucial, nonviolent sanctions were not the sole weapons. The success of Germany's other wartime enemies was obviously the critical factor in Denmark's liberation. Nevertheless, nonviolent resistance achieved significant victories when it came to protecting Danish citizens from the rigors of occupation.

PRINCIPLES OF DEVELOPMENT

Principle 1: Formulate Functional Objectives

The nonviolent protagonists conformed to this principle.

Two reasonably distinct periods were each dominated by a different ultimate objective, requiring somewhat different strategies and tactics. For the first three years, the agreed objective was simply the defense of Danes from the worst effects of occupation. For the last two, it was to act offensively against the Germans, less to eject them than to be seen as a factor in the Allied cause, negating the need for offensive Allied actions in Denmark.

Both policy objectives were functional, encouraging appropriate nonviolent sanctions. Strategic objectives were also highly functional, leading to valuable tactical encounters, such as the rescue of Danish Jews and the assault on some of the harsher measures of occupation. Internal struggle among advocates of different policies, however, consumed a great deal of time and energy. It is possible that a greater consensus about how to respond to the German occupation might have led to more effective resistance at each stage. Perhaps consensus would also have speeded the transition from a defensive to an offensive posture.

Principle 2: Develop Organizational Strength

The nonviolent protagonists conformed to this principle.

Denmark was a comparatively cohesive and well-organized society when the occupation began. The symbols of the nation and its democratic tradition, the king and the *Rigsdag,* were immediately available as rallying points and symbols of legitimacy. Because these elements performed well, the struggle was viable from the start. The Danish exhibited a high degree of ability to respond to specific challenges, to conceal, control, and motivate.

Functional leadership was provided first by the Cooperative Committee, then during the second phase by the Freedom Council. Each, for most of the period of its influence, had the requisite authority and efficiency to direct the struggle. The requirements of an operations corps in this instance were met by such groups as the youth associations and the underground DKP, which, owing to its own history, had experience in clandestine organization.

The populace at large was highly motivated and intelligently engaged. When mass participation was needed, it was forthcoming. General strikes showed an unusual degree of cohesion and participation. There were ties to external organizations (the Allied Command, the SOE, the BBC), which were helpful, though in no way exclusively nonviolent organizations.

Principle 3: Secure Access to Critical Material Resources

The nonviolent protagonists conformed to this principle.

As in the *Ruhrkampf*, resources in Denmark were a big part of the opponents' objective. The question with regard to this principle, however, is whether the Danes had what they needed to fight the occupiers. We find that most of what they needed was within their means, while protecting the overall resource base became a cat-and-mouse game with the Germans.

Two important methods for resupplying the struggle were improvised in Denmark. First, after 1943 when ministerial leadership was no longer key to the struggle, the ministers did what they could to reroute important resources to those underground organizations now in charge. Second, Allied forces became a source of material support for the underground.

There is also evidence of resource stockpiling for the population at large as a material hedge against repression. By 1943 most communications systems were co-optable by the resistance. The underground press developed the capability to publish and distribute annually over 10 million copies of two hundred and fifty different newspapers.

Principle 4: Cultivate External Assistance

The nonviolent protagonists conformed to this principle.

It would be difficult to overemphasize the relevance of this principle to the Danish case, given the context of the Second World War. The evolution of the conflict for Denmark was largely determined by the timing of the Nazi defeat. Therefore, collaboration by all anti-German forces, civilian and military, had a cumulative and beneficial effect. In this sense the war itself ensured that external assistance would be forthcoming.

Yet the relative importance of direct help from the outside in Denmark's case is hard to assess. Having to conduct a war on many fronts diluted the attention that Germany was able to give Denmark. Arguably Germany's preoccupations elsewhere defined the possibilities for Danish strategy more than any specific Allied intervention.

Still, specific outside assistance was also useful. Consistent with its own interests, England took early responsibility for supplying both intelligence and critical material support for the Danish resisters. Sweden's cooperation was pivotal in many operations, and especially in the great rescue of Jews in 1943. Once there was a Danish section of the SOE, the Allied High Command responded to the needs of the resistance, for example, by suspending air raids once factory sabotage took hold.

Principle 5: Expand the Repertoire of Sanctions

The nonviolent protagonists conformed to this principle.

The Danes performed extremely well, even though they were forced to do so under pressure and needed to improvise most of their tactics. The repertoire included many creative sanctions along the "cultural front," forms of economic and political noncooperation, especially stalling, and various strikes and work stoppages, which were consciously (and correctly) evaluated and adjusted during the heat of battle.

Since the opponents' objectives often create tactical opportunities, it is worth focusing on them here. Normalcy was important politically to the Germans, and methods of noncooperation are ideally suited to deny normalcy. Secure lines of supply were vital to the German war effort, so that factory sabotage and strikes were methods that took on direct relevance. Cultural hegemony, albeit a subordinate objective, was again something that could be resisted at low cost with a high yield in terms of resistance unity.

Finally, during the first phase of the conflict, political noncooperation was used adroitly on behalf of specific objectives rather than invoked as an indiscriminate style of resistance. Leaflets like the "Ten Commandments" were used with skill and deliberation expressly to develop the repertoire. Other sanctions, like the "go home early" campaign against curfews and time-restricted public demonstrations made clever use of special opportunities.

PRINCIPLES OF ENGAGEMENT

Principle 6: Attack the Opponents' Strategy for Consolidating Control

The nonviolent protagonists conformed to this principle.

The strategy for consolidating control rested on two pillars: legitimacy for the German occupation to produce normalcy and repression to produce compliance. Both were successfully challenged.

The Danes may have persisted with the Scavenian policy for too long, but it undeniably had the desired effect, namely, to keep the Germans off-balance and indecisive on the question of repressive measures. The Germans concluded that if some Danes would play ball, why not encourage them? The Germans knew that violent repression would not help Scavenius' credibility, which in turn would not help German legitimacy. Still, the Germans had to wonder whether certain Danes were really collaborating with them or distracting them from achieving better control.

This conundrum set the Germans up for a mistake in their control strategy: they allowed the election of 1942 to take place. They failed to realize that the results would lead to a consolidation of relatively nonpartisan leadership for the Danes, leading to more effective and unified Danish decisions as the fight went forward. An abrupt shift to a policy of repression, from efforts to produce normalcy, made the repression appear clumsy.

The Draconian measures of 1944 became opportunities for resistance. The strategy for control itself became a vulnerable target, which is the ideal manifestation of this principle. The Danes not only subverted the control but also won some important social objectives in the process.

Principle 7: Mute the Impact of the Opponents' Violent Weapons

The nonviolent protagonists only partially conformed to this principle.

The "getting out of the way" dimension of this principle is highly in evidence, reaching its zenith with the rescue of the Danish Jews, but also with other rescue operations, such as those of foreign pilots. Stalling and creating the illusion of compliance are other methods of avoiding violent repression and were hallmarks of the Danish resistance.[52]

Sabotage and executions by the resistance drew more violent repression than any other factor. In textbook fashion they became the excuse or rationale for Germany's expanding coercive measures to preserve order, including retaliatory bombings of public places such as theaters, social clubs, and civic buildings. Neither was the Danish violence successful in creating hesitations or subversion among the German troops.

Danes supported victims of violence and also did a good job garnering alternative foodstuffs to ensure that people did not go hungry. Consequently, the civilian population recuperated quickly from retaliatory blows while preserving anti-Nazi unity. The resistance was also quite effective in making the Germans indecisive about the value of repression. For example, one of the points at issue in the Copenhagen peoples' strike was the opponents' violent weapons, including the Schalburg Corps and military patrols. When the Germans withdrew, rescinding the curfew, they implicitly acknowledged that their repression had become impotent, at least in that encounter. This was a tremendous victory for the Freedom Council, with obvious ramifications on other fronts for shielding the citizens from additional violence.

Principle 8: Alienate Opponents from Expected Bases of Support

The nonviolent protagonists conformed to this principle.

Again, the wider war intrudes on our analysis of the Danish-German confrontation. Sides were more or less chosen up by the April invasion and occupation. There were hardly any unidentified external sources of German support to undermine.

However, existing bases of German support within Denmark were vulnerable, including the occupying troops, Danish Nazis, and moderate Danish bureaucrats. The complete isolation and negation of the Danish Nazis as a relevant factor in the conflict was a triumph, and illustrates this principle well. A large part of the success was the result of political discipline, especially after the 1942 election ensured that moderates did not, indeed, become collaborators.

As in several other cases, there is little evidence of a conscious attempt to undermine troop reliability. Given the wider war, there was probably too much polarization for this to be a viable option, except in special encounters with individual soldiers.

Principle 9: Maintain Nonviolent Discipline

This principle is not supported in the Danish case because of the unique circumstances of World War II. The occupation of Denmark was not an isolated conflict, so the complexities of the surrounding violent action require additional analysis.

In the early phase, the king's call for orderly and nonprovocative behavior had some of the effects envisioned in the principle. However, nonviolent discipline reached a point of diminishing returns as the Danes' problem became how to conduct sufficient resistance against the Germans in ways that would signal the Allies that the Danes were unambiguously on their side.

Unlike its effects in many other campaigns, violent sabotage in this instance was not necessarily counterproductive to strategic nonviolent conflict. Again this is because a much larger conflict was raging simultaneously throughout Europe. Certain violent sabotage by the Danes ended up having worthwhile net effects. For example, factory demolitions forced the Germans to evoke harsh countermeasures, which were no worse than the damage the Allied air strikes might have inflicted in the absence of sabotage. The German response also became the trigger for most of the large-scale strikes, contributing to a radical diminution in the level of repressive violence. Eventually the Danish underground came to appreciate that these strikes were the best arrow in their quiver. As the end of the conflict drew near, strikes were correctly viewed as a more powerful and less costly tool than sabotage.

PRINCIPLES OF CONCEPTION

Principle 10: Assess Events and Options in Light of Levels of Strategic Decision Making

The nonviolent protagonists conformed to this principle.
Immediately after the German invasion, there was a rudimentary

plan and an official body charged with making decisions. Highly provocative violent or nonviolent encounters requiring German retaliation were kept to a minimum. This was implicit in the Scavenian policy of protecting society rather than confronting the occupiers.

The challenge to this approach came in 1943 as the Germans escalated demands and pressure through threats and repression. Danish policy had to be reevaluated. An informal reassessment took place and a new plan emerged. The ultimate objective shifted from protection of Danish civilians and the defense of social and economic structures to the ejection of the occupation and to clarifying the country's position for the outside world. The Freedom Council was successful in bringing subordinate decisions into line with this new focus.

Principle 11: Adjust Offensive and Defensive Operations According to the Relative Vulnerabilities of the Protagonists

The nonviolent protagonists conformed to this principle.

The appropriate defensive adjustments exhibited by this case include: the emphasis, when needed, on rescue operations; the peoples' strike to contest harsh measures; workplace actions (in the sense that they were a functional substitute for, and therefore defense against, air raids); and disguised noncompliance, all of which had precisely the intended effects.

There were also many offensive adjustments designed to attack points of vulnerability. The Germans had a limited military commitment in Denmark, given the wider war. Mass actions were offensive in that they stretched repressive capacity to the breaking point. The Achilles' heel of the occupation was its need for normalcy, which was denied consistently when the Danes were on the offensive. The appearance of normalcy was, of course, exploited by the Danes in the early phase as defensive cover. Later on, such techniques as time-restricted demonstrations allowed for swings from offense to defense and back again.

Principle 12: Sustain Continuity Between Sanctions, Mechanisms, and Objectives

The nonviolent protagonists conformed to this principle.

During the first phase of the occupation, good continuity was achieved between the desired outcome (protection), the appropriate

mechanism (accommodation), and sanctions (political noncooperation, negotiation, and hidden noncompliance). There was no expectation that some form of conversion would move the Nazis out. It
was also understood that the Allies would be critical to German defeat. In phase two, the Scavenian policy lost its effectiveness under
the pressure of more extreme demands and harsher repression. The
national dialogue led to the identification of new objectives. In relation to these, more coercive weapons came into play along with a
more aggressive sense of what could happen to the opponent. The
principle of continuity was sustained, this time not by Scavenius but
by the Freedom Council.

NOTES

1. Sir Basil Liddell Hart, *History of the Second World War*, 53; David Littlejohn, *The Patriotic Traitors*, 9–10.
2. John Danstrup and Hal Koch, *History of Denmark* (in Danish), 14:35,
55; Werner Rings, *Life with the Enemy*, 25.
3. This was clearly a lesser objective, which would presumably come
about voluntarily after the anticipated *Endsieg*, or final victory.
4. Danstrup and Koch, *History of Denmark*, 14:56, 75.
5. Ibid., 14:73; Jorgen Haestrup, ed., *Occupation 1940–1945* (in Danish),
25. All translations by Lennart Bergfeldt.
6. Ibid.
7. Ibid. Christian X of Denmark often signed his communications "Rex"
or "R" for the Latin "king."
8. Danstrup and Koch, *History of Denmark*, 14:56, 75.
9. Ibid., 74; H. S. Nissen and H. Poulsen, *On the Basis of Danish Freedom*
(in Danish), 19; Ulrich Poch, "Anpassungspolitik," 249.
10. H. S. Nissen, *1940: Studies in the Policy of Negotiations* (in Danish),
197–98, 453, 598.
11. Jorgen Haestrup, *Secret Alliance*, 2:200.
12. Haestrup, ed., *Occupation 1940–1945*, 133.
13. Leo Buschardt et al., eds., *The Illegal Press 1940–1945: An Anthology*
(in Danish).
14. Haestrup, *Occupation 1940–1945*, 174.
15. Ibid., 96.
16. Danstrup and Koch, *History of Denmark*, 14:129; Poch, "Anpassungspolitik," 277.
17. Ibid., 284.
18. Rings, *Life with the Enemy*, 49. "SS" refers to the *Schutzstaffeln*, the Nazi
elite group for paramilitary struggle and terror.
19. Haestrup, *Occupation 1940–1945*, 217.
20. Hans Kirchhoff, *August Revolt, 1943* (in Danish), 1:173; Haestrup, *Occupation 1940–1945*, 222.

21. Kirchhoff, *August Revolt, 1943*, vol. 2, chap. 11; Ulrich Poch, *Der Dänische Widerstand*, 92.

22. Kirchhoff, *August Revolt, 1943*, 2:397.

23. Ibid., 2:443.

24. Haestrup, *Occupation 1940–1945*, 52.

25. Jorgen Haestrup, *For the Good of the Country* (in Danish), 21:71.

26. The camp they were taken to was Theresienstadt in Czechoslovakia.

27. Haestrup, *Secret Alliance*, 3:65.

28. Haestrup, *Occupation 1940–1945*, 88.

29. Ibid., 157.

30. Poch, *Der Dänische Widerstand*, 177.

31. Ibid., 172, quoting from the proclamation of the Freedom Council.

32. Haestrup, *Occupation 1940–1945*, 238.

33. Ibid., 67; and Poch, *Der Dänische Widerstand*, 178.

34. Ibid.

35. Ibid., 188.

36. Haestrup, *For the Good of the Country*, 1:341.

37. Haestrup, *Secret Alliance*, 2:159.

38. In Haestrup, *Occupation 1940–1945*, 67.

39. Haestrup, *For the Good of the Country*, 1:516.

40. In Poch, *Der Dänische Widerstand*, 281.

41. Haestrup, *Occupation 1940–1945*, 122.

42. Poch, *Der Dänische Widerstand*, 264.

43. Ibid., 281.

44. This statement by Herman Dedichen, contact person from the Freedom Council to the leading politicians, is quoted from Haestrup, *Secret Alliance*, 3:32.

45. Ibid., 2:352.

46. Haestrup, *Occupation 1940–1945*, 120, 122.

47. Ibid., 162–64.

48. Haestrup, *For the Good of the Country*, 2:149.

49. Ibid., 2:161–62, 252.

50. Haestrup, *Occupation 1940–1945*, 74.

51. Ibid., 80, 96; Danstrup and Koch, *History of Denmark*, 14:325.

52. This type of activity is commonly called "Schweikism," in reference to Jaroslav Hasek's *The Good Soldier Svejk* (Schweik), whose hero is its exemplar.

Chapter 7

El Salvador: The Civic Strike of 1944

The presidency of General Maximiliano Hernández Martínez lasted longer than any other in El Salvador's history. It began in December 1931, after a military coup removed Martínez' predecessor, and lasted until May 1944, when Martínez withdrew from office in the face of a civic strike which followed on the heels of an abortive violent uprising. His regime was popular at the outset because its economic programs and populist gestures offered something to every segment of the population, but it was also a dictatorship which concentrated power in the hands of the president and his small personal following. Broad initial support turned eventually to acquiescence in his rule that had to be reinforced by a variety of coercive means.

He maintained control over the armed forces by placing loyal supporters in key positions. A notorious spy system was coupled with a form of blackmail, putting officers caught in any financial transgressions on notice that the evidence against them would remain in the president's desk for future reference. Under a 1935 revision of the military code, subversive activities became punishable by death.

The armed forces ruthlessly repressed a communist-led peasant

Dr. Patricia Parkman served as a research consultant for this case study. Dr. Parkman provided all the primary research from Spanish sources and the initial descriptive historical copy. The modifications the authors have made to this material, including all analytical judgments which follow, are their responsibility alone. For a more detailed treatment of these events, see Dr. Parkman's excellent study, *Nonviolent Insurrection in El Salvador* (Tucson: University of Arizona Press, 1988).

uprising at the beginning of Martínez' regime in January 1932. Credible estimates of the number of people who were summarily executed range from ten thousand to thirty thousand. While Martínez obviously was no stranger to political violence, he never resorted to it on this scale again. Some people suffered long and arbitrary imprisonment, however, and some prisoners were physically maltreated and reportedly died at the hands of the authorities.

The state of siege which began during the 1932 insurrection continued throughout the Martínez era. A press law enacted in April 1933 made editors of all types of literature liable for prosecution for printing "willful criticism of officials and public employees, as well as . . . matter subversive of the existing social order."[1] The government permanently suppressed some periodicals and temporarily suspended the publication of others, including two respected San Salvador dailies. At least four newspaper editors suffered exile, and one was summarily, though briefly, imprisoned.

Labor unions were forced underground, and workers' mutual aid societies functioned under police surveillance. The University of El Salvador lost its autonomy in 1938 when key appointments became the prerogative of the president who proceeded to staff it with his supporters. Two years later the state rescinded the university's right to authorize individuals to practice the liberal professions. The government suppressed organizations of university and high school students, and finally even the bar association.

The only recognized political party which functioned during the Martínez era was the president's own *Partido Nacional Pro-Patria* (hereafter Pro-Patria), whose members were primarily public employees and others whose jobs depended on the goodwill of the government. The government-sponsored *Reconstrucción Social* (Social Reconstruction), which "purported to be comprised of workers 'from the shops and the fields' " and to "deal with unemployment and related social problems,"[2] served to keep workers in line and mobilize political support for the president.

After the 1933 election the National Legislative Assembly consisted only of administration supporters, and a critic complained that no bills even came before it without the president's prior approval.[3] Martínez further augmented the traditional powers of the presidency by suppressing the autonomy of municipal governments. Mayors became appointees of the national executive, and the municipalities lost their separate sources of revenue.

Government functionaries and paid informants monitored private expressions of opinion, and the president's secret police force was "reported to be the best in Central America."[4]

These methods of control undoubtedly contributed to Martínez' ability to maintain his office. Near the close of the term for which his predecessor had been elected, he handed the government over to his minister of war and ran for a term of his own. He was elected without opposition in 1935. Under the 1886 constitution in force at the time, he could not legally serve beyond the end of his term in 1940. In 1939, however, following procedures which critics condemned as illegal, the National Legislative Assembly decreed a new constitution. This constitution extended the presidential term to six years, preserving a long-standing ban on reelection except for the period from 1 March 1939 to 1 January 1945, for which the Assembly gave itself power to elect the president, and then promptly elected Martínez.

OPPOSITION DEVELOPS

Some opposition to Martínez' rule had always existed. Organized urban workers resented the curtailment of their rights. The Communist Party, which began to rebuild itself immediately after the disaster of 1932, was a consistent enemy of the regime. And between 1934 and 1939 dissident military officers were accused of at least four plots against the Martínez government.

The first significant defection of Martínez supporters came when the president's intention to seek a third term became apparent. The constitutional principle of "alternation in office" was one to which the Salvadoran elite attached great importance. Several of the president's most able and respected collaborators, including members of his cabinet, resigned over this issue. The attack on the university in the same year brought students into active conflict with the regime.

Opposition grew over the next four years. Some observers thought that the caliber of Martínez' associates declined as he surrounded himself with "yes-men" and refused to listen to anyone else. This restricted opportunities for professional white collar people who also objected to dictatorship in principle. Limited opportunities for promotion and low salaries alienated junior officers in the armed forces. When El Salvador entered World War II on the side of the Allies, it began to be flooded with U.S. propaganda promoting democratic values, boosting the legitimacy of those advocating democracy for Salvadorans. And the government's economic policies increasingly alienated the business community and the landowning and financial elite.

Finally, in 1943 the accumulated resentment, frustration, and fear of various segments of the population found a focus. Martínez intended to have the constitution amended again to remain in office beyond the term for which the National Legislative Assembly had elected him in 1939. Critics of the government looked on in dismay as a well-orchestrated campaign led up to the election of a new constituent assembly in early 1944, and the election of Martínez to a new term which began on 1 March of that year.

Nonviolent sanctions had been used with moderate success in Salvadoran politics before the Martínez era. Student political protests, including strikes, first appeared in 1890. Labor unions which organized and sometimes won strikes emerged in the 1920s, building on a heritage of worker associations going back to the mid-nineteenth century. Market women, supported by the banks, demonstrated against changes in currency values in 1922, leading to the resignation of the minister of finance. Women also marched for a reform presidential candidate of that era. In 1917 students led a protest against increased trolley fares, and twelve years later commuter buses were boycotted. In 1930 simultaneous boycotts of electric power by subscribers in half a dozen cities impelled fifty power companies to reduce their rates. When the depression left many agricultural workers without jobs and depressed wages by more than 50 percent, the leading labor federation brought eighty thousand demonstrators to San Salvador. Workers' demonstrations in city and country continued until the Martínez regime imposed the state of siege.

The first significant resistance directed at the Martínez regime itself came from San Salvador journalists. Having failed in their campaign to prevent passage of the restrictive 1933 press law, they suspended publication of the capital's newspapers for nine days of mourning. Similarly, when the university lost its autonomy in 1938, the rector resigned in protest and the students went on strike. Continuing student discontent found expression in *veladas* (theatrical performances poking fun at officialdom) and in a satirical magazine. A series of committees founded on one pretext or another served as cover for anti-Martínez activity. One, ostensibly devoted to sports, seized upon the fall of Paris in 1940 to organize the first public demonstration against the president, disguising an attack on his generally recognized fascist sympathies as a protest against Nazi aggression in Europe.

The war years also saw the formation of a number of anti-Axis organizations which provided a meeting ground for opponents of the dictatorship in El Salvador and contributed to the diffusion of democratic ideas. Of these, the most enduring and significant was *Acción Democrática Salvadoreña* (Salvadoran Democratic Action, hereafter ADS) founded in 1941 by a group which consisted largely of professional men, including former high officials of the Martínez government. ADS held two public meetings, at which the speakers attacked the Martínez regime and then went underground.

A MIXED STRATEGY EMERGES

By late 1941 ADS had set up two commissions to carry out anti-government activities. One of them openly published statements and undertook legal action. The other worked clandestinely, making contacts and producing subversive literature, and helped form with other unidentified people a group variously known as the Executive Committee of Opposition, Executive Committee of the Revolution, and Civil Committee which, sometime in 1943 if not earlier, began to prepare for violent insurrection.

Other key participants in the conspiracy came from the Mortgage Bank, which was the most important of the semi-public financial institutions created by the Martínez regime. A few student and labor organizations and the Communist Party probably played minor roles.

In mid-1943 the opposition launched an unprecedented offensive. The strategy embraced several lines of action which unfolded while plans for the violent insurrection moved forward. These included propaganda, a legal challenge to the president's continuation in power, and appeals to the other American republics, particularly the United States. All of these measures were aimed at pressuring Martínez to permit the election of a successor, while at the same time winning sympathy for an insurrection in the event that he remained obdurate.

The campaign opened with a barrage of anonymous leaflets (from June to September) which announced the existence of an organized opposition, presented its program, and appealed for support. The first leaflet proclaimed the platform of a Salvadoran Democratic Front, which promised to reestablish the constitutional principles of 1886, along with reforms necessary to restore the basic freedoms of thought, speech, press, assembly, travel, and property. In July an unsigned "Manifesto to the Salvadoran People" demanded a public declaration by Martínez that he would not seek a fourth term, that he would dissolve the Pro-Patria Party, schedule elections, and reestablish freedom of the press. Within a month, "reliable sources" estimated that over ten thousand copies of this manifesto had been distributed.[5]

In October some 300 people, many of them prominent citizens, signed a petition to the Supreme Court which challenged the constitutionality of a 1941 decree restricting political organizations and asked the court to declare it null and void. The publication of the petition created a sensation in San Salvador. The Supreme Court rejected the petition, but opponents of Martínez took heart from the fact that the court felt it necessary to respond at all. A student group organized a demonstration, ostensibly in support of the United Nations, on 11 December which attracted some 400 participants.

Meanwhile opposition leaflets proliferated, and the press carried on a continuing "guerrilla campaign" of pinpricks at the administration.[6] Innumerable articles and brief quotations extolling liberty and condemning tyranny appeared under the names of such worthies as Salvador de Madariaga, John Milton, Simón Bolívar, Winston Churchill, and Domingo Sarmiento. When a contestant in a radio quiz show failed to define "democracy," an editorial innocently asked, "but is it possible that we don't know what democracy is?"[7] and recommended a program of civic education. Criticism of fascist practices in Argentina subtly attacked dictatorship at home. All three of the opposition dailies of San Salvador displayed their contempt for the process leading up to the revision of the constitution by declining to print a single word about it. Behind the scenes, dissidents attempted unsuccessfully to mobilize international pressure against Martínez' continuation in power.

The government tried, with no great success, to repress the agitation. It imposed prior censorship on the press, imprisoned some opposition leaders, and harassed others. Meanwhile, anti-Martínez forces within the army had also formed a committee, with which the civilian Executive Committee reached an agreement around the end of 1943, designating a commander for the military uprising and a civilian-military junta to take over the government until a new president could be elected.

THE VIOLENT INSURRECTION
AND ITS AFTERMATH

The violent insurrection began on 2 April 1944. It proved an unmitigated disaster, characterized by overconfidence as well as mutual distrust among the principals. The fighting ended by the morning of 4 April with all of the rebel leaders either captured or in flight.

The incident might have been forgotten were it not for the government's response. Martínez declared martial law throughout the country and imposed a curfew on San Salvador for some weeks following the revolt. The police required persons traveling to other parts of the country to obtain safe conduct passes and killed a number of people found on the street during curfew. Several social clubs were shut down, and labor organizations ceased to function.

In a thorough and vindictive crackdown on suspected opponents of the president, the director of the military school received orders to dismiss six cadets related to persons implicated in the insurrection. The U.S. Embassy heard reports that "no person who signed the petition to the Supreme Court" could get a permit to enter or leave San Salvador and that Martínez had issued orders that none were "to be permitted to register deeds or issue any other legal or medical document," which, the ambassador commented, would "destroy the livelihood of many of the professional classes."[8] The police searched houses without warrants, and government agents investigated withdrawals from bank accounts, apparently in an effort to catch financial contributors to the uprising.

A new wave of arrests resulted in the detention of a number of prominent citizens. Some newspaper owners and journalists were also imprisoned, while others went into hiding or found asylum in foreign embassies, with the result that the three opposition dailies of San Salvador all suspended publication from 2 April until after the resignation of Martínez.

This was not all. Of all the military officers and civilians caught plotting against Martínez during the 1930s, only one had been executed. In contrast, the Extraordinary Council of War (impaneled to try the insurrectionists of 2 April) condemned ten officers to death within hours after it began its proceedings on 9 April. The next morning citizens of San Salvador, just returning from their Easter holiday, could hear the sound of the firing squad at work in the cemetery. In the next two weeks the Council of War sentenced twenty-five more officers and nine civilians to death, most of them in absentia. Three officers and one civilian were subsequently shot, making a total of forty-three death sentences and fourteen known executions. Moreover, it was widely believed that some prisoners died at the hands of the authorities without benefit of judicial proceedings. Numerous tales of atrocities and general accusations of maltreatment of prisoners circulated.

The violence of the repression inspired widespread fear, but it also solidified opposition to Martínez. Most significantly, it aroused lower-class Salvadorans, the group least committed to opposition before the insurrection. At the end of April, the U.S. military attaché reported that "market people, shopkeepers and civilians on the street are openly decrying the executions and tortures."[9] Members of the clergy joined in the general effort to save fugitives, as citizens of all ranks, from market vendors to the archbishop of San Salvador, pleaded for an end to the executions.

On 17 April the diplomatic corps as a group visited Martínez to urge that he adopt a policy of clemency toward the rebels. From beyond the borders of El Salvador, the Venezuelan Chamber of Deputies, Latin American labor leader Vicente Lombardo Toledano, and a group of Latin American physicians then resident in Baltimore, Maryland, sent similar petitions. Editorials attacking the bloodbath appeared in Panamanian, Venezuelan, and Ecuadoran newspapers, and no less a celebrity than the Chilean poet Pablo Neruda raised his voice in protest.

This burgeoning second-stage crisis created an increasingly serious dilemma for the United States, since both sides in the conflict saw North American influence as a factor that could be turned to their advantage.

The policy of the Roosevelt administration from 1934 on was one of noninterference in the internal politics of Latin American countries. Correspondence between the State Department and its embassy in San Salvador clearly indicates that Washington had no interest in the removal of Martínez, and indeed would probably have preferred to maintain the status quo for the duration of World War II.

Members of the embassy staff, however, inevitably looked at Salvadoran politics through the spectacles of North American political traditions, New Deal liberalism, and the ideological polarization of the world war, and disapproved of much of what they saw. They maintained extensive and friendly contacts with leading opponents of Martínez and listened sympathetically when those opponents challenged the United States to act on the democratic principles it professed. Early in January 1944, Ambassador Walter Thurston apprised the State Department of the dilemma in which he found himself:

> Our pronouncements such as the Atlantic Charter and the Declaration of the Four Freedoms . . . are accepted literally by the Salvadorans as official endorsement of basic democratic principles we desire to have prevail currently and universally. . . . It is difficult for them to reconcile these pronouncements with the fact that the United States tolerates and apparently is gratified to enter into association with governments in America which cannot be described as other than totalitarian. . . . The principal defect of a policy of non-intervention accompanied by propaganda on behalf of democratic doctrines is that it simultaneously stimulates dictatorships and popular opposition to them. Moreover, by according dictators who seize or retain power unconstitutionally the same consideration extended to honestly elected presidents we not only impair our moral leadership but foment the belief that our democratic professions are empty propaganda and that we are in fact simply guided by expediency.[10]

Thurston walked a tightrope, trying to keep the United States from being associated either with the perpetuation of the Martínez regime or with the activities of the opposition. A particularly painful decision was forced upon him during the 2 April insurrection when two of the insurgent officers appeared at the embassy asking for asylum. U.S. policy forbade giving anyone asylum in the embassy, and Thurston eventually turned them over to the government after receiving an assurance from Martínez himself "that they would be given the benefits of the process of the laws of El Salvador."[11] He subsequently called upon the president to urge him "to exercise clemency" and made a similar appeal to the minister and under-secretary of foreign affairs.[12] Both men were executed on 11 April. This incident probably accounts for reports of opposition bitterness toward the United States which frequently reached the embassy after the insurrection, although other reports had it that government officials thought the U.S. Embassy supported the rebels.

Up to this point it would seem that Thurston had succeeded in maintaining the embassy's neutrality. He probably found it difficult, however, to maintain his accustomed detachment in the face of recriminations against the United States following the failure of the insurrection. Also, he must have felt deep personal distress when the men he had delivered to the government were executed. Perhaps because he was anxious to avoid giving the opposition any further cause for complaint, the weight of the embassy's influence subtly shifted against the government.

THE CIVIC STRIKE

Contemporary observers had no doubt that Martínez' opponents would soon make another attempt to unseat him, but no one anticipated the form the new uprising would take. With the leaders of the insurrection conspiracy imprisoned, in exile, or in hiding, a new movement had to be improvised.

On 17 April, the day the university reopened after an extended Easter vacation, word reached San Salvador that Arturo Romero, one of the civilian leaders of the insurrection who had been sentenced to death in absentia, had been captured as he tried to cross the frontier into Honduras. He was severely wounded in the process and remained in the hospital in eastern El Salvador. Romero was a young physician who was very popular with poor people in San Salvador, many of whom he had treated without charge. He also had a following of medical students, who knew him as a good teacher in the public hospital where they received their training.

On 18 or 19 April "all of the medical students arrived at the university wearing black ties to signify that they were in mourning because of the capture and wounding of Dr. Arturo Romero and also because of the executions carried out by the government."[13] Meanwhile the sixth-year law students assembled and called a meeting of delegates from each class to consider the question of a university strike. They reached no agreement but did call a further meeting of representatives from all the university faculties, and sent representatives to meetings of delegates in other schools.

The next step was the election of some forty delegates, two each from the faculties of law, medicine, engineering, and pharmacy, and the formation of a small secret central committee to lay plans for a strike. The central committee called a meeting of the student body for 24 April. Meanwhile, it began making contacts outside the university, and issued its first anonymous leaflet calling upon the public to

> do something, but something effective, so as not to permit the blood of loved ones . . . to continue to be spilled by the aid of our passivity. . . .
>
> We are not in a position to provoke a revolution, nor is it necessary that more innocent blood be shed. But there are methods, which however unlawful they may be, could be considered honorable and praiseworthy. . . . We are fighting with an astute and sagacious man . . . then to this astuteness and sagacity let us oppose ours, which being that of an entire people . . . will now take by force that which has been usurped, ITS LIBERTIES.[14]

Some evidence exists that there were other spontaneous attempts to organize. One participant, then a law student who had stayed away from his own school for fear of being apprehended in connection with the 2 April insurrection, thought the idea of the civic strike originated with a group consisting of both students and nonstudents which met at the engineering school to consider protest action against the executions. He remembered a number of people independently organizing their own committees to promote the strike. An unidentified group also called for a demonstration on 23 April, variously reported as against the execution of Romero and in favor of clemency for all civilians imprisoned as a result of the 2 April insurrection. The police apparently prevented people who gathered for that purpose from marching

On 24 April the university student assembly declared:

> a suspension of all student activities in view of the present national events, which are cause for profound grief and for every Salvadoran citizen. . . . This suspension of activities extends to the hospital work of medical students, attendance in the courthouse by students of jurisprudence, the employment of engineering students in Development,

Public Works and Mejoramiento Social [social betterment], and atten-
dance at the dental clinic by students of Dentistry.[15]

By this time some students were probably already thinking of a
more far-reaching movement than a university strike in protest
against the executions. One of the leaders recalled that the unsuccessful university strike of 1938–1939 had convinced him, as well as
other students that "strikes of intellectuals were merely symbolic, that
they could serve to initiate movements of greater reach, but that by
themselves they were not sufficient to win political battles."[16] According to the student who proposed the idea of a national strike to
compel Martínez to resign in a meeting of the Central Committee:

> The fundamental thesis was the following: General Martínez domi-
> nated the Salvadoran scene militarily and by force. . . . Martínez, I
> maintained, was an individual who was capable of waging war without
> moderation. If he encountered a group to confront, or which con-
> fronted him, he shot at all, and he was capable of defeating anyone
> militarily. Therefore it was necessary to organize a popular movement
> which did not confront Martínez, so that he would not have anyone to
> shoot. From this was deduced the conclusion that the movement
> should be a movement not of the streets, but of hiding. And the *huelga
> de brazos caídos* [peaceful or passive strike] emerged. Nobody do any-
> thing. Simply stay in his house without going into the streets, so that
> there would not be possibilities for repression.[17]

The students chose a nonviolent strategy for purely pragmatic reasons. They lacked the means to do anything else. Nevertheless, it was
a clear and conscious choice. Their thinking, one of the leaders said,
was that "the use of nonviolence would attract more supporters than
if violence was used, and besides, we knew that if things became violent then the army would take a hand in the matter, would dissolve
the strike by pure force."[18] When one of the group suggested sniping at the police, the others squelched the idea. They also informed
the U.S. Embassy that "their revolt [was] a pacifist one. They plan to
paralyze the life of the country and thus force the President to relinquish power. They do not wish to see more blood shed."[19]

The strike committee originally aimed to shut San Salvador down
by 1 May, but later postponed to 5 May to allow more time for various acts of noncooperation to peak. It gave priority to closing the
banks and paralyzing transportation, which it viewed as the most vul-

nerable points of the Salvadoran economy. If they could achieve this, the students thought, other sectors of the economy would follow. Moreover, since the committee had no means of communicating outside San Salvador, it counted on the failure of the trains to appear on schedule to carry the message of the strike throughout the country. It also attached major importance to the psychological impact of closing commerce and of a strike by physicians, who enjoyed great public respect. In particular, the students felt that the loss of medical services and the closing of drugstores would push the general public to make a stand, either declaring for Martínez or demanding his resignation.

The strategy excluded street demonstrations so as not to provoke confrontations with government forces. However, student organizers did collaborate with the widows of some of the executed officers in planning a mass for the martyrs of the April uprising in the downtown Church of the Rosary on 5 May, which served to rally the public behind the movement.

Meanwhile, a steady stream of leaflets spread news of the developing revolt and called for support. Some were mimeographed, and the students eventually found a printer, but many were typed by hand and bore a request to the reader to make and circulate additional copies. Secretaries in offices, including some government departments, and students in secretarial schools joined in the effort. Hundreds of leaflets appeared in the city every night, "typewritten, mimeographed, or even scrawled by hand on coarse paper, pushed through window gratings, left in automobiles, tacked on walls."[20]

The organization of the strike involved a substantial outlay of money for striking workers, paper, printing, and transportation of people on strike business. Like other facets of the movement, the collection and disbursement of funds became decentralized. The Central Committee's initial cash came from the treasury of a student group, reimbursed from contributions which subsequently poured in. The committee's treasurer remembered receiving some donations as large as five thousand colones ($2,000 U.S.). Some of these large contributions no doubt reflected the efforts of the Finance Committee, formed early in May, which included the president of the Mortgage Bank and a leading coffee grower connected with another San Salvador bank. There were also informal committees of women who raised funds and distributed them to striking workers.

Persuading key groups to strike depended almost entirely upon personal contact. The student organizers initially divided up the work as far as possible along the lines of their natural associations: medical students approached physicians, law students, lawyers and employees of the courts, engineering students, engineers and employees of the Ministry of Public Works, pharmacy students, the drugstore employees. Other committees concentrated on commercial employees, railroad workers, and Palestinian proprietors. Convinced individuals took on the task of winning over their colleagues and neighbors. Small committees sprang up spontaneously, consisting largely of women, and went from door to door talking with shopkeepers.

Some proprietors, especially Palestinians and Chinese, feared retaliation from the authorities if they closed their doors. One former student activist remembered throwing stones at a few stores so the owners could say they had closed under duress. Others kept their shops open but declined to wait on customers. Most owners paid their employees for the time lost from work, and some contributed to the strike fund.

However, the movement inspired less than unanimous enthusiasm among the lower-class citizens. One of the students who dealt with the railroad workers recalled that "neither sufficient political consciousness nor political objectives which could interest them existed."[21] They evidently feared reprisals even more than the shopkeepers, for in addition to demanding their full salaries in advance they agreed to absent themselves from work only on condition that the strike committee find houses where they and their families could take refuge.

Buses and taxis, as well as the railroads, remained in service the day after virtually all commercial establishments had closed, and a meeting of *Reconstrucción Social* the night of 5 May drew "perhaps 1,300 persons."[22] On 10 May, the day after Martínez resigned, a member of the U.S. Embassy staff "overheard three independent groups of the poorer class peons gathered in the plazas talking in this vein—What difference does it make what crowd gets in. We gain nothing by it. The hell with both of them. . . . I have no money. Never had any. Damn them all. I have had no money since the strike began."[23]

One anonymous leaflet writer scolded the students for neglecting to win worker support, charging that the strike had "been translated into unemployment for them," a situation which Martínez could readily exploit.[24]

Nevertheless, working people did join the strike, though the means by which they were reached remain unclear. Contacts were apparently made with some of the legal workers' societies, in particular the Union of Commercial Employees, and the Communist Party probably served as a channel of communication with some clandestine unions.

The testimony of a taxi driver illustrated the way many workers must have become involved. He recalled that a representative of one of the leading bankers approached him to ask whether the taxi drivers would be willing to join the strike, and offered to provide a daily stipend to those who did. The informant then undertook to persuade the men at his stand and a number of others to keep their cars off the streets, and made daily rounds to distribute the allowances.

The natural leaders of the meat cutters, who had no formal organization, went to the university to offer the students their collaboration. The market women, whom Ambassador Thurston described as "a formidable factor in the less polite strata of Salvadoran politics," played a major role in the strike, not only abandoning their own business but persuading others to join the movement.[25]

The Church took no official position on the insurrection, but the attitude of many clergymen probably encouraged it. After the president's resignation, the archbishop of San Salvador went so far as to tell one member of the U.S. Embassy staff of "his dislike of the oppression and cruelties of the Martínez regime and his gratification when Martínez departed from the country."[26] Catholic schools closed, and churches were used for the distribution of food during and immediately after the strike, with Jesuit priests in charge of the distribution in one instance.

Despite gaps in participation, nearly all Salvadorans who lived through the strike remembered it as an expression of overwhelming national unity. Two participants described it as the product of a "very emotional force," something "mystical." Crime fell off as though "even the thieves had patriotism."[27]

While all the grievances which had motivated earlier opposition to the Martínez regime undoubtedly contributed to this highly contagious state of mind, accounts of the civic strike unanimously emphasized the impact of the death sentences and executions which fol-

lowed the insurrection of April. The imminent threat to Arturo
Romero's life moved not only his students and colleagues but also
taxi drivers and lower-class citizens. One upper-class participant,
whose brother and husband were among those sentenced to death in
absentia, recalled the desperation with which she and her friends
asked each other what they could do. A contemporary journalist captured that desperation in these words:

> People felt that the shootings were simply the beginning of a new
> nightmare. They feared Martínez' revenge. It was this collective fear,
> a coffee plantation owner told me, which gave us courage. We were
> deathly afraid of Martínez because we knew him to be a brave and
> decided man. Fear drove the students to strike. Fear forced the mer-
> chants to close their shops. Fear made the banks suspend operations.[28]

The strike gathered momentum over the following two weeks. By
26 April the interns at the public hospital and one private hospital
had left their posts, "practically all of the engineering students" employed by the Ministry of Development, Mejoramiento Social, and
other government agencies had resigned, and "law students who
were assigned cases in the Justice of the Peace Courts no longer attended the sessions."[29]

On 27 April some schoolteachers went on strike after police broke
up a novena which one of their number, the widow of an executed
officer, had attempted to organize for him. The next day brought
the walkout of secondary students and the national high school and
some private schools. By 3 May the strike was spreading among secondary schools and "younger professional employees of the government."[30]

Meanwhile, on 2 May the newly appointed director of the public
hospital called a meeting with the physicians on his staff, who seized
the opportunity to draft a memorandum to Martínez outlining the
following conditions for their continuing "full collaboration in behalf
of those needing it":

1. That all death sentences be commuted and that general amnesty be extended to all persons charged with political offenses;
2. That all doctors who have been removed from their posts because of political activities be returned to them; and

3. That democratic principles be respected and fulfilled, especially that concerning freedom of suffrage.[31]

Theater employees walked out on 3 May, and by 4 May market vendors had announced their intention to vacate their stands on 5 and 6 May. That night the engineers and technicians of the Cooperative Inter-American Public Health Service met and voted to join the strike. The dentists of San Salvador followed suit the next morning.

In the meantime Martínez had rudely rebuffed the director of the public hospital when the latter presented the physicians' statement to him. The director promptly resigned. On the morning of 5 May, as the strike officially began, sixty doctors signed a new and stronger statement in which they agreed to leave their posts in public institutions and to close their private clinics and offices pending a change in the "system of government in the country," which, they stated, "implies the immediate necessity of the deposit of the presidency in any designate, in order that he may call the people to free elections."[32]

Pharmacists, lawyers, and justices of the peace also went on strike that day, along with "virtually all employees of all banking institutions."[33] At the Church of the Rosary, a "huge" crowd waited in vain for the arrival of a priest to say mass, which the authorities had evidently forbidden.[34] Finally, the assembled worshipers dispersed throughout the city to "close everything." "Stores closed gradually as they went from store to store requesting the owners to lock their doors and asking the employees to return to their homes."[35] Office employees of the International Railways of Central America, Salvadoran Railways, the electric light company, Mejoramiento Social, and the credit cooperatives walked out, as did "hundreds [of] government employees."[36] The Sanitation Department became the first government agency to declare itself on strike "by order of its chiefs."[37]

On 6 May the Salvadoran Railway Company suspended operations. Employees of the Subsecretariat of Development walked out "in a body." Municipal employees and "subordinate personnel in several ministries including the Foreign Office" joined them.[38]

By this time the Central Committee, realizing that the strike could not be sustained indefinitely, had begun to consider the possibility of bringing people into the streets to intensify the pressure on Martínez. On Sunday, 7 May, an apparently nervous or trigger-happy policeman fired without warning into a group of boys on the street, killing seventeen-year-old José Wright instantly. Wright belonged to a prominent San Salvador family, and as the son of a North American father he was a U.S. citizen. Indignation banished fear as San Salvadorans poured into the streets. Literally thousands of people arrived at the Wright home that evening and at the funeral the next morning.

The strike leaders worried about the possibility of violence, as talk of killing policemen and other acts of revenge filled the air. At that point the leadership set up a peacekeeping force of some fifty students charged with the task of calming public feeling. Members of this group spoke in the streets on the night of 7 May, at Wright's funeral, and at the plaza in front of the National Palace where a crowd had gathered after the funeral.

Inside the National Palace on the morning of 8 May, five employees of the comptroller general's office presented their resignations and appealed to their fellow workers to join them, which they did. When the students announced the news over loudspeakers, all the other employees in the building joined the walkout. Buses disappeared from the streets that day, and the International Railways of Central America suspended all services except the delivery of gasoline from North American oil companies to Guatemala.

By this time the strike had begun to spread to other cities. There was an active strike committee in Santa Ana (then El Salvador's second city). Groups came to consult with students from more distant Ahuachapán and San Miguel. Some people went on strike in Sonsonate and Ahuachapán, students struck in Santa Ana and San Miguel on 5 May, and in Santa Ana physicians joined them. On the night of 7 May the department heads of Santa Ana's municipal government informed the mayor that the city's employees had decided to join the walkout. The next morning the city council passed a resolution supporting the employees' right to exercise their "political convictions" and promising that their jobs would be waiting for them at the conclusion of the strike.[39] On 8 May "the majority of the business firms" in Santa Ana shut down, banks closed in San Miguel, and schoolteachers in San Vicente joined the strike.[40]

MARTÍNEZ WITHDRAWS

The Martínez government could not deal with the new insurrection. Its ineffectual response reflected divisions within the administration and a general collapse of morale in the wake of the April uprising.

The army had already proven unreliable. Although no one doubted the loyalty of the minister and undersecretary of defense or the army chief of staff to Martínez, "disunity, mistrust and fear pervaded the whole officer corps."[41] Soldiers disappeared from the streets, leaving law enforcement in the hands of the police and National Guard.

Civilian officials lost confidence in the president's ability to govern. By 17 April some of his closest associates, including the president of the Mortgage Bank and three members of the cabinet, had reportedly reached the conclusion that Martínez' retirement was the only way to salvage the situation. A member of the U.S. Embassy staff heard that Finance Minister Hector Escobar Serrano had "spoken up in informal meetings of Government men against the . . . 'reign of terror,' counseling moderation and the cessation of killings and persecution," while Minister of Government Rudolfo Morales was "entirely out of sympathy with [the] present course of affairs and particularly anxious to get out of his present position." The diplomat concluded:

> there is little doubt that a feeling of apprehension, doubt and fear is developing among the ranks of the President's followers . . . not only because they feel the President's position is ill-advised, vengeful and likely to prove ruinous to all interests, but also because these men, and certainly a large number of minor officials, are beginning to think of their own personal and economic safety in the event that the Government is . . . overturned. . . . It seems that the desire to be non-committal, to hedge and to express no opinion and play safe, is becoming almost more marked among the followers of the President than among sympathizers of the revolution.[42]

The civic strike took everyone in the administration by surprise. The cabinet opposed repressive measures and favored a strategy of waiting out the strike, on the theory that the funds necessary to maintain it would eventually run out. Several actions of the government showed a desire to placate its adversaries and avoid confrontations. It lifted the curfew on 25 April, and on 4 May (too late to stem the rising tide of revolt) announced the release of all civilians still held in connection with the 2 April uprising, though an opposition leaflet attacked the announcement as fraudulent. At some point National Guardsmen were withdrawn from the streets of San Salvador.

An order for the arrest of "a number of University students" was reportedly issued around 1 May, but actual arrests did not go beyond the brief detention of a few people for possession of strike leaflets.[43] This probably reflected the reluctance of the cabinet, in particular Rudolfo Morales, whose ministry controlled the National Police, to sanction harsh measures. Moreover, the policemen themselves were not unanimous in supporting suppression of the strike. Some in fact sympathized with it, and agents who captured one group of organizers sent them off in another direction where no police were stationed.

The police did go to the homes of some strikers to compel them to return to work, although they found that most absent public servants had prudently taken refuge elsewhere. They offered protection to strike breakers, who were apparently recruited through *Reconstrucción Social*.

A few merchants reportedly reopened their shops under threats that they would lose their licenses or be expelled from the country. These threats probably came from Martínez himself, who "summoned the heads of many business establishments . . . and . . . strongly urged them to open their business . . . even though they were without employees for their proper management."[44] He also issued an order for the dismissal of certain physicians at the public hospital, which only antagonized the hospital director. In fact, although rumors circulated that employees of banks and other enterprises who failed to appear for work would lose their jobs, the anti-Martínez press reported the dismissal of only one government employee for promoting the strike.

Meanwhile a pro-government newspaper launched a propaganda campaign designed to identify the government with the interests of the masses and the opposition with those of the wealthy. On the night of 5 May Martínez went on the air, lavishly praising the honest workers who remained on the job and labeling the propaganda for the civic strike a Nazi tactic. A leaflet dated 6 May announced the formation of a "Workers Anti-Revolutionary Committee."

Several incidents on that day suggested an effort by government supporters to mobilize violence against participants in the strike. Also on 6 May, "groups of men" reportedly "forced open the doors of at least two drug stores, . . . in an effort to force the proprietors to open them for business."[45] According to other reports, "some doctors who were participating in the general strike . . . received anonymous threats of violence to their persons or property," and one of a group of men who tried unsuccessfully to lure a leader of the striking physicians out of his home "was heard to say to another, 'Let's see, who is next on the list.' "[46] A list of persons to be beaten or threatened subsequently appeared in one of the newspapers, which interpreted it as instructions given to Pro-Patria *orejas* ("ears," hence spies).

In fact, however, no pro-government demonstration, concerted campaign of intimidation, or serious violence developed. The U.S. Embassy staff member who attended the *Reconstrucción Social* meeting on 6 May at the request of the director reported that the director, while attacking the strike, urged his listeners to refrain from violence. The director subsequently testified that Martínez himself instructed him "to avoid trouble with the strikers."[47] In all probability the perpetrators of the few incidents cited above acted on their own, without official sanction.

Meanwhile action unfolded on other fronts. Two committees claiming to speak for the strikers emerged, but the one which maintained ties with the student organizers and received general recognition bore the imprint of the *Acción Democrática Salvadoreña*-Mortgage Bank network. On the night of 5 May representatives of the Mortgage Bank and its offshoots, the credit cooperatives, and Mejoramiento Social, the Central Reserve Bank, three private banks, an insurance company, the physicians, lawyers, dentists, pharmacists, students, commercial employees, market women, day laborers, and bus and taxi drivers met to elect a national strike committee which came to be known as the Committee of National Reconstruction. It was made up of five people: a student, a physician, a commercial employee, a prominent attorney whose clients included the Mortgage Bank, and a retired general, Salvador Casteneda Castro, evidently the favorite of anti-Martínez elements in the armed forces.

On 6 May the committee agreed on its final demands. In support of them they delivered to the U.S. Embassy a manifesto which asserted that passive resistance would continue until Martínez resigned. It offered "Martínez, his associates and partisans" guarantees against reprisals, while "recommending" that the president leave the country.[48]

On the diplomatic front, opposition leaders sought assistance of some sort from the U.S. ambassador and representatives of other foreign governments as well, though the precise timing and nature of these appeals is unknown. Documents in U.S. diplomatic archives contradict the assertion of some writers that Ambassador Thurston threatened Martínez with military intervention after the killing of José Wright. However, Thurston's attitude probably did contribute to the erosion of the president's support and the constriction of his options.

During the latter part of April, rumors had circulated that "in the event of new troubles in San Salvador" North American residents would be attacked. Thurston had attempted to "build a backfire" against this possibility "by pointing out that any premeditated and deliberate outrage upon the American colony certainly would bring very serious consequences."[49] The embassy files do not indicate to whom these remarks were directed or what the hearers may have understood by "very serious consequences," but the warning may well have influenced the Salvadoran government's policy of avoiding violence during the strike and contributed to the panic which Wright's death apparently stimulated in official circles.

Accounts of developments within the government during the night of 7 May vary. The police were speedily concentrated in their barracks, presumably on the authority of either Minister of Government Morales or President Martínez. All or most of the cabinet, alarmed by the appearance of crowds in the streets, which gave rise to the possibility of bloody repression, met and decided to present their collective resignation.

Martínez received the ministers at nine o'clock on the morning of 8 May. The army chief of staff appeared during that meeting to assure the president that the army supported him 100 percent and only wanted an order from him to disperse the crowds in the streets. When the spokesman for the cabinet told the president, "We cannot join you in any violent measure," Martínez interrupted him with the assertion that he did not favor violent measures either. He added that he had shown he was no coward in putting down the 2 April insurrection and would not hesitate to put the army in its place if it should rebel again. "But against the people," he said, "I am not going to take any violent measure. If the people now want me to retire, I am willing to do it without difficulty."[50]

Later that morning the five members of the Committee of National Reconstruction sat down with the ministers to discuss the terms of the president's retirement. Martínez had proposed that he continue in office until the end of the month and the selection of his successor. But the committee refused to yield, insisting that the strike would continue until Martínez left office.

Martínez also insisted that the transfer of power follow the procedure prescribed by the constitution of 1939. Under that procedure, the Legislative Assembly annually elected three designates, one of whom it chose as interim chief executive in case the presidency was suddenly vacant. The subservient Legislative Assembly could be expected to follow Martínez' wishes on his successor. Some elements of the opposition pressed for an interim president entirely unconnected with the regime, so the committee arrived at the second negotiating session with a list of persons from whom Martínez might choose his successor. After an hour-long discussion with the cabinet, the committee finally agreed to add the name of Minister of War Andrés I. Menéndez, who was one of the Assembly designates. The cabinet undoubtedly knew that Menéndez was the man Martínez wanted to succeed him. And the committee may have felt that its constituency would accept Menéndez because he was entirely lacking in political ambition and universally respected for his integrity.

As Martínez continued to try to delay his departure, tension mounted. National Guardsmen had replaced policemen on the streets in the early hours of the morning. They made no attempt to interfere with the crowds, and the soldiers whose appearance early in the afternoon gave rise to a brief flurry of alarm also made it clear that "their presence was only to protect the demonstrators themselves."[51] However, people were getting impatient, and the possibility existed that some incident would touch off a bloody clash. According to one report, a member of a second committee claiming to represent the groups on strike obtained an audience with the president himself late in the afternoon and warned him that if he "persisted in remaining in office there would be a great deal of bloodshed and trouble."[52] Martínez finally agreed to relinquish the presidency the next morning.

The transfer of office to Menéndez was accomplished smoothly on 9 May. Menéndez moved quickly to win the confidence of the opposition. In his first meeting with the Committee of National Reconstruction, the new president promised that the constitution would be reformed and elections held as soon as possible. "Authorized sources" also told the press that martial law would be lifted as soon as possible.[53] Late in the afternoon of 9 May the Legislative Assembly approved a decree of "full and unconditional amnesty to all those soldiers or civilians" implicated in acts of rebellion, sedition, or other political crimes prior to passage of the law.[54]

The strike continued, however, because two new issues had arisen and remained unresolved. The composition of Menéndez' cabinet became the focus of extended negotiations, and other citizens joined the student strike leaders in demanding Martínez' departure from the country. The cabinet appointments on 10 May included a nominee of the Committee of National Reconstruction and two members of the rival strike committee, but three members of Martínez' cabinet remained.

This obvious compromise did not please the students. The strike leaders could see, though, that the general public felt the fight had been won with the removal of Martínez, and they themselves were exhausted. When Menéndez promised the Committee of National Reconstruction on 10 May that Martínez would leave El Salvador the next day, both the committee and the students agreed to end the strike.

ANALYSIS

Outcome of the Campaign

The campaign's stated objective was to oust Martínez, and it accomplished that. If the end of military rule and a permanent resumption of civilian democratic government were implicit goals, the campaign fell short and should be seen as neither a complete victory nor a defeat.

PRINCIPLES OF DEVELOPMENT

Principle 1: Formulate Functional Objectives

The nonviolent protagonists only partially conformed to this principle.

Attacking Martínez and his cult of personal power was a highly functional objective. He became an easy target. His effrontery first alienated and then mobilized one group after another in El Salvador. The call for his removal from power was a tangible goal and progress toward it was measurable. Subsidiary goals focused on ending all forms of authoritarian behavior, including torture, imprisonment, press censorship, and banning of labor unions and academic associations. Each area suggested specific sanctions and natural participants.

If the movement had articulated more fully what it really wanted for El Salvador, it might have been something less personal. The return to civilian constitutional rule might have been the primary objective instead of overthrowing Martínez. The easy assumption that removing one dictator was somehow tantamount to civilian rule did not serve the opposition movement well. It left the door open for Martínez' cronies to play key roles in the next regime and to subversion of what should have been the broader objective. How could things have been different? If the dictator's resignation had been an important but not exclusive objective, there would probably have been more focus on the content of the final negotiations. Perhaps there should have been a fall-back position of returning to the struggle if the primacy of civil authority could not be firmly reestablished.

Principle 2: Develop Organizational Strength

The nonviolent protagonists conformed to this principle.

Mobilization occurred through informal networks and so quickly that deliberate efforts to strengthen individual components of organizational strength were precluded. ADS and the Mortgage Bank were the exceptions, as they played an early role in the opposition. Other groups joined the struggle as they were progressively alienated from the regime. Lower-class workers, however, were hesitant because they feared the economic consequences of a civic strike.

Committees were formed to stimulate action, but they were not able to direct or control it. As in the Russian case, contagion by groups occurred, but in this case the "operations corps" only hit its stride after the civic strike began. Existing civic organizations from railroad workers groups to physicians enlisted the support of their colleagues. Women were active in soliciting support from individual shopkeepers.

The Committee of National Reconstruction emerged, but only just in time to participate in negotiations for a settlement. This at least is positive, since without such a body, divide-and-rule tactics would have been a viable alternative for Martínez.

Principle 3: Secure Access to Critical Material Resources

This principle was inoperative.

Strike funds provided some support at the margin. Wealthy bankers provided stipends for taxi drivers to stop working. A reasonable clandestine communications net developed for the civic strike, including staff in government offices being recruited to transcribe messages from the underground. Despite these fragmentary developments, the whole contest was over too soon for material factors to be assessed.

Principle 4: Cultivate External Assistance

This principle was not operative.

The United States was sympathetic but not overtly helpful. In 1944 there was no particular reason for a confrontation with the government of an ally to be high among U.S. priorities. Indeed, the opposition movement's positive view of the United States was muddied after Ambassador Thurston handed over to Martínez' custody two men seeking asylum in the U.S. Embassy. Despite assurances, Martínez executed them ten days later. It is unclear how the external aid factor might have developed given the short duration of the contest.

Principle 5: Expand the Repertoire of Sanctions

The nonviolent protagonists conformed to this principle.

The opposition made good use of culturally accessible sanctions. Funeral masses, for instance, were used to marshal wider circles of opposition. Petitions, for which there was a tradition, were widely used. The civic strike itself was an innovation, and a highly effective one. Had the struggle extended, a wider repertoire would definitely have been required, but the sanctions developed were sufficient for this campaign.

PRINCIPLES OF ENGAGEMENT

Principle 6: Attack the Opponents' Strategy for Consolidating Control

The nonviolent protagonists conformed to this principle.

The strategy for exercising control in a long-entrenched, highly personalized dictatorship is often to depend on ever-increasing levels of repression. Any hesitation connotes weakness. However, to the extent that the dictator actually has to make good his threats, his usable power is weakened significantly.

Martínez had an established reputation for ruthlessness and blood-letting. Intimidation and threats of direct violence as well as lesser punishments were affecting an ever-widening circle of individuals, from the population at large to his own inner group. To move from resentment to action requires overcoming the initial fear that holds a dictatorship in place. Once Martínez' provocations provided suffi-cient incentive for a civilian reaction, his regime was quickly un-masked and put at risk. This dynamic was never more apparent than in response to executions, which had exactly the right effect from the resistance movement's point of view, and exactly the wrong one from Martínez'. Rather than being cowed by the grotesque and senseless killings, the population became enraged and emboldened.

Principle 7: Mute the Impact of the Opponents' Violent Weapons

The nonviolent protagonists conformed to this principle.

The casualties among the opposition were enough to infuriate, but not enough to intimidate, the groups engaging Martínez. We cannot identify those factors leading Martínez at the end to reject wholesale violence against civilians, or whether he even made a thoroughly considered conscious choice in this direction. The "operations corps"—that is, the most active opposition players—deliberately avoided exposing people to the risk of attack at critical junctures.

Principle 8: Alienate Opponents from Expected Bases of Support

The nonviolent protagonists conformed to this principle.

As noted under principle 4, the U.S. position was ambiguous and under-exploited by the Salvadoran opposition. While that is true in terms of overt U.S. aid to the struggle, we also have to consider that the U.S. posture must have looked at least as ambiguous and proba-bly hostile to Martínez. The lack of U.S. support may well have re-strained Martínez' treatment of the strike as it evolved.

Until the very end the military did not defect from Martínez, though the civic strike did cause some disruption in the ranks. On the other hand, many political moderates, ministerial officials, civil servants, and government workers, horrified at the prospect of a wider bloodbath, defected. These people would never have challenged the regime on their own initiative, but when a choice was posed by others, they took the opportunity to follow it.

Principle 9: Maintain Nonviolent Discipline

The nonviolent protagonists conformed to this principle.

A complex dynamic unfolded similar to that in the Danish campaign. The abortive uprising that preceded the strike was unmistakably violent. The unnecessary harshness of the reprisals it evoked became the spark that mobilized the civic strike, which did maintain nonviolent discipline. The Salvadoran civic strike, like the Copenhagen peoples' strike of the same year, might not have occurred at all without the violent provocation.

Once the nonviolent challenge was mounted, its discipline was used to good effect. The choice to deny Martínez visible targets for repression, and to avoid provoking his troops, was highly functional for the movement. It allowed even the comparatively restrained violence of the regime to seem gratuitous. Lethal sniping at the police, when proposed, was wisely rejected as inconsistent with the dominant strategy.

PRINCIPLES OF CONCEPTION

Principle 10: Assess Events and Options in Light of Levels of Strategic Decision Making

This principle is not operative because of the short duration of the struggle. Over time it may have come into play, but a conflict comprising two or three dramatic events leaves few options to assess.

Principle 11: Adjust Offensive and Defensive Operations According to the Relative Vulnerabilities of the Protagonists

The nonviolent protagonists conformed to this principle.

The regime's rigid control was the main source of its vulnerability.

Expressions of mass dissatisfaction were the best way to cause a breach, and then a hemorrhage, of support for the regime.

As a defensive ploy, the use of World War II themes to disguise agitation for democratic reform was inspired. As an ostensible ally of the United States, Martínez could hardly be seen to be suppressing such statements, even if his real sympathies were radically different. Each time the movement chose to escalate the conflict, they did so in relation to the opponent's newly exposed weaknesses. Momentum developed favorably, and its intensity accounts in part for the brevity of the campaign.

Principle 12: Sustain Continuity Between Sanctions, Mechanisms, and Objectives

The nonviolent protagonists only partially conformed to this principle.

With regard to the ouster of Martínez, the principle was fulfilled. The sanctions chosen were precisely the right ones to induce the dictator to retire, with a face-saving negotiation. Martínez' regime was facing imminent disintegration. Unlike India in the 1930s, there was never the temptation to believe that the regime could be converted into a more benign form.

Constitutional civil rule was assumed to be a natural consequence of the dictator's departure. As a result, the principle of continuity was never applied to that unarticulated objective. Full-scale coercion against Martínez was an appropriate mechanism to secure his resignation, but other mechanisms might have been pursued to restore constitutional rule.

NOTES

1. W. J. McCafferty, U.S. chargé d'affaires ad interim, El Salvador, to Secretary of State, despatch 282, April 1933, Decimal File 816.911/33, General Records of the Department of State, Record Group 59, U.S. National Archives, Washington, D.C. (hereafter RG 59, NA).

2. Everett A. Wilson, "The Crisis of National Integration in El Salvador, 1919–1935," 241; H. Gardner Ainsworth, U.S. vice consul, El Salvador, memorandum, 3 November 1943, enclosure to despatch 929, Decimal File 816.00/1153, RG 59, NA.

3. Anonymous memorandum by a member of the U.S. Embassy staff,

San Salvador, enclosure no. 1 to despatch 1156, 8 January 1944, Decimal File 816.00/1172, RG 59, NA.

4. Robert Varney Elam, "Appeal to Arms: The Army and Politics in El Salvador, 1931–1964," 55.

5. Gerhard Gade, U.S. chargé d'affaires *ad interim*, El Salvador, to Edward G. Trueblood, U.S. chargé d'affaires *ad interim*, Costa Rica, 8/21/43, Records of the Foreign Service Posts, Dept. of State, RG 84, San Salvador, 1943, SC 800, U.S. National Archives, Washington National Records Center, Suitland, Maryland (hereafter WNRC).

6. Tiburcio Santos Dueñas, *Aurora del dos de abril de 1944*, 15.

7. *La Prensa Grafica* (San Salvador), 2 September 1943.

8. Walter Thurston, U.S. Ambassador to El Salvador, despatch 1466, 4/14/44, Decimal File 816.00/1261, RG 59, NA.

9. Cited in Patricia Parkman, "Insurrection Without Arms," 133.

10. Thurston to Secretary of State, despatch 1154, 1/8/44, Decimal File 816.00/1171, RG 59, NA.

11. Thurston to Secretary of State, despatch 1448, 4/5/44, Decimal File 816.00/1249, RG 59, NA.

12. Thurston to Secretary of State, telegram 109, 4/5/44, Decimal File 816.00/1244, RG 59, NA.

13. "Revolutionary Activities in El Salvador," n.d., 13–14, Decimal File 816.00/1418, RG 59, NA.

14. "Los hijos del pueblos," [*sic*] "Salvadoreños," San Salvador, 19 April 1944. Typed carbon copy enclosed with a letter from Rufus A. Byers, Chief, U.S. Military Mission to El Salvador, to chief, Military Intelligence Service, War Department, 30 April 1944, file 3000-3020, Box 817, RG 165, WNRC.

15. "Al pueblo salvadoreño," as reproduced in *Opinión Estudiantil* (San Salvador), 8a época, no. 1, 20 May 1944.

16. "Un componente de la huelga de mayo habla para esta revista: El br. Reynaldo Galindo Pohl, hace importantes revelaciones," *Repertorio Salvadoreño* (San Salvador), 2a época, año 6, no. 6, 15 July 1946, p. 11.

17. Patricia Parkman's interview with Fabio Castillo, San José, Costa Rica, 15 October 1976.

18. Patricia Parkman's interviews with Jorge Bustamante, San Salvador, 22 March 1978.

19. E. M. [Estes?], memorandum, United States Embassy, 1 May 1944, RG 84, San Salvador, 1944, 800, WNRC.

20. Rose Harkness, untitled report, "Guatemala, May 4, 1944," quoted in A. B. Hannah, assistant U.S. military attaché, Guatemala, Report 1183, May 6, 1944, G-2 Regional File 1933–44, El Salvador, file 3000–3020, Box 817, RG 165, WNRC.

21. Parkman's interviews with Castillo, 15 October 1976.

22. Thurston to Secretary of State, despatch 1560, 12 May 1944, Decimal Files 816.504/42, RG 59, NA.

23. "AFM," U.S. Embassy, San Salvador, memorandum, 10 May 1944, RG 84, San Salvador, 1944 Decimal 800, WNRC.

24. "Estudiantes: La revolución se conquista, no se espera," n.p., n.d., typed carbon in "Apuntes de Política Patria," an album in the library of Dr. Manuel Gallardo, Santa Tecla, El Salvador.

25. Thurston to Secretary of State, despatch 1646, 29 May 1944, Decimal File 816.00/1425, RG 59, NA.

26. "Revolutionary Activities," n.d., 22.

27. Parkman interviews with Victor Lasso, San Salvador, 16 January 1978, and Mario Hector Salazar, San Salvador, 20 March 1978.

28. Cesar Ortiz, "AP Special Advance for AMS of Sunday, June 4," dateline San José, Costa Rica, 3 June [no year], marked at end, "sent June 1," G-2 Regional File 1933–44, El Salvador, file 3000–3020, Box 817, RG 165, WNRC.

29. "Revolutionary Activities," n.d., 14–15.

30. Thurston to Secretary of State, telegram 131, 3 May 1944, Decimal File 816.00/1291, RG 59, NA.

31. Original text in *El Diario Latino*, San Salvador, 10 May 1944.

32. Luís V. Velasco et al., memorandum beginning "Los infrascritos Médicos y Cirujanos de la Facultad: reunidos en sesión plena el día cinco de Mayo . . . ," *La Prensa Gráfica* (segunda extra), 12 May 1944.

33. Thurston to Secretary of State, telegram 133, 5 May 1944, Decimal File 816.00/1299, RG 59, NA.

34. Parkman's interview with Reynaldo Galindo Pohl, Washington D.C., 27 September 1977.

35. Parkman's interview with Bustamante, 22 February 1978.

36. "Revolutionary Activities," n.d., 21; Krehm to Johnson, 6 May 1944, RG 84, San Salvador, SC 811.11, WNRC.

37. *El Diario Latino*, 19 May 1944.

38. Ibid., 9 May 1944; Thurston, telegram 145, 6 May 1944, Decimal File 816.00/1306, RG 59, NA.

39. *El Diario Latino*, 24 May 1944.

40. "Revolutionary Activities," n.d., 21.

41. Overton G. Ellis, U.S. vice consul, El Salvador, memorandum dated 25 May 1944, RG 84, San Salvador, 800, WNRC.

42. Ellis, memorandum, 18 April 1944, RG 84, San Salvador, 1944, 800, WNRC.

43. E. M. E., memorandum, 1 May 1944.

44. Thurston to Secretary of State, telegram 145, 6 May 1944, Decimal File 816.00/1306, RG 59, NA.

45. "Revolutionary Activities," n.d., 30.

46. Ibid.

47. "W.W.S.," U.S. Embassy, San Salvador, memorandum, 7 June 1944, RG 84, El Salvador, 1944, Decimal 800, WNRC.

48. "Fellow Citizens," San Salvador, 6 May 1944, translated in Thurston to Secretary of State, despatch 1545, 6 May 1944, Decimal File 816.00/1347, RG 59, NA.

49. Thurston to John M. Cabot, San Salvador, 12 May 1944, RG 84, San Salvador, 1944, 800, WNRC.

50. Parkman, confidential interview, 1978.

51. *El Diario de Hoy*, San Salvador, 9 May 1944.

52. "Revolutionary Activities," n.d., 33.

53. *La Prensa Gráfica*, segunda extra, 9 May 1944.

54. *El Diario Latino*, 10 May 1944; Decreto número 36, *Diario Oficial* (San Salvador), 136:103 (10 May 1944). While dated 10 May, contemporary press reports make clear that the decree was issued on 9 May.

Chapter 8

Solidarity Versus the Polish Communist Party, 1980–1981

To speak about Polish communism is to speak about conflict and crisis. That is because Soviet-style communism was never indigenous to Poland. Its imposition by force and fraud in the aftermath of the Second World War represented a new chapter in the age-old story of Poland's suffering at the hands of various imperial neighbors, but primarily Russia's.[1]

Bloody uprisings against Russian domination had occurred in 1794, 1830, 1848, and 1863. In the Soviet period, the Polish-Soviet war of 1919–1922 rekindled traditional hostilities. The communist project in Poland was in trouble from the start. In addition to a virulent anti-Soviet nationalism, deeply rooted Catholicism was fundamentally at odds with the basic tenets of Marxism-Leninism. Finally, Poland was a largely agricultural society in which the total collectivization of land was destined to fail.

Because of the triple forces of nationalism, Catholicism, and private agriculture, the major aspects of the Soviet system failed to be incorporated into the triumph of communism in Poland. The leading role of the Communist Party, its pervasive ideology, an arbitrary and authoritarian system of law, political oligarchy, a centrally con-

Prof. Jan Zielonka served as a research consultant for this case study. Prof. Zielonka provided all the primary research from Polish sources and the initial descriptive historical copy. The modifications the authors have made to this material, including all the analytical judgments which follow, are their responsibility alone.

trolled economy, omnipresent police control, and censorship of mass communications all came to define political life in communist Poland.

Given these antithetical forces, the modern history of Poland is one of successive struggles against the communist authorities. In 1956, 1968, 1970, and 1976 significant challenges to the system were mounted. Each engagement followed a typical pattern, each involving some civilian resistance to provocation, various degrees of marginal violence, occasional short-term gains, and eventual defeat by repression.

For example, in 1956, workers in the Cegielski engineering plant in Poznan had made long and fruitless attempts to reverse new production targets and to get higher wages. On 26 June they sent a delegation to Warsaw to talk with the authorities who promised an immediate response and a new system for computing wages. Neither was forthcoming. On the morning of 28 June, the Cegielski plant workers struck and marched into Freedom Square in Poznan. Hearing of the action, workers from other enterprises stopped work and joined the march. Large numbers of people joined the demonstration, which turned into a riot when rumors spread that mass arrests were being conducted. The crowd stormed the District Security building, where it was turned away by security forces firing live ammunition. The shooting further outraged the demonstrators, and the riots continued for two days, leaving a total of fifty-three dead and hundreds wounded.[2]

In 1968 a student demonstration at Warsaw University demanded an end to the persecution of certain students and direct talks with the minister of education. The proctor negotiated with a student delegation, and a compromise was reached, but as the students were disbanding, squads of paramilitary police appeared at the main gate of the university and began a truncheon attack. Some students were beaten senseless, although no deaths were reported.

The next crisis began in December 1970 with a spontaneous mass meeting at the Gdansk shipyards to protest dramatic new price increases. This time workers demanded talks with the regional Party authorities. When no one fitting that description appeared, they marched to the regional Party Committee headquarters. A delegation of workers failed to gain access to the building but had mobilized other Gdansk workers as they marched. When a larger group returned to the Party Committee building, militia units attacked the crowd, which then rioted. At the same time in Szczecin, workers sent a delegation to their own regional committee. The delegation was promptly arrested, provoking strikes, marches, and ultimately attacks on Party headquarters.

In June 1976 a strike began at the General Walter metal factory in Radom, again culminating in riots. Workers notified other factories and formed a demonstration that marched toward the Regional Party Committee headquarters. The demonstrators called for official representatives to come out, and when none did, they entered the building. They found no one in authority, but they did find stores of goods, including some for which the prices had just been raised. Angered, they destroyed the interior of the building, eventually setting it on fire, and began marching again, this time smashing shop windows as they passed. Armed militia broke up the demonstrations, and many workers were imprisoned.

With the exception of the student action of 1968, each of these crises was spurred by economic complaints but led inexorably to the articulation of some basic political demands. Workers' participation, democratization of decision making, and basic freedoms of speech, religion, and association became linked to specific economic requests. Some of these crises brought about temporary liberalization and occasional changes in Party leadership after repression had run its course, but none resulted in fundamental reforms in political or economic structures.

Each skirmish took place against the backdrop of potential Soviet intervention. The invasions of Hungary in 1956 and Czechoslovakia in 1968 set the presumed limits of Soviet tolerance for significant dissent in Eastern Europe. The Polish opposition became skilled at staying within those limits, but the economic, social, and political crises only worsened over time. Each encounter deepened demoralization.

KOR CHANGES THE PATTERN OF CONFLICT

After the 1976 strikes the organizers created the Workers' Defense Committee, or KOR, to assist the victims of the crackdown. KOR stated that the trade unions could not help since these were controlled by the state. "Society can only defend itself against lawlessness through solidarity and mutual aid," KOR said in a September 1976

appeal. Established by a small group of intellectuals, KOR never as-
pired to be a mass political organization.[3] It provided food, legal aid,
money, and other practical assistance to persecuted workers and
their families. Though it was never intended to promote a political
or ideological program, KOR quickly became an influential pressure
group.

KOR's initial demands were met when the authorities passed two
successive Amnesty Acts in February and July 1977 and released all
imprisoned workers. At this juncture, KOR transformed itself into
the Social Self-Defense Committee (KSS-KOR). Leader Jacek Kuron
declared, "political opposition should immediately begin to organize
a network of social movements which would cooperate with the organization and which would express the aspirations of the whole society."[4]

The practical upshot was the creation of an ongoing resistance
movement based on social self-organization. The most well-known
groups responding to the appeal were the Movement for Defense of
Civil and Human Rights (ROPCIO) and the Confederation of Independent Poland (KPN). The concept spread, and soon there were
independent social movements springing up in most professional
sectors. The first independent trade unions emerged in the Silesia
district and on the Baltic coast region in early 1978. They focused on
typical industrial union issues, presenting a challenge to the official,
government-dependent trade unions. Lech Walesa was among the
original organizers of the new independent unions. He and other
activists later gained prominence as leaders of Solidarity.

Polish students established their own independent self-defense
committee in 1977 in reaction to the death of Stanislaw Pyjas, a student supporter of KOR who was presumed to have been killed by
the police.[5] By August 1978 the first "Temporary Committee of
Peasants Self-Defense" was formed in reaction to state repression of
peasants who refused to pay the obligatory subscription to a new
peasant retirement foundation.

This progressive institutionalization of opposition throughout Poland was accompanied by the creation of an independent information network, a variety of publishing activities, and initiatives for self-
education. By 1979 there were over thirty independent newspapers
and magazines in Poland, as well as a few independent publishing
houses.[6]

The new expressions of opposition were closely linked to the activity of some officially recognized bodies, especially Catholic ones. For instance, many people from the Club of the Catholic Intelligentsia (KIK), and the Catholic magazines *Wiez, Znak,* and *Tygodnik Powszechny,* worked closely with opposition groups. The Polish primate, Cardinal Stefan Wyszynski, received KOR members and encouraged them to "defend the culture and values of the nation."[7]

Opposition activity also received support from some communists. "Future and Experience," a group with many communist members, became notorious for a series of anti-government reports on the evolution of the Polish situation.

One of the defining features of the broad movement for social self-defense was its early and rigorous advocacy of nonviolence. Kuron stressed that any social movement "must get rid of the use of force and compulsion." Another KOR activist, Jan Jozef Lipski, said that "the iron principle of KOR was its refusal to use coercion." When Catholic intellectuals began a hunger strike in 1977 to protest the arrest of nine activists, they stated, "we have consciously chosen a hunger strike as a form of struggle for the rule of law and justice, a struggle without using force and violence."[8]

Sustained nonviolent opposition exposed a deep crisis in the communist system in Poland in a way that the earlier episodic challenges had not. Poles were becoming increasingly aware that three decades of communist rule had brought neither prosperity nor social justice. A grave economic crisis had begun to affect the whole population. The Party itself was in a state of internal disarray, weakened by years of corruption. Party slogans rang hollow next to the pronouncements of the Church and the organized opposition. Party chief Edward Gierek had become isolated within his own system, and civil, military, and business elites were openly critical of economic mismanagement and political malaise.

Gierek responded to the deteriorating situation by trying to avoid the open confrontation that had failed so conspicuously for his predecessor, Wladyslaw Gomulka. Gierek attempted to engage the Church in dialogue. He liberalized press constraints and eased harassment of the political opposition. He also promoted various sorts of cooperation with Western Europe and the United States. The reforms, however, were all too little and too late. Gierek was unable to deliver any significant economic or political reforms that could forestall the deepening crisis.

Gierek's attitude was conciliatory in comparison to that of the Soviet Union. The Soviet press openly attacked KOR and other opposition groups, and was caustically critical of the Church, whose right to exist was questioned.

When strikes began in the summer of 1980, the Polish authorities faced an unsympathetic public, a demoralized Party, and a Soviet Union hostile to the new civil initiatives and ambivalent toward the Gierek regime itself.

SUMMER 1980: SOLIDARITY TAKES THE OFFENSIVE

On 1 July 1980, the government introduced a new price system for meat which raised prices 90 percent to over 100 percent on some types. Workers at some major plants stopped work and established strike committees to demand compensatory wage increases. The first protest strikes began at the Ursus tractor plant near Warsaw, where some seventeen thousand workers (40 percent of the work force) were involved. More strikes followed at the vehicle parts factory in Tczew, at the Warsaw steel works, and in Lodz. Strikers' demands were settled quickly on the following day in direct talks between workers, represented by "workers' committees," and management, bypassing both the official trade union and Party apparatus. Pay raises of between 5 percent and 10 percent were granted as well as guarantees against reprisals.

Meanwhile, strikes began in other factories. Management's conciliatory attitude (suggestive of instructions from above) permitted agreement with successive workers' demands, and the process of industrial bargaining spread rapidly throughout the country. As the scale of pay settlements steadily rose, workers who had accepted a 5 percent increase in the first days of July struck again when they saw awards at other plants creeping up to an average 10 percent, and later reaching 15 percent and even 20 percent in some isolated cases.

On 18 July, KOR, which from the beginning had acted as a strike information agency, listed fifty-one factories which had received pay increases and at least seventeen others out on strike. On 26 July, Jerzy Urban, a government journalist, admitted in *Poltyka* that strikes had affected one hundred enterprises.

At first, strike solidarity was built on an occupational rather than a class basis. Separate strike committees were organized in individual factories. Local demands (mainly for wage increases) and local solutions were formulated largely because the authority to revert to the old price structure was delegated to the local administrative level.[9] The decentralized form of protest greatly reduced the threat to managers and the Party apparatus. On the other hand, differences between bargaining positions were narrow enough to prevent authorities from credibly invoking emotional appeals such as to "the national interest" as they had sometimes in previous situations.

Bargaining with management continued smoothly as long as the strikes were well organized, tension remained low, and workers' claims were mostly of a modest economic character. But a second and different wave of strikes began in the middle of August in the Baltic coast area and, in a period of ten days, swept over the country. Gdansk, Gdynia, and Szczecin had gone on strike in December 1970, and their cumulative experience since had clearly shown that progress on simple economic demands was not enough and the relatively decentralized pattern of occupational strikes was not adequate to meet political demands.[10]

Strike committees now formulated political demands. They included freedom of speech and information, authentic trade union representation, and the release of political prisoners.[11] The workers wanted negotiations at a higher than enterprise level, and suspended or restricted separate talks. For the first time they created an overarching interenterprise organization, the Strike Committee (MKS) in Gdansk.

The authorities were ready to make a number of concessions. In his speech on 18 August, Gierek promised a shift in priorities to the consumer by increasing meat import quotas, stabilizing prices of food staples and utilities, increasing family allowances, and introducing progressive wage increases for all groups of workers. He also created a multilateral committee of inquiry into workers' grievances. He admitted that the official trade unions were "too far from the working people," and promised to reform them.[12] But the authorities rejected the political demands and refused to discuss them with the MKS.

Though he had promised that force would not be used, Gierek now began castigating the "enemies of the people" and issued an emphatic warning that any challenges to the socialist state would not be tolerated. The governmental commission led by Deputy Pyka, which had been sent to Gdansk, refused to meet the strikers' commission on 19 August, preferring instead to deal with each separate factory's representatives. Another governmental delegation sent to Szczecin at the same time also proved intractable.

Despite the government's reaction, the strikers maintained two preconditions for resuming work: restoration of communication between the Baltic Coast and the rest of the country (which had been revoked at the outset of the strikes) and recognition of the MKS as the sole bargaining unit. A high level of organization enabled the strikers to stick to these essential preconditions.

The occupational strike, in which striking workers take over the workplace, had several inherent advantages. It protected workers against the kind of police reprisals that had been encountered in 1956, 1970, and 1976. It also turned the workplace into a tightly organized democratic forum and training ground. In relative safety, workers selected leaders and formulated demands in genuinely democratic discussions while maintaining morale and discipline. Moreover, valuable factories and equipment became "hostages," while the walls and fences surrounding the factories provided natural protection against repression and infiltration.

By August 1980, Polish shipyards looked like defense strongholds. Control was established over entrances, and a no-alcohol rule was enforced. Problems were debated openly with workers speaking directly to one another from special platforms or standing atop bulldozers. Lech Walesa was directly elected, as were other strike leaders, in this kind of setting. Walesa was also elected to head the MKS on 19 August.

Religious celebrations reinforced the unity of the strikers in occupied factories. So did various national and Catholic symbols. The now famous symbol of Solidarity, a carelessly hand-drawn inscription in red on a white background, became a rallying point for the entire movement.

Occupied factories were also a good place to negotiate with the government. The authorities' representatives could not help but feel under direct pressure from the physical presence of masses of workers. Observers have frequently described the moment when government negotiators came for the first time to the Lenin Shipyard. The distance from their bus to the negotiating table required them to walk a few hundred meters among workers loudly chanting "Walesa."[13] For their part, the workers' representatives had direct access to their constituents and could check their positions periodically in talks with the rank and file. In the Lenin Shipyard the proceedings were often broadcast directly to the strikers over the factory loudspeaker system.

Occupied factories also helped create a sense of unity on a regional and even national scale. On 23 August, the MKS already represented 370 strike committees and over four hundred thousand workers. It also controlled practically the entire Gdansk-Gdynia area, including determining which parts of the public transport system would continue to operate. It also directed the supply of provisions, not only to striking workers but to food stores of the region as well.

Intellectuals and churchmen began to endorse publicly the aims of the strikers. On 15 August, Cardinal Wyszynski delivered an Ascension Day sermon at the Jasna Gora shrine in Czestochowa, where he prayed for "spiritual freedom" and "the right of self-decision." He supported the strikes again on 17 and 26 August and called for calm and responsible behavior from the strikers.

On 21 August a group of 64 outstanding intellectuals issued an appeal to both parties to follow the path of negotiation and compromise. Within a week there were 239 signers. Expressions of support for the Polish workers began to pour in from foreign trade unions and socialist parties. At the same time hundreds of Polish and foreign journalists gravitated toward the Gdansk shipyard, and detailed news about the Polish workers' initiative began to reach the outside world.

This confluence of events brought powerful pressure to bear on the authorities. The first governmental delegation to Gdansk had to be recalled to Warsaw after it tried and failed to make separate deals with individual strike committees, using a mixture of promises and threats. At the same time, internal party politics led to some changes in leadership. A new negotiating team, led by Deputy Premier Jagielski, began serious negotiations with the MKS. The talks were facilitated by the arrival of two groups of academic experts in Gdansk to assist both sides in the conflict.

The MKS eventually developed a list of twenty-one demands. The government considered the demand for a free trade union as the biggest stumbling block in the list. In the meantime, however, strikes had already affected virtually all the industrial sectors and regions of Poland, and workers throughout the country were expressing solidarity with the MKS.

Somewhat cornered, Jagielski's delegation finally asked the MKS to define independent unions and to say what their attitude would be toward the "leading role of the communist party." The MKS accepted the principle of communist government, providing a temporary solution to the authorities' main political problem: the existence of working-class representation on both sides of the table. This solution encouraged the government to hope for the subordination of new workers' organizations to their institutionalized counterparts within the Communist Party. As a face-saving measure, this formula was equally important to the ruling elites of both Warsaw and Moscow.

Prior to 19 August, there had been virtually no mention in the Soviet media of labor unrest in Poland. But on that date, the Soviet news agency TASS, Radio Moscow, and Soviet television reported on Gierek's speech of the previous day. On 20 August, a summary of his speech was published in *Pravda*, which dwelt on the role of "anti-socialist elements" in the strike activity, and underlined Gierek's note about "efforts to make use of work stoppages to serve hostile political goals."[14]

Four days earlier TASS had announced routine maneuvers of the Warsaw Pact armies in East Germany and the Baltic area. The Soviet media intensified its criticism after 27 August, specifically attacking "the bourgeois media" which "orient themselves around the statements of those oppositional elements that are trying to awaken an anti-state anti-socialist feeling."[15]

On 1 September, *Pravda* published a sharp criticism of the "anti-socialist elements operating in a group of factories on the Polish coast," who use "economic difficulties for their own counter-revolutionary goals."[16] The timing of these comments could suggest criticism of the Polish Party's concessions as much as of the strikers themselves. The newspapers of the German Democratic Republic (GDR) depicted the Polish government's action as capitulation. They argued that the strikers' demands would "inflict direct damage upon socialism on Polish soil."[17] At that time there was no official government statement from any East European capital outside of Poland.

Despite this level of uneasiness throughout the communist world, three major agreements were signed in three strike centers: Szczecin (30 August), Gdansk (31 August), and Jastrzebie (3 September). The agreements were similar, and, among other concessions, they permitted the creation of free trade unions, promised wage increases and a five-day week, and guaranteed legal limitations on censorship. In content and in the way they were produced, the concessions were unprecedented in postwar East European politics.

A PERIOD OF MUTUAL TESTING

The signing of the agreement in Gdansk, reported by Polish television and radio, was cause for national celebration. With high emotion millions of Poles watched as Lech Walesa said of the negotiations, "We talked like Poles to the Poles." Despite the fact that some regional strikes continued, the Baltic Coast agreements ended the acute political crisis of August 1980. It was only the beginning, however, of a new political and industrial bargaining process in Poland.

The workers' demands had not been unlimited. They did not ask for the elimination of the "leading role" of the Party. Nor did they ask for the removal of Soviet troops from Polish soil or for free elections. They did not question the dominance of the public sector economy. But the accepted provisions were still far-reaching. New independent unions would have the right to strike, an institutionalized tool with which to struggle for further concessions. Political persecution of dissidents was supposed to cease, and press censorship was to be limited. Furthermore, if the economic and social welfare concessions were carried out seriously, they should lead to significant reforms in the Polish economy. Some highly important symbolic concessions were made as well. Notably, the government agreed that Sunday mass should be regularly broadcast on the radio, and promised to erect statues and monuments commemorating the December 1970 deaths of workers at the hands of the police.

While some strikers were disappointed, it was clear that full implementation of the agreements would mean significant changes in the communist system in Poland and create opportunities to push for further changes. The main challenge to the leadership of Solidarity, as the newborn union was to be called, was to deal with the practical problems of organizing. The Gdansk presidium, which had emerged as the natural leadership within the Lenin Shipyard, and then de facto became the national leadership, moved out of the shipyard after its first week of legal existence and into the old Hotel Morski in Gdansk. There, on 17 September, the first all-Poland meeting of Solidarity representatives established the nucleus of a "National Co-

ordinating Committee" (KKP). In the meantime, Walesa appointed
Kuron of KOR as chief advisor on union organization.

While Solidarity grappled with the problems of nascent organization, the Communist Party faced a new and deeper internal crisis.
Caveats aside, the Party had always claimed to be the sole representative of workers' interests, and now it appeared likely that many Party
members, who had played active roles in the strikes, would leave the
Party and/or join Solidarity. No matter what assurances had been
given, the very existence of an independent union had to undermine
the political position and legitimacy of the Party. Moreover, other
professional and social groups were now demanding their own representative organizations. Peasants created Rural Solidarity with the
strong backing of the Catholic Church. Students established the Independent Union of Students. Various cultural and educational associations elected new leadership and adopted goals divergent from
those of the Party. Gierek was replaced by a new Party chief, Stanislaw Kania, who faced the triple threats of Solidarity, his own demoralized rank and file, and a deeply concerned Soviet Union (although
after August the Soviet media were remarkably quiet on the subject
of Poland).

Under pressure, the government balked. It pulled back from, undermined, or otherwise failed to implement its August commitments.
Retreat from the Gdansk and Szczecin accords automatically increased friction with Solidarity. The first skirmishes occurred in September and centered on the government's reluctance to make good
on the anti-censorship provisions. Next there was a delay in wage
increases. But that problem was resolved soon after a one-hour nationwide strike—a symbolic affair, since most regional unions allowed selective participation of certain enterprises, and required only
supportive gestures (such as hoisting the Polish flag) of others. However, the message was unmistakable. When factory sirens wailed
across the land and signaled the start of the strike, Solidarity was
firmly in control of Polish labor.

Legal registration of the new unions became the next crisis. Although the court had registered some new independent unions (the
national airline LOT being the first), Solidarity, by far the largest
union, received only a letter from the court listing a series of complaints about its statutes. The court questioned Solidarity's claim to
operate nationally rather than regionally, its ban on Party members
and managers from holding office in the union, and reraised the

question of its attitude toward the Party's "leading role." Solidarity provided clarifications on these points, but the court still refused to register the union, ostensibly on Party instructions.

Frustrated, the National Coordinating Committee called for a general strike. The court registered Solidarity and accepted its statutes but ordered the insertion of a long clause repeating, among other things, that Solidarity recognized the socialist system and would use the strike weapon only within legal bounds. The court's interference convinced workers that they should go ahead with the general strike. The government countered by threatening to impose a state of emergency in Warsaw and elsewhere. And Solidarity prepared to go underground.

Several plant and regional branches of Solidarity devised plans for a state of emergency, specifying the organizational role various branches would play in a general strike. Before it was necessary to implement them, though, Walesa and the new premier, Pinkowski, resolved the issue. For the second time, muscle flexing had the desired effect.

Next came the arrest on 19 November of a print worker named Jan Narozniak. As he was the first Solidarity activist to be arrested, the Warsaw chapter of Solidarity warned that there would be a strike if the man was not freed within twenty-four hours. This time Solidarity had to make good on its threat. On 24 November a half dozen Warsaw factories stopped work, and leaflets and posters denouncing the security police began appearing around the city. Walesa himself warned that there might be strikes elsewhere in Poland unless Narozniak was released.

The situation was complicated by the fact that a two-hour strike of railway workers over a pay dispute had just evoked a sharp reaction from the Soviet Union. The Soviet newspaper *Izvestia* decried "activity aimed at heightening the tense situation in Poland" and warned that a rail strike could affect Poland's national defense interests and disrupt transit links across Poland.[18] On 25 November the U.S. State Department told journalists that Soviet troops near the Polish border had been placed on a higher state of alert than normal.[19]

The conflict was resolved this time through the mediation of some journalists, especially Stefan Bratkowski, chairman of the Association of Polish Journalists, who acted as an envoy between the Party and Solidarity leadership. Narozniak was released, and the strike ended.

But the situation was ripe for further conflict, and mutual testing continued for a number of reasons. The Party and Solidarity differed on the interpretation of the agreements, a fundamental source of conflict. Also, neither the Party nor Solidarity could control its rank and file sufficiently to relieve tension and facilitate the bargaining process, especially at the local level. Party officials at all levels were actively questioning the relative "independence" of such non-Solidarity organizations as the Union of Students or Rural Solidarity. Most difficult to resolve, Solidarity's basic impulses for dignity, justice, and truth in public life were ultimately incompatible with the Soviet system in Eastern Europe.

So far, the skirmishes followed a typical pattern. The Party would obstruct some provision of the agreements. Solidarity countered with a threat to strike or use other nonviolent sanctions. Negotiations ensued, leading to a compromise. Neither side wanted to escalate to the point where they might trigger Soviet intervention. The pattern was repeated on numerous occasions at the local level, where the Party apparatus was particularly vulnerable and defensive.

The biggest national confrontation to fit the pattern began on 19 March 1981 in Bydgoszcz. Local militia beat up some Solidarity activists after they refused to leave a meeting of the *Voivoship* (Peoples' Council) to which they had been invited. Solidarity's National Coordinating Commission asked the government for a full investigation of the incident, but they considered the subsequent official report inadequate. So a national general strike was announced, and a four-hour "warning strike" was staged on 27 March. The threat was sufficient to motivate direct talks between Lech Walesa and Deputy Premier Rakowski, resulting in a joint government-Solidarity statement on the events in Bydgoszcz.

The Bydgoszcz crisis, which nearly erupted in open confrontation, became an emotional focal point throughout Poland and abroad. The East European media intensified their criticism of Solidarity, emphasizing "the political nature" of its program and encouraged the Polish leadership to take a harder line against the "anarchy and lawlessness" spreading throughout Poland.[20]

At the same time, NATO held a special Atlantic Council meeting to discuss the situation in Poland. The NATO countries had expressed their deep concern about Poland as early as December 1980, when Soviet forces in the GDR, Czechoslovakia, and the western Soviet Union had begun taking up forward positions near the Polish borders.

The protracted political confrontation did nothing to improve the deep economic crisis brewing in Poland since the early 1970s. Worsening shortages of basic goods were a perennial source of discontent.

With both the political and economic stakes getting higher, Solidarity shifted strategy during the autumn of 1981. Originally, it had sought to play a role similar to a western trade union—stand outside the economic system, critique it, and name the conditions under which it was willing to provide its own principal resource, labor. Solidarity took no direct responsibility for the efficiency of industry or for the economy as a whole. Older state-sponsored experiments in worker self-management had resulted in the co-optation of labor and its neutralization as a political force. It was in reference to that dubious tradition that Lech Walesa had stated: "We do not want to be bureaucrats, but activist-examiners. We would like to do our job and examine."[21]

Solidarity's disengagement left the economy in the hands of the Party, which could only mean further decline and a negative spiral of more hardship, protest, and confrontation. The same argument applied to education, culture, and other areas of national life, which the Party was also mismanaging. The situation required more rather than less engagement by Solidarity in all aspects of Polish life.

This necessity demanded a new strategy which gradually emerged. At its First National Congress in October 1981, Solidarity elaborated a comprehensive program entitled the "Self-Governing Commonwealth." The objective of this program was nothing less than the political and economic transformation of Poland based on the gradual development of genuine self-management in all arenas of national life. Strikes and other forms of protest and noncooperation would drive the process forward, and phoney manifestations, such as the government's proposed Act of Farmers' Self-Government (as against a free peasants' union) would be rejected. Solidarity was beginning to look like a parallel government in Poland.

While risky, this new line of departure seemed the only way to address and eventually resolve Poland's multiple and endemic crises. The First National Congress of Solidarity, therefore, went well beyond the August agreements of 1980, by propounding a wider and deeper set of objectives for the movement. The Congress also consolidated the national leadership of Lech Walesa, took measures toward greater internal discipline (especially against wildcat strikes), and mapped out areas for negotiation with the authorities. Despite some internal dissent, the program and the leadership structure were confirmed through a democratic process that strengthened the union and enhanced its ability to bargain with the state. For the time being, advocates of open confrontation were a minority within Solidarity.

An entirely different process was taking place within the Communist Party. On the one hand, the Party leadership felt pressure from the rank and file who were asking for democratization. Many of them joined the Party's so-called "horizontal organization" which promoted programs similar to that of Solidarity. On the other hand, the Party's traditional bureaucracy, especially at the local administrative level, looked on any changes as a threat to its privileged position and urged confrontation with Solidarity. The Party was unable to resolve the dilemma at its Ninth Annual Conference. The ruling elite in Poland looked beyond the Party to preserve their power and, by the same token, Soviet domination. Their gaze fell on the army.

In the autumn of 1981, General Wojciech Jaruzelski, who already held the positions of prime minister and minister of defense, was elected first secretary of the Party. At the same time the first "military operational groups" began supervising local administration and functioning in what had always been the traditional role of the local Party committees. This was followed by a tougher approach to Solidarity.[22] The first act of open aggression took place on 2 December, when some one thousand police troops, following repeated warnings, entered the fire-fighting officers' academy in Warsaw, evicted the students occupying the premises, and arrested Solidarity's representatives. The government anti-Solidarity campaign had picked up.

Solidarity's appeals for national reconciliation were ignored, and successive proposals for bilateral negotiations on economic and social questions were refused.[23] Conciliatory efforts made by the Catholic Church were similarly ignored. The primate intervened directly in the country's politics by urging an end to social conflict. Writing on behalf of the entire episcopate, the Council of Bishops sent appeals to all members of parliament to refrain from passing recently proposed legislation that would give the government the right to use "extraordinary means" in dealing with social problems.

On 9 December, Archbishop Glemp and other members of the Church hierarchy met Lech Walesa and other Solidarity leaders. At the same time Radio Moscow, quoting a TASS report, claimed that counterrevolutionary forces in Poland were fighting an increasingly open struggle against the authorities and against socialism. The report stated that Solidarity had gone on a state of alert in several regions of Poland and that attacks on Party committees in various enterprises were continuing. It also accused the Roman Catholic Church of encouraging sermons "which discredited the government's actions for the defense of socialism in the country."[24]

MARTIAL LAW: THE PARTY COUNTERATTACKS

On Sunday, 13 December 1981, at 6 A.M., General Jaruzelski announced that the State Council had declared a state of war. For the duration of the martial law emergency the country was to be administered by the Military Council of National Salvation, consisting of Jaruzelski as head and twenty other military men. The military council began by suspending unions and introducing a curfew which closed down communications, domestic and foreign travel, meetings, strikes, and all independent activities. Solidarity activists were arrested, as well as intellectuals (some who had advised Solidarity and others) and some discredited Party officials. Soldiers surrounded the big industrial centers and began patrolling the streets in each big city. The mass media were silenced. Only one radio and television channel continued to function, and this was operated by soldiers.

Among those arrested were Lech Walesa and virtually the entire 107-man National Commission of Solidarity which had been meeting in Gdansk and had broken up only hours before the troops and tanks took up their positions. According to official Polish sources, a total of 6,309 people were interned in the operation.[25] Workers in key industries, including transport, communications, mining, power, and some key manufacturing plants, were placed under military law. This meant that failure to obey orders was punishable by death. Any activities contravening the new laws were to be judged by special military courts under the new procedures.

The earliest court verdicts signaled the government's intent to rule with an iron fist. Strike organizers were sentenced to five to nine years in prison. Ordinary life in Poland took on the classic features of a military occupation: censorship of correspondence, curfews, raids, searches, arrests, military courts and sentences, and the notion of collective responsibility for infractions.

The declaration of martial law came as a shock to most Poles. In part, they had been lulled by the protracted state of crisis going back to August 1980. Although they had gotten used to a state of permanent alert, no individual crisis until now had forced the authorities to make outright war on society.

Moreover, few Poles could have imagined in advance the Polish army suppressing society. A patriotic and sentimental confidence in the army was backed up by the notion that, if called in, the army could not possibly be effective against a Solidarity general strike. The sense of surprise was heightened by the fact that the Soviet Union, not the Polish army, had always been the presumed military threat.

People also hoped that conciliatory intervention by the Church would somehow bring about political stability, as it had in the past. Finally, there was a widespread conviction that the government would know that any move to crush Solidarity and renege on the August agreements would be patently counterproductive. It would risk moral outrage both within and without Poland, and seemed likely to lead to prohibitive political and economic costs for the regime.[26]

Recovering quickly from the general state of shock, Solidarity responded with courage and ingenuity. On 14 December strikes broke out in most of the larger plants in Lodz, Cracow, Warsaw, Wroclaw, and the entire Gdansk-Gdynia area, as well as in several of the Silesian coal mines. Motorized riot police units (ZOMO), with the assistance of the military, launched attacks on the strikers, first in the Warsaw foundry and at the Huta Katowice steel works, and later at the larger enterprises throughout the country. Now that the workers were in a state of open warfare with the state, the tactical advantages that they had earlier enjoyed inside their factories disappeared. In many cases tanks drove through factory walls and fences and the ZOMO forces attacked workers with gas, water canon, and guns. In some cases the government forces were reinforced by parachute landings.

The strikers generally followed Archbishop Glemp's appeals to avoid a violent response. Workers were severely beaten, and many died from police brutality, but they countered with violence only rarely. They appeared to understand that mass violent resistance could lead to even greater bloodletting.

Although street demonstrations risked more violent reaction than strike actions, a number did occur in the early days of martial law. In Gdansk, for instance, the eleventh anniversary of the December

1970 killings occasioned demonstrations and skirmishes in which over three hundred people were injured.[27]

Acts of disobedience or noncooperation among the government bureaucrats were not tolerated. By 15 December some *voivods* had already been replaced by military personnel because of "improper performance of their duties" and "for attempting to avoid performing tasks imposed on them by the emergency decree." Many senior industrial managers were also dismissed for similar reasons.[28]

Despite these early efforts, resistance wore down. The arrest of most of Solidarity's leaders had effectively broken communication throughout the country. Isolated strikes were attacked by specially trained units, and the resisting factories collapsed one by one. The last holdouts were in the coal district of Silesia, where miners sealed themselves off in shafts. To break through, ZOMO used heavy guns and live ammunition and killed seven at the Wujek mine. In some factories the striking workers would assemble in the main factory square, from there to be repulsed by the security forces, while maintaining their symbolic unity by keeping locked arms as they were pushed back.

The reaction of the Soviet authorities was constrained but approving. A long-term Soviet credit to Poland was announced on 6 January 1982, and four days later Josef Czyrek, Poland's minister of foreign affairs, went to Moscow for meetings with Soviet leaders.

The Western alliance reacted sharply but not in unison. U.S. President Ronald Reagan strongly condemned the repression of Solidarity and, after a few days, suspended credit and commercial ties with Poland. West German leaders, on the other hand, avoided criticism of the Polish military and received the Polish deputy premier, Mieczyslaw Rakowski, in Bonn on 30 December.

On 11 January 1982, NATO representatives held another special meeting in Brussels and decided to withhold further commercial credits except for those needed for food. They suspended negotiations on extending Poland's debt payments and offered to continue, even to increase, direct humanitarian aid to the Polish people.

The Soviet Union and Poland jointly condemned NATO actions and described them as gross interference with Poland's internal affairs. Finally, at the end of December, the last of the strikes were broken.

The pretext for martial law, as articulated by Jaruzelski, was that it was necessary to prevent anarchy and the complete breakdown of order in Polish society. But both Solidarity and the Church were in an overtly conciliatory posture when the state of war was declared. Their attempts to establish a new modus vivendi were brushed aside. There were shortages and discontent, to be sure, but no strikes were taking place, much less anything resembling "anarchy." Perhaps the Polish authorities felt they needed to preclude a military move by the Soviet Union, as recent statements by Jaruzelski have suggested.[29] It would be difficult to disprove this possibility, but it is hard to see why the Soviets would want to bear the costs of such an operation when it had willing surrogates to do the job for them.

The most probable explanation is that the government found the existence of well-organized independent unions irreconcilable with its own continued authority and system of government. The course taken in December 1981 was probably chosen sometime earlier and launched when the first glimmer of a valid pretext arose.

If that is the case, Solidarity during the autumn of 1981 may have played into the state's hands. It had sent, for example, a "letter of greeting" to the working people of Albania, Bulgaria, Czechoslovakia, the German Democratic Republic, Rumania, Hungary, and "all the nations of the Soviet Union" encouraging them to struggle for free trade unions of their own and calling for a sharing of experiences in this regard across national boundaries. Against the background of the new ideology of "self-governing commonwealth," it was undoubtedly inflammatory.

Solidarity's National Commission, meeting two days prior to the declaration of martial law, had further politicized the battle by calling for a national day of protest on 17 December and demanding a multipurpose referendum amounting to a vote of confidence on General Jarulzelski and the Communist Party. Most threatening were calls for free elections and reconsideration of future military cooperation with the Soviet Union. These gestures must have looked audacious to all the Communist bloc countries.[30] Therefore, while Solidarity may not have caused the state of war, the National Commission's provocations meant Solidarity would continue to seek to extract the greatest possible cost from the Party for having made war on the workers.

Ironically, the National Commission meeting simplified the government's task of rounding up leaders. By interning virtually the entire Solidarity leadership in one fell swoop, the architects of martial law created a perception of strength, decisiveness, and competence that they had not enjoyed since before August 1980.

Solidarity had chosen a self-limiting course. It had opted for gradual transformation of the communist system and tried to create pockets of social, political, and economic independence from Party control. It chose a method of nonviolent struggle toward this goal, both because nonviolence was tactically necessary for survival and because it implied the moral repudiation of a system based on violent and deceitful uses of power. If there was a failure in December 1981, it was not in the choice of nonviolent struggle but in the inability of Solidarity to appreciate and prepare for the lengths the communist system would go to defend itself from such a pervasive, albeit longer-term threat.

Solidarity had been counting on moderates within the system to engage with workers in a process of gradual reform. People who identified with the political center generally favored real accommodation between the Party and Solidarity. Martial law not only constrained Solidarity severely, it also effectively eliminated centrist politics within the Communist Party. By banning the union, it eliminated the possibility of any middle ground, and the center quickly lost its political base and its preferred program. Party centrists were appalled by the brutality of the suppression, and many found themselves in the same boat with Solidarity activists, that is, they were subject to significant reprisals themselves.

TOWARD A MUTUAL VETO

The application of nonviolent sanctions became extremely difficult after the imposition of martial law. By its sheer enormity, the military action was able to defeat the resistance and expose weaknesses in Solidarity's capacity for self-defense. The military remained loyal to the Military Council of National Salvation. Police units were able to isolate and break up occupation strikes. The capacity to mobilize strikes was in decline, after more than a year of perpetual crises, followed by the shock of brutal and paralyzing repression. The unspoken threat of possible Soviet action to back up Jaruzelski's coup contributed further to feelings of apathy and impotence. Many people no longer believed that nonviolent sanctions could deter or defeat military attack.

Nevertheless, Solidarity continued its struggle. The leading activists, both those who were interned and those who operated underground, argued against violent resistance. It would surely invite a Soviet invasion, and whether it succeeded or not, such action would dramatically increase the number of casualties. Further, to adopt violent methods now would be to give up an important comparative advantage. Military repression had evoked moral condemnation. Much of Solidarity's legitimacy derived from its repudiation of violence as a means for resolving political conflicts. Besides, the objective had always been the transformation of the communist system rather than its overthrow. So, despite disappointment and setbacks, underground Solidarity chose to stick to its program and methods, and retain its unique voice in Polish affairs by pressing on through strictly nonviolent means.

On 7 January, only two weeks after the imposition of martial law, the first issue of the underground paper *War Weekly* appeared in Warsaw. Two days later Zbigniew Bujak, head of the Warsaw chapter of Solidarity, who had been in hiding since martial law began, said that "the union was continuing its activities underground" and was "prepared to struggle through peaceful means against the military dictatorship." Bujak said, "the first shock of martial law has passed and now a spontaneous opposition is growing." He cited examples of passive resistance against political dismissals in factories, the fact that intellectuals were turning in their Party cards, and that people were banding together to refuse to sign loyalty oaths.[31]

At the same time there were also signs of emerging resistance among the peasants. The communist newspaper *Trybuna Ludu* warned peasants that the authorities might have to enforce compulsory deliveries of grain if the peasants continued to withhold deliveries to state procurement points.[32] In late January there was also a significant protest from Polish intellectuals who issued a petition to parliament signed by 130 academics, urging the authorities to stand down from confrontation. Polish bishops and the primate repeatedly called for freedom for all citizens and the nation as a whole.[33]

Popular discontent was inflamed by a governmental decision to increase substantially the prices of coal, electricity, water for heating radiators, and food. In the meantime, outside observers assessed Poland's industrial production to be running at some 50 to 60 percent of capacity. The Labor Social Affairs Institute said that at least a quarter of the population of Poland was living below the established poverty level.[34]

Not all protest was extinguished by martial law. For example, a huge street demonstration occurred in Gdansk on 30 January but was brutally attacked by the police. Two weeks later another big demonstration took place in Poznan. In mid-April a crowd gathered in Warsaw's central square to mark the deaths of twelve martial law victims. On 1 May there were demonstrations to counter May Day observances. Two days later police had to disperse another large gathering of Solidarity supporters in Warsaw. In April the first symbolic strikes began to appear. On 15 April Warsaw university students and teachers went on a fifteen-minute strike to protest the forced resignation of the university director. Two weeks later there was a fifteen-minute protest strike at the Gdansk Lenin Shipyard. On 13 May short strikes broke out in scattered factories to mark five months of martial law.

In the meantime discussions about an underground strategy of resistance began to develop. In February new underground newspapers appeared, among them the *Mazowsze Weekly* of Warsaw, which quoted Zbigniew Bujak advocating a mass campaign of support for the union through petitions and letters to the government. He also urged people to reaffirm their support for Solidarity in symbolic ways, such as refusing to buy newspapers on Wednesdays, and turning off the lights in their homes between 9 P.M and 9:30 P.M on the thirteenth day of every month. On that day people should also stop work for fifteen minutes at midday. Bujak's suggestions were widely carried out throughout the country. Observers noted that by the early spring of 1982:

> The resistance against the state's coercion is still spontaneous . . . spontaneous also are popular actions of placing flowers in symbolic places, of lighting candles, days of silence in schools, and the habit of wearing Solidarity badges on jackets . . . creation of the organized conspiracy (although still possible and probable) is not indispensable for the continuity of this resistance."[35]

Necessary or not, the underground movement did in fact become well organized, and so defeated one of the immediate objectives of martial law, namely, to deal a knockout blow to Solidarity. On 22

April, representatives of Solidarity's regional organizations set up an
Interim Coordinating Committee (TKK) whose goal was to coordinate resistance activities to nullify martial law. It also would seek the
release of political prisoners, the restoration of human and civil
rights, and the relegalization of Solidarity. The committee was composed of four Solidarity leaders who had eluded capture and remained underground. Lech Walesa recognized the TKK when he
was later released from internment and managed to meet secretly
with its members several times. Similar structures were created in
later months by Rural Solidarity and the Independent Union of Students.

On the government side, a new state organ, the "Patriotic Movement of National Rebirth," was supposed to unite various groups of
Polish society during this time. New trade unions were created by
the government to supplant the illegal Solidarity. Dissolved associations, such as the Association of Polish Journalists, were also replaced
by new state-controlled organs. Individual actors, writers, scientists,
and other intellectuals were invited to cooperate with the new regime. Solidarity leaders condemned any type of collaboration with
the government and a mass boycott of the pro-government organizations began to occur throughout Poland.

The contest for workers' loyalties was particularly sharp at the
shop and plant levels, where the government aggressively promoted
the new legal unions, only to be thwarted by workers who demonstrated their allegiance to Solidarity by continuing to pay Solidarity
membership fees.[36] Managers of most Polish enterprises continued
to consult former Solidarity representatives before proceeding with
major decisions affecting workers.[37]

The government was equally frustrated by intellectuals and artists.
Most actors refused to perform on radio and television. Journalists
boycotted communist newspapers. Teachers ignored instructions on
educational programs. Writers sent their work to clandestine publishing houses. Most prominent intellectuals refused to participate in
events organized by the authorities.

The outlawed leadership took heart. They felt vindicated in insisting on nonviolent discipline, and they took every opportunity to
reinforce it. Bujak condemned "any acts of violence, street battles,
hit-squads, acts of terror and armed organizations," and Adam Michnik of KOR wrote from prison in May 1982 that "armed actions

could only be conducted by fools or provocateurs and the underground should disassociate itself from any activity of this sort."[38]
Nonetheless they recognized the limitations, under present conditions, of particular kinds of nonviolent actions. Strikes and demonstrations especially elicited severe repression for comparatively little
gain, so they limited strike action to the symbolic sort.

It was also becoming clear that attempts to reconstitute Solidarity
as a monolithic organization capable of challenging the state directly
would create another target for Polish or Soviet repression. The obvious solution was to promote a "decidedly decentralized movement," adopting a less direct mode of action: "positional warfare," as
Bujak expressed it.[39] Individual groups and social networks would be
encouraged to create a bulwark of resistance against the monolithic
activities of the state in different areas of life by developing their
own mass movements and organizations. Through the independent
actions of peasants, students, craftsmen, and so on resistance would
become a new basis of social life.

While in factories resistance would mean the continued struggle
for independent unions, there should also exist committees for helping the needy and unemployed, independent publishing projects, educational councils, cultural and scientific networks, and professional
organizations for lawyers and doctors. All social and professional
groupings should follow the model of Solidarity, without explicit allegiance to it, to create a fait accompli of independence. Another underground Solidarity leader, Wiktor Kulerski, correctly predicted
that decentralization would lead to a situation in which "the authorities control empty shops but not the market, workers' employment
but not their livelihood, state owned mass media but not the circulation of information, printing houses but not publishing, the post and
telephones but not communications, the schools but not education."
According to Kulerski, this kind of sprawling social independence
could lead eventually to a situation where the state would be left
with the police and a few diehard collaborators, in which case the
government would either fall or turn to make its peace with society.[40]

This strategy was later elaborated in an official document of the
Interim Coordinating Committee, entitled "The Underground Society," and was gradually appropriated by the Solidarity rank and file
as well as supporters throughout society. Two years later, the underground society was well under way.

Hundreds of underground periodicals are being published more or less regularly, scores of new titles are added annually to the already rich library of underground book publishing. Some of them in quantities which would seem respectable even to Western commercial publishers. Living-room theater, underground cabaret, unofficial art exhibitions are flourishing. Tens of thousands of Poles attend unofficial adult education classes . . . participation in the underground fragmentally taps professional skills that the state does not call upon. A group of doctors·is at work on a report on an officially neglected health problem. Some lawyers are compiling a human rights report. A group of historians is making ready for publication—out of the country, and underground, of course—a vast history of Poland during the last forty years. The participants in such activities risk severe reprisals ranging from dismissal from their jobs, to long terms in prison under appalling conditions. Even so, their members appear to be growing.[41]

ANALYSIS

Outcome of the Campaign

This first campaign by Solidarity has to be seen as a short-term failure in that the stated objectives were not met. However, to a greater extent than India in 1932, Poland in 1982 was poised, as a result of the excellent defensive work accomplished during the early phases of martial law, to launch a new campaign and gain an overwhelming victory not many years later.

The worst thing that can be said about Solidarity's campaign of 1980–1981 is that, in terms of the singular objective, the legalization of an independent trade union, the campaign failed. It ended with Solidarity as such forced underground and greatly weakened as a formal organization. Nonetheless, Solidarity comported itself in adversity in such a way as to create a powerful mutual veto with the state. Solidarity could not function as it wished, but neither could the Communist Party rule as it desired.

In the longer term, we know that the prognosis for an alternative, underground society was perfectly correct. By the late 1980s, the Party needed resources and cooperation badly enough to resurrect Solidarity, to allow its participation in an open political process, and in the end to hand over major governmental responsibility to the organization it had once fiercely battled.

PRINCIPLES OF DEVELOPMENT

Principle 1: Formulate Functional Objectives

The nonviolent protagonists conformed to this principle.

The call for independent trade unions is one of the most perfectly framed objectives of the six cases. The opposition avoided the temptation of calling for the overthrow of the government, which would certainly have forced a Soviet response. The objective of free trade unions was also one whose progress could be readily measured.

The policy objective of demanding free trade unions flowed easily into functional strategic objectives. Moreover, the list of twenty-one demands were similarly functional as a means of crafting optimal tactical encounters.

The objectives at all levels of impact were concrete, touched vital interests, and generated wide support. Seeking to control particular social, political, and economic activities, however limited, was valuable in itself and contributed to further organization around the main objective.

All varieties of strikes and social and political noncooperation came to bear on the objective. The Poles were very effective in improvising variations on the known methods. The skillful selection of objectives by the leadership in this case can perhaps be attributed to lessons from the struggles of 1968, 1970, and 1976, which had more amorphous objectives.

Principle 2: Develop Organizational Strength

The nonviolent protagonists conformed to this principle.

Though at times unwieldy, Solidarity in 1980 was one of the best fighting organizations in the history of strategic nonviolent conflict. It was clearly a product of recent experience with related organizations like KOR, which gave Solidarity depth and breadth.

Walesa's charismatic leadership was mostly functional. The commitment of the Solidarity movement to democratic practices within its own structures had both a positive and a negative aspect. Democratic procedures meant the movement could only react slowly at certain decision points. On the other hand, adherence to these procedures meant that major choices once arrived at invoked more explicit support and authority than they might have otherwise. And, of course, whatever Walesa's limitations they were mitigated somewhat by disciplined collective decision making within the organization.

Besides the tight-knit operating corps within Solidarity, the society itself also offered many organizational opportunities. This was an ideal situation, in that it placed the maximum burden on the forces of repression, running in all possible directions to secure compliance. Widespread civilian involvement gave the movement the widest possible set of options to attack or defend with. Solidarity also took a page from Gandhi by requiring the maintenance of personal discipline (such as sobriety) in factories to keep people sharp and their endurance high.

Principle 3: Secure Access to Critical Material Resources

The nonviolent protagonists conformed to this principle.

The trade union movement, by virtue of its direct access to the infrastructure of Polish society, controlled the necessary material base, including transport and the supply of key provisions such as coal and grain.

A tradition of providing relief from organizations like KOR meant that there would be help for those who were hard-pressed. Though the economic situation was deteriorating for everyone, causing considerable strain, loss of specific economic resources did not weaken the resistance. In fact, price increases stimulated resistance.

The early "self-defense organizations" gave Polish resisters experience in clandestine organization. Their underground press and communications functioned impressively and could not be stopped, even after the onset of martial law.

Principle 4: Cultivate External Assistance

This principle was inoperative.

Outside support was never useful to Solidarity in 1980–1981 and was not really cultivated. The geopolitics of the East-West relationship in 1980 dictated that while the West would express great sympathy for the brave struggle of Solidarity, there was no pretence that any major confrontation would be risked in order to be of tangible assistance. Only when martial law was established did external economic sanctions, particularly from the United States, become a factor. They remained a minor factor, however, in comparison to the society's own direct actions.

Neither was there tangible help from within the communist bloc, as might have been expected later in the decade.

Principle 5: Expand the Repertoire of Sanctions

The nonviolent protagonists conformed to this principle.

The repertoire included: strikes, constructive work, underground press, parallel institutions, alternative education, creative use of symbolic protests, mass defiance, and illegal communications both inside and outside the zone of conflict. The opportunistic use of religious places (especially Catholic churches) and symbols were important. In-factory strikes, short demonstration strikes, and wildcat strikes were especially effective. Many of the sanctions were easily reproducible. During the course of the campaign, strikes affected over one hundred enterprises.

PRINCIPLES OF ENGAGEMENT

Principle 6: Attack the Opponent's Strategy for Consolidating Control

The nonviolent protagonists conformed to this principle.

The Polish Communist Party's strategy was dependent on unchallenged legitimacy. The Party was both overextended and undersupported, especially from Moscow. The Party was continuously susceptible to the risk of losing control. The Party's own membership was at points demoralized and wavering. In these circumstances, Solidarity's ideology and methods took the contest directly to them. The demand for free trade unions was a frontal assault on the Communist Party's primary means of control, which was exclusivity.

Early success was no doubt in part a product of the understanding that the Soviet Union was reluctant to put itself on the line, as long as a comparatively restrained strategy was waged by Solidarity. Thus, to the extent that the Communist Party's control depended on Soviet sponsorship, Solidarity's strategy was to take advantage of reduced Soviet aggressiveness in the region.

Principle 7: Mute the Impact of the Opponents' Violent Weapons

The nonviolent protagonists only partially conformed to this principle.

It seems clear that after the experience of 1970, Polish workers and the opposition understood the necessity to limit their direct exposure to the opponents' firepower. More recently, from 1976 they designed support systems for the families of victims of the repression to counteract extreme deprivation and bolster morale.

Using the factory as the venue for strikes, as opposed to the streets, made it logistically difficult for the government to use violence. The struggle was conducted in such a way that acts of governmental violence were magnified for the purposes of domestic and international media consumption. This eventually lead to inhibitions on the government's use of violence, even when the Soviets sporadically called for harsher measures.

On the negative side, the movement was set back significantly when it failed to anticipate the December 1981 roundup of its operatives. Good intelligence on the imminent imposition of martial law would have allowed dispersion of key people. While the arrests might still have occurred, they would have created a drawn-out melodrama and spectacle for the international community. Martial law would then have made heroes of the resisters and buffoons of the government.

Principle 8: Alienate Opponents from Expected Bases of Support

The nonviolent protagonists failed to conform to this principle.

Warsaw Pact countries were not yet willing or able to defy the dominant state in the region. This left the Polish government with a one-front campaign to fight. The Soviet Union was not likely to exert itself to support the Polish Communist Party, but this fact cannot be attributed to adherence to this principle. The Soviets were occupied with their own problems.

The other main source of support was that the Polish Communist Party would expect to maintain the reliability of its own soldiers. This was by no means assured, however, since they came out of the same alienated Polish society. As with other cases, not enough was deliberately done to see whether the soldiers could be converted and their service severed from the state.

Principle 9: Maintain Nonviolent Discipline

The nonviolent protagonists conformed to this principle.

Clear strictures against violence almost universally accepted by the opposition resulted in low overall casualties. There seemed to be little risk that people would become tempted to use violence as a response to repression. Neither was the movement tainted with violent provocateurs.

Kuron and Michnik, in their writings, were explicit on the need to remain nonviolent. Their ideas were respected in practice, perhaps because of a long, unsuccessful Polish history of mixing civilian resistance with violent encounters resulting in short-term gain and long-term loss.

PRINCIPLES OF CONCEPTION

Principle 10: Assess Events and Options in Light of Levels of Strategic Decision Making

The nonviolent protagonists only partially conformed to this principle.

After a period of mutual testing, tactical responses countered specific threats. All tactical maneuvers seemed to be consistent with strategy and policy. For example, throughout the autumn of 1980 quick, highly focused responses were made to all government attempts to back away from the August agreements, demonstrating the ideal interplay of strategic objectives and tactical execution to secure them.

The December 1981 "provocations," however, arose from a lost sense of strategic flexibility. Actions took on a go-for-broke quality. There was a misplaced urgency to do something that would be remembered after the widely anticipated crackdown. Energies would have been better focused on preventing, mitigating, or recovering from that crackdown. Decisions on the level of policy were otherwise excellent.

Principle 11: Adjust Offensive and Defensive Operations According to the Relative Vulnerabilities of the Protagonists

The nonviolent protagonists only partially conformed to this principle.

Offensive operations up through Gdansk were well chosen. The Gdansk negotiations were a magnificent example of an offensive operation that was appropriate to the strength that had been amassed and the relative vulnerability of the opponent. The events added to Solidarity's reputation and reduced the reputation of the government, signaling both a real and a symbolic shift of power.

Defensive operations against government retreats from the agreement were also well chosen and effective. Without these, the original gains would have been negated quickly, which is no doubt what the Party was counting on when they signed the Gdansk agreement. When the final escalatory tactics were developed, no corresponding defense emerged to counter the likely government response. This was the major single failing in the case, because it led to demobilization and dormancy. It seemed the resistance was lulled into a period of denial, because it did not distinguish between short- and long-term effects of martial law. Had this been recognized, leaders would have been better prepared for a counterattack.

Principle 12: Sustain Continuity Between Sanctions, Mechanisms, and Objectives

The nonviolent protagonists only partially conformed to this principle.

Because the objectives of the struggle were limited, the mechanism of change most likely to prevail was some form of accommodation. Given that premise, Solidarity did an excellent job selecting its preferred nonviolent sanctions.

The more difficult task, however, was to secure the concessions which, once won, were being taken back. Does the provocation of having your opponents renege on their agreements demand an escalation? Does the right mechanism to meet the objectives shift from accommodation to coercion?

The Poles faced just such questions, and while looking for the right answer, left themselves vulnerable to an all-out counterattack.

As it turns out, the key question was how to pursue the conflict after the imposition of martial law. When Solidarity reasserted itself, the ante was raised so the mechanism of change became disintegration, which, until then, had been believed to be impossible.

NOTES

1. The imposition of the Soviet system resulted from a combination of naked force, phony elections, and helpless acquiescence by the Western powers. See T. G. Ash, *The Polish Revolution,* and A. R. Rachwald, *Poland Between the Super-Powers,* for good treatments of the process.

2. Ash, *Polish Revolution,* 9.

3. Originally twelve members, KOR was thirty-three strong by the end of the 1970s. See J. J. Lipski, *KOR,* 48–53.

4. Jacek Kuron, *Co robic?,* 30.

5. Ibid., 124 ff.

6. J. Kwiatkowska, *Kultura* (Paris, 1979), 6:75.

7. Neal Ascherson, *The Polish August,* 116.

8. Jacek Kuron, *Zasady ideowe,* 49; J. J. Lipski, *Etos KOR,* 36; KOR, *Builetyn Informacyjny,* May (Warsaw, 1977). The operative concept here seems to be simply the avoidance of violence. The precise meanings of "coercion" and "force" are unclear, but they do not appear to imply a limitation to only bodily coercion. So a more positive approach to conflict may be being suggested; however, the combination of this concept of "nonviolence" with direct actions gives us the net result of a disciplined nonviolent action campaign.

9. J. Staniszkis, "The Evolution of Forms of Working-class Protest in Poland," 204–31.

10. Staniszkis, "Working-class Protest in Poland," 207.

11. W. F. Robinson, ed., *August 1980,* 12.

12. *Zycie Warszawy,* 19 August 1980.

13. Staniszkis, "Working-class Protest in Poland," 223.

14. PAP (Polish Press Agency), 20 August 1980.

15. TASS, 27 August 1980.

16. *Pravda,* 1 September 1980.

17. Robinson, ed., *August 1980,* 227.

18. *Izvestia,* 24 November 1980.

19. *International Herald Tribune,* 26 November 1980.

20. R. Stefanowski, *Poland: A Chronology of Events, August–December 1981,* 88.

21. Interview with leaders of Solidarity, *Polityka,* no. 44 (Warsaw, 1980). Particularly in the period 1956–1958, in response to the workers' uprising of 1956, workers' self-management councils had been created, but without any centralized leadership, so that the councils were easily manipulated by the Party. In fact, they were used as a source of social mobilization against

the old Stalinist Party clique, and once the new Party leadership had installed itself, the councils were quickly transformed into purely economic bodies, in the so-called Conference of Workers' Self-Government.

22. Previously, with the exception of some local episodes like Bydgoszcz, the authorities had not fully flexed their repressive muscle with Solidarity. Sometimes they had taken only symbolic actions to manifest their strength and determination. This occurred, for instance, in August 1981 in Warsaw, when a motorcade protesting over food issues was stopped by the police and its path blocked on security grounds. This resulted in a protest of parked vehicles in central Warsaw lasting for several days.

23. More about this problem in, for example, Jan Zielonka, *Pools Experiment.*

24. Stefanowski, *Chronology of Events,* 88.

25. Report on the Situation in Poland, presented by Under Secretary General Hugo Gobbi, United Nations, ECOSOC, in Geneva, 21 February 1983, p. 8.

26. As it turns out, martial law did indeed discredit the regime and entail such costs, but the fact that it would do so was not sufficiently clear to Jaruzelski to dissuade him from taking the gamble.

27. *International Herald Tribune,* 17 December 1981.

28. Stefanowski, *Chronology of Events,* 2.

29. *New York Times,* 4 March 1993. Jaruzelski is quoted as saying the threat of Soviet invasion "was real," and he could not have acted otherwise to prevent it.

30. Lawrence Wechsler, *The Passion of Poland,* 86.

31. *New York Times,* 16 January 1982.

32. *Trybuna Ludu,* 16 January 1982.

33. See "The Pastoral Letter of Catholic Bishops," 24 January 1982, distributed and read in all Polish churches.

34. Stefanowski, *Chronology of Events,* 10.

35. Solidarnosc, *Biuletyn Informacyjny* 45 (Paris, 1982), 16.

36. Ibid., 12.

37. Ibid., 24 (Paris, 1982), 9–10.

38. Bujak quoted in *Survey,* 3 (London, 1982), 89; Adam Michnik, "O oporze," in *Krytyka,* 13/14: 12.

39. In Solidarnosc, *Biuletyn Informacyjny* 16 (Paris, 1982).

40. W. Kulerski in Solidarnosc, *Biuletyn Informacyjny* 17 (Paris, 1982).

41. A. Neier, in the *International Herald Tribune,* 11 May 1984.

Chapter 9

Strategy and the Margin of Victory

An important audience for this study are leaders of social and political groups who are challenged by adversaries with opposing interests who are prepared to use military force. These leaders often face a dilemma: they are unwilling to surrender their group's vital interests, but they see no obvious way to mount a viable military campaign. An all-out military campaign would risk extensive destruction of property and too many casualties. The military alternative may even fail, exposing the civilian population to reprisals. The one bright spot is that in order for the adversaries to secure their goals fully, the resisting civilian population must cooperate to some degree. The potential therefore exists for waging strategic nonviolent conflict.

With the stakes so high once the conflict begins, the nonviolent protagonists need to question continuously how they are doing. Unfortunately the answer is seldom clear. It can be understood only in terms of probabilities. For in one moment victory can seem inevitable, while in the next it can unexpectedly slip away. The danger of miscalculation is great. If nonviolent strategists are too optimistic, they may expose their people to loss of life and property, all in a futile effort. If they are too pessimistic, they may give up too soon and unnecessarily encourage their followers to surrender their vital interests.

One of the goals of this book is to analyze what is required for the nonviolent protagonist to win. We identify this task in Chapter 1 as the next to complete in order to develop strategic nonviolent conflict.

The principles in Chapter 2 and the cases in Chapters 3 through 8 isolate and illustrate types of behavior helpful to the nonviolent strategist. Leaders who consider relying on nonviolent sanctions may be aware that "people power" has been used before. They may be skeptical, however, of finding easy historical road maps in specific cases, because they correctly believe that each conflict throws up unique obstacles along the path to victory. Still hungry for guidance, they are unlikely to dismiss patterns in historical data suggesting sensible strategic choices. The question, then, is what reference points are they likely to find in this body of case material that will help them gauge their prospects?

We would argue that when the six cases are compared and contrasted, they support the central hypothesis of this book: comprehensive adherence to a set of strategic principles enhances performance, which bears importantly on the outcome. But other factors determine the outcome as well. Leaders may assess the evolving conditions of the conflict by asking who has the greatest control of critical economic and social resources, or they may judge the current strength of their opponents, including their military capability as well as their ingenuity in using the nonviolent sanctions they too have at their disposal.

Still, nonviolent protagonists are likely to learn a great deal about how they are faring by evaluating their own behavior in the heat of battle. They may feel most confident of success while their own strategic performance is at a high level. When they are using nonviolent sanctions effectively, they are widening the margin of victory. Then current circumstances and the adversaries' capabilities and performance may be offset, as effective nonviolent power reshapes the conflict. Conversely, when the nonviolent protagonists fail to act in a strategically sound way, their fate becomes much more tenuous. When the margin of victory is allowed to narrow, any material change of conditions or any new initiative from the adversary can become a decisive blow.

INHERENT UNCERTAINTIES OF CONFLICT

Strategic nonviolent conflict is just as unpredictable as conflict between two military adversaries. In fact, the uncertainty may be greater because nonviolent sanctions rely so heavily on masses of people understanding and performing complex operations.

One interesting historical observation is that campaigns that seemed most hopeless for nonviolent protagonists at the beginning were not necessarily those that turned out the least successful at the end. As may be recalled, we selected the six cases in part for the diversity of adversaries. For example, Russia, India, El Salvador and Poland were campaigns against entrenched power. The *Ruhrkampf* and Denmark were campaigns against freshly established power. The campaigns against entrenched power resulted in one victory (El Salvador) and one defeat (Poland). Two other campaigns, Russia and India, failed to attain their stated goals, but they sorely tested their military opponents, bringing them to the brink of capitulation. In the case of nonentrenched power, there was one victory (Denmark) and one stalemate (*Ruhrkampf*). So, at least with respect to these six cases, there is no obvious correlation between entrenched power and the outcome.

One of the red herrings we mentioned in Chapter 1 assumes that strategic nonviolent conflict can be waged only against benign opponents. If this were true, it should have been a useful guide to the outcome of these six campaigns. We needed only to handicap the prospects for victory in inverse relationship to the opponent's perceived ferocity. The ranking might be roughly as follows: *Ruhrkampf*, Poland, India, Russia, El Salvador, and Denmark. Unfortunately, the rankings do not correspond to who prevailed.

The reader should not conclude, however, that the campaigns were unaffected by repression. Ample evidence suggests that timely use of military power frequently demoralized the nonviolent resisters. Protagonists about to wage strategic nonviolent conflict have already determined that they are willing to face the opponents' military onslaught. They therefore should look to other variables in their situation to determine whether they can win or lose. Most important, they must not forget that their case is unique.

The six cases offered no reliably recurring patterns. Each case was decided by conformity or lack of conformity to changing subsets of principles. There are so many unique factors driving each of the six campaigns that there is no common road map through them, no pat formula for winning with strategic nonviolent conflict. This is why strategists can never overlook the special aspects of their case by relying too heavily on what appear to be perfect analogies from past events. There are too many differences to consider.

For example, in the Russian campaign the elemental force of the movement was expressed through the fledgling civic organizations of the period that formed a new political base in society (see principles 2 and 6). However, ambivalence about adhering exclusively to nonviolent sanctions split the movement (see principle 2), restricted use of a full range of nonviolent sanctions, and led to a total failure to respond coherently to unfolding events after creation of the Duma (see principles 2, 5, and 10).

The exceptional strength of the Indian campaign was also found in the organizational prowess and execution capabilities of the Indian National Congress (see principles 2 and 5). The commitment to abstain from violence was at the heart of the campaign strategy (see principle 9). The campaign foundered, however, when the designated leader's decision to negotiate alone at the Round Table discussions dissipated the power of the campaign. This demonstrated a faulty understanding of what would make Britain concede (see principles 2 and 12).

The sophisticated "passive resistance" of the *Ruhrkampf* was an important example of the strength to be found in existing civic and commercial organizations (see principle 2). But failure to define the objectives of the campaign with more precision (see principle 1), as well as the inability to move to a less offensive mode (see principle 11), led to stalemate. The campaign in El Salvador, by way of contrast, succeeded without ever needing to shift from offense to defense (see principle 11). Martínez was overwhelmed and his regime disintegrated (see principle 12). The critical feature for Denmark was to cultivate its natural wartime allies and wait for the outcome of the World War, as long as it was expected to be favorable (see principles 5 and 10).

The Polish campaign's key strengths emerged with the leadership's definition of the aims of the campaign. Focus was placed on the adoption of independent trade unions rather than on the overthrow of the communist government (see principle 1). Because these aims were limited, they had substantial credibility at the policy level (see principles 1 and 10). The Poles' adherence to nonviolent discipline was crucial to utilizing a wide variety of sanctions to pressure the regime (see principle 5). In the final analysis, however, the nonviolent protagonists were unprepared and unable to sustain a viable resistance after the imposition of martial law (see principles 7 and 11).

None of the campaigns exhibit an obvious progression to victory or defeat. Surprise and quickly changing fortunes for both sides were the rule. Neither Father Gapon, Count Witte, nor the radicals expected Bloody Sunday to set off the firestorm of protest and strikes that marked the first Russian revolution. However, no one having experienced the extraordinary turbulence of 1905 expected the opposition to unravel at the zenith of success, shortly after the tsar's concession of the Duma. Leaders of the German government probably knew their resistance to the Franco-Belgian invasion of the *Ruhrkampf* would require enormous economic sacrifice. They probably did not expect their currency to be ravaged. Neither did they expect, after all but conceding defeat, that the Dawes Commission would gratuitously redeem part of their position on reparations.

Few members of the colonial administration believed the Indian independence movement would commence with such a competent nonviolent sanction as the Salt March. After the Indian National Congress demonstrated ongoing skill and prowess, there were predictions that the viceroy would have to make substantial concessions toward independence. Few could have foreseen how one of the most brilliant strategists of nonviolent conflict in history would be finessed into personally dismantling what was most threatening to British rule: continued and expanded resistance. To the amazement and chagrin of his Congress colleagues, Gandhi chose to participate in the Round Table Conference, which he had reason to know would be of dubious value.

The Danish campaign had its own unpredictable ebb and flow. The most important indicator—who was winning World War II— vacillated greatly from the start of the German occupation. Yet who could have foreseen the ingenuity of the Danish efforts to secretly send the Jewish community into safe havens? The surprise of El Salvador was that after decades of repression Martínez finally outraged so many segments of society that he lost the ability to rule. It was as though a bubble had burst. At a different time and under different circumstances, a similar one-dimensional offense may have led to failure and high civilian casualties.

The early surprise of the Polish campaign was the way seasoned leadership committed to nonviolent action skillfully crafted objectives and sanctions. The ruling party found themselves unexpectedly boxed into a reactive mode. Later, those who decided so wisely to seek free trade unions rather than the overthrow of communism were strangely incapable of preparing for the crackdown they ought to have known was coming.

Extreme volatility of events sometimes clouds optimal choice. But it also opens up unexpected opportunities for inspiration and genius. The strategist should take heart that military protagonists under the strain of uncertain events can also become disillusioned with their methods of fighting against nonviolent adversaries.

OPPONENTS' CAPABILITIES AND PERFORMANCE

While concentrating on the behavior of the nonviolent strategists, we cannot conclude that it doesn't matter how the opponents behave. We disputed the notion that a ferocious adversary is more likely to win. Now we take issue with the idea that a more benign adversary is more prone to lose. In fact, so-called "benign" adversaries who use their violent weapons sparingly and skillfully (even sometimes in conjunction with their own nonviolent sanctions) may be the more formidable foes. Aggressive, ruthless opponents, too quick to "pull the trigger," may destroy the props supporting their own regime.

The cases show that military opponents seem to do better when they can avoid the forced choice between repression and acquiescence. A strategy of sustaining steady pressure on the nonviolent protagonists seems to work best. To illustrate, contrast the Russian and Indian campaigns. Key advisors to the tsar and the viceroy offered similar advice at an analogous moment in the struggle. The advice came as the first wave of nonviolent action spread across both countries. At that moment Count Witte advised the tsar that he had two choices: full-scale repression or concessions. The viceroy received similar advice in the context of whether or how to imprison Gandhi. One governor suggested that Lord Irwin's choices were basically two: a full crackdown or immediate concessions toward independence.

The tsar was more inclined to bounce from one extreme policy to another. Clearly, he was less certain of his path than the viceroy. When the tsar conceded the Duma, he did so because the situation in Russia, from his viewpoint, had gotten out of control. The viceroy's hand was much steadier. The record shows that he decided to steer a course he called "steady pressure." It was his hope that at some point the energy of the movement would dissipate if he did not provoke its continuance.

There were similarities between the elemental political and social forces propelling the Russian and Indian campaigns, but there were substantial differences in the skill and precision with which the two conflicts were waged. For example, analysis of the Indian campaign finds no principles of conception with which the nonviolent protagonists' behavior "failed to conform." In the Russian campaign, the nonviolent protagonists failed to conform with two principles of conception and only partially conformed with one other (see Table 9.1).

One might wonder what the tsar would have done if confronted by a united opposition with skills equal to those found in the leadership of the Indian National Congress. Then the Duma may have had a longer life and profound impact on society. One might speculate about an opposition in India plagued with disparate voices similar to those of the *zemstvos* and the Bolsheviks. Then the viceroy might have made his job considerably easier by attacking radicals as their significance grew in the opposition. The Indian National Congress never gave him the chance. Similar contrasts exist between the cunning of the French against the Germans and the inflexibility of Martínez or the Polish communists.

In most of the cases, unlimited violence was not an option for the adversary. The tsar could hardly count on the army to carry out enforcement duties at home while reeling from losses to Japan. The French and Belgian invaders would have met strong resistance from the English had a greater number of Germans been killed. Repeated incidents of the magnitude of the Peshawar massacre in India would not have been easily tolerated by some segments of public opinion in England. The last thing the Germans wanted was to divert the military resources needed elsewhere to create a full-scale reign of terror in Denmark. It is highly questionable if Martínez could have commanded sufficient loyalty from his army to pit them against civilian protesters in the last weeks of his rule. Had the Polish authorities resorted to wholesale torture and murder against Solidarity, they would have immediately isolated themselves from the citizenry. Whether an invasion by the Warsaw Pact similar to that of Czecho-

Table 9.1
The Frequency of Conforming Behavior by Principle in Relation to Outcome

PRINCIPLES	SUCCESS		STALEMATE		FAILURE		All
	DENMARK	EL SALVADOR	RUSSIA	RUHR	INDIA	POLAND	
1. Formulate functional objectives	conformity	partial conformity	nonconformity	conformity	partial conformity	conformity	
2. Develop organizational strength	conformity	conformity	partial conformity	conformity	conformity	conformity	
3. Secure access to critical material resources	conformity	inoperative	inoperative	nonconformity	inoperative	conformity	
4. Cultivate external assistance	conformity	inoperative	nonconformity	partial conformity	inoperative	inoperative	
5. Expand the repertoire of sanctions	conformity	conformity	conformity	partial conformity	conformity	conformity	
6. Attack the opponents' strategy for consolidating control	conformity	conformity	partial conformity	nonconformity	partial conformity	conformity	
7. Mute the impact of the opponents' violent weapons	partial conformity	conformity	partial conformity	partial conformity	conformity	partial conformity	
8. Alienate opponents from expected bases of support	conformity	conformity	partial conformity	nonconformity	partial conformity	nonconformity	
9. Maintain nonviolent discipline	contradicted	conformity	nonconformity	nonconformity	conformity	conformity	
10. Assess events and options in light of levels of strategic decision making	conformity	inoperative	nonconformity	nonconformity	partial conformity	partial conformity	
11. Adjust offensive and defensive operations according to the relative vulnerabilities of the protagonists	conformity	conformity	partial conformity	nonconformity	partial conformity	partial conformity	
12. Sustain continuity between sanctions, mechanisms, and objectives	conformity	partial conformity	nonconformity	nonconformity	partial conformity	partial conformity	
Conformity	10	7	1	2	4	6	35
Nonconformity			5	7		1	9
Partial conformity	1	2	5	3	6	4	20
Contradicted	1						1
Inoperative		3	1		2	1	7
							72

slovakia in 1968 would have then provided a suitable umbrella for repression is a matter for conjecture. It might have been unlikely, given subsequent developments within the Soviet Union.

The cases show that military protagonists often do better with guile than by flexing their violent muscles. One of the consistent high points in the performance of military adversaries was how skillfully they used partial or temporary concessions. In several contests the military opponents gave ground to the nonviolent resisters and took it back later. As long as military adversaries retain the preponderance of control, it seems they are able to modify or even renounce their concessions with little negative effect. One of the most difficult tasks for nonviolent strategists, therefore, is to maintain successes won through accommodation.

A pattern of concessions and subsequent de facto renunciation of them runs through at least three of the six cases. In Russia the tsar granted the Duma in 1905 but by early 1907 had totally eviscerated it. Lord Irwin induced Gandhi to come to a Round Table Conference on the condition he suspend civil disobedience. Gandhi, we presume, must have felt there was an implicit concession toward independence by convening the conference. Others, like Nehru, did not. Ultimately the Round Table collapsed and Lord Willingdon renounced whatever goodwill and status Gandhi had achieved with the previous viceroy. In Poland, whatever successes Solidarity achieved were trampled in the wake of the imposition of martial law in 1981. Nearly all of Solidarity's leadership was arrested, making impossible the short-term enforcement of its gains.

The cases also show, however, that military opponents cannot renege on agreements with the same effect every time. Shifting from defensive (concessions) to offensive (reneging) modes is most effective in the later stages of a campaign. Also, the original concessions had to have been sufficiently dramatic that they enticed those waging strategic nonviolent conflict to stand down in lieu of continuing an exhausting, costly battle. Concessions and their subsequent renunciation are not always an optimal approach for the military protagonist. For example, Martínez had no maneuvering room for effective concessions. His position deteriorated too quickly after the resistance began. The French and Belgians hardly needed concessions. The cost of resisting them was mounting exponentially. Several months into the campaign it became clear to both sides that "passive resistance" could not be sustained indefinitely. Concessions as a German bar-

gaining chip in the Danish campaign were unlikely to halt the growing resistance. Once the opposition campaign shifted from a policy
of neutrality and preservation of lives and property to aggressive coordination with the Allies, the Germans had little to offer.

UTILITY OF THE PRINCIPLES

A principle has utility only to the extent that it guides nonviolent
strategists toward victory. To review briefly, in the analysis section
for each campaign the behavior of the nonviolent strategists was
evaluated in relation to each of the twelve principles. This evaluation
yielded one of three conclusions with respect to a specific principle:
(1) it was operative in the case; (2) it was not operative in the case;
or (3) it was contradicted by the case.

There were also three ways a principle could be operative. The
nonviolent protagonists' behavior could have conformed to the principle with positive results. The nonviolent protagonists could have
failed to conform to the principle with negative results. Or the nonviolent protagonists could have been in partial conformity to the principle with both positive and negative results.

When the principle was not operative, the nonviolent protagonist
exhibited no relevant behavior. When the principle was contradicted,
either conforming, nonconforming, or partially conforming behavior
elicited results that did not support the principle.

There were twelve principles reviewed for each of the six cases.
Hence, the concluding analyses yielded seventy-two instances in
which the utility of principles could be evaluated. Of the seventy-two
analyses, only seven concluded the principle was inoperative and
only one suggested the principle was contradicted.

We have acknowledged that six cases are far from a sufficient universe of data to be conclusive. However, it is hard to ignore that
nearly nine out of ten analyses suggest the relevant principles to be
operative. The expectation that this set of twelve principles can apply
to other cases outweighs the expectation that they cannot. Social scientists may resist this assertion without a broader sample of supporting evidence. Yet practitioners may feel more comfortable looking
for direction from these brief assessments. Their alternative—"wing-
ing it"—means operating as though history offered no strategic in-

sights whatsoever. This is a bad gamble for those with so much at stake.

However, both the scholar and the practitioner may feel more comfortable with the utility of these twelve principles by learning why in certain cases they were inoperative. The explanations invariably point to unique but understandable factors.

For three cases, principle 3 was inoperative. This principle demonstrates the importance of controlling material resources in pursuing a successful strategy. The reason the principle is inoperative for both Russia and India has to do with the vastness of those countries. Russia at the turn of the century was just beginning to see migration to the cities. It still was a largely agrarian society. India, with its hundreds of thousands of villages, was also largely agrarian. Neither the tsar nor the viceroy could control all the important resources because they were so widely dispersed. The civilian populations, teetering near poverty, were not dependent on complex centralized distribution systems for goods or services, as was the situation for later campaigns in the Ruhr, Denmark, and Poland. The Russian and Indian populations found everyday self-sufficiency largely independent of their governments.

The speed of the campaign in El Salvador rendered principle 3 inoperative. No one had time to secure any additional resources in contemplation of a longer campaign. Events transpired too quickly to think about a counterattack from Martínez that would threaten access to key resources.

Principle 4, which addresses the cultivation of outside assistance, was inoperative for India and Poland. The main reason was that both were relatively self-contained campaigns. There were no potentially friendly allies on the sidelines ready to join in the fray in a way that could have made a practical difference. India was a completely closed affair between the opposition and Britain. In Poland, efforts to cultivate outside assistance resulted in lots of posturing but little specific help. For example, the Vatican tried to influence events during the campaign. Yet its involvement was more inspirational and conducive to unity of purpose than it was tangible in pressuring the Jaruzelski regime. No additional outside involvement was forthcoming until the United States and Western Europe responded with trade sanctions after the imposition of martial law. By then the campaign was lost.

As with principle 3, principle 4 was inoperative in El Salvador because of the campaign's brevity. The only potential source to cultivate was the United States. American policy was ambivalent, fluctuating between Washington wanting to maintain relations with a wartime ally and the Embassy's disgust with Martínez' excesses. By the time the campaign was at full steam, it became clear that American involvement would prove of little significance.

Similarly, principle 10, which is the principle requiring accurate assessment of progress in conflict, proved irrelevant for El Salvador. A campaign that lasts less than a month is a metaphorical sprint through a wall: there is no time to gauge one's speed, or the wall's thickness. The pace of events would have made efforts to weigh evidence and adjust strategy unavailing. Had Martínez survived the onslaught, this principle may well have become operative as it was for the other five cases.

The only instance of a principle being contradicted is principle 9, which declares that nonviolent strategy should not be adulterated with violence. The Danish campaign provides the contradictory evidence. There is an explanation for this exception. Denmark is the only case where the adversaries were simultaneously embroiled in a military conflict for their survival outside the region of the campaign. Adversaries of Germany were potentially powerful allies of Denmark, to the extent that Denmark expressed hostility to Germany. The Allies offered the prospect of intervening with overwhelming military force. Certain types of violence by the Danes, to the extent they aided the military effort against Germany, were beneficial. Still, many of the negatives associated with violence pertained. Violence did invite repression with all the accompanying difficulties for the civilian population, although the repression had a catalytic effect on later nonviolent actions.

Strategists and scholars may wonder whether the twelve principles address all key requirements for waging strategic nonviolent conflict. A simple exercise lends weight to the conclusion that the principles do, in fact, speak to all of the most important choices exhibited by each case. To illustrate, it is useful to see how the operative principles are distributed through categories of conformity, nonconformity, and partial conformity.

A majority of cases exhibit either conformity or partial conformity for ten out of the twelve principles. As already noted, the two exceptions, principles 3 and 4, are inoperative in three cases each. However, of the remaining cases where principles 3 and 4 are operative, the majority also exhibit conformity or partial conformity. Therefore, none of the twelve principles shows nonconformity in a majority of the cases.

What is the significance of these observations? Remember, we are looking for behavior during conflict that is significant for the outcome but can only be explained by a principle other than the ones set forth here. But we see that principles having utility in one case tend to exhibit utility for all the other cases. Thus, for a principle to be overlooked it would have to be overlooked many times in many campaigns. Since that probability is low, it is unlikely that a strategic principle would remain hidden from view. Therefore, it is likely that the twelve principles are complete for the six cases analyzed. This conclusion does not diminish the expectation that other cases can, and probably will, uncover new patterns of behavior that in turn may suggest new principles.

Nonviolent strategists need to distinguish between what they should do and what they can do. It makes little sense to plan a route to victory that is "easier said than done." Certain principles are easier to conform to than others. For example, in these six cases, there existed less conformity with the principles of engagement and conception than principles of development. Conversely, the likelihood of being in nonconformity was higher for the principles of conception than for principles of engagement and development.

Among the principles of development, only eight out of twenty-four (33 percent) analyses yielded nonconforming behavior. Among the principles of engagement, thirteen out of twenty-three (57 percent) analyses concluded there was some nonconforming behavior. And among the principles of conception, thirteen out of seventeen (77 percent) of the analyses demonstrated nonconforming behavior.

What warning signals should we hear from this? First, it seems that it is easier to mobilize for conflict than to wage it. (This point, by the way, refutes the red herring claiming that the potential of strategic nonviolent conflict can be stunted through specific limitations of circumstance. Indeed, it turns out that these are the easiest limitations to overcome.) Second, it seems that the greatest source of counterproductive behavior is associated with the conception of nonviolent strategy.

Prior to this study, there have been few precise guidelines for the use of nonviolent sanctions. It has been long established that if nonviolent protagonists withhold cooperation, they may eventually deny the opponents their goals (assuming some degree of cooperation is a requisite). Unschooled nonviolent protagonists, however, do not typically think about the costs of noncooperation or the specific, optimal ways to direct its course.

Protagonists, to be realistic, have to decide whether they can adhere to the principles of engagement once they have identified them, or whether they are consigned to do no better than those in the past lacking this understanding. They can look at the cases and judge whether the principles of engagement were conformed to because of spontaneity and luck as much as calculation and design. Readers may also hypothesize about overlooked opportunities to comply with certain principles of engagement. We noted, for example, how vulnerable the tsarist regime was to a credit boycott (see principle 6), and we could see how concerned Lord Irwin was in India with stemming defections among the local police (see principle 8).

Insufficient conformity to principles of conception appears to be related to poor conformity to principles of engagement. If there is no basis on which to define, evaluate, and adjust for productive engagement with the military opponents, then nonviolent strategists can neither assess how they are doing vis-à-vis the opponents (see principle 10), see when to go on the offense or stay on the defense (see principle 11), nor select the most viable mechanism of change designed to lead to victory (see principle 12). Disorientation and even paralysis is a possible consequence.

Since it is impossible to know before a conflict which principles will likely become the most crucial, the nonviolent protagonists must optimize the choice of sanctions they use during the middle of the fray. One benchmark is that the most useful principles to conform to are those which engender conformity for the greatest number of additional principles. Principles with reinforcement potential may be identifiable while the campaign is in progress.

The Russian precampaign history with strikes (see principle 5) gave a sense of direction to the *zemstvos* and other civic organizations and kept the radicals' ideological penchant for violence on the back burner (see principle 2). Emphasis on the strike challenged the tsar's capacity to exert control (see principle 6) and gave a strong offensive impetus to the first two-thirds of the campaign (see principle 11). Therefore, strategists in the Russian campaign may have reasonably focused on perfecting the strike and other forms of noncooperation and knitting them into an operational whole.

In India a tradition of nonviolent discipline (see principle 9) shaped and expanded the range of sanctions available to the Congress (see principle 5). It also muted the British ability to use repression (see principle 7) and mobilized the maximum number of interests in the fight for independence (see principles 1 and 2). Gandhi understood the pivotal importance of nonviolent behavior and spent much of his leadership capital urging it on the Indian people.

In the *Ruhrkampf* the main objectives were to prevent the forcible extraction of resources and to have the reparations question reopened. These objectives, however, seemed to force a direct confrontation with the occupation, making its cessation also an objective. This reinforced several principles. It presented the objective as a test of national dignity and pride, and helped mobilize the population for maximum effort and sacrifice (see principles 2 and 7). It defined the sanctions available for use (see principle 5) and directed the tactical encounters in whatever direction the Franco-Belgian forces sought to dominate (see principle 6). Unfortunately the unrelenting demand for an immediate end of the occupation made it very difficult to fight in a slower gear (see principle 11). The economic pressure the Germans placed on themselves was overwhelming (see principle 3). Strategists can learn a lesson from the *Ruhrkampf*: too much emphasis on conformity to one principle can positively reinforce certain principles at the expense of others.

The campaigns in El Salvador and Denmark failed to illustrate instances where conformity to a single principle automatically led to conformity to other principles. El Salvador was too brief a campaign, and Denmark was dominated by external variables not controlled by the opposition's leadership. Strategists in an El Salvador-type situation should recognize that they are attempting a nonviolent equivalent of a *blitzkrieg* and cannot wait for other principles to become operative in delayed sequence. Strategists in Denmark-type campaigns should strive to stay flexible, given the constraints of external forces.

In Poland, unlike the *Ruhrkampf*, all the reinforcement provided by key principles led to conforming rather than partially conforming, behavior. Poland was like the *Ruhrkampf* in that Solidarity's choice of free trade unions as the primary objective led to a variety of additional positive results. First, it was a sufficiently grand objective to mobilize mass Polish support (see principles 1 and 2). Striving for this objective helped give workers an edge in control of resources (see principle 3). Focus (perhaps too much) was placed on strikes as the main sanction (see principle 5). The objective threatened an important base of Communist Party control (see principle 6). Because it was less threatening than a call for total revolt, it tended to inhibit the Soviet Union from intervening (see principle 8). Finally, the call for free trade unions allowed Solidarity to go on the offensive but retain the possibility of a defensive platform from which to withstand a counterattack (see principles 7 and 11).

It may be unfair to compare strategic performance between the *Ruhrkampf* and Poland. Perhaps the strategists from either campaign could not have molded things differently. The Ruhr invasion was a fresh offensive threatening the German people, whereas Poland's communism was decades old. It may therefore have been unrealistic for Germans in 1923 to accept minimalist objectives, build a defensive position, and wait patiently. The Poles clearly were more desirous of seeking incremental gains, since any objective achieved was better than the status quo. Still, strategists can see in both campaigns the critical linkage between the selection of objectives (see principle 1) and the capacity to shift from offense to defense (see principle 11).

Another general observation about the performance of nonviolent protagonists derived from the cases is that there is a common temptation to abbreviate the campaign and leave the so-called field of battle without retaining the capacity to return. In some cases this was a sin of omission, resulting from a fierce counterattack by the military opponents. In other cases it was a sin of commission, when ending the resistance seemed a worthwhile bargaining chip to negotiate away. Protagonists must never relinquish the capacity for continued strategic nonviolent conflict. Otherwise they will find their campaign vulnerable to fatal risk.

Gandhi's premature suspension of resistance has been well discussed. But consider also how different events may have been in Russia if this point had been understood. The purblind focus of the Bolsheviks on an armed rising led them to the barricades in December 1905. Having concentrated their urban forces as well as their expectations on inconsequential violent skirmishes, they literally ran out of strategic ideas. It is as though they were more interested in playing out a script consistent with their ideological beliefs than in winning. The thing most needed was a way to exert pressure with nonviolent sanctions as the Duma was sorting itself out. This could have kept the tsar at bay and provided the leverage to make the Duma a true countervailing force. Failing to do this made it easy for the tsar to shut the Duma down in 1907 and arrest everyone who went to Vyborg. By then it was too late to resurrect the intense opposition of 1905.

Another questionable decision was the refusal to consider moderating the intensity of "passive resistance" in the Ruhr. A more flexible response, but at a pace dictated by Germany, may have been a smarter approach than using the cessation of "passive resistance" as a bargaining chip against the French and Belgians. The Germans seemed to view "passive resistance" as something to pursue without surcease until victory, lest they be crushed. While this "all or nothing" strategic approach was usefully applied in the overthrow of Martínez, it was not workable for the *Ruhrkampf* against a more complex and formidable adversary. One may wonder, had "passive resistance" continued in any form, if a new dynamic more favorable to German interests could have developed over time. The irony that the Dawes Commission eventually came to Germany's defense offers some confirmation that a prolonged struggle at a reduced level of intensity may have been preferable to a rout by the Franco-Belgian invaders. El Salvador was a quick success. Yet, after Martínez was gone, the resisters could not easily regroup to use nonviolent sanctions to push their constitutional agenda. In the early Danish campaign the entire emphasis of the Scavenian policy was on resistance designed to avoid a severe crackdown by holding the potential of civilian resistance in reserve.

Sometimes the determination to use nonviolent sanctions even when defeated allows for continuity between campaigns. In Poland the commitment to continued nonviolent action was what made it possible for the resistance to retain the last breath of life after martial law was imposed. Though the campaign was effectively over, the resistance was not fully extinguished. When it came back to life in the late 1980s, it did so with its strategy intact. This staying power, maintained underground, was a key factor in the subsequent victory of Solidarity.

Once resistance is abandoned, it is hard to resuscitate. It took Russia a full decade to recover a comparable level of opposition after the dissolution of the Duma. India after 1930–1931 required almost a

decade and a half with an intervening world war to gain independence.

The last observation about the performance of the nonviolent protagonist returns to a point made by Stiehm in our discussion of principle 9 in Chapter 2. Strategists have every right to ask: how do we
know whether there may be a moment when a shift from strategic
nonviolent conflict to the use of violent sanctions would be decisive?
How can the possibility be reasonably ruled out? Stiehm's point is
that the mental energy consumed in looking for that perfect moment
throws the nonviolent protagonists off stride.

What do the cases show? Do any of the cases display an unutilized
opportunity for decisive violence? For example, would an assassination have worked to overthrow the tsar's regime? The answer is not
clear. The tsar would have been a martyr for many. There would
conceivably have been a split among the most conservative members
of the opposition hoping for an orderly succession to the monarchy.

Violence proved useless in the Ruhr and dissipated hope and energy. In Denmark violence made a positive contribution only when
it reinforced specific tactical objectives of the Allies or worked as an
indirect catalyst for more nonviolent sanctions. Otherwise sabotage
and related activities put the civilian population in unnecessary danger. Even if strategists look at the situation with arguably the highest
potential—the possible assassination of Martínez—the dangers and
imponderables are still enormous. What if the assassination attempt
were to fail? Would this have motivated Martínez to continue repression which he refused to do after the civic strike? Violence in India
and Poland would have paralyzed the entire thrust of those two campaigns. Besides, who was there to kill who couldn't be replaced by
the British Raj or the Polish communists? What provisions existed to
deal with the retaliation sure to follow?

The cases give added salience for the necessity to conform to principle 9. Not only does violence mix poorly with nonviolent action,
but even the contemplation of opportunistic violence weakens the
effectiveness of strategic nonviolent conflict.

LESSONS FOR THE CONDUCT OF STRATEGY

Often when a violent adversary places another political group under great pressure, that group may be reluctant to fight because a
military response is not viable. Since surrender of vital interests may

be intolerable, the use of nonviolent sanctions becomes preferable to acquiescence. A "hard-nosed" assessment of whether a nonviolent campaign can succeed may develop only after the conflict has started. Choosing the best route to victory may take a back seat to naive reliance on spontaneity and improvisation. An important purpose of this book is to show how the quality of strategic choice emerges as a critical factor in who wins and who loses. To demonstrate this point, we invited readers to think about the six cases as though they were taking the same risks as the nonviolent protagonists. This exercise, just completed, has yielded several important lessons.

The first lesson is that no set of specific conditions can be said to determine the victor. Each case was sui generis and manifested substantial uncertainties from start to finish. There was no "Holy Grail" or universal path for success. Early circumstances, both favorable and unfavorable, were highly erratic predictors of the final outcomes. During each campaign the prospects of both protagonists were highly volatile. Each campaign had a different subset of principles that proved most important.

The next lesson was that the opponents' willingness to use violent measures also proved a poor determinant for the fortunes of the nonviolent protagonist. Violent sanctions showed severe limitations. From a strategist's perspective, their use frequently proved ill-conceived and costly. Interestingly, the skillful use of nonviolent sanctions by the adversary often became more important. For example, an effective trap often used by otherwise violent protagonists was to seek the cessation of nonviolent action through fraudulent concessions.

The final lesson is that conformity to the strategic principles is likely to increase the prospects for success. In general, greater conformity allowed for more progress, while nonconformity led to setbacks. At least with respect to the six cases, the twelve principles represented a reasonably complete set of behavioral guidelines. There did not seem to be any overlooked principles within the data, though we anticipate the possibility of entirely new principles having utility for protagonists in other campaigns.

Some principles were easier to conform to than others, with those of development being the easiest and those of conception the most difficult. Principles of engagement were somewhere in between. In each campaign, conformity to certain principles became pivotal as they would create opportunities for other principles to come into play. The importance of staying mobilized to be able to continue the fight, while also maintaining the ability to adopt a defensive posture when necessary, was clearly demonstrated. The cases also reaffirmed the dubiousness of looking for opportunities to switch to violence for a final assault.

One overarching lesson can be learned from these cases: to win with strategic nonviolent conflict, nothing can be taken for granted. All avenues must be explored, reexplored, and then reanalyzed after each engagement. Nonviolent strategists must be *comprehensive* in assessing every aspect of the campaign as it develops. Only then will they widen their margin of victory.

PREMEDITATION, FORESIGHT, AND STRATEGIC CHOICE

Leaders face many urgent problems in the midst of conflict. So much can go wrong that they may wonder about the consequences of failing to achieve comprehensive adherence to the principles. It is no easy feat to follow all the strategic principles at once. Certain principles may suggest contradictory courses of action. For example, with respect to principle 1, the articulation of certain goals may alienate a minority of the civilian population, but keep a majority highly motivated. This may work until the minority's behavior becomes counterproductive. Yet when goals are restated to include the minority, the majority's enthusiasm to fight may evaporate.

Conforming to one principle may require compromising another. For example, full mobilization of the civilian population, which is deemed desirable according to principle 3, may contradict the need to protect the population from repression, as required by principle 7. Conversely, exposing only a limited group to the opponents' fiercest repression may reduce the impact of the engagement on the adversary's control, as indicated in principle 6.

It is difficult to determine the optimum pace or sequencing of principles. The Danes' more defensive efforts at the start of the German occupation correctly preceded more aggressive nonviolent sanctions as the war progressed. In many cases, including Russia, Germany, India, and Poland, more aggressive use of nonviolent sanctions late in the campaign may have muted substantial setbacks, but too slow a start may have left these movements stillborn. In El

Salvador there were no discernible phases to the conflict. Unremitting aggressiveness by the nonviolent resistors led to victory, while hesitation might have led to disaster. Clearly, different principles become critical at different junctures. In some circumstances conformity to one principle needs to precede conformity to another. So how can a leader penetrate the obscurity except in hindsight? And what about normal human errors and oversights? Surely it is unwise to rely on any strategy that requires perfect analysis and behavior, or that assumes that nonviolent protagonists' weaknesses will be hidden in the tumult of conflict. It is just the reverse: inadequacies in strategic performance are more likely to surface when the pressure is greatest.

Comprehensive adherence to all the principles may not be enough. We must wonder if what is being offered is a "counsel of perfection"—unattainable in the real world—that will, in the end, be nothing more than a built-in excuse for failure? To resolve this quandary, comprehensive adherence to the twelve principles of strategic nonviolent conflict must be viewed less as an ultimate goal and more as a flexible process in continuous flux. There is no reason to expect failure because comprehensiveness has not been achieved. Neither can success automatically be assumed when all forms of conforming behavior have been pursued exhaustively.

Nonviolent strategists are forced to operate in extremely volatile circumstances where at least one critical variable always remains out of control—the strategic performance of the adversary. If the opponents' skills are formidable, defeat can result no matter how skilled the nonviolent protagonists, but if the opponents are weak in one way or another, nonviolent sanctions can probe and enlarge their weakness. The opponents' competence is an intangible factor. Who ends as the victor and who the vanquished can frequently leave us surprised, whether the practitioners are violent or nonviolent. That the outcome of conflict is indeterminate does not lessen the need for making sound strategic choices. The margin of victory, that is the range of possibilities for winning, cannot be enhanced without the determination to do so.

Two additional qualities come into play when the desire to succeed is high. The first is premeditation. The second is foresight. Premeditation and foresight work together. The nonviolent protagonist, through premeditation, molds behavior to conform to the principles. The essential purpose of premeditation is to seek the optimal result by designing alternatives that can be integrated and coordinated at various levels of strategy. Then these alternatives must be evaluated in light of *the willingness of the opponents to continue fighting.* Adequate foresight would allow leaders to assess the effect of various nonviolent sanctions on the opponents' thinking. Premeditated behavior is unreliable without a good sense of the adversaries' likely response. Without some foresight there is no method to weigh the likely effectiveness of one strategic choice in relation to another. Premeditation and foresight do not ensure all strategic choices will be good ones. Yet without these two qualities leaders can only hope that what they are doing will have a better than random chance of conforming to the principles.

As noted in the introduction, the structuralist argument against strategic nonviolent conflict is that certain obstacles to its success are overwhelming. But premeditation and foresight allows for one strategic choice properly made to lead to another and then another. This doesn't happen all at once, or necessarily in obvious ways. The unfolding of strategic opportunity is like peeling an onion layer by layer. If the opponents' perception of their own invincibility and control can be pierced by a succession of nonviolent sanctions, a conflict can be won. Victory against overwhelming military odds can come by increments, but only the foolhardy and lazy should hope that the right strategic choices will miraculously appear.

The margin of victory cannot be widened by wishful thinking. Strategists must make the best decisions possible, based on their estimation of the opponents' likely response. Too few who use nonviolent sanctions, or who seek to prove their futility, understand how critical the exercise of premeditation and foresight can be. If this book succeeds in highlighting these qualities, it will have achieved something new and important.

CONTINUITIES WITH CONTEMPORARY CAMPAIGNS

Our formal observations began with Russia's Bloody Sunday in 1905. They ended with the suppression of Solidarity in 1981. The period since then has been full of new examples of "people power." Indeed, as was previously noted, this phrase was made popular during the struggle to overthrow Ferdinand Marcos in the Philippines in 1986. This conflict and those in Panama, China, the Middle East, East Central Europe, the former Soviet Union, and South Africa, briefly touched on in the introduction, undoubtedly are among the defining events of the late twentieth century. Given their importance and complexity, they will require time to be fully understood. Until then, whole subindustries of scholarship will be devoted to discovering their meaning. This is why, despite their current significance, we felt it premature to include these cases in our basic analysis.

Though the dust has not yet settled on these episodes, we feel confident that they will affirm the link between strategic performance and the margin of victory. We would venture further by claiming that these campaigns will not be fully understood without explaining the role of strategic nonviolent conflict. The brief narratives that follow need to be read with the twelve principles in mind. One can then sense areas where future research may demonstrate continuities between the contemporary cases and the older ones presented in previous chapters.

The Philippines, 1986

Although it is known as the "people power revolution," nonviolent direct action by civilians was only one of the key ingredients attending the departure of Ferdinand Marcos from power in February 1986, after fourteen years of one-man rule. Other prominent factors included a grave economic crisis and a guerrilla insurgency which had already loosened Marcos' grip on power, the disaffection of important elements of his own armed forces, and the slow but ultimately decisive attrition of U.S. support for his position.

Still, it is difficult to imagine the outcome we know without the final drama of the civilian population, in a climate of religious fervor, interposing itself between the tanks and armored personnel carriers of the Marcos loyalists and those elements of the military that had mutinied and who, by 22 February, had endorsed Mrs. Corazon Aquino, the unified opposition candidate, as the legitimate president elect. From then on it was impossible for pro-Marcos voices in the Reagan administration to maintain that helping Marcos remain in power served either the interests of democracy in the Philippines or those of the United States in the region.[1] With the final withdrawal of U.S. backing, the dictator's only option was to concede defeat and leave the country.

Prior to the conflict's dramatic conclusion, nonviolent action had already played an important role. The election that brought Mrs. Aquino to power, and which Marcos had sought to subvert, stimulated a nationwide defensive operation, conducted by the National Movement for Free Elections, or NAMFREL. NAMFREL volunteers protected polling places from tampering through direct nonviolent intervention (interposing their bodies between ballot boxes and those who would tamper with them), and reported fraud systematically when it occurred, often at great risk to themselves.

Without the poll monitoring or the disciplined demonstrations at the end of the conflict, it would have been impossible to legitimize the Aquino victory. "People power" enabled the dissident military and the U.S. government to endorse and support Mrs. Aquino. While we have been careful, in developing our analytical framework, to avoid overemphasis on the prospects for external support (since it is rarely subject to full control by nonviolent strategists), this is clearly a case in which withdrawal of external support for the old regime, along with dissension in the military, were decisive factors. While nonviolent action was not the controlling element, it was one of several indispensable elements in determining the outcome of the conflict.

Panama, 1987–1988

Just over a year later, in the summer of 1987, another dictatorship encountered a nonviolent challenge. After a military crony exposed the corruption, brutality, and essentially criminal nature of General Manuel Noriega's regime in Panama, a new opposition movement calling itself the National Civic Crusade was born. As a nonpartisan network of over two hundred organizations, associations, and enterprises, the Crusade conducted an astonishingly energetic campaign of nonviolent actions over the next year and a half.

In some ways reminiscent of the Philippines and the earlier case of El Salvador, the movement sought to shift power back to civil society by rendering Panama ungovernable. The movement's hallmark was a relentless series of mass demonstrations in which hundreds of thousands, people from all walks of life, waved white handkerchiefs and religious symbols in denunciation of the regime. The

demonstrations were backed up by economic and political noncooperation, a series of short general strikes, and international economic
sanctions that eventually shut Panama's economy down to nearly half
its normal volume. A coup attempt involving some 20 percent of
Noriega's officer corps failed but left the impression that his last supports were eroding.

How was it possible, then, for Noriega to retain power until the
civilian struggle was preempted by U.S. military invasion in December 1989? At least part of the answer lies in what Roberto Eisenman,
editor of *La Prensa* and one of the Crusade's leaders, has called
"narco-militarism."[2]

This is an especially challenging case, since the theory of nonviolent action holds that if the governed systematically withdraw their
cooperation and support from a regime that oppresses them, that
regime should decline and fall as its sources of power dry up. This
assumes, of course, that the regime has some interest in governing a
functioning society. Panamanian society, at considerable cost to itself,
rendered itself ungovernable, but the military clique in control of the
state apparatus did not seem to care.

Eisenman's "narco-militarism" describes a situation in which a ma-
fia-type organization controls the machinery of state for the primary
purpose of participating in the international drug trade, along with
sundry other illicit rackets. If this depiction of Noriega's regime is
correct, the normal calculation of costs that one would expect a national leader to make when faced with widespread civilian insurrection may never have occurred.

The Crusade made as its objective the recapturing of society. It
tried to take the streets back from the army, expending itself continuously in mass demonstrations and strikes. Demonstrations were often billed as "the final mobilization," though none came close to fulfilling that promise, perhaps because Noriega had too little incentive
to return society to normal.

Only the Panamanian Defense Force, Noriega's ultimate power
base, and the revenues generated by the regime's illegal activities
kept the dictator in power. The movement never seriously threatened either of these supports. In other words, the Civic Crusade
failed in part because it never properly analyzed its opponent's designs, did not identify a functional objective, and could not account
for continuity between that objective, its available sanctions, and a
realistic mechanism for removing the dictator.

China, 1989

Another monumental event involving nonviolent action that requires attention is that of the Chinese democracy movement in the spring and early summer of 1989. Taking advantage of the international media coverage attending a state visit by Mikhail Gorbachev in early May, pro-democracy students challenged the Communist Party's stranglehold on power, first with a hunger strike in early May, and then with mass demonstrations in the heart of the nation's capital. The passion, discipline, and commitment of the students demanding reform was etched indelibly into the world's collective memory as surely as the brutal massacre on 4 June that seemed to put an end to their struggle for change.

For many observers, the Beijing massacre seemed to set the outside limit on the possibilities for civilian resistance. That conclusion, however, amounts to making an absolute strategic judgment based on a limited tactical encounter. The events in Tiananmen Square did not prove that nonviolent struggle was not possible against a regime that was willing to kill thousands. Rather, it should have been seen as an indication that concentrated demonstrations against reliable soldiers is not advisable and that a movement limiting itself to that method may very well fail.

Subsequent discussions of Tiananmen have focused on whether the students should have declared victory and withdrawn after the Thirty-eighth Army was peacefully denied access to the square. That is arguable, and it was argued by some at the time. It is also possible that the students needed to stay for the very purpose of forcing an encounter that would unmask the regime, despite the cost to themselves. The strategic failure, in this case, was not that the repression was allowed to occur but that its occurrence did not trigger enough subsequent sanctions to punish the regime for its folly. There were no strikes, no mass (nonstudent) defiance, and no international responses sufficient to make the regime reconsider its course. So the wave of repression that continued throughout the summer and beyond was allowed to appear decisive.

When nonviolent strategists have among their conceptual tools the option of making appropriate defensive adjustments and a clear focus on the need to prepare many and varied nonviolent sanctions in order to make flexible adjustments possible, they guard against this kind of unnecessary defeat. They can select from a whole range of options the ones that will keep them in the struggle, albeit in a defensive posture, until the time is right for a counterattack. As in military conflict, a battle need not be the war. Just as the Poles learned from the experiences of 1970 and 1980–1981, in order to triumph later in the decade, China, one of the world's last communist autocracies, may yet be transformed by strategic nonviolent action.

East Central Europe, 1989–1991

"The death knell of communist rule," writes Adam Roberts, "which has now ended in all European countries, was sounded not by nuclear weapons, nor even for the most part by the use of military force, but by civil resistance."[3] Roberts is quick to add that these revolutions were not exclusively nonviolent, one reason why we may not think of them entirely in terms of strategic nonviolent conflict. As we saw in the Philippines, several factors were at work.

The analysis must take into account forty years of debilitating military and economic competition from the West. Nor can we ignore the internal paralysis and demoralization of the Soviet Communist Party and similar crises of self-confidence and direction in the Soviet satellite countries. Economic strains loomed large in rousing the people to take direct action. It is difficult to sort out cause and effect in the great sea change in Soviet tolerance for dissent and openness to real reforms represented by Gorbachev. But there is no avoiding his special role, embodied in the policies of *glasnost* and *perestroika,* in creating the environment in which popular struggles blossomed.

Even if all they did was to deliver the death blow, the peoples of East Central Europe, the Baltics, and the successor states to the Soviet Union needed to act to reclaim their societies, and act they did, with intelligence and skill, from the candlelight demonstrations of Leipzig, to the festive dismantling of the Berlin Wall, to the reverential gatherings of Czechs and Slovaks in Wenceslas Square, and finally to the stunning defeat of the Soviet military coup in August 1991. The least that can be said about these episodes is that well-prepared and deliberate nonviolent sanctions were applied to exploit the biggest opening for the restoration of political freedom in living memory.

In terms of strategic nonviolent conflict, what factors will likely emerge as having made an important contribution in this series of struggles? Certainly the careful and deliberate development of organizational strength, exemplified by groups like Civic Forum in Czechoslovakia and New Forum in East Germany, was the basis for much of the successful action that followed. And, as we saw in Poland, many of the national movements were at pains to articulate objectives that were at once compelling to their compatriots and challenging to their opponents without being needlessly provocative.

Nonviolent discipline, though not universally adhered to, no doubt made repression harder and accommodation easier for communist authorities throughout the region. Various broadcast and print media, which were often the objects of defensive "people power" operations, because of their crucial importance in keeping the astonishing changes of this period foremost in the eyes of the world, had a similar effect.

Seen as dimensions of strategic performance, these now-familiar aspects of the revolutions of 1989 and 1991 emerge as an indispensable part of any attempt to explain the shape of East Central Europe, the Baltics, and the Commonwealth of Independent States today.

South Africa

The South African liberation struggle should also be part of any overview, however brief, of this period. It represents a complex admixture of violent and nonviolent methods in the same conflict, over time and in somewhat different theaters or campaigns, raising a number of interesting questions.

The struggle to end apartheid and to establish democracy in South Africa, led primarily by the African National Congress, has been said to rest on four "pillars": an externally based guerrilla insurrection, international economic sanctions, mass mobilization (i.e., nonviolent direct action by civilians), and negotiations for constitutional reform. In reality, the various "pillars" have been invoked, emphasized, or developed somewhat unevenly over time.

The military arm, which was never a match for the South African Defense Force, has at times been celebrated at the expense of more usable options. Nonviolent action, nominally repudiated as a realistic option after the Sharpeville Massacre in 1960, came back in force in the late 1970s and early 1980s under the rubric of mass mobilization. Huge stay-at-homes, boycotts, protest funerals, noncooperation of all sorts to pursue local as well as national issues, and a welter of legal and illegal political organizing typified the 1980's. In tandem with the international sanctions, these efforts helped to create a situation in which President F. W. De Klerk was forced to release long-term political prisoners, including Nelson Mandela, in February 1990, and to move toward negotiations.

At this juncture, the ultimate outcome of those negotiations is uncertain. In any event, even a constitutional settlement will scarcely begin to address the grievances and systemic problems engendered first by colonialism and then by apartheid. What this indicates is that the methods that helped to produce the current opening are likely to be a salient part of the political repertoire in South Africa for the indefinite future. The methods of nonviolent action should not be expected to operate in a strategic vacuum or be allowed to be identified with passivity or defeatism, as has happened at times in the past. The methods of nonviolent action should be recognized for what they are: the levers of power that a struggling people will need to defend themselves throughout the transformation of their country.

The Middle East

While it strains credulity to define the Palestinian struggle of the late 1980s strictly as a nonviolent conflict, it was certainly another case of mixed struggle with a large nonviolent component. It included merchant boycotts, civil disobedience, the creation of parallel institutions, mass demonstrations, protest funerals, and so on. Even the low-level violent actions that came to symbolize the Intifada (stone throwing and occasional use of Molotov cocktails) were seen by the outside world as restrained and largely symbolic. At least for its first three years, the struggle was more nonviolent than violent. The choice by the movement's so-called Unified Command to ban firearms from this campaign led to a redefinition of the conflict, one in which Israel's repressive violence was made to appear both gratuitous and dysfunctional.

Another critical choice was made when Palestinian Liberation Organization (PLO) Chairman Yasir Arafat renounced international terrorism as a method of struggle in the winter of 1988, while maintaining the right to keep the military wing of the movement intact outside of the Occupied Territories. This kept the initiative in Palestinian hands, levered the United States ever so slightly away from Israel and toward the PLO, and gave the movement a renewed and unified purpose, by removing one of the principal stumbling blocks to meaningful negotiations.

The Middle East peace process, of course, was eclipsed for a time by Iraq's invasion of Kuwait in August 1990 and the Persian Gulf War. Much of the goodwill and sympathy won by the self-restrained conduct of the Intifada evaporated when it appeared that many Palestinians were siding with Saddam Hussein. The fact that the movement had achieved a tactical separation between the methods used by its internal and external wings, and had even managed to make this distinction effectively for the purposes of international political consumption, was no protection from the criticism, after the Gulf War, that the Intifada's use of nonviolent methods had only been opportunistic.

Summary

The South African and Palestinian cases underscore the complexity of the relationship between violent and nonviolent action in mixed conflicts. As we saw in the case of Denmark under German occupation, it cannot be stated categorically that violent action never has indirectly beneficial consequences at the strategic level. However the political and moral liabilities of violent methods and their inherent unpredictability combined with the difficulties of distinguishing them from nonviolent methods so that the latter can operate effectively, reaffirm the principle of nonviolent discipline when strategic nonviolent conflict has been chosen.

In all of these recent episodes, even when deliberate strategy has been absent or poor, the principles of strategic nonviolent conflict can be seen to have explanatory value. They help us to understand the forces at work and some of the factors likely to have a bearing on the outcome in each case. Remember, this is not an argument that says nonviolent action will always win or will always be the most important influence on the outcome of a fight. Rather, it is clear that while it will take a long time to understand fully both the detailed history and the ultimate significance of these and other similar post-1981 cases, strategic nonviolent conflict is evident as an important component in each of them, and no analysis will be completely persuasive without its consideratioin.

THE DEVELOPMENT OF STRATEGIC
NONVIOLENT CONFLICT

We have noted that since the start of the 1980s, nonviolent sanctions have appeared frequently in major conflicts. Civilians, by virtue of their ingenuity and determination, molded the course of these campaigns and proved once again that the possibilities for nonviolent action are limited only by peoples' imagination and may never fully be extinguished by repression. The question for consideration now is whether this knowledge will be increasingly relevant to the post–Cold War world. As we argued in the introduction, it is our contention that it will be impossible to explain power, acute conflict, and the future of international relations without analyzing how civil society mobilizes itself for nonviolent action. We do not argue that strategic nonviolent conflict will be the dominant or controlling variable in future conflicts, but we do feel that all visions of the future will be incomplete unless they address the strategic potential of nonviolent sanctions.

Popular civilian struggles are reshaping our understanding of the international system. Scholars trying to understand the post–Cold War security environment find themselves in a particularly difficult position. Once comfortable with the paradigm of superpower antagonism—especially as it tended to reduce the variables for analysis to developments in military hardware and the logic of their deployment—these observers are now struggling to develop additional conceptual tools. In the process of groping for new ways to view security issues, there has been a general call for a broadening of focus. John Chipman, Director of the International Institute of Strategic Studies, writes, "The deployment and engagement of military force may be the anchor of the strategist's concerns, but it will be political, economic and social factors that permit or constrain, that inspire or foreclose, the decision to use military force that must be at the center of any investigation."[4]

We applaud the efforts of those seeking to widen the scope of security studies, and we urge that it be widened still further to include the study of nonviolent conflict. Common wisdom all too easily overlooks the fact that today even well-conceived violent insurgencies regularly falter. Yet the civilian, operating within and between complex interdependent societies, can do more to undermine the militarily aggressive protagonist seeking domination than in any period of history. This potential should not be ignored the moment one party begins military hostilities.

The end of the Cold War unleashed forces of change simmering below the surface of a bipolar system. As a result, conflict between large social and political groups is likely to continue to unfold in unpredictable patterns. Technological change means the nature of warfare is undergoing revolutionary transformation. There is reason to believe that nonviolent sanctions will have a growing relevance in conflict and could, in many instances, supplant the use of military force. Skeptics ask: "What does 'nonviolence' have to do with the extremely lethal activity we see today in Somalia, Cambodia, Bosnia-Herzegovena, Azerbaijan, and Iraq?" One answer is that those who are unsure of their chances in a military confrontation are derelict if they fail to assess other approaches to their fight. Nonviolent sanctions open a range of possibilities to change the risk-reward equation in uncertain and dangerous environments. This volume has tried to address the concerns of protagonists needing to make timely decisions under extraordinary pressures. Mistakes may be fatal, and only protagonists themselves can judge whether their skills and resources are up to the challenge.

New opportunities may emerge as practitioners think through their positions from the perspective of strategic nonviolent conflict. Why should that be surprising? If nonmilitary factors are now recognized as increasingly important in setting the *context* for conflict, these same factors embodied in the exercise of strategic nonviolent conflict might also be critical for the *waging* of conflict. Nonviolent sanctions, including well-planned acts of mass protest, noncooperation, and intervention need more, not less, study given the dramatic events the world has recently experienced. The principles of development, engagement, and conception outlined in Chapter 2, as well as additional principles conceived of by others, may be considered while future nonviolent protagonists face their adversaries.

The primary thrust of this study has been devoted to identifying relationships between behavior in conflict and its outcome. Can similar relationships be found between the study of strategic nonviolent conflict and its development? Can we expect this book, or any similar project, to promote such development? We are hopeful the answer for both scholars and practitioners will be yes, given a shared under-standing of what development entails.

For us development begins by recognizing there are unexplored possibilities for strategic nonviolent conflict, and continues by analyz-ing how its potential can be exploited to enhance the prospects for victory. We believe that history provides the starting point for a growing understanding of the strategic uses of nonviolent sanctions. Energies have focused on older campaigns where the historical re-cord is relatively clear, thereby avoiding debates over the interpreta-tion of more contemporary events that could cloud our basic purpose.

We have tried to show that there does indeed exist a common set of principles and that they are operative in a series of campaigns spread throughout the twentieth century. We present these princi-ples fully aware that nonviolent action has often been more impro-vised than planned, yet hopeful that the strategic choices yet to be made will increasingly feature premeditation and foresight. We feel confident that principles that were useful historically are still useful today. We welcome all efforts to take the lessons about the impor-tance of comprehensive adherence to a set of strategic principles and apply them rigorously to contemporary campaigns. Yet no one should be surprised if, after the post-1981 events are exhaustively researched, new principles emerge to deepen knowledge in this field.

We believe a gap has emerged in war and peace studies. Height-ened emphasis on conflict avoidance or amelioration through negoti-ation, mediation, and other "peaceful" approaches has diminished emphasis on the study of what happens when these approaches fail. There is a tendency to view the commencement of hostilities with despair as events seem to spin out of control, ushering forth destruc-tion of relentless intensity on an unstoppable trajectory.

Intellectual focus has been diverted away from some of the most intriguing of all strategic phenomena. These are the behavioral sig-nals key to understanding the evolving motivations of adversaries during the course of the conflict. Lacking the necessary insights from such observations, many parties act contrary to their best interests just when the stakes are highest. Under conditions of extreme ten-sion and fear, they are too frequently deprived of the creativity needed to explore their options to the fullest extent possible. The sad fact is that those engaged in crucial struggles often become incapable of recognizing when it is better to act like a civilian than a soldier. The result of this oversight can be defeat or death.

Lacking the motivation to break out of the same restrictive conceptual mold, some scholars blithely accept the conventional wisdom whispered from many quarters: "nonviolent action doesn't work." Uncritically they assume protagonists can learn nothing useful about radically different ways of acting in the heat of battle. Consequently, protagonists are seen as the embodiment of dichotomous behavior: they will either argue their interests or look for the biggest gun. The latter choice, time and again, promises extraordinary danger for those in a militarily inferior position. Strategic nonviolent conflict swings an axe at the root of the conventional lament: "But what can one do against so formidable a military opponent?"

Will there come a time when leaders seek guidance from past nonviolent campaigns, the way generals do from past wars? We have a few anecdotes about Gandhi's consciousness of the Russian Revolution of 1905 and Dr. Martin Luther King, Jr.'s study of Gandhi. Still, at present, scarce evidence exists that specific strategic lessons are transmitted from campaign to campaign. This should not be a source of discouragement. As long as we have a concrete, yet evolving, set of principles to evaluate in the light of future conflicts, we know that "people power" is developing. With that realization and that hope we ask others to join us in the next steps.

NOTES

1. Richard J. Kessler, "The Philippines: The Making of a 'People Power' Revolution," in J. A. Goldstone, T. R. Gurr, and F. Moshiri, *Revolutions of the Late Twentieth Century*, 210–11; James B. Goodno, *The Philippines: Land of Broken Promises*, 101.

2. Roberto Eisenman, "Panama and Narco-Militarism," *The Boston Sunday Globe*, 29 May 1988, A25.

3. Adam Roberts, *Civil Resistance in the East European and Soviet Revolutions*, 1.

4. John Chipman, "The Future of Strategic Studies: Beyond Even Grand Strategy," *Survival*, 34:110.

Bibliography

Ackerman, Peter. "Strategic Aspects of Nonviolent Resistance Movements." Ph.D. diss., Tufts University, 1976.

Albin, Cecilia. "The Politics of Terrorism: A Contemporary Survey." In *The Politics of Terrorism: Terror as a State and Revolutionary Strategy*, edited by Barry Rubin. Baltimore: Johns Hopkins University, Foreign Policy Institute, 1989.

Ali, Tariq. *The Nehrus and the Gandhis: An Indian Dynasty*. London: Pan Books, 1985.

Angell, Norman. *The Great Illusion*. London: Heinemann, 1935.

Artaud, Denise. "A propos de l'occupation de la Ruhr." *Revue d'histoire moderne et contemporaine* 17 (1970):1–21.

Ascherson, Neal. *The Polish August: The Self-Limiting Revolution*. New York: Viking Press, 1982.

Ash, Timothy Garton. *The Polish Revolution: Solidarity, 1980–1982*. London: Jonathan Cape, 1983.

Attali, Jacques. *Millennium: Winners and Losers in the Coming World Order*. New York: Random House, 1991.

Beaufre, André. *An Introduction to Strategy*. New York: Frederick A. Praeger, 1965.

Bergfeldt, Lennart. "Experiences of Civilian Resistance—The Case of Denmark 1940–1945." Ph.D. diss., University of Uppsala, Sweden, 1992.

Bergmann, Carl. *The History of Reparations*. Boston: Houghton-Mifflin, 1927.

Böhnke, Wilfried. *Die NSDAP im Ruhrgebiet 1920–1923*. Bonn-Bad Godesberg: Verlag Neue Gesellschaft, 1974.

Bonnell, Victoria E. *Roots of Rebellion: Workers, Politics and Organization in St. Petersburg and Moscow, 1900–1914*. Berkeley: University of California Press, 1983.

Bose, Subhas Chandra. *Indian Struggle 1920–1942*. Bombay: Asia Publishing House, 1964.

Brown, Judith M. *Gandhi: Prisoner of Hope*. New Haven: Yale University Press, 1989.

Buschardt, Leo, et al., eds. *Den illegale presse 1940–1945: En antologi* (The illegal press 1940–1945: An anthology). Copenhagen: N.p., 1965.

Charques, Richard. *The Twilight of Imperial Russia*. London: Oxford University Press, 1958.

Chipman, John. "The Future of Strategic Studies: Beyond Even Grand Strategy." In *Survival* 34, no. 1 (1992). London: International Institute for Strategic Studies.

Clausewitz, Karl von. *On War*, edited by Anatol Rapoport. Harmondsworth: Penguin Books, 1968.

Cornebise, Alfred Emile. "Some Aspects of the German Response to the Ruhr Occupation, January–September 1923." Ph.D. diss., University of North Carolina at Chapel Hill, 1965.

Craig, Gordon A. *Germany: 1866–1945*. New York: Oxford University Press, 1978.

Crelinsten, R. D. "Terrorism as Political Communication: The Relationship Between the Controller and the Controlled." In *Terrorism*, edited by Paul Wilkinson and Alasdair Stewart. Aberdeen: Aberdeen University Press, 1987.

Danstrup, John, and Hal Koch, eds. *Danmarks historie* (History of Denmark). Copenhagen: Politikens Forlag, 1978.

Earl of Halifax [Lord Irwin]. *Fullness of Days*. London: Collins, 1957.

Ebert, Theodor. "Preparations for Civilian Defence." In *Civilian Defence: An Introduction*, edited by T. K. Mahadevan, Adam Roberts, and Gene Sharp. New Delhi: Gandhi Peace Foundation, 1967.

Elam, Robert Varney. "Appeal to Arms: The Army and Politics in El Salvador, 1931-1964." Ph. D. diss., University of New Mexico, 1968.

Eliasberg, George. *Der Ruhrkrieg von 1923*. Bonn-Bad Godesberg: Verlag Neue Gesellschaft, 1974.

Ellis, Anthony, ed. *Ethics and International Relations*, Fulbright Papers, vol. 2. London: Manchester University Press and the Fulbright Commission, 1986.

Emmons, Terence. "Russia's Banquet Campaign." *California Slavic Studies* 10 (1977):45–86.

Engelstein, Laura. *Moscow, 1905: Working-Class Organization and Political Conflict*. Stanford, Calif.: Stanford University Press, 1982.

Erdmann, Lothar. *Die Gewerkschaften im Ruhrkampfe*. Berlin: Verlagsgesellschaft des Allgemeinen Deutschen Gewerkschaftsbundes, 1924.

Erdmann, Karl Dietrich, and Martin Vogt, eds. *Das Kabinett Stresemann. I.* Boppard am Rhein: Harald Boldt, 1978.

Eyck, Erich. *A History of the Weimar Republic*. 2 vols, translated by Harlan P. Hanson and Robert G. L. Waite. Cambridge: Harvard University Press, 1962.

Fischer, George. *Russian Liberalism: From Gentry to Intelligensia*. Cambridge, Mass.: Harvard University Press, 1958.

Fischer, Louis. *The Life of Mahatma Gandhi.* New York: Harper & Row, 1950.

Fraenkel, Ernst. *Military Occupation and the Role of Law in Government: Occupation in the Rhineland 1918–1923.* London: Oxford University Press, 1944.

Freedman, Lawrence. "Order and Disorder in the New World." In *Foreign Affairs: America and Around the World 1991–1992.* New York: Council on Foreign Relations, 1992.

Gandhi, Mohandas K. "When I Am Arrested." *Young India,* 27 February 1930.

———. "Open Letter to a British Viceroy." *Young India,* 12 March 1930.

———. *Collected Works of M. K. Gandhi.* Vols. 42–51. Delhi: Publications Division, Government of India, 1963.

Gante, Thilo. *Die Besetzung der Stadt Dortmund durch Französiche Truppen vom 16 Januar 1923 bis zum 22 Oktober 1924.* Stuttgart: Verlag von Ferdinand Enke, 1928. Reprinted in *Defeat, Revolution and the Occupation of the Ruhr: Birthpangs of the Weimar Republic,* part 3, vol 3, *Seeds of Conflict,* series 5. Nendeln, Liechtenstein: Kraus Reprint, 1976.

Gapon, Georgii. *The Story of My Life.* New York: E. P. Dutton, 1906.

Gates, David. *Non-Offensive Defense: An Alternative Strategy for NATO?* London: Macmillan, 1991.

Gilder, George. *Life After Television: The Coming Transformation of Media and American Life.* New York: W. W. Norton, 1992.

Gobbi, Under Secretary General Hugo. *Report on the Situation in Poland.* Geneva: United Nations, ECOSOC, 21 February 1983.

Goodno, James B. *The Philippines: Land of Broken Promises.* London: Zed Books, 1991.

Gopal, Ram. *How India Struggled for Freedom.* London: Frederick Muller, 1967.

Gopal, Sarvepalli. *The Viceroyalty of Lord Irwin 1926–1931.* Oxford: Clarendon Press, 1957.

Graml, Hermann. *Europa zwischen den Kriegen.* Munich: Deutscher Taschenbuch Verlag, 1969.

Greer, Guy. *The Ruhr-Lorraine Industrial Problem: A Study of the Economic Inter-Dependence of the Two Regions and Their Relation to the Reparation Question.* New York: Macmillan, 1925.

Grimm, Friedrich. *Vom Ruhrkrieg zur Rheinlandräumung: Erinnerungen eines deutschen Verteidigers vor französischen und belgischen Kriegsgerichten.* Hamburg: Hanseatische Verlagsanstalt, 1930.

Gurko, V. I. *Features and Figures of the Past: Government and Opinion in the Reign of Nicholas II,* translated by Laura Matveev, edited by J. E. Wallace Sterling, Xenia J. Eudin, and H. H. Fisher. Stanford, Calif. Stanford University Press, 1939.

Gurr, Ted Robert. "Minorities at Risk: The Dynamics of Ethnopolitical Mobilization and Conflict, 1945–1990." Paper prepared for the International Studies Association Meetings, Vancouver, April 1991.

Haestrup, Jorgen. . . . *til landets bedste* (For the good of the country). 2 vols. Copenhagen: Gyldendal, 1966, 1971.

———. *Secret Alliance: A Study of the Danish Resistance Movement, 1940–1945,* translated by Alison Borch-Johnson. 3 vols. Odense, Denmark: Odense University Press, 1976–77.

———, ed. *Besaettelsen 1940–1945: Politik, modstand, befriese* (Occupation 1940–1945). Copenhagen: Politikens Forlag, 1979.

Harbeck, Karl-Heinz, ed. *Das Kabinett Cuno*. Boppard am Rhein: Harald Boldt, 1968.

Harcave, Sidney. *First Blood: The Russian Revolution of 1905*. New York: Macmillan, 1964.

Hasek, Jaroslav. *The Good Soldier Svejk* (Schweik). London: Penguin Books, 1973.

Henrikson, Alan K. "Toward a Practical Vision of Collective Action for International Peace and Security." Paper presented at a Roundtable on Defining a New World Order at the Fletcher School of Law and Diplomacy, Tufts University, 1991.

Holst, Johan Jorgen. *Civilian-based Defense in a New Era*. Cambridge: Albert Einstein Institution Monograph Series no. 2, 1990.

Hufbauer, Gary Clyde, Jeffrey J. Schott, and Kimberly Ann Elliott. *Economic Sanctions Reconsidered*. 2d ed. Washington, D.C.: Institute for International Economics, 1990.

Kasure, M. Abdul Qadir. *Young India*, 8 May 1930.

Kennan, George. "The Breakdown of the Tsarist Autocracy." In *Revolutionary Russia*, edited by Richard Pipes. Cambridge: Harvard University Press, 1968.

Kennedy, Paul. *The Rise and Fall of the Great Powers*. New York: Random House, 1987.

Kessler, Richard J. "The Philippines: The Making of a 'People Power' Revolution." In *Revolutions of the Late Twentieth Century*, edited by Jack A. Goldstone, Ted Robert Gurr, and Farrokh Moshiri. Boulder, Colo.: Westview Press, 1991.

Kirchhoff, Hans. *Augustopröret 1943* (August Revolt, 1943). Copenhagen: Gyldendal, 1979.

Kumarappa, J. C. *Young India*, 29 May 1930.

Kuron, Jacek. *Co robic?* Paris: Instytut Literacki, 1978.

———. *Zasady ideowe*. Paris: Instytut Literacki, 1978.

Kwiatkowska, J. *Kultura*. Paris, 1979.

Lademacher, Horst. "Nördlichen Rheinlande von der Rhein provinz bis zur Bildung des Landschaftsverbandes Rheinland (1815–1953)." In *Rheinische Geschichte*. 3 vols. Düsseldorf: Schwann, 1976.

Liddell Hart, Sir Basil. *Strategy: The Indirect Approach*. New York: Praeger, 1967.

———. "Lessons from Resistance Movements." In *Civilian Resistance as a National Defence*, edited by Adam Roberts. Harmondsworth: Penguin Books, 1969.

———. *History of the Second World War*. New York: Putnam, 1979.

Lipski, J. J. *Etos KOR*. London: 1983.

———. *KOR: A History of the Workers' Defense Committee in Poland, 1976–1981*. Berkeley: University of California Press, 1985.

Littlejohn, David. *The Patriotic Traitors*. London: Heinemann, 1972.

Luttwak, Edward N. *Strategy: The Logic of War and Peace.* Cambridge: Harvard University Press, 1987.

McDougall, Walter A. *France's Rhineland Diplomacy, 1914–1924: The Last Bid for a Balance of Power in Europe.* Princeton, N.J.: Princeton University Press, 1978.

MacKinlay, John. "The Requirements for a Multinational Force Capability." In *Collective Security in a Changing World.* Providence, R.I.: The Thomas J. Watson, Jr. Institute of International Studies, Brown University, 1992.

Maier, Charles S. *Recasting Bourgeois Europe: Stabilization in France, Germany and Italy in the Decade After World War I.* Princeton, N.J.: Princeton University Press, 1975.

Malvour, James. *An Economic History of Russia.* 2d ed. New York: E. P. Dutton, 1925.

Mann, G. *The History of Germany Since 1789.* London: Pelican, 1974.

Massie, Robert K. *Nicholas and Alexandra.* New York: Atheneum, 1968.

Mehlinger, Howard D., and John M. Thompson. *Count Witte and the Tsarist Government in the 1905 Revolution.* Bloomington: Indiana University Press, 1972.

Michaelis, Herbert, and Ernst Schraepler, eds. *Ursachen und Folgen: Vom deutschen Zusammenbruch 1918 und 1945 bis zur staatlichen Neuordnung Deutschlands in der Gegenwart.* Vol. 5. Berlin: Dokumenten-Verlag Dr. Herbert Wendler, n.d.

Michnik, Adam. "O oporze." *Krytyka* 13/14 (Warsaw, 1983).

Nehru, Jawaharlal. *Toward Freedom.* Boston: Beacon, 1971.

Nissen, Henrik S. *1940: Studier i forhandlingspolitikken of samarbejdspolitikken* (1940: Studies in the Policy of Negotiations). Copenhagen: Gyldendal, 1973.

Nissen, Henrik S., and Hennig Poulsen. *På donsk friheds grund* (On the basis of Danish freedom). Copenhagen: Gyldendal, 1963.

Olgin, Moissaye J. *The Soul of the Russian Revolution.* New York: Henry Holt, 1917.

Pares, Sir Bernard. *The Fall of the Russian Monarchy.* London: J. Cape, 1939.

Parkman, Patricia. "Insurrection Without Arms: The General Strike in El Salvador, 1944," Ph. D. diss., Temple University, 1980.

———. *Nonviolent Insurrection in El Salvador: The Fall of Maximiliano Hernández Martínez.* Tucson: University of Arizona Press, 1988.

Pattabhi Sitaramayya, B. *The History of the Indian National Congress.* Vol. 1. Madras: The Working Committee of the Congress, 1935.

Petras, Harri. *Der Ruhrkampf im Spiegel der Ereignisse im Hattinger Raum. Hattinger Heimatkundliche Schriften.* Grosse Reihe, vol. 2, 1973.

Pfleiderer, Otto. "Die Reichsbank in der Zeit der grossen Inflation, die Stabilisierung der Mark und die Aufwertung von Kapitalforderungen." In *Wahrung und Wirtschaft in Deutschland 1876–1975,* edited by Deutsche Bundesbank. Frankfurt: Fritz Knapp, 1976.

Philips, Cyril Henry, ed. *The Evolution of India and Pakistan 1858–1947.* London: Oxford University Press, 1962.

Poch, Ulrich. "Anpassungspolitik ohne Kollaboration" (A policy of accommodation). In *Ziviler Widerstand*, edited by Theodor Ebert. Düsseldorf: Bertelsmann Universitätsverlag, 1970.

———. *Der Dänische Widerstand in den Jahren 1943–1945* (The Danish Resistance between 1943 and 1945). Berlin: Studiengruppe Soziale Verteidigung, 1971.

Postgate, Raymond William. *Revolution from 1789 to 1906*. Boston: Houghton-Mifflin, 1923.

Poupard, E. *L'occupation de la Ruhr et le droit des gens*. Paris: Les presses universitaires de France, 1925.

Rachwald, A. R. *Poland Between the Super-Powers*. Boulder, Colo.: Westview Press, 1983.

Raun, Toivo U. "The Revolution of 1905 in the Baltic Provinces and Finland." *Slavic Review* 6 (Fall 1984):453–67.

Reimer, Klaus. *Rheinlandfrage und Rheinlandbewegung (1919–1933): Ein Beitrag zur Geschichte der regionalistischen Bestrebungen in Deutschland*. Frankfurt: Peter Lang, 1979.

Rings, Werner. *Life with the Enemy: Collaboration and Resistance in Hitler's Europe, 1939–1945*, translated by J. Maxwell Brownjohn. Garden City, N.Y.: Doubleday, 1982.

Roberts, Adam. *Civil Resistance in the East European and Soviet Revolutions*. Cambridge: Albert Einstein Institution Monograph Series, no. 4, 1991.

Robinson, W. F., ed. *August 1980: The Strikes in Poland*. Munich: Radio Free Europe Research, 1980.

Rupieper, Hermann-Josef. "Politics and Economics: The Cuno Government and Reparations, 1922–1923." Ph.D. diss., Stanford University, 1974.

Sablinsky, Walter. *The Road to Bloody Sunday: Father Gapon and the St. Petersburg Massacre of 1905*. Princeton, N.J.: Princeton University Press, 1976.

Santos Dueñas, Tiburcio. *Aurora del dos de abril de 1944*. San Salvador, 1944.

Schelling, Thomas C. "Some Questions on Civilian Defence." In *Civilian Resistance as a National Defence*, edited by Adam Roberts. Harmondsworth: Penguin Books, 1969.

Schmidt, Royal Jae. *Versailles and the Ruhr: Seedbed of World War II*. The Hague: Martinus Nijhoff, 1968.

Schneiderman, Jeremiah. *Sergei Zubatov and Revolutionary Marxism: The Struggle for the Working Class in Tsarist Russia*. Ithaca, N.Y.: Cornell University Press, 1976.

Severing, Carl. *Mein Lebensweg*. Vol. 1. Cologne: Greven Verlag, 1950.

Sharma, Tagdish Saran, ed. *India's Struggle for Freedom: Selected Documents and Sources*. Delhi: S. Chand & Co., 1962.

Sharp, Gene. *Gandhi Wields the Weapon of Moral Power*. Ahmedabad: Navajivan Press, 1960.

———. *The Politics of Nonviolent Action*. 3 vols. Boston: Porter Sargent, 1973.

———. *Gandhi as a Political Strategist*. Boston: Porter Sargent, 1979.

———. *Civilian-Based Defense: A Post-Military Weapons System*. Princeton, N.J.:Princeton University Press, 1990.

————. "What Is Happening in the World Concerning Nonviolent Struggle?" In *Thinking About Nonviolent Struggle: Trends, Research, and Analysis.* Cambridge, Mass.: Albert Einstein Institution, 1990.

Shridharani, Krishnalal. *War Without Violence: A Study of Gandhi's Method and Its Accomplishments.* New York: Harcourt, Brace, 1939.

Spear, Percival. *A History of India.* Vol. 2. Harmondsworth: Penguin Books, 1965.

Spethmann, Hans. *Zwölf Jahre Ruhrbergbau.* Vol. 3, *Der Ruhrkampf 1923 bis 1925 in seinen Leitlinien.* Berlin: Verlag von Reimar Hobbing, 1929.

————. *Der Ruhrkampf 1923 bis 1925: Das Ringen um die Kohle,* vol. 4. Berlin: Verlag von Reimar Hobbing, 1930.

Staniszkis, J. "The Evolution of Forms of Working-class Protest in Poland: Sociological Reflections on the Gdansk-Szczecin Case." *Soviet Studies* 2 (August 1980):204–31.

Stefanowski, R. *Poland: A Chronology of Events, August–December 1981.* Munich: Radio Free Europe Research, 1982.

Stiehm, Judith. "Contemporary Theories of Non-violent Resistance." Ph.D. diss., Columbia University, 1969.

Strange, Susan. "The Name of the Game." In *Sea Changes: American Foreign Policy in a World Transformed,* edited by Nicolas X. Rizopoulos. New York: Council on Foreign Relations Press, 1990.

Stresemann, Gustav. *Vermächtnis: Der Nachlass.* Vol. 1. Berlin: Ullstein Verlag, 1932.

Toffler, Alvin. *Power Shift.* New York: Bantam, 1990.

Trotsky, Leon. *1905,* translated by Anya Bostock. New York: Random House, 1971.

Ulam, Adam B. *Russia's Failed Revolutions.* New York: Basic Books, 1981.

Van Crevald, Martin. *On Future War.* London: Brassey's, 1991.

Waite, Robert G. L. *Vanguard of Nazism: The Free Corps Movement in Postwar Germany, 1918–1923.* Cambridge: Harvard University Press, 1952.

Walder, David. *The Short Victorious War.* London: Hutchinson, 1973.

Waters, Mary Alice, ed. *Rosa Luxemburg Speaks.* New York: Pathfinder, 1970.

Weschler, Lawrence. *The Passion of Poland.* New York: Pantheon, 1984.

Wheeler-Bennett, John W., and Hugh Latimer. *Information on the Reparation Settlement.* London: George Allen & Unwin, 1930.

Williams, Marc, ed. *International Relations in the 20th Century.* 2d ed. London: Macmillan, 1990.

Wilson, Everett A. "The Crisis of National Integration in El Salvador, 1919–1935." Ph. D. diss., Stanford University, 1970.

Witte, Sergei. *The Memoirs of Count Witte,* translated by Abraham Yarmolinsky. Garden City, N.Y.: Doubleday, 1921.

Wright, Robin, and Doyle McManus. *Flash-Points: Promise and Peril in a New World.* New York: Alfred Knopf, 1991.

Zielonka, Jan. *Pools Experiment.* Leeuwarden: Uitgeverij Eisma, B. V., 1982.

Zimmermann, Ludwig. *Frankreichs Ruhrpolitik von Versailles bis zum Dawesplan,* edited by Walther Peter Fuchs. Göttingen: Musterschmidt, 1971.

Zum Ruhreinbruch: Tatsachen und Dokumente. Berlin: Walter de Gruyter u. Co., 1923. Reprinted in *Defeat, Revolution and the Occupation of the Ruhr: Birthpangs of the Weimar Republic,* part 3, vol. 3, *Seeds of Conflict,* series 5. Nendeln, Liechtenstein: Kraus Reprint, 1976.

Index

About the Authors

PETER ACKERMAN is Managing Director of Rockport Financial, Ltd. and Rockport Partners, Inc. in London. He was a Visiting Scholar at the International Institute of Strategic Studies until 1992.

CHRISTOPHER KRUEGLER is President of The Albert Einstein Institution, Inc. in Cambridge, Massachusetts. He is editor-in-chief of the forthcoming *Encyclopedia of Nonviolent Action* (1996).